STATE
TROOPER
EXAM

**OTHER TITLES OF INTEREST FROM
LEARNINGEXPRESS**

Math for Law Enforcement Exams
Reasoning for Law Enforcement Exams

STATE TROOPER EXAM

2nd Edition

LEARNINGEXPRESS®

NEW YORK

Copyright © 2010 LearningExpress, LLC.

All rights reserved under International and Pan-American Copyright Conventions.
Published in the United States by LearningExpress, LLC, New York.

Library of Congress Cataloging-in-Publication Data:
State trooper exam.—2nd ed.
    p. cm.
ISBN 978-1-57685-735-9
1. Police, State—United States—Examinations, questions, etc. 2. Police—United States—Examinations, questions, etc. I. LearningExpress (Organization)
  HV8143.S73 2010
  363.2076—dc22

                                                    2009032219

Printed in the United States of America

9 8 7 6 5 4 3 2 1

ISBN: 978-1-57685-735-9

For information on LearningExpress, other LearningExpress products,
or bulk sales, please write to us at:
  2 Rector Street
  26th Floor
  New York, NY 10006

Or visit us at:
  www.learnatest.com

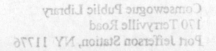

LIST OF CONTRIBUTORS ▶

The following individuals contributed to the content of this book.

Kimberly Collica, PhD, has a doctorate in Criminal Justice and is a professor in the Justice Studies/Criminal Justice Department at Berkeley College. She has many years of experience working within the state prison and county jail systems. Her research focuses on HIV, correctional populations, rehabilitation, and reintegration.

Gennifer Furst, PhD, has a doctorate in Criminal Justice and is an assistant professor in the Sociology Department at William Paterson University. Her research focuses on issues related to incarceration, prison-based animal programs, and the use of animals by the criminal justice system.

Dorothy Moses Schulz, PhD, is a professor at John Jay College of Criminal Justice (CUNY). She is a retired captain with the Metro-North Commuter Railroad Police Department and its predecessor railroad, Conrail. She was the first woman to hold a management rank in both departments. Dr. Schulz is a life member of the International Association of Chiefs of Police (IACP) and other police and history associations; speaks frequently at police and academic gatherings; and has published material about a variety of historical and current police topics, particularly in areas concerning transit and railroad police, and women in policing.

Walter Signorelli was a member of the New York City Police Department for 31 years. He retired with the rank of inspector after serving in the Patrol Bureau, the Narcotics Division, the Detective Division, the Organized Crime Control Bureau, and the Personnel Bureau. He is a graduate of St. John's University School of Law and is licensed to practice law in New York State. He is an assistant professor of law and police science at John Jay College of Criminal Justice.

CONTENTS

INTRODUCTION ▶

State Trooper Exam is more than just a guide to taking and passing the state trooper exam. It is also more than merely a collection of practice tests. This book provides you with an overview of who state police officers are and what they do, the steps in the hiring process, academy training, and conditions of employment. It also explains how you should design your approach to taking the exam so that you have the best possible chance of passing it.

When you take the practice tests, do not just answer the questions and hope for the best—if you do that on the exam, you are not likely to do your best. After taking a practice test, make sure to review your answers thoroughly, particularly the ones that were incorrect. Each practice exam provides explanations for both correct and incorrect answers. If you use this book as a guide to understanding *how* the exam is structured and *what* you are being asked to do, your chances of passing will increase considerably. Remember, a prepared test taker is a better test taker. No book can promise you a higher score, but a book can offer you tips and hints to better understand how to study for an exam and how to analyze the patterns of the skills that are being tested. To help you understand each of those skills, there are sections devoted to different types of questions you might see on the written state trooper exam.

Most state police departments begin the formal hiring process with a written exam. In virtually all states, it will be the first step you take after applying for the job and after your application is checked to assure you have the minimum requirements for entry into the department you are testing for.

Because the written test is only the first step you must take to become a state trooper, there are also chapters on how to prepare for the oral appraisal, the physical and medical exams, and the psychological exam. Not all agencies make use of an oral appraisal; some consider it too costly or time-consuming to have applicants from all over the state—or even all over the nation—come to a test site to be interviewed by a panel of policing experts. Even if the agency you are applying for does not require an oral exam, the chapter on oral appraisal exams can help you prepare for any type of interview that may occur in the hiring process.

Physical, medical, and psychological exams are common steps in the applicant process for almost all police positions. The exams may not be exactly the same, and they may not take place in the same order in every agency, but eventually, if you are successful in passing the written exam, you will be called to appear for one or all of these tests. Of the three, the physical exam is the easiest to prepare for. Not only can you work to get yourself into excellent physical condition, but many state police agencies now provide information on their websites about what you will be asked to do when you report for the physical exam.

Start training as soon as possible. If you are not in the best physical shape, four to six months of training may be necessary. You should familiarize yourself with the agency's physical agility requirements, and then you should train expressly for those requirements. Most departments require a timed 1½ mile run. Do not try to train for the run by engaging in alternative types of exercise such as racquetball, swimming, etc. The only way to prepare for a run is to consistently run. This means you should be running at least three to four times per week. Make sure you practice on a regulation track; do not train for the run by using a treadmill. Focus all of your training sessions on the specific physical agility requirements and nothing else. Furthermore, do all of the requirements in one setting in the exact order you will be tested (i.e., a sprint, sit-ups, push-ups, and 1½ mile run). These tasks may be easy for you to do individually, but when you have to do them all back to back, it becomes a bit more challenging.

Statistics show that this is the most difficult portion of the exam for female applicants, but "difficult" does not mean "impossible." In addition to publicizing the physical test requirements, a number of agencies also provide training plans to prepare an applicant for what will be expected. Some schedule pre-physical meetings or even training sessions to help applicants prepare for this rigorous step in the hiring process.

Remember that even if you never get to take the physical, the healthy habits you have learned will stay with you and benefit you throughout your lifetime. On average, individuals who eat well and exercise regularly have fewer health problems than those who make unhealthy nutritional choices and live a sedentary lifestyle. Exercise can also decrease stress and subsequently improve your overall quality of life. A sound mind and a sound body will better prepare you for any law enforcement career.

It is more difficult to prepare for the medical and psychological exams, although the training program you develop to pass the physical may help you to pass the medical if you have no serious ailments. The medical may also include a drug test. This is one area where different agencies set different standards as to past drug use, but no agency will hire an applicant who tests positive for drugs at the medical exam. Check your desired employer's minimum qualifications for past drug experimentation so you are neither disappointed nor embarrassed when you appear for testing.

The psychological exam is the hardest to study or practice for. Although policies differ among agencies, you will most likely be asked to complete a number of paper-and-pencil tests that have been determined successful at assessing the traits considered most important for a successful police career. Generally, these traits include self-confidence (but not arrogance), honesty, integrity, compatibility (ability to work with a team), diplomacy, independence, dependability, and decisiveness. To you, some of these may actually appear contradictory, but the series of tests you will take have been shown to analyze whether you have these traits in the proper combination. The best way to prepare for this test is to be relaxed, minimize stress in your life before appearing for the test, and answer honestly. Do not try to fool the test; you may be asked a different version of the same question more than once, and if you answer dishonestly, it is very likely that the results will show this.

The last part of the applicant hiring process could include a polygraph examination. Although infrequent, there are some agencies, like the North Carolina State Highway Patrol, that require a polygraph exam in order to qualify as a state trooper. You cannot train for the polygraph exam, and attempting to "beat" the exam will automatically disqualify you from employment. There are plenty of websites that provide information on how to "beat" a polygraph, (i.e., keeping your body tense through the entire procedure, biting your tongue, moving your extremities, taking deep breaths, fidgeting). A trained examiner will know exactly what you are doing. This behavior will unequivocally damage your credibility. The best preparation for a polygraph is to relax, tell the truth, and disclose any information to the examiner beforehand that you think might be problematic.

How to Use This Book

Now that you have a good idea of what the book contains, you should consider how you will use it to your best advantage. The first thing to remember is that, just as in the test you will be taking, there are no shortcuts. Do not practice only the tests; practice the *skills* you will need for the test. Do this by carefully reading the material in each chapter and by thinking about how that topic will help you become a state police officer. Even if you have done well in high school or college, you need to remember that careful reading is not the same as just reading the words. Reading this book carefully is an important way to practice for the test. If you do not read the test questions carefully, you will probably answer them incorrectly.

Throughout the United States, educators have been worrying about the drop in SAT scores within the last decade. Maybe you were faced with concern over the SAT when you were in high school and thinking about attending college. Because many state police agencies now require some college or even a four-year degree from their applicants, it is likely that you have already faced timed aptitude tests that can play a large role in your future. One of the findings of those studying the drop in SAT scores was that students took too many shortcuts in studying. For instance, they studied vocabulary lists rather than more complex reading material. This did not help the students, because reading is more than just a list of words; it also means understanding the words in context so that you understand a situation.

Thus, reading this book carefully will help you in a number of ways. Just by reading each section carefully, you will enhance your comprehension skills; these skills are exactly what will be tested in the reading portions of the entry exam.

Many states include math on their entry exams. You might wonder why. While the average trooper may not need advanced calculus to get through the day, basic math is required when estimating speed or distance, when totaling the value of found or stolen property, and even for calculating such simple things as mileage or expenses. Your math skills will be tested in conjunction with your reading skills; rather than just being asked to add up a list of numbers or determine a percentage of items lost or found, you might be asked to read a passage on a situation and then to do some arithmetical calculations. If you haven't read the situation properly, there is a good chance you will not calculate properly, either.

None of this information is meant to intimidate you, only to impress on you the importance of studying for the written exam, and to help you understand how *State Trooper Exam* can give you an extra boost of knowledge and confidence that may translate into the difference between passing and failing.

1 ▶ WHAT STATE TROOPERS DO

CHAPTER SUMMARY

State police and highway patrols provide many services, although the roles of officers in highway patrol departments may be somewhat more limited than those in full-service state police departments.

State police have concurrent (or shared) jurisdiction or responsibility with local police departments. Forty-nine of the 50 states in the United States have some form of a state police agency; Hawaii is the only state without such an agency. State police agencies were originally designed to handle crime in non-urbanized areas and to deal with crimes that spanned across multiple cities in the same state. State police are not limited by county politics, and their jurisdiction is only bound by state lines. Their area of law enforcement authority is much larger than that of local police municipalities. In about half the states, state troopers, whether in full-service agencies or in highway patrols, have primary responsibility for enforcing traffic laws on interstate highways, turnpikes, and other major roadways.

In some states, state police are responsible for criminal investigations and are frequently called upon by small local police departments and some small sheriffs' offices to provide leadership and expertise in many complex criminal investigations. Many form partnerships with Federal Law Enforcement Agencies, such as the Office of Homeland Security, to aid in criminal investigations and buttress counter-terrorism efforts. Full-service state police agencies are sometimes referred to as operating in the centralized model of state law enforcement because all the state's policing functions are combined in one large department.

These full-service departments also provide crime lab services for local police and sheriffs. This might include ballistic and drug testing, DNA analysis, and analysis of evidence in major crimes. These departments may also maintain the state records on criminal history of offenders, including sex offender records, and may operate a state computer network that is similar to the one maintained at the federal level by the Federal Bureau of Investigation (FBI). Certain departments, such as the New York State Police, maintain an account of all handgun transactions within the state and can provide a history of ownership records to law enforcement agencies nationally on a weapon that was used during the commission of crime. About two-thirds of state police agencies operate recruit training academies; some of these permit officers from local departments to attend. Many state police departments also take leadership roles in supervisory, management, and specialized training for local police officers, particularly those in small rural police departments.

Some state police even fulfill the role of local police in small towns and unincorporated areas of a state. This may be because there is no local police department or because the local department is too small to provide coverage 24 hours a day, seven days a week. In these cases, troopers may be assigned full-time to provide all general police services to a town or area, in effect becoming the town's police force. In some states, such as New Jersey, towns may pay the state police to act as their police force; this is often termed *contract policing*, and obligates the state police to provide whatever services are outlined in the contract just as a private security firm might do for a client.

Some states limit the roles of the state police because they also have formed bureaus of investigation to undertake criminal and civil investigations on a statewide basis. This is often referred to as a decentralized model of state law enforcement, because there is a distinction between highway traffic enforcement and other state-level law enforcement functions. In these states, agencies, often with names like *bureau of investigation*, are state versions of the FBI; agents are sworn police officers but rarely, if ever, work in uniform or are involved in non-investigatory police activities.

The decentralized model is more often found in southern and midwestern states, although some western states also follow this type of organization. Generally, the state police agencies that operate in a decentralized model can be recognized by the word *highway* or *patrol* in their name. Examples are the Ohio State Highway Patrol, the North Carolina Highway Patrol, and the Wyoming Highway Patrol. Many of the decentralized agencies have fewer officers than the full-service state police agencies, in part because their responsibilities are more limited, but also because they are often found in states with smaller populations and lower population density. This means that highway patrol officers must often patrol long stretches of roadway alone, with their backup many miles away.

Interestingly, both the largest and the smallest state patrol agencies are decentralized. The largest is also the best known—the California Highway Patrol (CHP). Despite its fame through a television show and its almost 7,000 sworn officers, the CHP shares law enforcement duties with the California Division of Law Enforcement, the state's investigative agency. And as an indication that labels do not always tell the entire story, in 2001 and 2002, CHP was honored with the Herman Goldstein Award by the Police Executive Research Forum (PERF) for its efforts in problem-oriented policing, a philosophy more commonly associated with municipal policing than with highway patrol. In contrast with the size of CHP, the North Dakota Highway Patrol is the smallest decentralized agency, with approximately 150 officers patrolling throughout the entire state.

What does all this mean to you—the applicant? It means that there are many career paths to follow. Although virtually all state police agencies assign new officers to uniformed patrol in marked vehicles on roadways, there are many career options to which a trooper may aspire.

The New Jersey State Police (NJSP), for instance, lists more than 120 units in which its officers might work. Although the choices do not run from A to Z, they do run from A to V. Troopers may work in alcoholic beverage control enforcement, as armorers (those who test, maintain, and repair firearms), in the aviation unit, or in the victims services unit. The range between these duties is vast; some assignments are action-oriented and require working mostly nights with teams of other officers, while other assignments may appeal to those who require a more normal work-week to care for children or other dependents. To say there is something for everyone is not an exaggeration, although, of course, no one is guaranteed the assign-ment of his or her choice. The NJSP's range of duties is particularly wide, but is not that different from other full-service state agencies. In the New York State Police (NYSP), officers might work in crime analysis, forensics, drug enforcement, or the warrant squad. They also have positions within their aviation, bomb, canine, and motorcycle units, or their bicycle and snowmobile patrols. Perhaps you might be interested in marine detail by patrolling New York's waterways, in addition to providing water search and rescue ser-vices. The Arizona Highway Patrol's Illegal Immigra-tion Prevention and Apprehension Cooperative Team investigates crimes associated with illegal immigra-tion, including human trafficking. The Illinois State Police (ISP), which began as a highway patrol in 1919 but grew into a full-service agency, maintains the state's criminal statistics and criminal history records, registers firearm owners, and has gained an enviable reputation for its various labs and electronic data pro-cessing and computer center.

With this wide range of assignments open to you, it is important not to forget that the most basic responsibilities of any state trooper are to protect life and property and to promote highway safety. You may respond to all types of crime calls, including burglaries, assaults, robberies, and homicides, and also to such service calls as finding lost or missing children or adults, evacuating those in danger due to natural disasters or vehicle accidents, or assisting fire or medical personnel in handling other health or safety emergencies.

These basic requirements mean that all troop-ers must know how to operate a motor vehicle; must be prepared to work all hours of the day and night, including weekends and holidays; must be prepared to carry a firearm and use it if the situation warrants deadly physical force; patrol wide areas, generally in one-officer patrol cars; interact with people of all races and from all social classes; investigate crimes; take notes based on a series of events or interviews; make arrests; conduct searches; testify in court or before a grand jury; and fulfill a number of roles that may develop on short notice and that require tact and good judgment.

Contemporary Concerns Lead to New Roles

In addition to these varied tasks that state police have performed for decades, the twenty-first century has brought new responsibilities. Since September 11, 2001, state police have become involved in anti-terrorism and homeland security activities. Most Americans know that after the 9/11 attacks, the federal government passed the Homeland Security Act of 2002, forming the Department of Homeland Secu-rity (DHS). This new cabinet-level department has brought together about 170,000 employees working for 22 agencies that protect Americans overseas and domestically, and maintain safe transportation, cargo, and borders. Less well known are the state-level activi-ties to increase homeland security, many of which were assigned to state police departments, resulting in career paths that had not previously existed. State police officers are now involved in investigating sus-pected terrorists or terrorist-inspired crimes.

Although foreign terrorists have received con-siderable press and law enforcement attention, there are numerous domestic terrorist groups operating around the nation. Additionally, whether the terror-ists themselves are foreign or domestic, acts of terror-ism are essentially local issues that must be addressed primarily by local police acting in conjunction with state and federal agencies. State police departments participate in multiagency joint terrorism task forces and serve as the lead agency for many new statewide intelligence-gathering networks. In rural areas, anti-terrorism resources are usually staffed by state police officers, who also frequently provide training for local police.

State homeland security directors, whether working out of the offices of their respective governors or other arrangements, frequently rely on the state police for expertise and personnel to undertake specialist assignments. The NYSP worked closely with U.S. Customs and Border Patrol officers who were assigned to checkpoints along the Canadian border, a task that the NYSP was not assigned prior to the September 11 attacks. Additional emerging areas of specialization are enforcement of regulations to control or safeguard the handling and shipping of hazardous materials, conducting threat analyses to prevent terrorist acts such as bombings, and assistance in such newly emerging specialties as risk analysis and threat and vulnerability recognition and resolution. State police are also working to prevent terrorist acts involving weapons of mass destruction, including chemical, biological, and radiological weapons.

Just as computers have become a way of life in many parts of the country and a lifeline for teens and businesspeople, they have also fostered new types of crimes that are often beyond the capability of local police to investigate but are not broad enough to involve federal law enforcement agencies. Many state police agencies have assumed investigative and enforcement responsibilities for computer-generated crimes, particularly those involving financial fraud, identity theft, or dissemination of prohibited material. Although computer crime is vast, like many more traditional modes of criminal behavior, it can be divided into categories. Cyber-criminals who strike businesses are often insiders (current or former employees); hackers are outsiders who want to hurt a company or institution or, sometimes, just prove they are able to break into an institution's computer network; virus writers may be motivated by financial gain or, again, just want to impress those in the know with their ability to curtail or even stop computer traffic; and criminal groups mostly use computers to engage in some form of theft or fraud.

Another large category of computer criminals are sex offenders, who use the Internet to prey on young victims. State police have been involved in so-called "stings," posing as underage boys and girls online and then arranging to meet those who seek sexual contact with minors. Pornographers, too, have been able to use the Internet to circulate pictures and movies of children engaged in sexual behavior. The resources to investigate these types of complex crimes are often beyond the capabilities of most small police departments, and to fill the void, in many states, state police investigators have gained expertise in these areas and are working with federal agents, banks, and financial institutions to prosecute cyber-criminals.

The History of State Policing

The history of state police agencies in the United States is not as long as the histories of municipal or federal policing, but it is far more varied and colorful than you might expect. Many applicants who take the exams for state police departments are surprised to learn that the job is far more than patrolling state highways and rural byways. This surprise often comes because books on policing have portrayed the creation of state police merely as attempts to provide highway enforcement at a time when cars were becoming commonplace throughout the country. The development of state police agencies is one of the most neglected areas of police history.

The roots of state policing can be traced to experiments that began when, upon gaining independence from Mexico in 1835, Texas formed the Texas Rangers. Since Texas was a republic at the time, rather than a state, the Rangers did not officially become a state police force until 1845, when Texas became a state. Similar mounted forces were formed in 1901 and 1905 by the territories of Arizona and New

Mexico, respectively. Although today these forces are considered the pioneers in state policing, since most of their tasks involved patrolling the border with Mexico, they were actually more like today's federal Border Patrol than like the state police departments that followed in their footsteps.

The earliest state police department that would be familiar to today's applicants was formed in Connecticut in 1903, followed by the Pennsylvania State Constabulary (now the Pennsylvania State Police) in 1905. Eventually, all 50 states except Hawaii formed some type of state police agency—either a full-service department, such as those in New York, Connecticut, New Jersey, Pennsylvania, and Illinois, or an agency primarily assigned to highway patrol, such as the California Highway Patrol, the Ohio State Highway Patrol, and the South Carolina Highway Patrol.

The Pennsylvania State Constabulary in some ways set the tone for all state police agencies. Although it has changed over the years, the Pennsylvania force was highly centralized and as much like a militia as a police force. Its organization, and the fact that officers played a large role in controlling strikes, led to its unpopularity with both business leaders and laborers. Setting the tone for many later controversies involving police, business leaders felt the constabulary was unreliable as a strike-breaking force, and laborers believed they were the victims of unnecessary police violence, going so far as to compare them to Cossacks.

Although the Pennsylvania State Police (PSP) has changed considerably over the years, state police agencies to this day are more formal in their manner and more military in training and attitude than most municipal police departments. They also tend to demand a higher level of physical agility during training and throughout a trooper's career.

The creation of the state police in New York was also controversial; again, the issues revolved around business versus labor and urban versus rural interests. Many of those who favored the state police tried to convince those in rural portions of the country that they were being overrun by crime, in part due to the new availability of vehicles. This perception, and the fact that many state police agencies were not formed until the 1920s and 1930s, is part of the reason the development of state policing is generally viewed as primarily a response to the newfound mobility of criminals. Other departments that formed before the 1920s, and prior to the advent of the automobile as a major issue in crime control, include Michigan in 1917 and West Virginia in 1919.

Despite a number of critics who argued that small, rural police and sheriffs' departments were unable to meet the crime-fighting needs of rural America, many residents of these areas, including New York state, were concerned that supporting state police forces would result in higher taxes and that the forces could become agents of repression, particularly in labor disputes. Organized labor was also against state police, but in New York, a coalition of upstate and suburban legislators overcame the opposition by including a prohibition against using the state police within city limits to suppress riots and disorders, unless directed to do so by the governor or unless requested by the mayor of the city and approved by the governor. With this limitation, the authorization passed both houses of the New York State Legislature and the bill was signed into law by Governor Charles S. Whitman.

Setting the early military style of the department, Governor Whitman named his friend Dr. George Fletch Chandler, a surgeon who had served in the U.S. Army's 10th Infantry, as the first commander. The first recruits trained at a National Guard camp and appeared in public for the first time in September 1917, when 232 troopers were assigned to the New York State Fairgrounds near Syracuse. Troopers were appointed for two years subject to the approval of the superintendent. It was a misdemeanor to quit without consent until 1938, the year appointments became permanent. Although early NYSP troopers were required to know how to ride horseback, and many did so in the course of their duties, by 1918 the force had added Model T Fords and motorcycles, especially for what were termed *hurried calls*.

Troopers in many states lived in barracks, worked long hours, and needed permission to marry. In 1958, troopers in New York State saw their average workday change to an eight-hour, five day a week schedule from the previous 12-hour schedule. Although no troopers are still required to live in barracks, state police agencies are generally more military in their training styles and have a much smaller percentage of women in their ranks than municipal police departments and most federal law enforcement agencies.

2 ▶ BECOMING A STATE TROOPER

CHAPTER SUMMARY

Not only is state policing newer than municipal and federal policing, it also has the fewest agencies and employs the fewest number of officers of the three branches (federal, state, local) of policing. In the year 2000, the 49 state police agencies employed about 56,000 full-time, sworn officers. Reflecting that patrol is the major component of the job, more than 65% of the officers spent their workday on patrol. This small number of positions compared to municipal policing, which in 2000 employed more than 440,000 sworn officers, means that each applicant for a state police position will face intense competition for the few positions that become available.

Eligibility/Basic Qualifications

It is very important for anyone who aspires to a position as a state police officer to review the eligibility requirements carefully. Although it might seem surprising, considering the similarity in the organization and roles of many state police departments, the basic requirements may differ substantially from agency to agency. The differences may have little to do with job responsibilities or with geography. As an example, the NYSP requires an applicant to be 20 years old on application date and 21 at the time of appointment, and no older than 30 without a military-service exemption. However, the NJSP requires that applicants be at least 21 on the date the initial application is submitted, but may attend and graduate from the academy up to age 35. The ISP demands that an applicant be between 21 and 36 years old. The PSP accepts applicants who are least 20 when they complete the application, but new troopers (cadets) must be at least 21 and under 40 at the time of appointment.

Educational requirements are also different. The NYSP requires a high school diploma or equivalent at the time of application and completion of 60 college credits by the time of appointment, although there are at least two categories of exemptions to the educational requirements. The NJSP requires a four-year bachelor's degree or 60 college credits plus at least two years of satisfactory employment or military experience and 30 college credits. The ISP has a number of educational options, all of which require an applicant to have an average of C or better, and to have some combination of education and work experience, with military duty often substituting for the years of work. The PSP requires an associate's degree or 60 college credits at the time of application (different from the time of appointment), but will accept some waivers if the candidate has military training or has two years of full-time police experience, including having been certified by the state's Municipal Police Officers' Education and Training Commission (MPOETC). The departments also differ as to how military training counts in place of other education or work experience, and whether and how veterans' preference points are added to an applicant's test score.

Just as with other types of police employment, candidates must be U.S. citizens by the time of appointment but need not always have attained citizenship at the time of application. Virtually all state police agencies require an applicant to have a valid driver's license, sometimes from the state of appointment, sometimes from any state. Similarly, some require that you be a resident of the state at the time of appointment, others at the time you begin or graduate from the police academy.

Other areas that may differ are past drug use, past conviction records (although no agency will employ someone who has a felony on his or her record), and past driving or credit records. Having been less than honorably discharged from any branch of the military will usually disqualify an applicant, as will having been fired from a government job, especially if that job is with another law enforcement agency. Testing positive for current drug use will also disqualify a candidate.

Few agencies have specific height and weight standards any longer, instead requiring that candidates pass the physical ability test. The vision requirements, once universally set at 20/20 uncorrected, are now more flexible. Color blindness remains an automatic disqualification for virtually all police jobs. A new standard in many police departments concerns tattoos. The NYSP, for instance, according to its website, requires all officers to *present a neat and professional appearance at all times* and specifies that this means that tattoos, brands, body piercings, and other body art may not be visible while an officer is in uniform or dressed in other business attire. The NJSP has a policy regarding tattoos that states: *No tattoos/body art/brands on an enlisted member's face, head, neck, scalp, hands, or any parts of the exposed body shall be visible when on duty*. The PSP website was updated in June 2009 to include the requirement that at the time of appointment, the officer *shall have no tattoos or brandings which would be visible to the public when wearing the summer uniform shirt—collared, short-sleeved dress shirt*. Also, *ear plugs shall be removed with the ear repaired upon appointment*. The department retains the right to make that determination and requires that those that do not conform be altered or removed.

Regulations on other matters are equally specific for many of the agencies. Applicants should become familiar with the requirements of the agency or agencies they plan to apply to. Because the regulations may be similar in some cases or substantially different in others, understanding the specific requirements of the agency is vital to your job search.

Career Information Resources

For those who want to apply to only one state police agency or to multiple agencies that do not require residency, the best place to begin a search for information is on the Internet. All state police agencies, like many municipal and virtually all federal agencies, have web pages, and they are full of useful information. Use any search engine to find the website of your agency of choice. Once you've gotten to the pages you are seeking, bookmark them so you can go back anytime you want to check something or to see if the requirements or other information provided has changed. Because the headquarters of state police agencies are often located in rural parts of their states, it may be hardest for those living in big cities to learn about their state police agencies firsthand. It is for these applicants that the websites will be exceptionally useful. Many of the websites are interactive and provide you with the opportunity to ask questions and receive personalized answers from a member of the force.

If you are in college, attend your school's career fairs or visit with a career counselor. Many state police agencies, even those that do not require a college education, are eager to recruit college students into their ranks. Particularly if you are attending a college with a criminal justice or a police studies program, there is a strong possibility that your own state's police agency will be at the career fair; often, neighboring states will also attend to increase interest in their agencies. Some job fairs are strictly informational, offering material for further study. Others will provide you with an opportunity to talk to officers from the department who are assigned to the recruitment office. Come prepared with resumes, since some departments will take your information and place you on a list to receive the latest test applications and schedules as they are developed. If you attend a college that does not have a criminal justice program, contact a local college that does and see if you might be permitted access to its fair. Be forewarned: A number of colleges are instituting dress codes to attend job fairs.

Many state police agencies exhibit at state and county fairs. While their primary purpose at these events may be to promote highway safety or various community-based programs, general career informa-

tion will probably be available. Because these exhibits are usually staffed by troopers, they present excellent opportunities to speak with someone on the job who can give you a good idea of what the work is like and help you decide if the position fits your interests and aspirations.

State police agencies tend to have smaller percentages of women and racial and ethnic minorities than large municipal police departments. To help them find candidates who often do not look for them, agencies have expanded their recruitment to some less traditional venues. Some agencies have begun recruiting at gyms and sporting events, while others have set up career events with scouting groups and groups that have large minority or female memberships. If you belong to any such groups and are interested in a career in state policing, have your group leader contact the state police recruitment unit, which may be happy to send information or even a recruiter to talk personally with potential applicants.

The Job Search

Similar to learning basic eligibility standards and information about your agency of choice, the best way to learn about vacancies, exam periods, steps in the application process, and whatever else you need to know leading up to the actual written test is from the agency's website. If you have met with a recruitment officer or contacted the agency via mail or phone, you may have already received an applicant package. If not, requirements, samples, and actual applications may be available on the agency's website. Even if the application itself is not there, you can often fill out a form to request this material.

Generally, the first step in the selection process will be completing the application. Read carefully what you are being asked and make sure you answer everything honestly and correctly. The application may ask you to list every place you have lived for the past seven or ten years. "Every" means just that; do not decide that somewhere you lived for only four or five months doesn't count. If you lived in a college dorm but it wasn't your legal address for voting, reread the form to see what is being asked of you. If you can't determine, consider e-mailing or calling to be sure. A form that is incorrectly filled out may disqualify you if the reader finds lies or inconsistencies. This is not a good time to guess. Make a copy of the application so you can make edits and corrections should the need arise. Once you have thoroughly reviewed your draft, neatly complete the final application and submit it to the agency.

What you write on the application will form the basis of your initial screening and your more detailed background investigation. The initial check is to assure you meet the minimum entry requirements. Are you the correct age to be eligible to sit for the written exam? If there is a residency requirement, and have you fulfilled it? Do you have a valid driver's license, or is it only necessary for you to have this at the time of actual appointment? If it is determined that you have intentionally made a false statement, you will be disqualified before you even get to the written exam.

Some applicants are disqualified not because they lied—but simply because they did not follow instructions. Did you complete the application? Did you sign and date the application?

Most state police agencies have specific filing periods for upcoming exams. Only a few agencies have rolling applications, which means you may apply at any time and your application will be held until the next test date. If you are filing for a specific exam, the easiest way to be disqualified is by not mailing the application in enough time for it to be postmarked before the application deadline. Parents and teachers may have given you second chances; it is unlikely the state police will. The first step in the early elimination of applicants is the application process. Just as the written exam is meant to test your reading and comprehension skills, so is the application. Read carefully and follow the instructions.

If you have carefully read and followed the instructions and you meet all the minimum eligibility requirements, you will be advised, usually by mail, of the next steps in the application process. Some agencies may ask you for a resume, but many will not. This is where the hiring process differs from many civilian positions. You may be asked to submit documents to support your claim of minimum eligibility, such as a birth certificate, a high school diploma, a college transcript, or military discharge papers, but even these may not be asked of you until after you have passed the written exam. The reason for this is that the written exam eliminates many applicants, and many agencies do not want to invest the time and costs related to checking documentation of applicants who may not pass the written exam. You probably know this already, which may be the reason you have invested in this study guide to help you get over the first hurdle.

Steps in the Hiring Process

Although different agencies may arrange the steps in the hiring process differently, virtually all will include the following steps:

1. Completing the written application (possibly online)
2. Successfully passing the written exam
3. Passing the physical fitness (or ability) tests
4. Passing the background investigation
5. Passing the medical and psychological examinations

Depending on the agency to which you have applied, other steps might include an oral appraisal exam and a polygraph exam. A drug-screening exam (generally a urinalysis) will also be administered, either at the physical fitness test or during the medical exam. Generally, you must pass each step in the process to be permitted to move on to the next phase of the application process.

Some agencies may ask for letters of recommendation; others, such as the PSP, specifically advise candidates that no recommendations will be accepted and that, in fact, they will be discarded if received. Some agencies may ask for a traditional resume, while others will expect you to provide all required information on the application form itself. Agencies that accept military service in lieu of educational requirements or that offer veterans' preference points will ask you to provide a non-returnable copy of the Certificate of Release or Discharge from Active Duty (Form DD-214, Member 4 copy). If you are applying while still an active duty member of the military, there are other requirements you must fulfill, which are generally available on the agency's website or obtainable by a telephone call or e-mail to the recruitment section.

Hiring Trends

It is difficult to discuss hiring trends in state policing because the sizes of the agencies vary so greatly. Remember that the smallest state police agency has only about 150 employees, while the largest has over 7,000. In addition, state policing is not a career that someone enters casually. Most of those who become state troopers have sought the position for many years. The voluntary turnover rates are low; most of those who pass all the steps in the hiring process and who successfully complete the academy remain for their entire work lives, usually retiring after 20 or 25 years of service. It can be estimated that even the larger agencies hire no more than 100 or 200 troopers each year. Because there are mandatory retirement ages for troopers in many states (usually 55 or 60), the number of vacancies may depend on whether the agency increased in size at particular times in its history. If there was a large increase in staff at a particular period, this may mean that there will be a disproportionately large number of retirements in a particular year. Current applicants are at somewhat of an advantage because new roles for state police

agencies in combating terrorism, illegal immigration, and computer-related crimes have resulted in some increases in staff complements.

Regardless of these small increases, the position is selective. The NYSP is an excellent example. In 2008, the agency reported on its website that for its most recent exam, more than 19,000 applicants took the exam and 15,700 passed. Until recently, the NYSP usually conducted two academy classes each year, but budget constraints have changed this. Although class size may vary from about 100 to 250 recruit officers per class, what generally does not vary is the statistic that it takes about ten candidates to fill one vacancy. What this means is that for every ten people who pass the written exam, nine do not pass the later portions of the applicant process. This means that about 1,000 people who passed the written exam are contacted for processing to fill 100 positions. Other states do not differ substantially.

Some agencies may have even higher rates of applicants who pass the written exam but do not reach the point of entering an academy. Rather than making the written exam less important, this fact highlights the importance of doing well. Most agencies contact applicants in the order they ranked on the written exam. Thus, the higher your score, the earlier you will have the opportunity to enter into the rest of the hiring process—and the sooner you may be called to attend an academy class.

Training

What can you expect when you attend an academy class? The first thing to know is that state police training is not like a vacation or camp. Depending on the state in which you are hired, you can expect to attend the academy for between five and eight months. Generally, you will be expected to live on the academy grounds at least from Sunday evening to Friday night. Some academies do not permit recruit officers to go home at all until they are partway through the training period. This means that if you have dependent children or other relatives, you will have to make provisions for their care in your absence. The same is true if you have pets.

Academy training is a full-time responsibility, and you will live under paramilitary organization conditions for the 27-week duration of the academy training. The PSP considers the normal training day to begin at 5:30 A.M. and end at 10:45 P.M. While you may not be busy for all these hours, you should expect some nighttime training and other activities that may be scheduled for after the dinner period. You will not be permitted to hold any type of job or attend any other schools while in the academy. You can expect to be up early in the morning, generally starting the day with an inspection of your living space and your uniform, participating in some physical activity, and then attending a full day of classroom activities. You will be advised on what you are expected to bring with you on the first day of training; the PSP's website lists 20 items of training uniforms and materials you are to have on the first day of the academy. The list ranges from uniforms to gym clothing, civilian attire, toiletry and bath items, and 30 hangers of the same color. In that respect, it might seem like summer camp or a college dorm, but the discipline will be far stricter than at either of those places. Candidates with a military background will have a more realistic idea of what to expect. Other agencies may be somewhat less specific, but the expectations are similar.

Much has been written about the rigors of the physical training at most state police academies. Of course, you will have to be in excellent physical shape to pass the preemployment physical, but the regimen may still be taxing. Remember that by the time you get to most academies, you will already have passed a strenuous physical ability test, but you will be expected to stay in top shape and can expect to be tested frequently on your flexibility, strength, and cardiovascular health. Using the PSP, one of the most rigorous academies, as an example, upon arrival at the academy, cadets are expected to pass the same physical

fitness test they took for entry, and to participate in a program that includes calisthenics, weight training, fighting techniques, boxing, and defensive tactics.

Depending on the policies of your department, you may be taught to drive a variety of vehicles in addition to a passenger vehicle. In every state, you will receive firearms training, at least in your sidearm and a shotgun, and, in some states, in a wider variety of weapons. Expect to run daily in the morning, the evening, or both. You can also expect swimming, water rescue, and emergency medical training, although only a few states expect you to go beyond Red Cross basic first-aid training. Those who are or want to become certified emergency medical technicians or even paramedics may be provided with the opportunity to take this training or refresh their certifications.

Although physical training is a vital part of the state police academy training, mental activity is also emphasized. You will also have a full range of classroom activities, including pencil-and-paper exams, oral presentations, and projects that you will have to work on individually or as part of a group. Virtually all academies expect you to maintain an academic average of at least 70% to successfully complete the classroom portion of the training. Recruits at the NJSP Academy are issued laptop computers that are used throughout the training.

Classroom instruction will range from the history of policing and the history of your agency to modern theories of community policing and crime prevention. You will study all aspects of law, including criminal law, motor vehicle law, drug law, and various aspects of civil law. You will also learn about crimes against children and how to interview juveniles and adults, including elderly persons who may need special attention. There are explanations of what constitutes domestic violence and how best to respond to these types of complaints. Additional training topics include decision making, responding to critical incidents, accident investigation and reconstruction, and other investigatory techniques. Practical police training will include how and when to make an arrest, how and when to search someone or something (particularly a motor vehicle), and general patrol techniques. There is also ethical training, dealing with moral dilemmas and how to deal with the authority and power that comes with being a police officer. This is all in addition to your other practical training on firearms, first aid, water safety, and possibly fire rescue and extracting injured persons from motor vehicles.

Most of your courses will be taught by senior members of the department, but outside experts, including attorneys, medical personnel, and community leaders, may be brought in for certain subjects. Many academies encourage student officers to form study groups in the evening, and many candidates also spend evening hours in the gym to help them meet the rigorous physical requirements.

The last set of academy requirements will involve personal grooming and maintaining your living quarters. Again, different from high school or college but similar to the military, state police recruits are expected to maintain military-style personal grooming standards, as well as keeping their dorm rooms and bunks clean. The length of hair and the permissibility of sideburns will be specified. Men can expect that beards and/or mustaches will be prohibited. Women may be expected to cut their hair so that it does not extend beyond the bottom of the uniform collar, or they may be permitted to keep their hair longer as long as it can be pinned up under all agency hats, helmets, or other headgear. Jewelry is generally not permitted, and cologne or makeup may also be prohibited.

Conditions of Employment

What will the job be like after all this, and how much can you expect to earn? Once again, the answers will depend on the agency. Salaries can normally be found on the agency's website. Full-service agencies may pay slightly higher than some highway patrol agencies, but because salaries come from government sources and because many agencies are unionized, the salary will be based in part on what a state can pay and what the officers' union representatives are able to obtain at the collective bargaining table. Some examples based on 2009 salaries may not be representative of all agencies, but can give you some idea of annual wage levels.

The NYSP starting salary as of April 1, 2009 was over $50,000 during academy training, and rising to more than $70,000 upon graduation. After annual raises, based on the current contract, troopers with five years' experience earned more than $87,000. There are also location expenses for certain urban counties and New York City. NJSP salaries are comparable; in 2009, troopers earned a starting salary of nearly $56,000 (which included a uniform allowance), and over $62,000 in their second year of service. Salaries are lower in other locations. There is also often overtime pay or compensatory time off and, in some cases, additional pay or time off for working holidays, nights, or weekends. Obviously, if you take and pass a promotion exam, your salary will be considerably higher in each of the agencies.

Each of the departments offers full medical benefits, including dental and life insurance for yourself and for your dependents, although you may have to contribute to dependents' coverage. All departments offer vacation benefits, generally starting at a minimum of two weeks and increasing with longevity. Such benefits are usually accrued monthly (often, one sick day for each month worked), and most agencies have policies that give you time off for work-related injuries and do not require you to use your own time. Candidates who are active in sports, where they may become injured, or candidates who are thinking of becoming parents at some point in their careers should investigate policies pertaining to use of time off for non-work-related events that may limit the ability to work full duty.

One reason that vacancies do not occur frequently in state police agencies is that retirement policies are usually more generous than in private industry. Once again, different agencies may differ, but generally, troopers are able to retire at half-pay or higher with some combination of age and years of service. A common combination is age 50 with 25 years of service or age 55 with 20 years of service. In many agencies, if you stay beyond the minimum age and years of service formula, you add considerably to your retirement package. Although many agencies have eliminated mandatory retirement regulations, some require you to retire at age 55, 60, or 63.

In return for this generous benefit package, you will be asked to give up some other benefits that you might have in your present employment. As explained earlier, virtually all agencies will expect you to live at the training facility while you are in the academy and to give up personal freedom as to going out, grooming, and other decisions you may now take for granted. Virtually all agencies assign new troopers to road patrol, and you will most likely have no say in what part of the state you are assigned and the hours and days you will work, although generally you will not be expected to work more than 40 hours a week without overtime pay.

You will be expected to work armed and in uniform in all types of weather and to handle all types of police calls to which you are dispatched. Most often, you will work in a marked patrol car alone and will be expected to handle your calls independently until another officer is available to respond. This is a major difference between state policing and policing in a large metropolitan police department. In a large department, you may work with a partner, or other officers may be only minutes away; in state policing, the closest member of your own department may be hours away, and even officers from smaller neighboring departments may be 30 minutes or more away. This is why physical training, judgment, and handling yourself in emergencies are such an important part of academy training.

3 ▶ ABOUT THE STATE TROOPER WRITTEN EXAM

CHAPTER SUMMARY
To select the best candidates to become state troopers, state governments employ a series of screening devices, including medical and physical examinations, character and background investigations, psychological assessments, and written tests. The written test is competitive.

How the Exam Is Scored

Those who score the highest marks have the greatest chance of being selected, but others who pass the exam also can be selected. Merely passing the exam is not to be disparaged. These exams are challenging, and the passing mark is set at a point deemed effective for selecting qualified candidates.

When the cutoff mark is set, one point on the grading scale becomes the difference between passing and failing. It may seem arbitrary that, for example, a candidate who scores 80% passes the exam, while a candidate who scores 79% fails, but a line must be drawn somewhere; otherwise, administering a written examination would be meaningless.

For candidates, the lesson to be drawn from this is that every point counts, whether the exam is difficult or relatively easy. Most of the exams are organized and graded like exams you have taken throughout your educational career, and are also similar to many of the exams given in the military to test candidates for entry and for specific specializations. These are traditional paper-and-pencil tests that, for ease of scoring, will usually be based on a total of 100 points. This may mean either 100 or 200 questions; most often, your score will be expressed as a percentage.

Your goal must be to score a higher mark than most of the other candidates. If the candidate is exceptionally brilliant, perhaps he or she need not worry about the competition; but for most candidates taking the exam, their preparation, practice, and perseverance—rather than sheer brilliance—is what separates the winners from the losers.

Establish a Study Game Plan

Establishing a study schedule is essential. These schedules are like game plans, and just like a football or basketball coach's game plan, they must be carried out successfully on the field or on the court. Going through the motions will not result in a win; full commitment to the game plan is required.

A candidate cannot succeed by going through the motions of reading the material and logging in the hours on the schedule. You must thoroughly study and master the material. This includes concentrating, making notes, restudying questions that you answered incorrectly, and working until you get 100% of the practice questions right. This is hard work, and requires motivation. Therefore, the first step is to find the motivation.

The desire to succeed on any test provides a basic level of motivation for most people, especially when passing the test opens an opportunity for employment. However, the best motivation for a candidate is to decide that becoming a state police officer is his or her number one career choice. That is the kind of commitment and motivation that a candidate needs to compete successfully, because the majority of the other candidates are just as committed to becoming state troopers.

A career as a state trooper is not an ordinary job. It is not merely a civil service position; it is an extraordinary position. It is a career that gives the officer a special status in society. It is a career that engenders respect and admiration for those who carry out their responsibilities honorably, courageously, fairly, and intelligently. A state trooper is endowed with substantial authority and responsibility to protect life and property, to preserve the peace, to protect the rights of citizens, to prevent crime, and to apprehend criminals. When necessary, a state trooper has the authority to use physical force and even deadly physical force.

We entrust the trooper with this authority, and we expect him or her to perform these duties in an exemplary manner. The functions that state troopers perform cover a wide spectrum of activities, including, but not limited to: investigating reported crimes, arresting lawbreakers, counseling youths, disarming dangerous criminals, enforcing traffic laws, investigating organized crime and terrorist networks, rendering aid and assistance to accident victims, reconstructing accident scenes, handling demonstrations and public disorders, and testifying at hearings and trials.

Each state trooper may be called upon to perform any of these functions, and all need to possess the skills that will enable them to do so. With training, they learn to perform these functions efficiently and effectively. However, before candidates are hired and before they are trained, they must demonstrate that they have the capability to perform these functions properly. They must demonstrate that they have the ability to assess situations and to make the proper judgments as to what action, if any, to take.

The written test is the primary means of ascertaining whether a candidate possesses the necessary capabilities. Written tests are not the perfect means of assessing candidates, but they have proven to be the most practical and effective. The written exam is, in many ways, the most important step in the hiring process, because it serves as an important gate-keeping function. The candidate who does not pass the written exam may be in excellent physical condition or may have other qualifications, but it will make no difference if he or she is unable to pass the written exam.

The Three Ps

Some states, in addition to the written test, employ oral question and answer tests to select candidates, but you must pass the written test before moving on to the oral test. Whether the process includes only a written test or requires both oral and written tests, the three Ps—preparation, practice, and perseverance—are the keys to success.

Preparation

Preparation includes not only the time spent studying the relevant material and guides, but also a full-time commitment to obtaining the knowledge and abilities that will make you a successful candidate and an excellent state police officer. You should study previous tests that were given for the position. Every day, you should devote a substantial amount of time to reading about law-enforcement topics. You should have a comprehensive, up-to-date police administration textbook as a reference. You should also read newspaper articles pertaining to police work, and focus on current police-related issues and controversies that are raised in the media.

As part of your preparation, you should endeavor to improve your vocabulary. In the course of your studies and when taking practice tests, you must look up every word about which you are unsure. In law enforcement, as in any specialized profession, there are words, terms, and jargon (specialized expressions used primarily in certain professions but not in others) that are repeatedly used. Candidates should be familiar with them and should understand how they are used in the context of law-enforcement terminology. Unfamiliarity with or an erroneous understanding of a word during the written exam can cause substantial difficulty, especially in a reading comprehension question. Because many exam questions are structured in a series format, an erroneous interpretation of one word can cause a series of errors.

Practice

Practice tests are invaluable tools for candidates to improve their test-taking skills. The best way to take practice tests is to replicate as closely as possible the actual test conditions. Uninterrupted privacy is a must, and the tests should be completed in one sitting. Training for written exams is similar to training for physical contests. Endurance is essential. The exams can be viewed as mental marathons. An exam of several hours tests a person's mental and emotional endurance. Those who have not trained will tire and as a result will make mistakes. Those who have trained will be better suited to remain focused and clearheaded until the end of the exam.

With rare exceptions, your written exam will be similar to the exams given in past years. Familiarity with previous exams is invaluable. Being familiar with the structures of individual questions and of questions in a series will allow you to quickly note the question format and proceed to the content of the questions. This will save time and considerable mental energy.

The types of questions are each described in later chapters of this book. The most common types of questions are reading-based (comprehension); writing and information ordering; mathematics; spatial and directional orientation (generally map reading); memory and observation; and problem solving, which includes reasoning, judgment, and sensitivity. Generally, there will be anywhere between five and 15 questions in each category, although some categories may be stressed more strongly than others. The most common response pattern will be multiple choice (select from **a** through **d**), although true/false or short response questions may also be included.

Sometimes, the examiners will employ a new format for the entire exam or for a section of the exam. In the event that the exam uses a new format, candidates who are thoroughly familiar with past exams will recognize that a new format is being employed. With this knowledge, you can avoid panic, because you will know that all the other candidates taking the exam will be as unfamiliar with the new format as you are.

Perseverance

Perseverance is the product of motivation and commitment. Studying past exam questions repeatedly until you get them all right, constantly working to improve your vocabulary, working out math problems, and sticking to good and consistent study habits is hard work. If you have a year to prepare, it is a long haul. If you have only a few short months, the concentrated effort to prepare can be arduous. To overcome any discouragement that may arise, and to overcome any tendency to put off work that needs to be done today, you must periodically revisit and, if necessary, revise your motivations and commitments. You should have in mind a set of articulated goals, and remember the benefits of becoming a state police officer—the pride, the respect, the accomplishment. State police officers have the opportunity to help others, to make a difference in society, and to preserve and improve the community. Success in these things brings success in life.

By any measure, the yearly salary is not exorbitant, but over the course of a career, the security of the steady salary, pay raises, health benefits, pension benefits, and the opportunity for promotions provide substantial value that many higher paying jobs do not offer.

Moreover, becoming a state police officer may be only the first step on the ladder to higher ranks, further career advancement, higher salaries, and greater opportunities. To become a sergeant, a lieutenant, a captain, a colonel, or a chief, you must first pass the initial written exam for entry into the agency. To move up the ranks, you must do your best at the very beginning of your career, because the higher the mark you score, the sooner you will be hired, and the sooner you will have the opportunity to take the exam for promotion to sergeant. The written promotion exam will follow the same format as the entry exam, so the good study habits you developed at the beginning of your career will help you excel again. Then, of course, the sooner you become a sergeant, the sooner you can move up further in the ranks.

With these opportunities for advancement, you should realize that the written exam to become a state police officer is much more than a single test. It is only the first step on the ladder. In a cost-benefit analysis, you should not calculate the time and effort you expend preparing and practicing versus the benefit of becoming an officer, but rather the expenditure versus the opportunity of achieving higher rank and the opportunities that will follow.

Just as you did for initial information about job qualifications and other portions of the hiring process, visit the website of the agency of your choice to learn more about the written exam. Some agencies post sample questions and study hints similar to those in this book. Equally important is the information on test dates and application deadlines. Most agencies test no more than twice a year, some less frequently than that. There are also cut-off dates by which your application must have been received for you to be permitted entry into a test site. If this information is not available on the website, contact the agency by e-mail or telephone or reach out to your recruiter for relevant details.

4 ▶ THE LEARNINGEXPRESS TEST PREPARATION SYSTEM

CHAPTER SUMMARY

Taking a state trooper exam can be tough, and your career in law enforcement depends on passing the exam. The Learning-Express Test Preparation System, developed exclusively for LearningExpress by leading test experts, gives you the discipline and attitude you need to succeed.

Taking the state trooper written exam is no picnic, and neither is getting ready for it. Your future career depends on passing the test, but there are all sorts of pitfalls that can keep you from doing your best on this all-important exam. Here are some of the obstacles that can stand in the way of your success:

- Being unfamiliar with the format of the exam
- Being paralyzed by test anxicty
- Leaving your preparation to the last minute
- Not preparing at all
- Not knowing vital test-taking skills: how to pace yourself through the exam, how to use the process of elimination, and when to guess
- Not being in tip-top mental and physical shape
- Arriving late at the test site, having to work on an empty stomach, or shivering through the exam because the room is cold

What's the common denominator in all these test-taking pitfalls? One word: control. Who's in control, you or the exam?

Now the good news: The LearningExpress Test Preparation System puts you in control. In just nine easy-to-follow steps, you will learn everything you need to know to make sure that you are in charge of your preparation and your performance on the exam. Other test takers may let the test get the better of them; other test takers may be unprepared or out of shape—but not you. You will have taken all the steps you need to take to get a high score on the state trooper written exam.

Here's how the LearningExpress Test Preparation System works: Nine easy steps lead you through everything you need to know and do to get ready to master your exam. Each of the following steps includes both reading about the step and one or more activities. It is important that you do the activities along with the reading, or you won't be getting the full benefit of the system.

Step 1: Get Information
Step 2: Conquer Test Anxiety
Step 3: Make a Plan
Step 4: Learn to Manage Your Time
Step 5: Learn to Use the Process of Elimination
Step 6: Know When to Guess
Step 7: Reach Your Peak Performance Zone
Step 8: Get Your Act Together
Step 9: Do It!

If you have several hours, you can work through the whole LearningExpress Test Preparation System in one sitting. Otherwise, you can break it up and do just one or two steps a day for the next several days. It is up to you—remember, you are in control.

Step 1: Get Information

Activities: Read Chapter 3, "About the State Trooper Written Exam," and use the suggestions there to find out about your requirements.
Knowledge is power. Therefore, first, you have to find out everything you can about the state trooper exam. Once you have your information, the next steps will show you what to do about it.

Part A: Straight Talk about the State Trooper Written Exam

Why do you have to take this exam, anyway? State policing is an attractive career option to many people, and the number of candidates often exceeds the number of job openings. To ensure that they hire the most qualified candidates, your state or the agency you want to work for will require you to take a written exam.

It is important for you to remember that your score on the written exam does not determine how smart you are or even whether you will make a good state trooper. There are all kinds of things a written exam like this can't test: whether you are likely to show up late or call in sick a lot, whether you can follow orders, or whether you can become part of a unit that works together to accomplish a task. Those kinds of things are hard to evaluate on a written exam. Meanwhile, it is easy to evaluate whether you can correctly answer questions about your job duties.

This is not to say that correctly answering the questions on the written exam is not important! The knowledge tested on the exam is knowledge you will need to do your job, and your ability to enter the profession depends on passing this exam. And that's why you are here—to achieve control over the exam.

Part B: What's on the Test

If you haven't already done so, stop here and read Chapter 3 of this book, which gives you an overview of the written exam. Later, you will have the opportunity to take the sample practice exams in Chapters 5, 13, 14, 15, 16, and 17.

Step 2: Conquer Test Anxiety

Activity: Take the Test Anxiety Quiz on page 22.
Having complete information about the exam is the first step in getting control of the exam. Next, you have to overcome one of the biggest obstacles to test success: test anxiety. Test anxiety can not only impair your performance on the exam itself, it can even keep you from preparing! In this step, you will learn stress management techniques that will help you succeed on your exam. Learn these strategies now, and practice them as you complete the exams in this book so that they will be second nature to you by exam day.

Combating Test Anxiety

The first thing you need to know is that a little test anxiety is a good thing. Everyone gets nervous before a big exam—and if that nervousness motivates you to prepare thoroughly, so much the better. Many well-known people throughout history have experienced anxiety or nervousness—from performers such as actor Sir Laurence Olivier and singer Aretha Franklin to writers such as Charlotte Brontë and Alfred, Lord Tennyson. In fact, anxiety probably gave them a little extra edge—just the kind of edge you need to do well, whether on a stage or in an examination room.

Stop here and complete the Test Anxiety Quiz on the next page to find out whether your level of test anxiety is something you should worry about.

Stress Management before the Test

If you feel your level of anxiety getting the best of you in the weeks before the test, here is what you need to do to bring the level down again:

- **Get prepared.** There's nothing like knowing what to expect and being prepared for it to put you in control of test anxiety. That's why you are reading this book. Use it faithfully, and remind yourself that you are better prepared than most of the people taking the test.
- **Practice self-confidence.** A positive attitude is a great way to combat test anxiety. This is no time to be humble or shy. Stand in front of the mirror and say to your reflection, "I'm prepared. I'm full of self-confidence. I'm going to ace this test. I know I can do it." If you hear it often enough, you will start to believe it.
- **Fight negative messages.** Every time someone starts telling you how hard the exam is or how it is almost impossible to get a high score, start telling them your self-confidence messages. If the someone with the negative messages is you, telling yourself *you don't do well on exams* or *you just can't do this*, don't listen.
- **Visualize.** Imagine yourself reporting for duty on your first day as a state trooper. Visualizing success can help make it happen—and it reminds you of why you are working so hard to pass the exam.
- **Exercise.** Physical activity helps calm down your body and focus your mind. Besides, being in good physical shape can actually help you do well on the exam. Go for a run, lift weights, go swimming—and do it regularly.

You need to worry about test anxiety only if it is extreme enough to impair your performance. The following questionnaire will provide a diagnosis of your level of test anxiety. In the blank before each statement, write the number that most accurately describes your experience.

0 = Never   1 = Once or twice   2 = Sometimes   3 = Often

_____ I have gotten so nervous before an exam that I simply put down the books and didn't study for it.

_____ I have experienced disabling physical symptoms such as vomiting and severe headaches because I was nervous about an exam.

_____ I have simply not shown up for an exam because I was scared to take it.

_____ I have experienced dizziness and disorientation while taking an exam.

_____ I have had trouble filling in the little circles because my hands were shaking too hard.

_____ I have failed an exam because I was too nervous to complete it.

_____ **Total: Add up the numbers in the blanks above.**

Your Test Stress Score

Here are the steps you should take, depending on your score. If you scored:

- **Below 3,** your level of test anxiety is nothing to worry about; it's probably just enough to give you that little extra edge.
- **Between 3 and 6,** your test anxiety may be enough to impair your performance, and you should practice the stress management techniques listed in this chapter to try to bring your test anxiety down to manageable levels.
- **Above 6,** your level of test anxiety is a serious concern. In addition to practicing the stress management techniques listed in this chapter, you may want to seek additional, personal help. Call your local high school or community college and ask for the academic counselor. Tell the counselor that you have a level of test anxiety that sometimes keeps you from being able to take the exam. The counselor may be willing to help you or may suggest someone else you should talk to.

Stress Management on Test Day

There are several ways you can bring down your level of test anxiety on test day. They will work best if you practice them in the weeks before the test, so you know which ones work best for you.

- **Deep breathing.** Take a deep breath while you count to five. Hold it for a count of one, then let it out for a count of five. Repeat several times.
- **Move your body.** Try rolling your head in a circle. Rotate your shoulders. Shake your hands from the wrist. Many people find these movements very relaxing.
- **Visualize again.** Think of the place where you are most relaxed: lying on the beach in the sun, walking through the park, or whatever makes you feel good. Now close your eyes and imagine you are actually there. If you practice in advance, you will find that you need only a few seconds of this exercise to experience a significant increase in your sense of well-being.

When anxiety threatens to overwhelm you right there during the exam, there are still things you can do to manage the stress level.

- **Repeat your self-confidence messages.** You should have them memorized by now. Say them quietly to yourself, and believe them!
- **Visualize one more time.** This time, visualize yourself moving smoothly and quickly through the test, answering every question correctly, and finishing just before time is up. Like most visualization techniques, this one works best if you have practiced it ahead of time.
- **Find an easy question.** Skim over the test until you find an easy question, and answer it. Getting even one circle filled in gets you into the test-taking groove.
- **Take a mental break.** Everyone loses concentration once in a while during a long test. It is normal, so you shouldn't worry about it. Instead, accept what has happened. Say to yourself, "Hey,

I lost it there for a minute. My brain is taking a break." Put down your pencil, close your eyes, and do some deep breathing for a few seconds. Then you will be ready to go back to work.

Try these techniques ahead of time, and see which ones work best for you.

Step 3: Make a Plan

Activity: Construct a study plan.
Maybe the most important thing you can do to get control of yourself and your exam is to make a study plan. Too many people fail to prepare simply because they fail to plan. Spending hours poring over sample test questions the day before the exam not only raises your level of test anxiety, but also will not replace careful preparation and practice over time.

Don't fall into the cram trap. Take control of your preparation time by mapping out a study schedule.

Even more important than making a plan is making a commitment. You can't review everything that might be on the test in one night. You need to set aside some time every day for study and practice. Try for at least 20 minutes a day. Twenty minutes daily will do you much more good than two hours on Saturday—divide your test preparation into smaller pieces of the larger work. In addition, making study notes, creating visual aids, and memorizing can be quite useful as you prepare. Each time you begin to study, quickly review your last lesson. This routine will help you retain all you have learned and help you assess whether you are studying effectively. You may realize you are not remembering some of the material you studied earlier. Approximately one week before your exam, try to determine the areas that are still most difficult for you.

Don't put off your study until the day before the exam. Start now. A few minutes a day, with half an hour or more on weekends, can make a big difference in your score.

Learning Styles

Each of us absorbs information differently. Whichever way works best for you is called your dominant learning method. If someone asks you for help constructing a new bookcase, which may be in many pieces, how do you begin? Do you need to read the directions and see the diagram? Would you rather hear someone read the directions to you—telling you which part connects to another? Or do you draw your own diagram?

The three main learning methods are visual, auditory, and kinesthetic. Determining which type of learner you are will help you create tools for studying.

1. **Visual learners** need to see the information in the form of maps, pictures, text, words, or math examples. Outlining notes and important points in colorful highlighters and taking note of diagrams and pictures may be key in helping you study.
2. **Auditory learners** retain information when they can hear directions, the spelling of a word, a math theorem, or poem. Repeating information aloud or listening to your notes on a tape recorder may help. Many auditory learners also find working in study groups or having someone quiz them is beneficial.
3. **Kinesthetic learners** must *do*! They need to draw diagrams, or write directions. Rewriting notes on index cards or making margin notes in your textbooks also helps kinesthetic learners to retain information.

Mnemonics

Mnemonics are memory tricks that help you remember what you need to know. The three basic principles in the use of mnemonics are imagination, association, and location. Acronyms (words created from the first letters in a series of words) are common mnemonics. One acronym you may already know is **HOMES**, for the names of the Great Lakes (**H**uron, **O**ntario, **M**ichigan, **E**rie, and **S**uperior). **ROY G. BIV** reminds people of the colors in the spectrum (**r**ed, **o**range, **y**ellow, **g**reen, **b**lue, **i**ndigo, and **v**iolet). Depending on the type of learner you are, mnemonics can also be colorful or vivid images, stories, word associations, or catchy rhymes such as "Thirty days hath September . . ." created in your mind. Any type of learner, whether visual, auditory, or kinesthetic, can use mnemonics to help the brain store and interpret information.

Step 4: Learn to Manage Your Time

Activities: Practice these strategies as you take the sample tests in this book.

Steps 4, 5, and 6 of the LearningExpress Test Preparation System put you in charge of your exam by showing you test-taking strategies that work. Practice these strategies as you take the sample tests in this book, and then you will be ready to use them on test day.

First, you will take control of your time on the exam. Most state trooper exams have a time limit, which may give you more than enough time to complete all the questions—or may not. It is a terrible feeling to hear the examiner say, "Five minutes left," when you are only three-quarters of the way through the test. Here are some tips to keep that from happening to you.

- **Follow directions.** If the directions are given orally, listen to them. If they are written on the exam booklet, read them carefully. Ask questions before the exam begins if there's anything you don't understand. If you are allowed to write in your exam booklet, write down the beginning time and the ending time of the exam.
- **Pace yourself.** Glance at your watch every few minutes, and compare the time to how far you have gotten in the test. When one-quarter of the time has elapsed, you should be a quarter of the way through the test, and so on. If you are falling behind, pick up the pace a bit.

- **Keep moving.** Don't spend too much time on one question. If you don't know the answer, skip the question and move on. Circle the number of the question in your test booklet in case you have time to come back to it later.
- **Keep track of your place on the answer sheet.** If you skip a question, make sure that you also skip the question on the answer sheet. Check yourself every 5–10 questions to make sure that the number of the question still corresponds with the number on the answer sheet.
- **Don't rush.** Though you should keep moving, rushing won't help. Try to keep calm and work methodically and quickly.

Step 5: Learn to Use the Process of Elimination

Activity: Complete worksheet on Using the Process of Elimination (see page 27).

After time management, your next most important tool for taking control of your exam is using the process of elimination wisely. It is standard test-taking wisdom that you should always read all the answer choices before choosing your answer. This helps you find the right answer by eliminating wrong answer choices. And, sure enough, that standard wisdom applies to your state trooper exam, too.

Let's say you are facing a vocabulary question that goes like this:

"Biology uses a binomial system of classification." In this sentence, the word *binomial* most nearly means
a. understanding the law.
b. having two names.
c. scientifically sound.
d. having a double meaning.

If you happen to know what *binomial* means, of course you don't need to use the process of elimination, but let's assume you don't. So, you look at the answer choices. "Understanding the law" sure doesn't sound very likely for something having to do with biology. So you eliminate choice **a**—and now you have only three answer choices to deal with. Mark an X next to choice **a**, so you never have to read it again.

Now, move on to the other answer choices. If you know that the prefix *bi-* means *two*, as in *bicycle*, you will flag choice **b** as a possible answer. Mark a check mark beside it, meaning "good answer, I might use this one."

Choice **c**, "scientifically sound," is a possibility. At least it's about science, not law. It could work here, though, when you think about it, having a "scientifically sound" classification system in a scientific field is kind of redundant. You remember the *bi-* in *binomial*, and probably continue to like answer **b** better. But you're not sure, so you put a question mark next to **c**, meaning "well, maybe."

Now, choice **d**, "having a double meaning." You're still keeping in mind that *bi-* means *two*, so this one looks possible at first. But then you look again at the sentence the word belongs in, and you think, "Why would biology want a system of classification that has two meanings? That wouldn't work very well!" If you're really taken with the idea that *bi-* means *two*, you might put a question mark here. But if you're feeling a little more confident, you'll put an X. You already have a better answer picked out.

Now your question looks like this:

"Biology uses a binomial system of classification." In this sentence, the word *binomial* most nearly means
X a. understanding the law.
✓ b. having two names.
? c. scientifically sound.
? d. having a double meaning.

You've got just one check mark for a good answer. If you're pressed for time, you should simply mark choice **b** on your answer sheet. If you have the time to be extra careful, you could compare your check-mark answer to your question-mark answers to make sure that it's better. (It is: The *binomial* system in biology is the one that gives a two-part genus and species name, like *Homo sapiens*.)

It is good to have a system for marking good, bad, and maybe answers. We recommend this one:

> **X** = bad
> **✓** = good
> **?** = maybe

If you don't like these marks, devise your own system. Just make sure you do it long before test day—while you are working through the practice exams in this book—so you won't have to worry about it during the test.

Even when you think you are absolutely clueless about a question, you can often use the process of elimination to get rid of at least one answer choice. If so, you are better prepared to make an educated guess, as you will see in Step 6. More often, you can eliminate answers until you have only two possible answers. Then you are in a strong position to guess.

Try using your powers of elimination on the questions in the worksheet on page 27, Using the Process of Elimination. The questions are not about law enforcement; they are just designed to show you how the process of elimination works. The answer explanations for this worksheet show one possible way you might use the process to arrive at the right answer.

Step 6: Know When to Guess

Activity: Complete worksheet on Your Guessing Ability (see page 28).

Armed with the process of elimination, you are ready to take control of one of the big questions in test taking: Should I guess? The answer is *Yes*. Some exams have what's called a "guessing penalty," in which a fraction of your wrong answers is subtracted from your right answers—but state trooper exams don't tend to work like that. The number of questions you answer correctly yields your raw score. So you have nothing to lose and everything to gain by guessing.

The more complicated answer to the question "Should I guess?" depends on you—your personality and your guessing intuition. There are two things you need to know about yourself before you go into the exam:

1. Are you a risk taker?
2. Are you a good guesser?

You will have to decide about your risk-taking quotient on your own. To find out if you are a good guesser, complete the Your Guessing Ability worksheet on page 28.

Step 7: Reach Your Peak Performance Zone

Activity: Complete the Physical Preparation Checklist.

To get ready for a challenge like a big exam, you have to take control of your physical, as well as your mental, state. Exercise, proper diet, and rest in the weeks prior to the test will ensure that your body works with, rather than against, your mind on test day, as well as during your preparation.

Use the process of elimination to answer the following questions.

1. Ilsa is as old as Meghan will be in five years. The difference between Ed's age and Meghan's age is twice the difference between Ilsa's age and Meghan's age. Ed is 29. How old is Ilsa?
   a. 4
   b. 10
   c. 19
   d. 24

2. "All drivers of commercial vehicles must carry a valid commercial driver's license whenever operating a commercial vehicle."

   According to this sentence, which of the following people need NOT carry a commercial driver's license?
   a. a truck driver idling his engine while waiting to be directed to a loading dock
   b. a bus operator backing her bus out of the way of another bus in the bus lot
   c. a taxi driver driving his personal car to the grocery store
   d. a limousine driver taking the limousine to her home after dropping off her last passenger of the evening

3. Smoking tobacco has been linked to
   a. increased risk of stroke and heart attack.
   b. all forms of respiratory disease.
   c. increasing mortality rates over the past ten years.
   d. juvenile delinquency.

4. Which of the following words is spelled correctly?
   a. incorrigible
   b. outragous
   c. domestickated
   d. understandible

Answers

Here are the answers, as well as some suggestions as to how you might have used the process of elimination to find them.

1. **d.** You should have eliminated choice **a** off the bat. Ilsa can't be four years old if Meghan is going to be Ilsa's age in five years. The best way to eliminate other answer choices is to try plugging them in to the information given in the problem. For instance, for choice **b**, if Ilsa is 10, then Meghan must be 5. The difference in their ages is 5. The difference between Ed's age, 29, and Meghan's age, 5, is 24. Is 24 two times 5? No. Then choice **b** is wrong. You could eliminate choice **c** in the same way and be left with choice **d**.

2. **c.** Note the word not in the question, and go through the answers one by one. Is the truck driver in choice **a** "operating a commercial vehicle"? Yes, idling counts as "operating," so he needs to have a commercial driver's license. Likewise, the bus operator in choice **b** is operating a commercial vehicle; the question doesn't say the operator has to be on the street. The limo driver in choice **d** is operating a commercial vehicle, even if it doesn't have a passenger in it. However, the cabbie in choice **c** is not operating a commercial vehicle, but his own private car.

3. a. You could eliminate choice **b** simply because of the presence of the word all. Such absolutes hardly ever appear in correct answer choices. Choice **c** looks attractive until you think a little about what you know—aren't fewer people smoking these days, rather than more? So how could smoking be responsible for a higher mortality rate? (If you didn't know that mortality rate means the rate at which people die, you might keep this choice as a possibility, but you would still be able to eliminate two answers and have only two to choose from.) And choice **d** is unlikely, so you could eliminate that one, too. You are left with the correct choice, **a**.

4. a. How you used the process of elimination here depends on which words you recognized as being spelled incorrectly. If you knew that the correct spellings were outrageous, domesticated, and understandable, then you were home free.

Your Guessing Ability

The following are ten really hard questions. You are not supposed to know the answers. Rather, this is an assessment of your ability to guess when you don't have a clue. Read each question carefully, just as if you did expect to answer it. If you have any knowledge of the subject, use that knowledge to help you eliminate wrong answer choices.

1. September 7 is Independence Day in
 a. India.
 b. Costa Rica.
 c. Brazil.
 d. Australia.

2. Which of the following is the formula for determining the momentum of an object?
 a. $p = MV$
 b. $F = ma$
 c. $P = IV$
 d. $E = mc^2$

3. Because of the expansion of the universe, the stars and other celestial bodies are all moving away from each other. This phenomenon is known as
 a. Newton's first law.
 b. the big bang.
 c. gravitational collapse.
 d. Hubble flow.

4. American author Gertrude Stein was born in
 a. 1713.
 b. 1830.
 c. 1874.
 d. 1901.

5. Which of the following is NOT one of the Five Classics attributed to Confucius?
 a. *I Ching*
 b. *Book of Holiness*
 c. *Spring and Autumn Annals*
 d. *Book of History*

6. The religious and philosophical doctrine that holds that the universe is constantly in a struggle between good and evil is known as
 a. Pelagianism.
 b. Manichaeanism.
 c. neo-Hegelianism.
 d. Epicureanism.

7. The third chief justice of the U.S. Supreme Court was
   a. John Blair.
   b. William Cushing.
   c. James Wilson.
   d. John Jay.

8. Which of the following is the poisonous portion of a daffodil?
   a. the bulb
   b. the leaves
   c. the stem
   d. the flowers

9. The winner of the Masters golf tournament in 1953 was
   a. Sam Snead.
   b. Cary Middlecoff.
   c. Arnold Palmer.
   d. Ben Hogan.

10. The state with the highest per capita personal income in 1980 was
   a. Alaska.
   b. Connecticut.
   c. New York.
   d. Texas.

Answers

Check your answers against the correct answers below.

1. c.
2. a.
3. d.
4. c.
5. b.
6. b.
7. b.
8. a.
9. d.
10. a.

How Did You Do?

You may have simply gotten lucky and actually known the answers to one or two questions. In addition, your guessing was probably more successful if you were able to use the process of elimination on any of the questions. Maybe you didn't know who the third chief justice was (question 7), but you knew that John Jay was the first. In that case, you would have eliminated choice **d** and therefore improved your odds of guessing right from one in four to one in three.

According to probability, you should get two and a half answers correct, so getting either two or three right would be average. If you got four or more right, you may be a really terrific guesser. If you got one or none right, you may be a poor guesser.

Keep in mind, though, that this is only a small sample. You should continue to keep track of your guessing ability as you work through the sample questions in this book. Circle the numbers of questions you guess on as you make your guess; or, if you don't have time while you take the practice tests, go back afterward and try to remember which questions you guessed at. Remember, on a test with four answer choices, your chance of guessing correctly is one in four. So keep a separate "guessing" score for each exam. How many questions did you guess on? How many did you get right? If the number you got right is at least one-fourth of the number of questions you guessed on, you are at least an average guesser—maybe better—and you should always go ahead and guess on the real exam. If the number you got right is significantly lower than one-fourth of the number you guessed on, you would be safe in guessing anyway, but maybe you would feel more comfortable if you guessed only selectively, when you can eliminate a wrong answer or at least have a good feeling about one of the answer choices.

Because the state trooper exam has no guessing penalty, even if you are a play-it-safe person with lousy intuition, you are still safe guessing every time.

Exercise

If you don't already have a regular exercise program going, the time during which you are preparing for an exam is actually an excellent time to start one. And if you are already keeping fit—or trying to get that way—don't let the pressure of preparing for an exam fool you into quitting now. Exercise helps reduce stress by pumping feel-good hormones called *endorphins* into your system. It also increases the oxygen supply throughout your body, including in your brain, so you will be at peak performance on test day.

A half hour of vigorous activity—enough to raise a sweat—every day should be your aim. If you are really pressed for time, every other day is okay. Choose an activity you like and get out there and do it. Jogging with a friend always makes the time go faster, or take a portable radio or MP3 player.

But don't overdo it. You don't want to exhaust yourself. Moderation is the key.

Diet

First of all, cut out the junk. Go easy on caffeine and nicotine, and eliminate alcohol from your system at least two weeks before the exam. What your body needs for peak performance is simply a balanced diet. Eat plenty of fruits and vegetables, along with protein and carbohydrates. Foods that are high in lecithin (an amino acid), such as fish and beans, are especially good "brain foods."

The night before the exam, you might carbo-load the way athletes do before a contest. Eat a big plate of spaghetti, rice and beans, or whatever your favorite carbohydrate is.

Rest

You probably know how much sleep you need every night to be at your best, even if you don't always get it. Make sure you do get that much sleep, though, for at least a week before the exam. Moderation is important here, too. Extra sleep will just make you groggy.

If you are not a morning person and your exam will be given in the morning, you should reset your internal clock so that your body doesn't think you are taking an exam at 3 A.M. You have to start this process well before the exam. The way it works is to get up half an hour earlier each morning, and then go to bed half an hour earlier that night. Don't try it the other way around; you will just toss and turn if you go to bed early without having gotten up early. The next morning, get up another half an hour earlier, and so on. How long you will have to do this depends on how late you are used to getting up.

Step 8: Get Your Act Together

Activity: Complete the Final Preparations worksheet.

You are in control of your mind and body; you are in charge of test anxiety, your preparation, and your test-taking strategies. Now it is time to take charge of external factors, like the testing site and the materials you need to take the exam.

Find out Where the Test Is and Make a Trial Run

The testing agency or your recruiter will notify you when and where your exam is being held. Do you know how to get to the testing site? Do you know how long it will take to get there? If not, make a trial run, preferably on the same day of the week at the same time of day. Make note, on the worksheet Final Preparations on page 33, of the amount of time it will take you to get to the exam site. Plan on arriving at least 10–15 minutes early so you can get the lay of the land, use the bathroom, and calm down. Then figure out how early you will have to get up that morning, and make sure you get up that early every day for a week before the exam.

Physical Preparation Checklist

For the week before the test, write down what physical exercise you engaged in and for how long and what you ate for each meal. Remember, you're trying for at least half an hour of exercise every other day (preferably every day) and a balanced diet that's light on junk food.

Exam minus 7 days

Exercise: _____ for _____ minutes

Breakfast: _____

Lunch: _____

Dinner: _____

Snacks: _____

Exam minus 6 days

Exercise: _____ for _____ minutes

Breakfast: _____

Lunch: _____

Dinner: _____

Snacks: _____

Exam minus 5 days

Exercise: _____ for _____ minutes

Breakfast: _____

Lunch: _____

Dinner: _____

Snacks: _____

Exam minus 4 days

Exercise: _____ for _____ minutes

Breakfast: _____

Lunch: _____

Dinner: _____

Snacks: _____

Exam minus 3 days

Exercise: _____ for _____ minutes

Breakfast: _____

Lunch: _____

Dinner: _____

Snacks: _____

Exam minus 2 days

Exercise: _____ for _____ minutes

Breakfast: _____

Lunch: _____

Dinner: _____

Snacks: _____

Exam minus 1 day

Exercise: _____ for _____ minutes

Breakfast: _____

Lunch: _____

Dinner: _____

Snacks: _____

Gather Your Materials

The night before the exam, lay out the clothes you will wear and the materials you have to bring with you to the exam. Plan on dressing in layers; you won't have any control over the temperature of the examination room. Have a sweater or jacket you can take off if it is warm. Use the checklist on the Final Preparations worksheet on the following page to help you pull together what you will need.

Don't Skip Breakfast

Even if you don't usually eat breakfast, do so on exam morning. A cup of coffee doesn't count. Don't eat doughnuts or other sweet foods, either. A sugar high will leave you with a sugar low in the middle of the exam. A mix of protein and carbohydrates is best: Cereal with milk, or eggs with toast, will do your body a world of good.

Step 9: Do It!

Activity: Ace the state trooper exam!

Fast forward to exam day. You are ready. You made a study plan and followed through. You practiced your test-taking strategies while working through this book. You are in control of your physical, mental, and emotional states. You know when and where to show up and what to bring with you. In other words, you are better prepared than most of the other people taking the state trooper exam with you.

Just one more thing: When you are done with the exam, you deserve a reward. Plan a celebration. Call up your friends and plan a party, or have a nice dinner for two—whatever your heart desires. Give yourself something to look forward to.

And then do it. Go into the exam, full of confidence, armed with test-taking strategies you have practiced until they are second nature. You are in control of yourself, your environment, and your performance on the exam. You are ready to succeed. So do it. Go in there and ace the exam. And look forward to your future career as a state trooper!

Getting to the Exam Site

Location of exam site: _____

Date: _____

Departure time: _____

Do I know how to get to the exam site?   Yes ____   No ____   (If no, make a trial run.)

Time it will take to get to exam site: _____

Things to Lay out the Night Before

Clothes I will wear   ____

Sweater/jacket   ____

Watch   ____

Photo ID   ____

Four #2 pencils   ____

Other Things to Bring/Remember

_____   _____

_____   _____

_____   _____

_____   _____

5 ▶ STATE TROOPER PRACTICE TEST 1

CHAPTER SUMMARY

This is the first practice test in the book based on the most commonly tested areas on the state trooper exam. By taking Practice Test 1 before you begin studying for the state trooper exam, you will get an idea of how much you already know and how much you need to learn.

The skills tested on the exam that follows are the ones that have been tested in the past on state trooper exams that focus on job-related skills. The exam you take may look somewhat different from this exam, but you'll find that this exam provides vital practice in the skills you need to pass a state trooper exam.

The practice test consists of 100 multiple-choice questions in the following areas: reading comprehension, writing and information ordering, mathematics, spatial and directional orientation, memory and observation, and problem solving. You should give yourself two hours to take this practice test. The time limit of the actual state trooper exam can vary from region to region.

State Trooper Practice Test 1

1. (a) (b) (c) (d)
2. (a) (b) (c) (d)
3. (a) (b) (c) (d)
4. (a) (b) (c) (d)
5. (a) (b) (c) (d)
6. (a) (b) (c) (d)
7. (a) (b) (c) (d)
8. (a) (b) (c) (d)
9. (a) (b) (c) (d)
10. (a) (b) (c) (d)
11. (a) (b) (c) (d)
12. (a) (b) (c) (d)
13. (a) (b) (c) (d)
14. (a) (b) (c) (d)
15. (a) (b) (c) (d)
16. (a) (b) (c) (d)
17. (a) (b) (c) (d)
18. (a) (b) (c) (d)
19. (a) (b) (c) (d)
20. (a) (b) (c) (d)
21. (a) (b) (c) (d)
22. (a) (b) (c) (d)
23. (a) (b) (c) (d)
24. (a) (b) (c) (d)
25. (a) (b) (c) (d)
26. (a) (b) (c) (d)
27. (a) (b) (c) (d)
28. (a) (b) (c) (d)
29. (a) (b) (c) (d)
30. (a) (b) (c) (d)
31. (a) (b) (c) (d)
32. (a) (b) (c) (d)
33. (a) (b) (c) (d)
34. (a) (b) (c) (d)
35. (a) (b) (c) (d)
36. (a) (b) (c) (d)
37. (a) (b) (c) (d)
38. (a) (b) (c) (d)
39. (a) (b) (c) (d)
40. (a) (b) (c) (d)
41. (a) (b) (c) (d)
42. (a) (b) (c) (d)
43. (a) (b) (c) (d)
44. (a) (b) (c) (d)
45. (a) (b) (c) (d)
46. (a) (b) (c) (d)
47. (a) (b) (c) (d)
48. (a) (b) (c) (d)
49. (a) (b) (c) (d)
50. (a) (b) (c) (d)
51. (a) (b) (c) (d)
52. (a) (b) (c) (d)
53. (a) (b) (c) (d)
54. (a) (b) (c) (d)
55. (a) (b) (c) (d)
56. (a) (b) (c) (d)
57. (a) (b) (c) (d)
58. (a) (b) (c) (d)
59. (a) (b) (c) (d)
60. (a) (b) (c) (d)
61. (a) (b) (c) (d)
62. (a) (b) (c) (d)
63. (a) (b) (c) (d)
64. (a) (b) (c) (d)
65. (a) (b) (c) (d)
66. (a) (b) (c) (d)
67. (a) (b) (c) (d)
68. (a) (b) (c) (d)
69. (a) (b) (c) (d)
70. (a) (b) (c) (d)
71. (a) (b) (c) (d)
72. (a) (b) (c) (d)
73. (a) (b) (c) (d)
74. (a) (b) (c) (d)
75. (a) (b) (c) (d)
76. (a) (b) (c) (d)
77. (a) (b) (c) (d)
78. (a) (b) (c) (d)
79. (a) (b) (c) (d)
80. (a) (b) (c) (d)
81. (a) (b) (c) (d)
82. (a) (b) (c) (d)
83. (a) (b) (c) (d)
84. (a) (b) (c) (d)
85. (a) (b) (c) (d)
86. (a) (b) (c) (d)
87. (a) (b) (c) (d)
88. (a) (b) (c) (d)
89. (a) (b) (c) (d)
90. (a) (b) (c) (d)
91. (a) (b) (c) (d)
92. (a) (b) (c) (d)
93. (a) (b) (c) (d)
94. (a) (b) (c) (d)
95. (a) (b) (c) (d)
96. (a) (b) (c) (d)
97. (a) (b) (c) (d)
98. (a) (b) (c) (d)
99. (a) (b) (c) (d)
100. (a) (b) (c) (d)

State Trooper Practice Test 1

Directions: Read the following passage, and then answer questions 1 through 4.

Trained criminal justice professionals are not the only people involved in the criminal justice system. Any ordinary person who has been victimized by crime is also included, but with a limited role. Once a crime has been committed, the government, or state, takes over the part of a victim. In criminal law, the government, often represented by an assistant district attorney, prosecutes or accuses the alleged perpetrator. The accused is the defendant who is presumed innocent. It is up to the prosecution to show, beyond a reasonable doubt, that the accused committed the crime(s) he or she is being put on trial for. Victims of crime often complain that they are left out of the criminal justice process. The defendant's lawyer, whether a private attorney or public defender, often negotiates outside the court with the prosecutor with the hope of avoiding a trial. The victim does not take part in these talks, which can determine the defendant's punishment. Victims often feel that when a "deal" is reached, the offender is not being adequately punished. If a trial does take place, a victim may not be told when key events, such as the testifying of a certain witness, are going to occur.

It is widely known that our court system is overwhelmed and there are many reasons for postponing or continuing with the proceedings at a later date. However, for the victim, it may feel that "justice delayed is justice denied." It is common for victims to be frustrated by the slow speed with which cases advance through the criminal justice system. There are signs that the system is moving toward increased recognition of victims' rights. A growing number of states will automatically contact the victim and/or witnesses when the offender is being released from incarceration.

1. The main purpose of the passage is to
   a. argue that the police are too rude to victims.
   b. question the use of public defenders.
   c. describe how a crime victim may experience the criminal justice system.
   d. specify the stages that a criminal case moves through the system after arrest.

2. According to the passage, which of the following is not a common experience of a crime victim?
   a. Victims are frustrated by the speed of case processing.
   b. Victims are included in decisions made by the prosecutor.
   c. Victims may be informed of their perpetrator's release back into the community.
   d. The victim's interests are represented by the government.

3. How might sentencing decisions be made?
   a. through lawyers' negotiations
   b. through consultation with the arresting officer
   c. based on what a judge deems is best
   d. through consultation with the victim

4. The passage suggests
   a. law enforcement should be more sensitive to victims' rights.
   b. lawyers should demand judges hear cases without delay.
   c. judges may be able to hear more cases a day than they do now.
   d. a victim may be frustrated by a number of factors in the processing of his or her criminal case.

Directions: Read the following passage, and then answer questions 5 through 8.

Police officers must read suspects their Miranda rights upon taking them into custody. When a suspect who is merely being questioned incriminates himself or herself, he or she might later claim to have been in custody, and seek to have the case dismissed on the grounds of not having been apprised of his or her Miranda rights. In such cases, a judge must make a determination as to whether or not a reasonable person would have believed himself or herself to have been in custody, based on certain criteria. The judge must determine whether the suspect was questioned in a threatening manner (for example, if the suspect was seated while both officers remained standing) and whether the suspect was aware that he or she was free to leave at any time. Officers must be aware of these criteria and take care not to give suspects grounds for later claiming themselves to have been in custody.

5. What is the main idea of the passage?
   a. Officers must remember to read suspects their Miranda rights.
   b. Judges, not police officers, make the final determination as to whether or not a suspect was in custody.
   c. Officers who are merely questioning a suspect must not give the suspect the impression that he or she is in custody.
   d. Miranda rights needn't be read to all suspects before questioning.

6. According to the passage, a suspect is not in custody when he or she is
   a. free to refuse to answer questions.
   b. free to leave the police station.
   c. apprised of his or her Miranda rights.
   d. not apprised of his or her Miranda rights.

7. When must police officers read Miranda rights to a suspect?
   a. while questioning the suspect
   b. before taking the suspect to the police station
   c. while placing the suspect under arrest
   d. before releasing the suspect

8. A police officer questioning a suspect who is not under arrest must
   a. read the suspect his or her Miranda rights.
   b. allow the suspect a phone call.
   c. advise the suspect of his or her right to a lawyer.
   d. inform the suspect that he or she is free to leave.

Directions: Read the following passage, and then answer questions 9 through 14.

Stalking is defined as the "willful, malicious, and repeated following and harassing of another person." The act of stalking can probably be traced back to the earliest episodes of human history, but in the United States, no substantive law existed to protect the victims of stalkers until 1990. Prior to this, the most that police officials could do was arrest the stalker for a minor offense or suggest the victim obtain a restraining order, a civil remedy often ignored by the offender. Frightened victims had their worst fears confirmed: They would have to be harmed—or killed—before anything could be done.

Stalking was brought into the public eye in 1989 by the stalker-murder of television star Rebecca Schaeffer, and then by the 1990 stalker-murders of four women in Orange County, California, in a single six-week period. When it was discovered that one of the Orange County victims had a restraining order in her purse when her stalker murdered her, California reacted by drafting the first anti-stalking law. Now most states have similar laws.

The solution is not perfect: Some stalkers are too mentally deranged or obsessed to fear a prison term, and on the flip side, there is the danger, however small, of abuse of the law, particularly in marital disputes. Most importantly, law enforcement officials and general society need to be better educated about stalking, especially about its gender-related issues. (The majority of stalking victims are women terrorized by former husbands or boyfriends.)

But the laws are a vast improvement, and they carry the threat of felony penalties of up to ten years in prison for those who would attempt to control or possess others through intimidation and terror.

9. Based on the passage, which of the following is likely the most common question asked of police by stalking victims prior to 1990?
 a. How can I get a restraining order?
 b. Does he have to hurt me before you'll arrest him?
 c. Why is this person stalking me?
 d. Is it legal for me to carry a weapon to protect myself?

10. Which of the following best expresses the main idea of the passage?
 a. More education is needed about sexism, because sexism is the most important element in the crime of stalking.
 b. Stalking is thought of as a new kind of crime, but has probably existed throughout human history.
 c. The new anti-stalking legislation is an important weapon against the crime of stalking, though it is not a complete answer.
 d. Today, almost every state in the United States has a very effective, if not perfect, anti-stalking law.

11. Which of the following is NOT mentioned in the passage as a weakness in the new anti-stalking legislation?
 a. The laws alone might not deter some stalkers.
 b. A person might be wrongly accused of being a stalker.
 c. The police and public do not completely understand the crime.
 d. Victims do not yet have adequate knowledge about anti-stalking laws.

12. Based on the passage, why are restraining orders ineffective in preventing stalking?
 a. Only civil charges can be leveled against the violator.
 b. Prior to 1990, restraining orders could not be issued against stalkers.
 c. Law enforcement officials do not take such orders seriously.
 d. Restraining orders apply only to married couples.

13. Which of the following is NOT a stated or implied motive for stalking?
 a. to own the victim
 b. to terrify the victim
 c. to rob the victim
 d. to badger the victim

14. Based on the information in the passage, which of the following did the murders of Rebecca Schaeffer and the Orange County women mentioned in the second paragraph have in common?
 a. The murders provided impetus for anti-stalking laws.
 b. The victims sought, but could not obtain, legal protection.
 c. The victims were stalked and killed by a husband or lover.
 d. The murders were the result of sexism.

Directions: Read the following passage, and then answer questions 15 through 17.

Law enforcement officers often do not like taking time from their regular duties to testify in court, but testimony is an important part of an officer's job. To be good witnesses, officers should keep complete notes detailing any potentially criminal or actionable incidents. When on the witness stand, officers may refer to those notes to refresh their memory about particular events. It is also very important for officers to listen carefully to the questions asked by the lawyers and to provide only the information requested. Officers should never volunteer opinions or any extra information that is beyond the scope of a question.

15. According to the passage, an officer who is testifying in court
 a. will be questioned by the judge.
 b. may refer to his or her notes while on the witness stand.
 c. must do so without pay.
 d. appreciates taking a break from routine assignments.

16. This passage is probably taken from a(n)
 a. memo entitled "Proper Arrest Procedure."
 b. newspaper article about crime prevention.
 c. recruitment pamphlet for law enforcement officers.
 d. officers' training manual.

17. According to the passage, testifying in court is
 a. an important part of a law enforcement officer's job.
 b. difficult, because lawyers try to trick witnesses.
 c. less stressful for law enforcement officers than for other witnesses.
 d. a waste of time, because judges usually let criminals off.

Directions: Read the following passage, and then answer questions 18 through 20.

Most criminals do not suffer from antisocial personality disorder; however, nearly all persons with this disorder have been in trouble with the law. Sometimes labeled *sociopaths*, they are a grim problem for society. Their crimes range from con games to murder, and they are set apart by what appears to be a complete lack of conscience. Often attractive and charming, and always inordinately self-confident, they nevertheless demonstrate a disturbing emotional shallowness, as if they had been born without a faculty as vital as sight or hearing. These individuals are not legally insane, nor do they suffer from the distortions of thought associated with mental illness; however, some experts believe they are mentally ill. If so, it is an illness that is exceptionally resistant to treatment, particularly since these individuals have a marked inability to learn from the past. It is this latter trait that makes them a special problem for law enforcement officials. Their ability to mimic true emotion enables them to convince prison officials, judges, and psychiatrists that they feel remorse. When released from incarceration, however, they go back to their old tricks, to their con games, their impulsive destructiveness, and their sometimes lethal deceptions.

18. Based on the preceding passage, which of the following is NOT likely a characteristic of the person with antisocial personality disorder?
 a. delusions of persecution
 b. feelings of superiority
 c. inability to suffer deeply
 d. inability to feel joy

19. Which piece of information is NOT provided in the passage?
   a. the crimes commonly committed by a person with antisocial personality disorder
   b. the likelihood of effective medicinal treatment
   c. the legal definition of insanity
   d. the ability of a person with antisocial personality disorder to be effectively rehabilitated with punishment

20. Based on the passage, which of the following words best sums up the inner emotional life of the person with an antisocial personality?
   a. angry
   b. empty
   c. anxious
   d. repressed

Directions: For questions 21 through 24, choose the answer choice that best rephrases the underlined portion of the given sentence.

21. This was the fifth of five speeches the mayor gave during this the month of May.
   a. This was the fifth of the five speeches the mayor gave during this the month of May.
   b. Of the five speeches the mayor gave during May, this was the fifth one.
   c. Thus far during the month of May, the mayor gave five speeches and this was the fifth.
   d. This was the fifth speech the mayor gave during the month of May.

22. The mechanic put the car in his garage, so as to be able to put it on a lift and examine the car's exhaust pipe underneath.
   a. so as to be able to put it on a lift and examine the car's exhaust pipe underneath.
   b. put it on a lift, and examined the car's exhaust pipe from underneath.
   c. and to examine it from underneath, put it on his lift and examined the exhaust pipe.
   d. and because he wanted to examine the car's exhaust pipe from underneath, put the car on the lift to inspect it.

23. Along with your membership to our health club or two months of free personal training.
   a. Along with your membership to our health club and
   b. Along with your membership to our health club comes
   c. With your membership to our health club,
   d. In addition to your membership to our health club being

24. To determine the speed of automobiles: radar is often used by the state police.
   a. To determine the speed of automobiles, radar is often used by the state police.
   b. In determining the speed of automobiles, the use of radar by state police is often employed.
   c. To determine the speed of automobiles, the state police often use radar.
   d. Radar by state police in determining the speed of automobiles is often used.

25. Three of the sentences below contain one or more grammatical or spelling errors. Select the answer choice that is correct as is.
   a. Ethics and the law having no true relationship.
   b. There is no true relationship between ethics and the law.
   c. Between ethics and the law, no true relationship.
   d. Ethics and the law is no true relationship.

26. Three of the sentences below contain one or more grammatical or spelling errors. Select the answer choice that is correct as is.
   a. Some people say jury duty is a nuisance that just takes up their precious time and that we don't get paid enough.
   b. Some people say jury duty is a nuisance that just takes up your precious time and that one doesn't get paid enough.
   c. Some people say jury duty is a nuisance that just takes up precious time and doesn't pay enough.
   d. Some people say jury duty is a nuisance that just takes up our precious time and that they don't get paid enough.

27. Three of the sentences below contain one or more grammatical or spelling errors. Select the answer choice that is correct as is.
   a. The art professor, along with several of her students, is planning to attend the gallery opening tomorrow evening.
   b. The art professor, along with several of her students, are planning to attend the gallery opening tomorrow evening.
   c. The art professor, along with several of her students, plan to attend the gallery opening tomorrow evening.
   d. The art professor, along with several of her students, have planned to attend the gallery opening tomorrow evening.

28. Three of the sentences below contain one or more grammatical or spelling errors. Select the answer choice that is correct as is.
   a. A longer happier life, caused by one's owning a pet.
   b. Owning a pet, for one to live a longer, happier life.
   c. To live a longer, happier life by one's owning a pet.
   d. Owning a pet can help one live a longer, happier life.

29. Three of the sentences below contain one or more grammatical or spelling errors. Select the answer choice that is correct as is.
   a. In mysteries, Sherlock Holmes and Dr. Watson solved mysteries written by Sir Arthur Conan Doyle.
   b. Sherlock Holmes and Dr. Watson solving mysteries writing by Sir Arthur Conan Doyle.
   c. Sherlock Homes and Dr. Watson solved mysteries written by Sir Arthur Conan Doyle.
   d. Sherlock Holmes and Dr. Watson having solved mysteries written by Sir Arthur Conan Doyle.

30. Three of the sentences below contain one or more grammatical or spelling errors. Select the answer choice that is correct as is.
   a. I don't like fish as much as my sister does.
   b. I don't like fish as much as my sister.
   c. Fish isn't liked by me as well as my sister.
   d. My sister likes it, but I don't like fish as much.

31. Identify the sentence that contains a mistake in capitalization, punctuation, grammar, or spelling. If you find no mistakes, select choice **d**.
   a. Our class took a field trip, going to the art museum.
   b. There are rocky cliffs along the coast.
   c. We saw Dr. Mason because our doctor was on vacation.
   d. no mistakes

32. Identify the sentence that contains a mistake in capitalization, punctuation, grammar, or spelling. If you find no mistakes, select choice **d**.
   a. Make sure your seatbelt is fastened.
   b. I'm afraid of spiders George is too.
   c. Yes, I will bring the dessert.
   d. no mistakes

33. Identify the sentence that contains a mistake in capitalization, punctuation, grammar, or spelling. If you find no mistakes, select choice **d.**
   a. They traveled south and hiked in the desert.
   b. "Don't shout at me," she yelled back.
   c. Joshua enters lots of contests, therefore he knows he can't win.
   d. no mistakes

34. Identify the sentence that contains a mistake in capitalization, punctuation, grammar, or spelling. If you find no mistakes, select choice **d.**
   a. Where's my blue jacket?
   b. The prizes were awarded to Juan and me.
   c. After midnight, you will turn into a pumpkin.
   d. no mistakes

35. Identify the sentence that contains a mistake in capitalization, punctuation, grammar, or spelling. If you find no mistakes, select choice **d.**
   a. When I heard the alarm, I jump out of bed.
   b. Mr. Fox is the president of his own company.
   c. At night, I listened to jazz on the radio.
   d. no mistakes

36. Identify the sentence that contains a mistake in capitalization, punctuation, grammar, or spelling. If you find no mistakes, select choice **d.**
   a. The book cost more than the course are.
   b. I like to listen to the radio when I study.
   c. Speed limits are determined by the state, not the federal government.
   d. no mistakes

37. Look at the four numbered sentences below. Choose the sentence order that would result in the best paragraph.
   (1) During the parole period, he is supervised by a parole officer.
   (2) The parole officer must also be concerned, however, about the safety of the community.
   (3) After a prisoner has served his sentence, he may be paroled to the county where he was tried.
   (4) A parole officer has a certain amount of latitude in supervising her parolees' transition from prison life.
   a. 1, 4, 2, 3
   b. 2, 1, 4, 3
   c. 4, 1, 3, 2
   d. 3, 2, 4, 1

38. Look at the four numbered sentences below. Choose the sentence order that would result in the best paragraph.
   (1) The banks asked the federal government for help, or a bailout.
   (2) When the banks are stable, it contributes to the overall stability of the American economy.
   (3) Banks made loans to people who could not pay them back.
   (4) People unable to make their mortgage payments to the banks faced home foreclosure.
   a. 2, 3, 1, 4
   b. 3, 4, 1, 2
   c. 1, 2, 3, 4
   d. 3, 2, 1, 4

39. Look at the four numbered sentences below. Choose the sentence order that would result in the best paragraph.

(1) Visits, especially from family members, can aid in a prisoner's rehabilitation.

(2) Usually, this means that a prisoner and his visitors may not have physical contact with each other.

(3) Therefore, they are separated by a pane of glass and must talk by phone.

(4) However, in order to maintain prison safety, family visits cannot be unrestricted.

a. 2, 4, 1, 3
b. 1, 4, 2, 3
c. 1, 2, 3, 4
d. 3, 1, 2, 4

40. The following question consists of four numbered sentences. Choose the sentence order that would result in the best paragraph.

(1) Therefore, persuading another person to commit a crime by discussing a specific crime with the intention that the crime be carried out is considered solicitation.

(2) First, the person must have persuaded another person to commit a crime.

(3) Second, the person must have been discussing a specific crime and must have had the intention that the act would be done.

(4) Police officers may become aware of a person who did not actually commit a crime, but solicited another person to do so.

a. 1, 3, 4, 2
b. 2, 4, 1, 3
c. 4, 2, 1, 3
d. 4, 2, 3, 1

41. Find the quotient of 12,440 and 40.

a. 497,600
b. 12,480
c. 12,400
d. 311

42. $540 \div 6 + 3 \times 24 =$

a. 2,232
b. 1,440
c. 1,260
d. 162

43. 3^3 is equal to

a. 9
b. 27
c. 81
d. 52

44. $376 - 360 + 337 =$

a. 663
b. 553
c. 453
d. 353

45. The fraction $\frac{12}{144}$ is equivalent to which of the following?

a. $\frac{1}{12}$
b. $\frac{2}{3}$
c. $\frac{1}{5}$
d. $\frac{1}{4}$

46. $\frac{4}{5} + \frac{1}{6} =$

a. $\frac{5}{6}$
b. $\frac{5}{11}$
c. $\frac{7}{15}$
d. $\frac{29}{30}$

47. $(23 + 47)(79 - 69) =$

a. 70
b. 218
c. 240
d. 700

48. In a department store, a woman's handbag was stolen while she was shopping. The handbag is worth approximately $150. Inside the handbag were the following items:

- 1 leather makeup case: $65
- 1 vial of unopened perfume: $75
- 1 pair of earrings: $150
- cash: $178

Officer Beatriz Ceballos is writing the police report. What should she write as the value of the stolen cash and property?
- **a.** $468
- **b.** $608
- **c.** $618
- **d.** $718

49. $\frac{17}{20}$ is equivalent to what percent?
- **a.** 17%
- **b.** 65%
- **c.** 85%
- **d.** 90%

50. 192 is evenly divisible by
- **a.** 3
- **b.** 5
- **c.** 7
- **d.** 9

51. If 14 workers can complete a job in 2 days, how long will it take 4 workers to complete the same job? Assume all workers work at the same rate.
- **a.** $\frac{4}{7}$ day
- **b.** 5 days
- **c.** 6 days
- **d.** 7 days

52. If a police car travels at the speed of 62 miles per hour for 15 minutes, how far will it travel? (Distance = Rate × Time)
- **a.** 9.3 miles
- **b.** 15.5 miles
- **c.** 16 miles
- **d.** 24.8 miles

53. If a truck is traveling at a constant speed of 50 miles per hour for a total time of 1 hour and 30 minutes, how many miles does it travel? (Distance = Rate × Time)
- **a.** 75 miles
- **b.** 50 miles
- **c.** 5 miles
- **d.** 130 miles

54. The prison inmates need 3 square yards of cloth to make one uniform. There are 23,789 inmates. How many square yards of cloth are needed?
- **a.** 11,895 square yards
- **b.** 71,367 square yards
- **c.** 87,986 square yards
- **d.** 91,475 square yards

55. A squad car uses 16 gallons of gas to travel 448 miles. How many miles per gallon does the car get?
- **a.** 22 miles per gallon
- **b.** 24 miles per gallon
- **c.** 26 miles per gallon
- **d.** 28 miles per gallon

Directions: Answer questions 56 through 60 based on the following map. The arrows indicate traffic flow. One arrow indicates a one-way street going in the direction of the arrow; two arrows represent a two-way street. You are not allowed to go the wrong way on a one-way street.

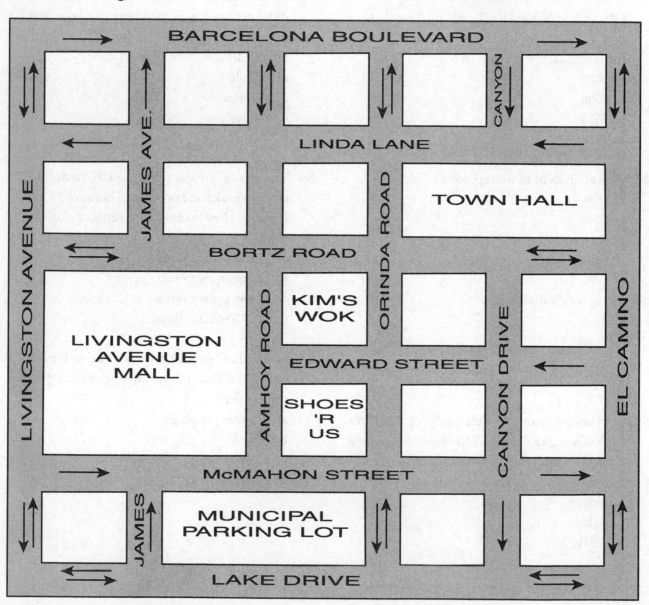

56. Your unit has been called to the scene of a car accident at the Livingston Avenue Mall at the southeast corner of the building. While you are there, dispatch notifies you of an alarm going off in a residence located at the northwest corner of Canyon Drive and Linda Lane. What is the quickest route for your unit to take from the mall to the residence?

   a. Turn north on Amhoy Road, then east on Linda Lane, then north on Canyon Drive.

   b. Turn east on McMahon Street, then north on El Camino, then west on Linda Lane, then north on Orinda Road, then east on Barcelona Boulevard to Canyon Drive, and south on Canyon Drive.

   c. Turn north on Amhoy Road, then east on Barcelona Boulevard, then south on Canyon Drive.

   d. Turn north on Amhoy Road, then east on Bortz Road, then north on Orinda Road, then east on Barcelona Boulevard, and south on Canyon Drive.

57. Your unit is southbound on Canyon Drive and has just crossed Edward Street when a call comes in that someone has been hit by a car at a bus stop located at Livingston Avenue and Bortz Road. What is the quickest route for your unit to take to the bus stop?

   a. Turn west on McMahon Street, then north on Livingston Avenue.

   b. Turn east on McMahon Street, then north on El Camino, then west on Bortz Road.

   c. Turn east on Lake Drive, then north on Canyon Drive, then west on Bortz Road.

   d. Turn east on Lake Drive, then north on El Camino, then west on Linda Lane, then south on Livingston Avenue.

58. State Trooper Scalzo has just come off duty and is driving east on Lake Drive. She makes a left on Orinda Road, then a right on McMahon Street, and then a left on Canyon Drive. What building will she meet up with if she continues on Canyon Drive?

   a. Shoes 'R Us

   b. Livingston Avenue Mall

   c. Town Hall

   d. Kim's Wok

59. A state trooper is escorting an important public official from the northwest corner of Livingston Avenue and McMahon Street to Town Hall. If the entrance to Town Hall is located a few feet to the left of the northeast corner of the building, how many turns will the state trooper make, taking the most direct route?

   a. one

   b. two

   c. three

   d. four

60. State Trooper Bassett is driving south on Livingston Avenue. She makes a left onto Lake Drive, then a left onto James Avenue, then a right onto McMahon Street, and then a right onto Orinda Road. What direction is she facing?

   a. east

   b. south

   c. west

   d. north

Directions: Answer questions 61 through 65 based on the following map. The arrows indicate traffic flow. One arrow indicates a one-way street going in the direction of the arrow; two arrows represent a two-way street. You are not allowed to go the wrong way on a one-way street.

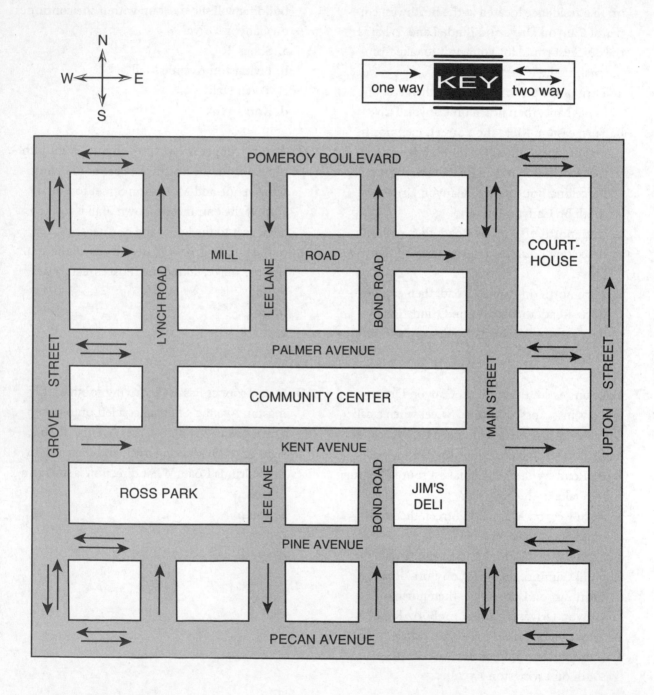

61. Your unit is eastbound on Kent Avenue at Lee
Lane when a call comes in from dispatch about
an explosion at a residence located at the northeast corner of Lynch Road and Mill Road. What
is the quickest route for your unit to take?

   a. Continue east on Kent Avenue, then turn
   north on Main Street to Mill Road, then
   west on Mill Road to the northeast corner of
   Lynch Road and Mill Road.

   b. Continue east on Kent Avenue, then turn
   north on Main Street, then east on Pomeroy
   Boulevard, then south on Lynch Road.

   c. Continue east on Kent Avenue, then turn
   south on Main Street, then west on Pine
   Avenue, then north on Grove Street, then
   east on Mill Road to Lynch Road.

   d. Continue east on Kent Avenue, then turn
   north on Main Street, then west on Palmer
   Avenue, then north on Lynch Road to Mill
   Road.

62. Officer McElhaney is off duty and driving by
the courthouse, northbound on Upton Street.
He receives a call on his cell phone about a
bomb having gone off at Ross Park on the
Grove Street side of the park. He decides he
may be able to be of some help. What is the
most direct route for McElhaney to take?

   a. Continue north on Upton Street, turn west
   on Pomeroy Boulevard, then south on Main
   Street, then west on Kent Avenue to Grove
   Street.

   b. Continue north on Upton Street, then turn
   west on Pomeroy Boulevard, then south on
   Grove Street to Ross Park.

   c. Continue north on Upton Street, then turn
   west on Pomeroy Boulevard, then south on
   Main Street, then west on Palmer Avenue,
   then south on Grove Street to Ross Park.

   d. Make a U-turn on Upton Street, then go
   west on Palmer Avenue, then south on
   Grove Street to Ross Park.

63. State Trooper Kearney just had lunch at Jim's
Deli and is now heading west on Pine Avenue.
She turns left on Lee Lane, then left again onto
Pecan Avenue. She turns left on Main Street
and finally turns right on Palmer Avenue.
What direction is she facing?

   a. west
   b. south
   c. north
   d. east

64. State Trooper Gurick is driving east on Pecan
Avenue. He makes a left onto Bond Road, then
a right on Kent Avenue, then a left on Main
Street, and then another left on Pomeroy Boulevard. What direction is he facing?

   a. north
   b. south
   c. east
   d. west

65. You are dispatched from the courthouse, facing
south on Upton Street, to an altercation occurring at the southeast corner of the community
center. Which is the most direct legal way to
drive there?

   a. south to Palmer Avenue and south on Main
   Street

   b. south to Palmer Avenue and west onto Kent
   Avenue

   c. south to Palmer Avenue, west onto Grove
   Street, and south onto Kent Avenue

   d. north to Pomeroy Boulevard, south on Lee
   Lane, east on Palmer Avenue, and south on
   Main Street

Directions: Answer questions 66 through 70 based on the following map. The arrows indicate traffic flow. One arrow indicates a one-way street going in the direction of the arrow, and no arrows represent a two-way street. You are not allowed to go the wrong way on a one-way street. Smaller boxes within the building outline indicate building entranceways.

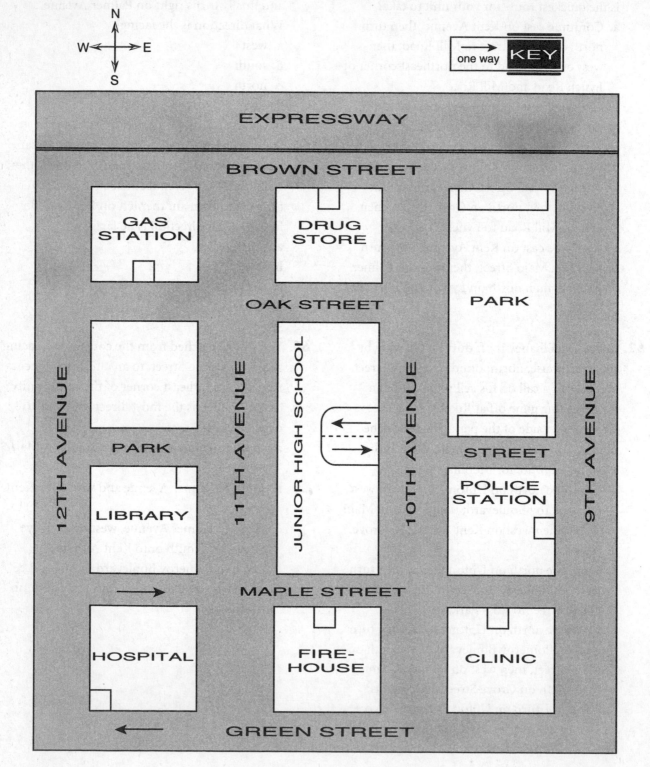

66. There is a vehicular accident at the corner of Brown Street and 9th Avenue, and a fire has started. What is the most direct legal way for the fire engine to travel from the fire station to the accident scene?
   a. east on Maple Street and north on 9th Avenue to the accident
   b. west on Maple Street, north on 12th Avenue, and east on Brown Street to the accident
   c. east on Maple Street and north on 11th Avenue to the accident
   d. west on Maple Street, north on 11th Avenue, and east on Brown Street to the accident

67. What streets run east and west of the junior high school?
   a. Maple Street and Oak Street
   b. Green Street and Brown Street
   c. 12th Avenue and 11th Avenue
   d. 11th Avenue and 10th Avenue

68. A civilian leaving the clinic needs to drive to the drugstore. If you were giving her directions from the clinic, what would be the most direct route?
   a. east on Maple Street, north on 9th Avenue, and west on Brown Street to the store entrance
   b. west on Maple Street, north on 10th Avenue, and west on Brown Street to the store entrance
   c. west on Green Street, north on 12th Avenue, and east on Brown Street to the store entrance
   d. east on Oak Street, north on 11th Avenue, and east on Brown Street to the store entrance

69. Someone at the junior high school has been injured and needs to go to the hospital. What directions would you give to the ambulance driver?
   a. Go north on 10th Avenue, west on Brown Street, and south on 12th Avenue to the hospital entrance.
   b. Go south on 10th Avenue and west on Green Street to the hospital entrance.
   c. Go north on 10th Avenue and south on Brown Street to the hospital entrance.
   d. Go south on 10th Avenue, south on Maple Street, and east on Green Street to the hospital entrance.

70. You are leaving work at the police station and need to fill your gas tank before you go home. What is the quickest legal route to the gas station?
   a. south on 9th Avenue, west on Maple Street, north on 11th Avenue, and west on Oak Street to the entrance
   b. north on 9th Avenue and west on Brown Street
   c. south on 9th Avenue, west on Maple Street, north on 12th Avenue, and east on Oak Street to the entrance
   d. north on 9th Avenue, west on Park Street, north on 10th Avenue, and west on Oak Street to the entrance

Directions: You will have ten minutes to read and study the following passage. Then, answer questions 71 through 80 without referring back to the passage.

Often in the course of routine patrol, a police officer needs to briefly detain a person for questioning without an arrest warrant or even probable cause. The officer may also feel that it is necessary to frisk this person for weapons. This type of detention is known as a "Terry Stop," after the U.S. Supreme Court case *Terry vs. State of Ohio*. In that case, the Court determined that a Terry Stop does not violate a citizen's right to be free from unreasonable search and seizure, as long as certain procedures are followed. First, the person must be behaving in some manner that arouses the police officer's suspicion. Second, the officer must believe that swift action is necessary to prevent a crime from being committed or a suspect from escaping. Finally, in order to frisk the individual, the officer must reasonably believe that the person is armed and dangerous. We will now look at each of these elements in more detail.

In determining whether an individual is acting in a suspicious manner, a police officer must rely on his or her training and experience. Circumstances in each case will be different, but an officer must be able to articulate what it was about a person's behavior that aroused suspicion, whether it was one particular action or a series of actions taken together. For example, it may not be unusual for shoppers in a store to wander up and down the aisles looking at merchandise. However, it may be suspicious if a person does this for an inordinate period of time, seems to be checking the locations of surveillance equipment, and is wearing loose clothing that would facilitate shoplifting. Similarly, it is not unusual for a person wearing gym shorts and a T-shirt to be running through a residential neighborhood; however, a person dressed in regular clothes might legitimately be suspect. It is important to note that a person who appears out of place based simply on the manner in which he or she is dressed is not alone cause for suspicion on the part of a police officer.

In addition to the behavior that arouses an officer's attention, the officer must believe that immediate action must be taken to prevent the commission of a crime or a suspect from escaping. In some situations, it may be better to wait to develop probable cause and arrest the person. One important element of this decision is the safety of any other people in the area. In addition, a police officer may determine that his or her immediate action is necessary to avert the commission of a crime, even if no people are in danger. If the suspect appears, for example, to be checking out parked cars for the possibility of stealing one, an officer may well be able to wait until the crime is in progress (thereby having probable cause for an arrest) or even until the crime is actually committed, when patrol cars can be dispatched to arrest the individual. However, a person who appears to be planning a car-jacking should be stopped before the occupants of a car can be hurt. The officer must make a quick decision based on all the circumstances.

Once an officer has detained a suspicious person, the officer must determine if it is necessary to frisk the individual for weapons. Again, an officer should rely on her or his training and experience. If the officer feels that the detainee poses a threat to his or her safety, the suspect should be frisked. For example, although there may certainly be exceptions, a person suspected of shoplifting is not likely to be armed. On the other hand, a person suspected of breaking and entering may very well be carrying a weapon. In addition, the officer should be aware of the behavior of the person once the stop is made. Certain behavior indicates the person is waiting for an opportunity to produce a weapon and threaten the officer's safety. The safety of the officer and any civilians in the area is the most important consideration.

71. According to the reading passage, a Terry Stop is
   a. an arrest for shoplifting.
   b. the brief detention and questioning of a suspicious person.
   c. an officer's frisking a suspect for weapons.
   d. the development of a case that results in an arrest warrant.

72. According to the passage, a Terry Stop includes the frisking of a suspect if
   a. the officer sees evidence of a weapon.
   b. the person is suspected of breaking and entering.
   c. there are civilians in the area.
   d. the officer or others are in danger.

73. An officer on foot patrol notices two people standing on a street corner. The officer observes the two, and after a moment, one of the people walks slowly down the street, looks in the window of a store called McFadden's, walks forward a few feet, and then turns around and returns to the other person. They speak briefly, and then the other person walks down the street, performing the same series of motions. They repeat this ritual five or six times each. The officer would be justified in performing a Terry Stop based on her suspicion that the people
   a. appeared to be carrying weapons.
   b. looked out of place.
   c. might be planning to rob McFadden's.
   d. were obstructing the sidewalk.

74. According to the passage, an officer may choose to conduct a Terry Stop to
   a. discourage loitering.
   b. prevent a crime from being committed or a suspect from escaping.
   c. find out if a person is carrying a concealed weapon.
   d. rule out suspects after a crime has been committed.

75. According to the passage, the determination that a person is suspicious
   a. depends on the circumstances of each situation.
   b. means someone looks out of place.
   c. usually means someone is guilty of planning a crime.
   d. usually indicates a person is carrying a concealed weapon.

76. An officer has stopped a suspicious individual. The suspect seems to be trying to reach for something under her coat. The officer should
   a. call for backup.
   b. arrest the suspect.
   c. frisk the suspect.
   d. handcuff the suspect.

77. An officer observes a person sitting on a bench outside a bank at 4:30 P.M. The officer knows the bank closes at 5:00. The person checks his watch several times and watches customers come and go through the door of the bank. He also makes eye contact with a person driving a blue sedan that appears to be circling the block. Finally, a parking space in front of the bank becomes vacant, and the sedan pulls in. The driver and the man on the bench nod to each other. The officer believes the two are planning to rob the bank just before it closes. What is the first thing the officer should do?
   a. Begin questioning the man on the bench, since it appears he's going to rob the bank.
   b. Begin questioning the driver of the sedan, since it appears she's driving the getaway car.
   c. Go into the bank, warn the employees, and ask all the customers to leave for their own safety.
   d. Call for backup, because it appears the potential robbers are waiting for the bank to close.

78. According to the U.S. Supreme Court, a Terry Stop
   a. is permissible search and seizure.
   b. often occurs in the course of police work.
   c. should be undertaken only when two officers are present.
   d. requires probable cause.

79. According to the passage, persons suspected of shoplifting
   a. should never be frisked, as shoplifters rarely carry weapons.
   b. may legitimately be the subjects of a Terry Stop.
   c. always wear loose clothing and wander in the store a long time.
   d. may be handcuffed immediately for the safety of the civilians in the area.

80. An officer in a squad car is patrolling a wealthy residential neighborhood. She notices one house in which a light will come on in one part of the house for a few minutes, then go off. A moment later, a light will come on in another part of the house, then go off. This happens several times in different parts of the house. The officer also notes that the garage door is standing open and that there are no cars parked there or in the driveway. The officer believes there may be a burglary in progress, and pulls over to observe the house. While she is watching the house, a man wearing torn jeans and a dirty T-shirt walks by the house. According to the passage, the officer should NOT
   a. allow the man to see her, as he may be dangerous.
   b. involve the neighbors by asking them if they have information.
   c. stop the man, as there is no indication he is involved in criminal activity.
   d. radio headquarters until she is absolutely sure a crime is being committed.

81. At 9:30 P.M., while parked at 916 Woodward Avenue, Police Officers Whitebear and Morgan were asked to respond to an anonymous complaint of a disturbance at 826 Rosemary Lane. When they arrived, they found the back door open and the jamb splintered. They drew their weapons, identified themselves, and entered the dwelling, where they found Mr. Darrell Hensley, of 1917 Roosevelt Avenue, sitting on the couch. Mr. Hensley calmly stated he was waiting for his wife. At that point, two children emerged from a hallway: Dustin Hensley, age 7, who lives in the dwelling, and Kirstin Jackson, age 14, Dustin's babysitter, who lives at 916 Ambrose Street. Kirstin stated she and Dustin had been sitting at the kitchen table when the back door was kicked in and Mr. Hensley entered, shouting obscenities and calling for Karen Hensley, Dustin's mother. Kirstin then hid with Dustin in a hallway storage closet. The officers contacted Mrs. Hensley at her place of employment at O'Reilley's Restaurant at 415 Ralston. At 9:55, she returned home and showed an Order of Protection stating that Mr. Hensley was not to have contact with his wife or child. Mr. Hensley was placed under arrest and taken in handcuffs to the station house. Based on Darrell Hensley's behavior when he first arrived at his wife's house, what was his most likely motivation for being there?
   a. to see his child, for a scheduled visitation
   b. to force his wife to speak with him
   c. to have a place to stay that night
   d. to peacefully reconcile with his family

82. An off-duty state trooper was seated in a diner when two armed teenagers entered and robbed the cashier. The officer made no attempt to prevent the robbery or apprehend the teenagers. The state trooper later justified his conduct, stating that an off-duty officer is a private citizen with the same rights and obligations as all private citizens. The state trooper's conduct was

a. correct; the state trooper was out of uniform at the time of the robbery.

b. correct; it would have been a mistake for him to intervene when outnumbered by the armed robbers.

c. incorrect; a state trooper must attempt to prevent crimes and apprehend criminals at all times.

d. incorrect; he should have obtained the necessary information and descriptions after the armed robbers left.

83. During her night patrol, State Trooper Griffin notices a well-dressed man break a car window with a rock, open the door, and get into the car. Of the following, the most essential action for the officer to take is to

a. approach the car and ask the man for proof of ownership.

b. take down the license plate number of the car and a description of the man in case the car is later reported stolen.

c. enter the car and order the man to drive to the nearest police station to explain his actions.

d. approach the car and ask the man to explain his actions.

84. When approaching a suspect to make an arrest, it is least important for a state trooper to prevent a suspect from

a. running away.

b. being armed.

c. spreading a disease.

d. using physical force.

85. While on foot patrol downtown, Officer Parker is approached by Ms. Ivy Vedder, who says that a man snatched a shopping bag she was carrying. It was full of the following gifts:

- 3 pairs of gold earrings, valued at $95 each
- 1 gold ring, valued at $237
- 1 wool sweater, valued at $86
- 1 diamond bracelet, valued at $379

Later, Officer Parker receives a call from Ms. Vedder who says she found her receipt and that she only bought two pairs of gold earrings and each was worth $104. What is the difference between the originally reported stolen amount and the actual stolen amount?

a. $77

b. $892

c. $987

d. $1,879

86. Officer Kemp has worked more night shifts in a row than Officer Rogers, who has worked five. Officer Miller has worked 15 night shifts in a row, more than Officers Kemp and Rogers combined. Officer Calvin has worked eight night shifts in a row, fewer than Officer Kemp. How many night shifts in a row has Officer Kemp worked?
a. eight
b. nine
c. ten
d. 11

87. For the past two months, stereo shops all over the city have been hit by burglars in the early morning hours. Sergeant Adams tells Officer Bryant that he should carefully watch the stores in his area that specialize in stereo equipment. Which one of the following situations should Officer Bryant investigate?
a. a truck with its motor running, backed up to the rear door of the House of Stereos at 1:00 A.M.
b. a lone man going through a dumpster at the rear of the House of Stereos at 2:00 A.M.
c. a delivery van marked "House of Stereos" parked in the rear of the store at 2:00 A.M.
d. two teenage boys intently examining a stereo system in the window of House of Stereos just after midnight

88. Four eyewitnesses saw a vehicle being stolen and noted the license plate number. Each wrote down a different number listed below. Which one is probably right?
a. KLV 017
b. XIW 007
c. XIW 017
d. XIV 017

Directions: Use the following procedures to answer questions 89 and 90.

An officer responding alone to the scene of a burglar alarm call should do the following:
- Turn off siren and emergency lights as soon as possible to keep from alerting suspects.
- Park the patrol car away from the building.
- Notify the dispatcher of his or her arrival and location.
- Begin checking the outside of the building for signs of entry.
- Notify the dispatcher if signs of entry are discovered.
- Wait for backup if it is available before going inside a building where entry has been made.
- Tell backup officers where to position themselves as they arrive.

89. Officer Kim is dispatched to a burglar alarm call at 100 South Main Street, where the Quik Stop convenience store is located. The store closed at 1 A.M., and it is now 3 A.M. Officer Kim is parked in the parking lot of the pawnshop next door, writing a report, when the call comes out. Officer Kim's next step should be to
a. walk up to the building from the side so her approach is undetected.
b. wait for backup before approaching the building.
c. inform the dispatcher that she has arrived at 100 South Main Street.
d. check the outside of the building for signs of entry.

90. Officer Smith is sent to 1313 Milbury Way on a residential burglary alarm call at 1 P.M. Traffic is heavy on the way to the call, and he turns on his emergency lights to help clear the way. Officer Smith is notified that no backup is available in his sector. What is the next thing Officer Smith should do?
- **a.** Park his patrol car a house or two away from 1313 Milbury Way.
- **b.** Inform the dispatcher when he arrives.
- **c.** Approach the front door, since any suspects are probably gone by now.
- **d.** Turn off his emergency lights as soon as he can safely do so.

91. Police officers may find themselves in situations in which using a normal, conversational tone of voice is not enough to get an individual to do what the officer needs done. Which situation below calls for an officer to shout using a firm, authoritative tone of voice?
- **a.** asking to see a driver's proof of automobile insurance after an accident
- **b.** advising a new partner of a recently implemented departmental policy
- **c.** chasing a burglar out of a house
- **d.** asking a boy why he is not in school on a Monday morning

92. On Thursday evening, Officers Gossard and Barinski responded to a burglary call. The owner of First Class Hauling, a trucking company, reported the following as missing:

- 4 cell phones, valued at $123 each
- 2 handheld computers, valued at $287 each
- 1 printer, valued at $99
- 1 answering machine, valued at $55
- 3 laptop computers, valued at $679

Officer Barinski is preparing a report on the burglary. What should she write as the total value of the stolen property?
- **a.** $1,243
- **b.** $2,970
- **c.** $3,257
- **d.** $3,936

93. In a four-day period—Monday through Thursday—each of the following officers worked only one day, each a different day. Officer Johnson was scheduled to work on Monday, but she traded with Officer Carter, who was originally scheduled to work on Wednesday. Officer Falk traded with Officer Kirk, who was originally scheduled to work on Thursday. After all the switching was done, who worked on Tuesday?
- **a.** Carter
- **b.** Falk
- **c.** Johnson
- **d.** Kirk

94. Mrs. Oneida called the police to report that a man was looking into her bedroom window last night around 9:45 P.M. Officer Williams talks to residents in the area and finds out that several people have seen a white male dressed in black walking up and down the street at about 10 P.M. for the past week. Officer Williams decides to patrol the area closely and is in the area by 9:30 P.M. Which of the following situations should she investigate?
 a. two teenagers in jeans and dark T-shirts sitting on the curb, smoking cigarettes
 b. a man wearing black jogging shorts and dark shoes stretching his legs in the driveway of a house
 c. a man dressed in dark jeans and a navy blue turtleneck walking rapidly away from some shrubbery at the side of a house
 d. a man in dark clothing attaching a water hose to the faucet on the side of a house

95. Four people witnessed a mugging. Each gave a different description of the mugger. Which description is probably right?
 a. He was average height, thin, and middle-aged.
 b. He was tall, thin, and middle-aged.
 c. He was tall, thin, and young.
 d. He was tall, of average weight, and middle-aged.

96. All police officers are expected to know how to properly package evidence after the decision has been made to collect it. The following steps should be carried out in the order listed:
 1. Place each item in a separate container.
 2. Seal each container in such a way that it cannot be opened without breaking the seal.
 3. The officer collecting the evidence should write his or her name or employee number on the seal.
 4. Place a tag on the container that identifies the case number, the date and time collected, where the item was found, what the item is, who collected it, and what condition the item is in.
 5. Turn the evidence in personally to the Property Room without breaking the chain of custody by allowing someone else to do it.

Officer Jones is the first officer to arrive at the scene of a burglary at Wiggin's Liquor Store. After making sure the scene is secure, he begins to collect evidence. The first item he finds is a screwdriver lying on the sidewalk in front of the glass doors leading into the store. The second item he sees is a small flashlight on the floor inside the building. Officer Jones places the screwdriver in a small plastic bag. What is the next thing he should do?
 a. Lock the screwdriver in the trunk of his car.
 b. Seal the bag with evidence tape so that the bag cannot be opened.
 c. Write the case number and other information about the evidence on the outside of the bag.
 d. Put the flashlight in the bag with the screwdriver.

97. Officers Roberts and Reed are on bicycle patrol in the downtown area. Sergeant McElvey tells them that a white male has been committing robberies along the nearby bike path by stepping out of the bushes and threatening bicyclists with an iron pipe until they give him their bicycles. There have been three separate incidents, and the suspect descriptions are from three different victims.

Robbery #1: Suspect is a white male, 20–25 years old, 5′9″, 145 pounds, with a shaved head, wearing a skull earring in the left ear, baggy white T-shirt, worn light blue jeans, and black combat boots.

Robbery #2: Suspect is a white male, 25–30 years old, dark brown hair in a military-style crew cut, 6′2″, 200 pounds, wearing a white T-shirt with the words "Just Do It" on the back, blue surgical scrub pants, and black combat boots.

Robbery #3: Suspect is a white male, 23 years old, 5′10″, skinny build, no hair, wearing a Grateful Dead T-shirt, blue baggy pants, dark shoes, and one earring.

Three days after Sergeant McElvey told the officers about the robberies, Officer Reed arrested a suspect for attempting to take a woman's mountain bike from her on the bicycle path. The description of the suspect is as follows:

Robbery #4: Suspect is a white male, 22 years old, 140 pounds, 5′10″, with a shaved head and one pierced ear, wearing a plain white T-shirt two sizes too large for him, faded baggy blue jeans, and scuffed black combat boots.

After comparing the suspect description with those in the first three robberies, Officer Reed should consider the arrested man as a suspect in which of the other robberies?

a. Robbery #1, Robbery #2, and Robbery #3
b. Robbery #1, but not Robbery #2 or Robbery #3
c. Robbery #1 and Robbery #3, but not Robbery #2
d. Robbery #1 and Robbery #2, but not Robbery #3

98. Officers are required to immediately report to their supervisor any damage to a patrol car. In which situation should an officer call the supervisor to report a damaged car?

a. A teenager kicks the front right tire of the car.
b. An angry crime victim throws a cup of coffee on the windshield of the car.
c. The officer is sideswiped by another car in a high-speed car chase.
d. An elderly woman spits on the patrol car.

99. The first officer to respond to the scene of a sexual assault has many responsibilities. The officer should take the following steps in the order listed:

1. Aid the victim if necessary by calling for an ambulance or administering first aid.
2. Try to calm and comfort the victim as much as possible.
3. If the attack is recent, get a suspect description from the victim and radio the dispatcher to put out a be-on-the-lookout broadcast.
4. Find out from the victim where the crime occurred.
5. Determine if there is any physical evidence on the victim that may need to be preserved, such as pieces of the suspect's skin or blood under the victim's fingernails.
6. If possible, have the victim change clothing, and then take the clothing he or she was wearing as evidence.
7. Convince the victim to undergo a medical exam for his or her health and safety and so that evidence may be gathered.

Officer Augustine is at 2101 Reynolds Street talking to Betty Smith, the victim of a sexual assault. Ms. Smith is uninjured and is very calm. She gives Officer Augustine a detailed description of her attacker and says she thinks he may be headed for a nearby tavern. At this point, Officer Augustine should
a. get into his patrol car and drive to the tavern.
b. give the dispatcher the description of the suspect.
c. take the victim straight to the hospital for a medical exam.
d. have the victim change clothing.

100. Fred is a business owner downtown who makes it well known that he hates police officers and thinks they are all corrupt. Fred runs a red light downtown, almost causing a van to hit him, and then pulls over in front of his store, cursing loudly about the other driver's driving skills. Officer Martinez was standing on the corner and watched Fred run the light. What should she do?
a. Write Fred a citation for running a red light.
b. Warn Fred not to run red lights and hope this improves Fred's opinion of police.
c. Suggest to Fred that he take defensive driving classes.
d. Look into having someone retime the lights in the downtown area.

Answers

1. c. Although the post-arrest processes are discussed, the main idea is about the experiences of crime victims.

2. b. The only answer not mentioned in the passage is the consulting of victims by prosecutors.

3. a. The arresting officer is not mentioned, nor is the judge. The victims are not consulted, and lawyers negotiate sentences between themselves.

4. d. The only statement made in the passage is that victims may be frustrated by the speed of the criminal justice system's processing of cases.

5. c. Although choices **a** and **b** are also true, they are not the main idea, which should be supported by the whole passage and spelled out in the last sentence.

6. b. This is implied in the next-to-last sentence of the passage.

7. c. See the first sentence of the passage.

8. d. Miranda rights are read only when the suspect is taken into custody. The right to call a lawyer (choice **c**) and the right to a phone call (choice **b**) are included in the Miranda rights.

9. b. See the last sentence of paragraph 1, which discuss the stalking victim's *worst fear*.

10. c. The last two paragraphs of the passage discuss why modern anti-stalking laws are more effective than previous methods, but also how they are flawed. The other answer choices are mentioned in the passage, but they are not the central argument.

11. d. The victim's knowledge or lack of knowledge about anti-stalking laws is not discussed anywhere in the passage. All the other choices are mentioned in the third paragraph.

12. a. The first passage states that a restraining order is a *civil remedy often ignored by the offender*.

13. c. Nowhere in the passage does it state that a stalker's motive is to rob or steal from his or her victim. All the other choices are mentioned in the final paragraph.

14. a. See the second paragraph. Choices **b** and **c** apply only to the Orange County women; choice **d** cannot be shown to apply to either example.

15. b. The second and third sentences of the passage state that *officers should keep complete notes detailing any potentially criminal or actionable incidents* and that the officers *may refer to those notes to refresh their memory about particular events*.

16. d. The passage provides information for law enforcement officers; choice **d** is therefore the most logical choice. Choice **a** refers to a memo directed to police officers, but the subject matter is incorrect. The subject matter of choice **b** is also incorrect. The wording and tone of the passage do not seem to be attempting recruitment, as in choice **c**.

17. a. The very first sentence of the passage states that testimony *is an important part of an officer's job*.

18. a. The discussion of the traits of a person with antisocial personality disorder specifies that such a person does not have distortions of thought. The passage speaks of the antisocial person as being *inordinately self-confident* (choice **b**) and of the person's *emotional shallowness* (choices **c** and **d**).

19. c. The other items are discussed in the passage.

20. b. The passage mentions *emotional shallowness*. The other choices hint at the capacity to feel meaningful emotion.

21. d. This is the only choice that does not contain excessive wordiness or redundancy. In choice **a**, the phrase *the fifth of five* is a redundancy. Choice **b** also repeats by using both *five* and *fifth*. Choice **c**, although constructed differently, makes the same error.

22. b. It is the most succinct way to express the idea. Choice **a** is the same as the original sentence. Choice **c** repeats the word *examine*. Choice **d** is too wordy.

23. b. This choice is the only one that is a complete sentence.

24. c. This choice is best because it is written in the active voice, and the sentence is constructed so that all modifiers are appropriately placed.

25. b. Choices **a** and **c** are sentence fragments. Choice **d** represents confused sentence structure as well as a lack of agreement between the subject and verb.

26. c. The other choices contain unnecessary shifts in person, from *people* to *their* and *we* in choice **a**, to *your* and *one* in choice **b**, and to *our* and *they* in choice **d**.

27. a. The subject of the sentence *art professor* is singular and takes the singular verb *is planning*.

28. d. This is a complete sentence; the other choices are fragments.

29. c. This is the only sentence without a grammatical error. Choice **a** is repetitive. In choice **b**, the verb should not be in present tense. Choice **d** contains verbs that are erroneously in the past tense.

30. a. This sentence is clearest. In choice **b**, the speaker likes his or her sister better than fish. Choice **c** is confusing. Choice **d** has an unclear pronoun: The use of *it* makes it unclear whether fish or the sister is referenced.

31. a. This sentence has faulty subordination; the word *going* should be deleted and the comma should be eliminated.

32. b. This is a run-on sentence.

33. c. The connecting word between the two clauses creates an illogical statement. The word *therefore* should be changed to the word *but*.

34. d. There are no errors.

35. a. This sentence makes an illogical shift from the past to the present tense.

36. a. Choice **a** contains a singular noun and a plural verb.

37. c. Sentence 4 is the topic sentence. Sentence 1 provides detailed information, and sentence 3 provides further detail about the information in sentence 1. Sentence 2, with the word *however*, adds to the information.

38. b. Sentence 3 is the topic statement. Sentence 4 provides more information about the topic. Sentence 1 describes the action taken, and sentence 2 explains why the action was taken.

39. b. Sentence 1 provides a general rule. Sentence 4, with the word *however*, notes an exception to the general rule. Sentence 2, with the word *usually*, gives an example of the exception. Sentence 3 tells how the example is applied in practice.

40. d. Sentence 4 introduces the topic of solicitation and explains how it might come up. Sentence 2 gives the first part of the definition of *solicitation*; sentence 3 gives the second part of the definition. Sentence 1 refers to all the elements mentioned in sentences 2 and 3.

41. d. A quotient results from division. $12{,}440 \div 40 = 311$.

42. d. Consider **PEMDAS**: *parentheses, exponents, multiplication, division, addition, subtraction*. Here you must solve the division first: $540 \div 6 = 90$. The equation becomes $90 + 3 \times 24$. Again, considering PEMDAS, you know you should calculate the multiplication first. $3 \times 24 = 72$, so the equation reduces to $90 + 72 = 162$.

43. b. $3 \times 3 = 9$, and then $9 \times 3 = 27$.

44. d. Do this problem in the order it is presented; first subtract, then add.

45. a. You can reduce this fraction in steps: $\frac{12}{144} \div \frac{12}{12} = \frac{1}{12}$.

46. d. The quickest way to find a common denominator is to multiply the two given denominators. $5 \times 6 = 30$, so the new denominator will be 30. To convert $\frac{4}{5}$ into 30ths, multiply by $\frac{6}{6}$: $\frac{4}{5} \times \frac{6}{6} = \frac{24}{30}$. To convert $\frac{1}{6}$ into 30ths, multiply by $\frac{5}{5}$: $\frac{1}{6} \times \frac{5}{5} = \frac{5}{30}$. Next, add: $\frac{24}{30} + \frac{5}{30} = \frac{29}{30}$.

47. d. Perform the operations in parentheses first: $23 + 47 = 70$ and $79 - 69 = 10$. Then go on to multiply the results from the parentheses.

48. c. The values added together total $618. If you chose choice **a**, you forgot to add the value of the handbag ($150) to the total.

49. c. First, set up a proportion: $\frac{17}{20} = \frac{?}{100}$. Cross multiply to get $17 \times 100 = 20 \times ?$, or $1,700 = 20 \times ?$. Divide both sides by 20 to get $? = 85$. Thus, the answer is 85%, choice **c**.

50. a. 192 is evenly divisible by 3. $192 \div 3 = 64$. The other choices cannot be divided evenly into 192.

51. d. Set up a proportion when confronted with this scenario: $\frac{14 \text{ workers}}{2 \text{ days}} = \frac{4 \text{ workers}}{? \text{ days}}$. Notice that the ? in the denominator of the second ratio will necessarily be smaller than the 2 days in the denominator of the first ratio. If 14 workers can complete the job in 2 days, it will take one person 14 times as long to complete the same job: 28 days. It will take 4 people $\frac{1}{4}$ as long to complete this amount of work, or 7 days.

52. b. Solving this problem requires converting 15 minutes to 0.25 hour, which is the time, then using the formula: 62 mph $\times$ 0.25 hour = 15.5 miles, choice **b**.

53. a. The truck travels for 1 hour and 30 minutes, which is 1.5 hours. According to the formula, then, the distance traveled is 1.5 hours times 50 mph, or 75 miles, choice **a**.

54. b. Each inmate requires 3 yards of cloth, so multiply the number of inmates (23,789) by 3 to get 71,367 total square yards of cloth required.

55. d. Take the total number of miles and find the average by dividing: $448 \div 16$ gallons = 28 miles per gallon.

56. c. This is the simplest way around the one-way streets and Town Hall. Because Linda Lane is one-way going the wrong way, some backtracking is inevitable. However, the residence is only one block off Barcelona Boulevard, and so turning eastbound on Barcelona requires the least amount of backtracking. Choice **a** directs your unit to turn the wrong way down a one-way street. Choice **b** requires too much backtracking because Barcelona Boulevard is a one-way street going east. Choice **d** requires too many turns and is the least direct route.

57. b. This is the most direct route because it requires the fewest turns. Choice **a** requires your unit to go the wrong way on McMahon Street. Choice **c** is not correct because Canyon Drive is a one-way street going south. Choice **d** is a much longer route.

58. c. If Scalzo is driving east on Lake Drive and makes a left on Orinda Road, then a right at the next corner onto McMahon Street, and a left going north on Canyon Drive, she will be facing the Town Hall.

59. c. The state trooper needs to make a right onto Bortz Road, a left onto El Camino, and a left onto Linda Lane. This is the most direct route. If you chose choice **a**, you may have thought the trooper could just make a right onto Linda Lane, but this is a one-way street heading west. If you chose choice **b**, you may have thought the trooper arrived at the final destination by reaching the northeast corner of Town Hall. However, the entrance is to the left of the northeast corner of the building, so the trooper must make a left onto Linda Lane.

60. b. If State Trooper Bassett turns right onto Orinda Road, he will be facing south.

61. d. This is the most direct route because it does not require any backtracking. Choice **a** is not correct because it would require your unit to go the wrong way on Mill Road. Choice **b** requires your unit to go the wrong way on Lynch Road. Choice **c** is not as direct because it requires your unit to move in the opposite direction from the call.

62. b. This is the fastest route, requiring the fewest turns. Choice **a** is not correct because Kent is a one-way street going east. Choice **c** requires too many turns and is not the most direct route. Choice **d** is not correct because Upton Street is one-way, going north.

63. d. A left turn onto Lee Lane turns Trooper Kearney south. Another left turn onto Pecan Avenue turns her east. A left onto Main Street turns her north, and the final right turn onto Palmer turns her back east, choice **d.**

64. d. He is facing west. After going east on Pecan Avenue, a left on Bond Road turns him north, a right on Kent Avenue turns him east, a left on Main Street turns him north, and a left on Pomeroy Boulevard leaves him facing west.

65. a. Choice **b** takes you the wrong way on Kent Avenue. Choices **c** and **d** are not the most direct routes.

66. a. The other routes are impossible or illegal.

67. a. Maple and Oak Streets run east and west of the school.

68. a. The other routes are impossible or illegal.

69. b. The other routes are impossible (choices **c** and **d**) or circuitous (choice **a**).

70. d. Choices **a** and **c** take you the wrong way on Maple Street. Choice **b** will not get you to the entrance of the gas station.

71. b. A Terry Stop is described in the first three sentences of the first paragraph of the passage.

72. d. See the fourth paragraph. If the officer feels that the suspect poses a threat to the officer's safety, the suspect should be frisked.

73. c. Based on the actions described, an officer's training and experience would indicate that the people were planning a robbery.

74. b. See the third-to-last sentence of the first paragraph.

75. a. See the second sentence of the second paragraph.

76. c. See the fourth paragraph.

77. d. See the third paragraph.

78. a. See the third and fourth sentences of the first paragraph.

79. b. Refer to the fourth sentence of the second paragraph.

80. c. See the sixth sentence of the second paragraph.

81. b. You can approach this question by asking why Mr. Hensley has forced open the door and has told police he is waiting for his wife. Choice **a** is incorrect; Mr. Hensley's child hid from him in a closet, and he evidently didn't try to get his son to come out. Choice **c** is incorrect because Mr. Hensley has a residence of his own at 1917 Roosevelt. Mr. Hensley evidently didn't intend peaceful reconciliation (choice **d**), because he kicked the door in.

82. c. Even when he or she is not on official duty, a state trooper must fulfill the police role if a crime is taking place in his or her presence.

83. a. This is the quickest way to find out if the man is the owner of the car or if he is committing a criminal act.

84. c. The state trooper must be concerned that the suspect might try to escape, be armed, or use physical violence. The state trooper must be least concerned with diseases the suspect may carry, but this is still a valid concern.

85. a. The originally reported total was $987, and the amended total was $910. The difference is $77.

86. b. Officer Kemp has worked more shifts in a row than Officer Calvin; therefore, Kemp has worked more than eight shifts. The number of Kemp's shifts plus the number of Rogers's shifts (five) cannot equal 15 or more, the number of Miller's shifts. Therefore, Kemp has worked nine shifts in a row (5 + 9 = 14).

87. a. A truck with the motor running, backed up to the rear door of a closed business at 1:00 A.M., is suspicious. Delivery vans owned by businesses are commonly parked on store property after hours (choice **c**). A lone man going through a dumpster would have no way to carry stereo equipment (choice **b**), and it would not be unusual for teenage boys to be looking at a stereo system in the window, even at midnight (choice **d**).

88. c. The elements of the license plate number that most often repeat in the descriptions are XIW and 017. Therefore, the correct license number is most likely XIW 017.

89. c. The officer has already done steps 1 and 2 because she is already at the location. Her next step would be to let the dispatcher know that she is on the scene (step 3).

90. d. Officer Smith should turn off his emergency lights as the first step in answering a burglar alarm call.

91. c. It would not be appropriate to shout in the situations described in choices **a**, **b**, or **d**. An officer would shout at a burglar because the situation calls for identifying himself or herself as a police officer. A loud, authoritative shout in this situation is part of the voice control officers should exercise as the first step in the use of force.

92. c. The total of the cell phones is $492. The total of the handheld computers is $574. The printer and answering machine are worth $154. The value of the three laptops is $2,037. The total is $3,257.

93. d. After all the switches were made, Officer Kirk worked on Tuesday. Officer Carter worked on Monday, Officer Johnson on Wednesday, and Officer Falk on Thursday.

94. c. The officer is looking for a suspect dressed in dark clothing who has been seen walking up and down a residential street during a specific time span—a window peeper. Choices **a**, **b**, and **d** suggest normal neighborhood activity because all the people involved are out in the open. The shrubbery the man in choice **c** is walking away from suggests a hiding place near a window.

95. b. Tall, thin, and middle-aged are the elements of the description repeated most often and are therefore the most likely to be accurate.

96. b. Sealing the bag is step 2 on the list of procedures.

97. c. The suspect described in Robbery #2 has a crew-cut hairstyle, is at least five inches taller than the other suspects, and is about 60 pounds heavier. The other three descriptions are much more likely to be of the same man because they all describe a similar build and mention one earring or a pierced ear.

98. c. No damage has been done in choices **a**, **b**, or **d**.

99. b. The officer has already taken care of steps 1 and 2: The victim doesn't need immediate medical help, and she is calm. Step 3 tells the officer to radio the suspect description to the dispatcher so a be-on-the-lookout bulletin can be issued.

100. a. Fred's opinion of police has nothing to do with the situation. Officer Martinez should write the ticket because the situation was dangerous, and that is what she would do under normal circumstances. A warning is not appropriate because a collision was narrowly averted.

6 ▶ READING TEXT, TABLES, CHARTS, AND GRAPHS

CHAPTER SUMMARY

State troopers need to have the ability to read—pure and simple. They also need to be able to understand what they are reading. Reports, procedure explanations, forms, suspect descriptions, and many other documents are regularly referred to in the law enforcement profession. This chapter provides tips and exercises that will help you improve your reading comprehension and improve your test score in this area.

The reading comprehension portion of the written test is designed to measure how well applicants understand what they read. The tests are usually multiple choice and will likely have questions based on brief passages, much like the standardized tests offered in schools. This chapter focuses on the specifics you will need to know to ace the reading comprehension questions on your exam. Once you are armed with the strategies that are explained in this chapter, you will be better able to understand what you read. Be sure to spend plenty of time with this chapter so that you can accurately assess your reading comprehension ability and increase your level of skill in this area.

Types of Reading Comprehension Questions

You have probably encountered reading comprehension questions before, where you are given a passage to read and then have to answer multiple-choice questions about it. This kind of question has two advantages for you as a test taker:

1. Any information you need to know is right in front of you.
2. You're being tested only on the information provided in the passage.

The disadvantage, however, is that you have to know where and how to find that information quickly in an unfamiliar text. This makes it easy to fall for one of the incorrect answer choices, especially since they're designed to mislead you.

The best way to excel on this passage/question format is to be very familiar with the kinds of questions that are typically asked on the test. Questions most frequently fall into one of the following four categories:

1. fact or detail
2. main idea or title
3. inference or interpretation
4. vocabulary definition

In order to succeed on a reading comprehension test, you need to thoroughly understand each of these four types of questions.

Fact or Detail

Facts and details are the specific pieces of information that support the passage's main idea. Generally speaking, facts and details are indisputable—things that don't need to be proven, like statistics (18 million people) or descriptions (a green overcoat). While you may need to decipher paraphrases of facts or details, you should be able to find the answer to a fact or detail question directly in the passage. This is usually the simplest kind of question; however, you must be able to separate important information from less important information. The main challenge in answering this type of question is that the answer choices can be confusing because they are often very similar to each other. You should read each answer choice carefully before selecting one.

Main Idea or Title

The main idea of a passage is the thought, opinion, or attitude that governs the whole passage. It may be clearly stated, or only implied. Think of the main idea as an umbrella that is general enough to cover all of the specific ideas and details in the passage. Sometimes, the questions found after a passage will ask you about the main idea, while others use the term *title*. Don't be misled; main idea and title questions are the same. They both require you to know what the passage is mostly about. Often, the incorrect answers to a main idea or title question are too detailed to be correct. Remember that the main idea of a passage or the best title for a passage is general, not specific.

If you are lucky, the main idea will be clearly stated in the first or last sentence of the passage. At other times, the main idea is not stated in a topic sentence but is implied in the overall passage, and you will need to determine the main idea by inference. Because there may be a lot of information in the passage, the trick is to understand what all that information adds up to—what it is that the author wants you to know. Often, some of the wrong answers to main idea questions are specific facts or details from the passage. A good way to test yourself is to ask, "Can this answer serve as a net to hold the whole passage together?" If not, chances are you have chosen a fact or detail, not a main idea.

Inference or Interpretation

Inference or interpretation questions ask you what the passage means, implies, or suggests, not just what it says. They are often the most difficult type of reading comprehension question.

Inference questions can be the most difficult to answer because they require you to draw meaning from the text when that meaning is implied rather than directly stated. Inferences are conclusions that we draw based on the clues the writer has given us. When you draw inferences, you have to be something of a detective, looking for clues such as word choice, tone, and specific details that suggest a certain conclusion, attitude, or point of view. You have to read between the lines in order to make a judgment about what an author was implying in the passage.

A good way to test whether you've drawn an acceptable inference is to ask, "What evidence do I have for this inference?" If you can't find any, you probably have the wrong answer. You need to be sure that your inference is logical and that it is based on something that is suggested or implied in the passage itself—not by what you or others might think. Like a good detective, you need to base your conclusions on evidence—facts, details, and other information—not on random hunches or guesses.

Vocabulary Definition

Questions designed to test vocabulary are really trying to measure how well you can figure out the meaning of an unfamiliar word from its context. *Context* refers to the words and ideas surrounding a vocabulary word. If the context is clear enough, you should be able to substitute a nonsense word for the one being sought, and you would still make the correct choice because you could determine meaning strictly from the sentence. For example, you should be able to determine the meaning of the following italicized nonsense word based on its context:

The speaker noted that it gave him great *terivinix* to announce the winner of the Outstanding Leadership Award.

In this sentence, *terivinix* most likely means

    a. pain.
    b. sympathy.
    c. pleasure.
    d. anxiety.

Clearly, the context of an award makes choice **c**, *pleasure*, the best choice. Awards don't usually bring pain, sympathy, or anxiety.

When confronted with an unfamiliar word, try substituting a nonsense word and see if the context gives you the clue. If you're familiar with prefixes, suffixes, and word roots, you can also use this knowledge to help you determine the meaning of an unfamiliar word.

You should be careful not to guess at the answer to vocabulary questions based on how you may have seen the word used before or what you think it means. Many words have more than one possible meaning, depending on the context in which they're used, and a word you've seen used one way may mean something else in a test passage. Also, if you don't look at the context carefully, you may make the mistake of confusing the vocabulary word with a similar word. For example, the vocabulary word may be *taut* (meaning *tight*), but if you read too quickly or don't check the context, you might think the word is *taunt* (meaning *tease*). Always make sure you read carefully and that what you think the word means fits into the context of the passage you're being tested on.

Now it is time to practice answering the four types of reading comprehension questions.

Practice Passage 1

The following is a sample test passage, followed by four questions. Read the passage carefully, and then answer the questions, based on your reading of the text, by circling your choice. Note under your answer which type of question has been asked. Correct answers appear immediately after the questions.

In the last decade, community policing has been frequently touted as the best way to reform urban law enforcement. The idea of putting more officers on foot patrol in high crime areas, where relations with police have frequently been strained, was initiated in Houston in 1983 under the leadership of then-Commissioner Lee Brown. He believed that officers should be accessible to the community at the street level. If officers were assigned to the same area over a period of time, those officers would

Before the test:

- Practice, practice, practice!
- Working with a friend or family member, select paragraphs from an article in the newspaper and have your partner create questions to ask you about it.
- Read short passages from articles or books and make up questions for yourself.

During the test:

- Read the questions first, before you read the passage, so you will know what words and ideas to look out for.
- Focus your attention; don't let your mind wander during the reading of the test passages.
- If one part of a passage confuses you, just read on until you are finished. Then go back and look at the confusing part again.
- Look at each one of the multiple-choice answers, then compare each with the paragraph to see which ones can be eliminated.
- Focus on the main idea of the text. What is the passage mostly about?
- Don't skip any sentences when reading the passage.
- Don't let your own knowledge of the subject matter interfere with your answer selection. Stick with the information that is given in the passage.
- Read the passage actively, asking yourself questions about the main idea and jotting down notes in the margin.

---

eventually build a network of trust with neighborhood residents. That trust would mean that merchants and residents in the community would let officers know about criminal activities in the area and would support police intervention. Since then, many large cities have experimented with Community-Oriented Policing (COP) with mixed results. Some have found that police and citizens are grateful for the opportunity to work together. Others have found that unrealistic expectations by citizens and resistance from officers have combined to hinder the effectiveness of COP. It seems possible, therefore, that a good idea may need improvement before it can truly be considered a reform.

1. Community policing has been used in law enforcement since
   a. the late 1970s.
   b. the early 1980s.
   c. the Carter administration.
   d. Lee Brown was New York City police commissioner.

Question type: _____

2. The phrase *a network of trust* in this passage suggests that
   a. police officers can rely only on each other for support.
   b. community members rely on the police to protect them.
   c. police and community members rely on each other.
   d. community members trust only each other.

Question type: _____

3. The best title for this passage would be
   a. Community Policing: The Solution to the Drug Problem.
   b. Houston Sets the Pace in Community Policing.
   c. Communities and Cops: Partners for Peace.
   d. Community Policing: An Uncertain Future?

Question type: _____

4. The word *touted* in the first sentence of the passage most nearly means
   a. praised.
   b. denied.
   c. exposed.
   d. criticized.

Question type: _____

Answers

Don't just look at the correct answers and move on. The explanations are the most important part, so read them carefully. Use these explanations to help you understand how to tackle each kind of question the next time you come across it.

1. b. Question type: 1, fact or detail. The passage says, "The idea of putting more officers on foot patrol in high crime areas, where relations with police have frequently been strained, was initiated in Houston in 1983 under the leadership of then-Commissioner Lee Brown." Do not be confused by the opening phrase, *In the last decade* because the passage does not include the current date, so you have no way of knowing which decade the passage is referring to. This information doesn't help you even if you know that a decade is a period of ten years. Don't be misled by trying to figure out when Carter was president. Also, if you happen to know that Lee Brown was New York City's police commissioner at one time, don't let that information lead you away from the information contained in the passage alone. Brown was commissioner in Houston when he initiated community policing.

2. c. Question type: 3, inference. The *network of trust* referred to in this passage is between the community and the police, as you can see from the sentence where the phrase appears. The key phrase in the question is *in this passage.* You may think that police can rely only on each other, or one of the other answer choices may appear equally plausible to you. But your choice of answers must be limited to the one suggested in this passage. Another tip for questions like this: Beware of absolutes! Be suspicious of any answer containing words like *only*, *always*, or *never*.

3. d. Question type: 2, main idea. A good title usually expresses the main idea. In this passage, the main idea comes at the end. The sum of all the details in the passage suggests that community policing is not without its critics and that therefore its future is uncertain. Another key phrase is *mixed results*, which means that some communities haven't had full success with community policing.

4. a. Question type: 4, vocabulary. The word *touted* is linked in this passage with the phrase *the best way to reform.* Most people would think that a good way to reform something is praiseworthy. In addition, the next few sentences in the passage describe the benefits of community policing. Criticism or a negative response to the subject doesn't come until later in the passage.

Practice Passage 2

Answer the questions that follow this passage. Circle the answers to the questions, and note under your answer which type of question has been asked. Then check your answers against the key that appears immediately after the questions.

There is some evidence that crime rates are linked to social trends, such as demographic and socio-economic changes. Crime statistics showed a decline in the post-World War II era of the 1940s and '50s. Following the Vietnam War in the 1970s, however, reported crimes were on the rise again, only to be followed by lower numbers of such reports in the 1980s. One of the reasons for these fluctuations appears to be age. When the population is younger, as in the 1960s when the baby boomers came of age, there is a greater incidence of crime nationwide. A second cause for the rise and fall of crime rates appears to be economic. Rising crime rates appear to follow falling economies. A third cause cited for the cyclical nature of crime statistics appears to be the ebb and flow of public policy decisions, which sometimes protect personal freedoms at the expense of government control. A youthful, economically disadvantaged population that is not secured by social controls of family and community or by government authority is likely to see an upswing in reported crimes.

1. Crime statistics seem to rise when populations are
  a. younger.
  b. older.
  c. veterans.
  d. richer.

  Question type: _____

2. The main idea of the passage is that
  a. times of prosperity show lower crime statistics.
  b. when the economy slows, crime statistics rise.
  c. incidence of reported crime is related to several social and economic variables.
  d. secure families are less likely to be involved in crime.

  Question type: _____

3. The best title for this passage would be
  a. Wars and Crime Statistics.
  b. Why Crime Statistics Rise and Fall.
  c. Youth and Crime Statistics.
  d. Poverty and Crime Statistics.

  Question type: _____

4. Crime statistics show that crime is
  a. random.
  b. cyclical.
  c. demographic.
  d. social.

  Question type: _____

Answers

1. a. Question type: 1, detail. This is a fairly clear example of how you can look quickly through a passage and locate a clearly stated detail. The word *young* appears in relation to the baby boomers; the idea is also suggested in the last sentence by the word *youthful*.

2. c. Question type: 2, main idea. The other answer choices are details—they're all in the passage, but they're not what the passage is *mostly* about. Choice **c** is the only one that combines several details into a statement that reflects the first sentence, which is also the topic sentence, of the paragraph.

3. b. Question type: 2, main idea. Each of the other choices expresses a detail, one of the reasons listed in the passage for fluctuation in crime rates. Choice **b** is the only one that expresses the sum of those details.

4. b. Question type: 1, detail. The passage mentions *the cyclical nature of crime statistics*. Other phrases that suggest this answer include *fluctuations, rise and fall,* and *ebb and flow*.

Practice Passage 3

Answer the questions that follow this passage. Circle the answers to the questions, and note under your answer which type of question has been asked. Then check your answers against the key that appears immediately after the questions.

In recent years, issues of public and personal safety have become a major concern to many Americans.

Violent incidents in fast-food restaurants, libraries, hospitals, schools, and offices have led many to seek greater security inside and outside of their homes. Sales of burglar alarms and high-tech security devices such as motion detectors and video monitors have skyrocketed in the last decade. Convenience stores and post offices have joined banks and jewelry stores in barricading staff behind iron bars and safety glass enclosures. Communities employ private security forces and encourage homeowners to keep trained attack dogs on their premises. While some people have sympathy for the impetus behind these efforts, there is also some concern that these measures will create a siege mentality leading to general distrust among people that could foster a dangerous isolationism within neighborhoods and among neighbors.

1. The passage suggests which of the following about community security?

   a. Communities are more dangerous today than they were ten years ago.
   b. Too much concern for security can destroy trust among neighbors.
   c. Poor security has led to an increase in public violence.
   d. Isolated neighborhoods are safe neighborhoods.

Question type: _____

2. The word *foster* in the last sentence of the passage most nearly means
   a. adopt.
   b. encourage.
   c. prevent.
   d. secure.

Question type: _____

3. The author believes that
   a. more security is needed to make neighborhoods safer.
   b. people should spend more on home security.
   c. people should not ignore the problems created by excessive safety concerns.
   d. attack dogs and high-tech devices are the best protection against violent crime.

Question type: _____

4. In the last sentence, the phrase *siege mentality* means
   a. hostility.
   b. defensiveness.
   c. fear.
   d. corruption.

Question type: _____

Answers

1. b. Question type: 4, inference. The key word here is *distrust*, which implies that neighbors become suspicious of each other if they are worried about safety.

2. b. Question type: 3, vocabulary. The first answer choice is meant to confuse you if you associate the word *foster* with foster care and, by extension, with adoption. *Foster* means *nurture* or *help to grow*. Look again at the sentence. What could *a general distrust* (the thing that fosters) do to *a dangerous isolationism* (the thing being fostered)? A general distrust could *encourage* a dangerous isolationism.

3. c. Question type: 4, inference. By using phrases like *dangerous isolationism*, the author suggests that he or she doesn't approve of the move toward more use of security devices. The other answer choices all indicate the author's approval of the trend being discussed.

4. b. Question type: 3, vocabulary. The key word here is *siege*. People who perceive themselves to be under attack tend to stick together in the face of a common enemy. They become quick to defend themselves against that enemy.

Create Your Own Questions

A good way to solidify what you've learned about reading comprehension questions is for you to write the questions. Here's a passage, followed by space for you to create your own questions. Write one question of each of the four types: fact or detail, main idea or title, inference or interpretation, and vocabulary definition.

As you create your own questions and answers, you will have the chance to understand how multiple-choice questions work. Typically, incorrect answers are incorrect because the reader has misunderstood, has a predisposition, uses unsound reasoning, or is only casually reading the passage. Knowing how multiple-choice questions work gives you a definite advantage when taking your written exam.

In recent years, law enforcement officers have welcomed the advent of a number of new technologies that have aided them greatly in their work. These include long-range eavesdropping devices and computer scanners that allow police to identify possible suspects by merely typing a license number into a computer in the patrol car. The scanner allows instant access to motor vehicle and criminal records and gives officers the opportunity to snare wrongdoers, even when they are not involved in criminal activity at the time. Police departments have praised the use of the computers, which they say help them get criminals off the streets and out of the way of honest citizens. Not all of those citizens agree with this attitude, however; some believe that

arrests made solely on the basis of scanner identification constitute an invasion of privacy. They regard the accessing of records as illegal search and seizure. In New Jersey, Florida, and Arizona, lawsuits have been filed by citizens who believe that their constitutional rights have been violated. They believe that much computer-generated information is inaccurate and vulnerable to hackers who invade computer databases. Some believe that such information from scanners could be used to charge innocent citizens with crimes, or to target particular neighborhoods for harassment.

1. Detail question: _____
_____

    a.
    b.
    c.
    d.

2. Main idea question: _____
_____

    a.
    b.
    c.
    d.

3. Inference question: _____
_____

    a.
    b.
    c.
    d.

4. Vocabulary question: _____

_____

a.

b.

c.

d.

Possible Questions

Following is one question of each type, based on the passage. Your questions may be very different, but these will give you an idea of the kinds of questions that could be asked.

1. *Detail question:* Computer scanners allow police to
   a. identify suspects.
   b. access computer databases.
   c. locate wrongdoers.
   d. all of the above

2. *Main idea question:* Which of the following best expresses the main idea of the passage?
   a. New technologies are available to police officers.
   b. Police are skeptical of new policing technologies.
   c. New technologies raise questions of privacy.
   d. New technologies may be discriminatory.

3. *Inference question:* The writer implies, but does not directly state, that
   a. computer technologies must be used with care.
   b. high-tech policing is the wave of the future.
   c. most citizens believe that high-tech policing is beneficial.
   d. most police officers prefer using the new technologies.

4. *Vocabulary question:* In this passage, the word *snare* means
   a. question.
   b. interrupt.
   c. capture.
   d. free.

Answers

1. d.
2. c.
3. d.
4. c.

Reading Tables, Graphs, and Charts

State trooper exams may also include a section testing your ability to read tables, charts, and graphs. These sections are really quite similar to regular reading comprehension sections, but instead of pulling information from a passage of text, you will need to answer questions about a graphic representation of data. The types of questions asked about tables, charts, and graphs are actually quite similar to those about reading passages, though there usually aren't any questions on vocabulary. The main difference in reading tables, charts, or graphs is that you're reading or interpreting data represented in tabular (table) or graphic (picture) form rather than textual (sentence and paragraph) form.

Tables

Tables present data in rows and columns. The table that follows is a very simple table that shows the number of accidents reported in one county over a 24-hour period. Use it to answer question 1.

When nonnative speakers of English have trouble with reading comprehension tests, it's often because they lack the cultural, linguistic, and historical frame of reference that native speakers enjoy. People who have not lived in or been educated in the United States often don't have the background information that comes from reading American newspapers, magazines, and textbooks.

A second problem for non native English speakers is the difficulty in recognizing vocabulary and idioms (expressions like chewing the fat) that assist comprehension. In order to read with good understanding, it's important to have an immediate grasp of as many words as possible in the text. Test takers need to be able to recognize vocabulary and idioms immediately so that the ideas those words express are clear.

The Long View

Read newspapers, magazines, and other periodicals that deal with current events and matters of local, state, and national importance. Pay special attention to articles that are related to law enforcement.

Be alert to new or unfamiliar vocabulary or terms that occur frequently in the popular press. Use a highlighter pen to mark new or unfamiliar words as you read. Keep a list of those words and their definitions. Review them for 15 minutes each day. Though at first you may find yourself looking up a lot of words, don't be frustrated—you will look up fewer and fewer words as your vocabulary expands.

During the Test

When you are taking your written exam, make a picture in your mind of the situation being described in the passage. Ask yourself, "What did the writer mostly want me to think about this subject?"

Locate and underline the topic sentence that carries the main idea of the passage. Remember that the topic sentence—if there is one—may not always be the first sentence. If there doesn't seem to be one, try to determine what idea summarizes the whole passage.

TIME OF DAY	NUMBER OF ACCIDENTS
6:00 A.M.–9:00 A.M.	11
9:00 A.M.–12:00 P.M.	3
12:00 P.M.–3:00 P.M.	5
3:00 P.M.–6:00 P.M.	7
6:00 P.M.–9:00 P.M.	9
9:00 P.M.–12:00 A.M.	6
12:00 A.M.–3:00 A.M.	5
3:00 A.M.–6:00 A.M.	3

1. Based on the information provided in this table, at what time of day do the most accidents occur?
a. noon
b. morning rush hour
c. evening rush hour
d. midnight

The correct answer is **b**, morning rush hour. You can clearly see that the highest number of accidents (11) occurred between 6:00 A.M. and 9:00 A.M.

Graphs

Now, here's the same information presented as a graph. A graph uses two axes rather than columns and rows to create a visual picture of the data.

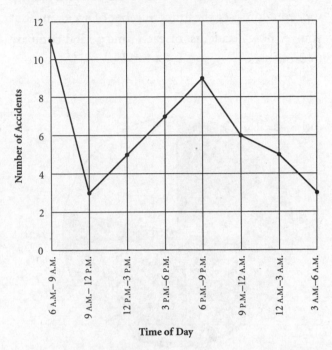

Here you can actually see the time of the greatest number of accidents represented by a line that corresponds to the time of day and number. These numbers can also be represented by a box in a bar graph, as follows.

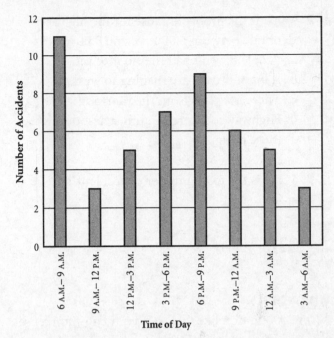

When reading graphs, the key is to be sure that you know exactly what the numbers on each axis represent. Otherwise, you're likely to misinterpret the information. On the bar graph, you see that the horizontal axis represents the time of day, and the vertical axis represents the number of accidents that occurred. Thus, the tallest box shows the time of day with the most accidents.

Practice

Like regular reading comprehension questions, questions on tables, charts, and graphs may also ask you to make inferences and maybe even do basic math using the information and numbers presented on the table, chart, or graph. For example, you may be asked questions like the following on the information presented in the preceding table, line graph, and bar graph. The answers follow immediately after the questions.

2. What is the probable cause for the high accident rate between 6:00 A.M. and 9:00 A.M.?

  a. People haven't had their coffee yet.

  b. A lot of drivers are rushing to work.

  c. There is a glare from the morning sun.

  d. Highway construction is heaviest during those hours.

3. What is the total number of accidents?

  a. 48

  b. 51

  c. 49

  d. 53

Answers

2. b. A question like this tests your common sense as well as your ability to read the graph. Though there may indeed be sun glare and many drivers may have not yet had their coffee, these items are too variable to account for the high number of accidents. In addition, choice **d** is not logical because construction generally slows traffic down. Choice **b** is the best answer, because from 6:00 to 9:00 A.M. there is consistently a lot of rush-hour traffic. In addition, many people do rush, and this increases the likelihood of accidents.

3. c. This question, of course, tests your basic ability to add. To answer this question correctly, you need to determine the value of each bar and then add those numbers together if you are given the bar graph. If you are given the table, you merely add up the column of numbers to find the total.

Charts

Finally, you may be presented information in the form of a chart like the one that follows. Here, the accident figures have been converted to percentages. In this figure, you don't see the exact number of accidents, but you see how accidents for each time period compare to the others.

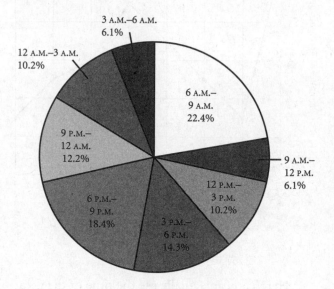

Practice

Try the following questions to hone your skill at reading tables, graphs, and charts.

Answer questions 1 and 2 on the basis of the following pie chart.

Causes of household fires

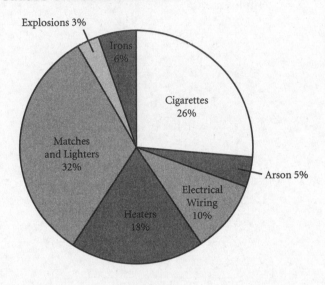

1. What is the percentage of smoking-related fires?
a. 26%
b. 32%
c. 58%
d. 26–58%

2. Based on the information provided in the chart, which of the following reasons applies to the majority of these fires?
a. malicious intent to harm
b. violation of fire safety codes
c. carelessness
d. faulty products

Answer questions 3 and 4 on the basis of the following graph.

Number of paid sick days per year of employment

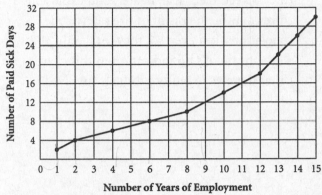

3. At what point does the rate of increase of sick days change?
a. one year of employment
b. four years of employment
c. three years of employment
d. nine years of employment

4. During what years of employment is the number of sick days equal to double the number of years of employment?
a. 1, 4, and 12
b. 13, 14, and 15
c. 1, 2, and 15
d. 2, 4, and 10

Answers

1. d. Of the causes presented in the chart, both cigarettes (26%) and matches and lighters (32%) are related to smoking. But not all match fires are necessarily smoking related. Thus, the best answer allows for a range between 26% and 58%.

2. c. Fires from cigarettes, heaters, irons, and matches and lighters—82% in total—are generally the result of carelessness. Only 5% of fires are arsons, so choice **a** cannot be correct. Electrical, heater, and explosion fires may be the result of fire safety code violations, but even so, they total only 31%. Finally, there's no indication in this chart that there were faulty products involved.

3. c. In the first two years of employment, employees gain an additional two sick days. In the third year, employees gain only one additional day, that is, from four to five days.

4. c. In the first year, the number of sick days is two; in the second, four; and not until the fifteenth year does the number of sick days (30) again double the number of years of employment.

7 ▶ GRAMMAR

CHAPTER SUMMARY

Besides being able to read well, state troopers must be able to write correctly and have a good grasp of the English language. This chapter reviews the sentence-level writing skills often tested on multiple-choice exams, including complete sentences, capitalization, punctuation, subject-verb agreement, verb tenses, pronouns, and confusing word pairs.

There is plenty of writing involved in state police work; just ask any trooper you see. The grammar section of the written exam helps the state determine whether or not applicants are capable of this aspect of the job. The tips and exercises in this chapter will help you improve your skills in this area and assess how much practice you need before taking the actual test.

Complete Sentences

Sentences are the basic unit of written language. Most writing is done using complete sentences, so it's important to distinguish sentences from fragments. A sentence expresses a complete thought, while a fragment requires something more to express a complete thought.

Fragments

Look at the following pairs of word groups. The first in each pair is a sentence fragment; the second is a complete sentence.

FRAGMENT	COMPLETE SENTENCE
The officer on foot patrol.	The officer was on foot patrol.
Exploding from the barrel of the gun.	The bullet exploded from the barrel of the gun.

These examples show that a sentence must have a subject and a verb to complete its meaning. The first fragment has a subject, but it needs a helping verb. Adding *was* before *on* completes the sentence. The second fragment has neither a subject nor a verb. Only when a subject and verb are added is the sentence complete.

Now look at the next set of word groups. Mark those that are complete sentences.

1. a. We saw the squad car approaching.
   b. When we saw the squad car approaching.

2. a. Before the prison was built in 1972.
   b. The prison was built in 1972.

3. a. Because we are on duty in the morning.
   b. We are on duty in the morning.

If you chose **1. a, 2. b,** and **3. b,** you were correct. You may have noticed that the groups of words are the same, but the fragments have an extra word at the beginning. These words are called subordinating conjunctions. If a group of words that would normally be a complete sentence is preceded by a subordinating conjunction, something more is needed to complete the thought.

In the following three sentences, the thoughts have been completed.

- When we saw the squad car approaching, we flagged it down.
- Before the prison was built in 1972, the old jailhouse was demolished.
- Because we were on duty in the morning, we went to bed early.

Here is a list of words that can be used as subordinating conjunctions.

after	that
although	though
as	unless
because	until
before	when
if	whenever
once	where
since	wherever
than	while

Run-On Sentences

If you can tell when a group of words isn't a sentence, then you can tell when one or more sentences have been run together, sometimes with a comma in between. Some tests will ask you to find run-on sentences. Each of the following sentences is a run-on sentence. Can you find where to put a period and begin a new sentence?

1. We went to the academy, we had a good time.
2. Without exception, the prisoners conformed to the new ruling they kept their cells clean.
3. The defense needed time to examine the new evidence, the lawyer asked for an extension.

If you noticed that a new sentence begins after academy in the first sentence, after ruling in the second, and after evidence in the third, you were right. Generally, you can tell whether you're looking at a run-on by covering the second half of the sentence and asking yourself whether the first half by itself is a sentence.

Then cover the first half. Is the second half a sentence by itself? If your answer to one or both questions is no, then the sentence is fine. If you answered both questions with yes—both halves of the sentence could be sentences by themselves—then you've got a run-on, unless there happens to be a semicolon (;) between the two halves.

Practice

Some of the questions on a state trooper exam may test your ability to distinguish a sentence from a fragment or a run-on. Check for a subject and a verb, as well as for subordinating conjunctions. Practice answering the following sample questions.

1. Which of the following groups of words is a complete sentence?
   a. The contraband buried beneath the floorboards beside the furnace.
   b. After we spent considerable time examining all of the possibilities before making a decision.
   c. In addition to the methods the detective used to solve the crime.
   d. The historical account of the incident bore the most resemblance to fact.

2. Which of the following groups of words is a complete sentence?
   a. This was fun to do.
   b. We looking.
   c. Before the door opened.
   d. If we ever see you again.

3. Which of the following groups of words is a run-on?
   a. Whenever I put on my uniform, I am filled with a sense of pride.
   b. The special services unit completed its work and made its report to the chief.
   c. Unless we hear from the directors of the board before the next meeting, we will not act on the new proposal.
   d. We slept soundly, we never heard the alarm.

Answers

1. d.
2. a.
3. d.

Capitalization

You may encounter questions that test your ability to capitalize correctly. Here is a quick review of the most common capitalization rules.

- Capitalize the first word of a sentence. If the first word is a number, write it as a word.
- Capitalize the pronoun *I*.
- Capitalize the first word of a quotation: I said, "What's the name of your dog?" Do not capitalize the first word of a partial quotation: He called me "the most diligent officer" he had ever seen.
- Capitalize proper nouns and proper adjectives. See the following table for more about proper nouns and adjectives.

The following passage contains no capitalized words. Circle those letters that should be capitalized.

when i first saw the black hills on january 2, 2005, i was shocked by their beauty. we had just spent new year's day in sioux falls, south dakota and had

CAPITALIZATION	
CATEGORY	EXAMPLE (PROPER NOUNS)
days of the week, months of the year	Friday, Saturday; January, February
holidays, special events	Christmas, Halloween; Two Rivers Festival, Dilly Days
names of individuals	John Jay, Rudy Giuliani, George Billeck
names of structures, buildings	Lincoln Memorial, Principal Building
names of trains, ships, aircraft	Queen Elizabeth, Chicago El
product names	Corn King hams, Ford Mustang
cities and states	Des Moines, Iowa; Juneau, Alaska
streets, highways, roads	Grand Avenue, Interstate 29, Deadwood Road
landmarks, public areas	Continental Divide, Grand Canyon, Glacier National Park
bodies of water	Atlantic Ocean, Mississippi River
ethnic groups, languages, nationalities	Asian-American, English, Arab
official titles	Mayor Daley, President Johnson
institutions, organizations, businesses	Dartmouth College, Lions Club
proper adjectives	English muffin, Polish sausage

headed west toward our home in denver, colorado. as we traveled along interstate 90, i could see the black hills rising slightly in the distance. president calvin coolidge had called them "a wondrous sight to behold." i understood why. after driving through the badlands and stopping at wall drug in wall, south dakota, we liked the way the evergreen-covered hills broke the barren monotony of the landscape. my oldest daughter said, "dad, look! there's something that's not all white." we could see why the lakota regarded the hills as a native american holy ground. we saw mount rushmore and custer state park, the home of the largest herd of buffalo in north america. we also drove the treacherous spearfish canyon road. fortunately, our jeep cherokee had no trouble with the ice and snow on the winding road.

Check your circled version against the corrected version of the passage that follows.

When I first saw the Black Hills on January 2, 2005, I was shocked by their beauty. We had just spent New Year's Day in Sioux Falls, South Dakota and had headed west toward our home in Denver, Colorado. As we traveled along Interstate 90, I could see the Black Hills rising slightly in the distance. President Calvin Coolidge had called them "a wondrous sight to behold." I understood why. After driving through the Badlands and stopping at Wall Drug in Wall, South Dakota, we liked the way the evergreen-covered hills broke the barren monotony of the landscape. My oldest daughter said, "Dad, look! There's something that's not all white." We could see why the Lakota regarded the hills as a Native American holy ground. We saw Mount Rushmore and Custer State Park, the home of the largest herd of buffalo in North America. We also drove the treacherous Spearfish Canyon Road. Fortunately, our Jeep Cherokee had no trouble with the ice and snow on the winding road.

Practice

Now try these sample questions. Choose the option that is capitalized correctly.

4. **a.** This year we will celebrate christmas on Tuesday, December 25 in Manchester, Ohio.
b. This year we will celebrate Christmas on Tuesday, December 25 in manchester, Ohio.
c. This year we will celebrate Christmas on Tuesday, December 25 in Manchester, Ohio.
d. This year we will celebrate christmas on Tuesday, December 25 in manchester, Ohio.

5. **a.** Abraham Adams made an appointment with Mayor Burns to discuss the building plans.
b. Abraham Adams made an appointment with Mayor Burns to discuss the Building Plans.
c. Abraham Adams made an appointment with mayor Burns to discuss the building plans.
d. Abraham Adams made an appointment with mayor Burns to discuss the Building Plans.

6. **a.** Abigail Dornburg, md, was named head of the review board for Physicians Mutual.
b. Abigail Dornburg, md, was named Head of the Review Board for Physicians Mutual.
c. Abigail Dornburg, md Was named head of the review board for Physicians mutual.
d. Abigail dornburg, md, was named head of the review board for Physicians Mutual.

Answers

4. c.
5. a.
6. a.

Punctuation

A section on the written exam may test your punctuation skills. Make sure you know how to use periods, commas, and apostrophes correctly.

Periods

Here is a quick review of the rules regarding the use of a period.

- Use a period at the end of a sentence that is not a question or an exclamation.
- Use a period after an initial in a name: Millard K. Furham.
- Use a period after an abbreviation, unless the abbreviation is an acronym.
  Abbreviations: Mr., Ms., Dr., A.M., General Motors Corp., Allied Inc.
  Acronyms: NASA, AIDS, MTV
- If a sentence ends with an abbreviation, use only one period. (We brought food, tents, sleeping bags, etc.)

Commas

Using commas correctly can make the difference between presenting information clearly and distorting the facts. The following chart demonstrates the necessity of commas in written language. How many people are listed in the sentence?

COMMAS AND MEANING	
Number undetermined	My sister Diane John Carey Melissa and I went to the fair.
Four people	My sister Diane, John Carey, Melissa, and I went to the fair.
Five people	My sister, Diane, John Carey, Melissa, and I went to the fair.
Six people	My sister, Diane, John, Carey, Melissa, and I went to the fair.

Here is a quick review of the most basic rules regarding the use of commas.

- Use a comma before and, but, so, or, for, nor, and yet when they separate two groups of words that could be complete sentences.
Example: The S.W.A.T. leader laid out the attack plan, and the team executed it to perfection.
- Use a comma to separate items in a series.
Example: The student driver stopped, looked, and listened when she got to the railroad tracks.
- Use a comma to separate two or more adjectives modifying the same noun.
Example: The hot, black, rich coffee tasted great after an hour in below-zero weather. (Notice that there is no comma between rich [an adjective] and coffee [the noun rich describes]).
- Use a comma after introductory words, phrases, or clauses in a sentence.
Examples: Usually, the class begins with a short writing assignment. [introductory word]
Racing down the street, the yellow car ran a stoplight. [introductory phrase]
After we responded to the call, we returned to our normal patrol. [introductory clause]
- Use a comma after a name followed by Jr., Sr., or some other abbreviation.
Example: The class was inspired by the speeches of Martin Luther King, Jr.
- Use a comma to separate items in an address.
Example: The car stopped at 1433 West G Avenue, Orlando, Florida, 36890.
- Use a comma to separate a day and a year, as well as after the year.
Example: I was born on July 21, 1954, during a thunderstorm.
- Use a comma after the greeting of a friendly letter and after the closing of any letter.
Example: Dear Uncle Jon,
Sincerely yours,

- Use a comma to separate contrasting elements in a sentence.
Example: Your essay needs strong arguments, not strong opinions, to convince me.
- Use commas to set off appositives (words or phrases that explain or identify a noun).
Example: My partner, a rookie, is named Ron.

The following passage contains no commas or periods. Add commas and periods as needed.

Dr Newton Brown Jr a renowned chemist has held research positions for OPEC Phillips Petroleum Inc Edward L Smith Chemical Designs and R J Reynolds Co His thorough exhaustive research is recognized in academic circles as well as in the business community as the most well-designed reliable data available Unfortunately on July 6 1988 he retired after a brief but serious illness He lives in a secluded retirement community at 2401 Beach Sarasota Springs Florida

Check your version against the following corrected version.

Dr. Newton Brown, Jr., a renowned chemist, has held research positions for OPEC, Phillips Petroleum Inc., Edward L. Smith Chemical Designs, and R.J.Reynolds Co. His thorough, exhaustive research is recognized in academic circles, as well as in the business community, as the most well-designed, reliable data available. Unfortunately, on July 6, 1988, he retired after a brief but serious illness. He lives in a secluded retirement community at 2401 Beach, Sarasota Springs, Florida.

Apostrophes

Apostrophes communicate important information in written language. Here is a quick review of the two most important rules regarding the use of apostrophes.

- Use an apostrophe to show that letters have been omitted from a word to form a contraction.
  Examples: do not = don't; national = nat'l; I will = I'll; it is = it's
- Use an apostrophe to show possession. See the following table for more examples.
  Examples: Juan's dog; Nikia's house

Practice

Practice with these sample test questions. For each question, choose which of the four options is punctuated correctly.

7.
a. Although it may seem strange, my partners purpose in interviewing Dr. E.S. Sanders Jr. was to eliminate him as a suspect in the crime.
b. Although it may seem strange my partner's purpose in interviewing Dr. E.S. Sanders, Jr. was to eliminate him, as a suspect in the crime.
c. Although it may seem strange, my partner's purpose in interviewing Dr. E.S. Sanders, Jr., was to eliminate him as a suspect in the crime.
d. Although it may seem strange, my partner's purpose in interviewing Dr. E.S. Sanders, Jr. was to eliminate him, as a suspect in the crime.

8.
a. After colliding with a vehicle at the intersection of Grand, and Forest Ms. Anderson saw a dark hooded figure crawl through the window, reach back and grab a small parcel, and run north on Forest.
b. After colliding with a vehicle at the intersection of Grand, and Forest, Ms. Anderson saw a dark hooded figure crawl through the window, reach back and grab a small parcel, and run north on Forest.
c. After colliding with a vehicle at the intersection of Grand and Forest Ms. Anderson saw a dark, hooded figure crawl through the window, reach back and grab a small parcel, and run north on Forest.
d. After colliding with a vehicle at the intersection of Grand and Forest, Ms. Anderson saw a dark, hooded figure crawl through the window, reach back and grab a small parcel, and run north on Forest.

9.
a. When we interviewed each of the boys and their fathers, we determined that the men's stories did not match the boy's versions.
b. When we interviewed each of the boys and their fathers, we determined that the men's stories did not match the boys' versions.
c. When we interviewed each of the boys and their fathers, we determined that the mens' stories did not match the boys' versions.
d. When we interviewed each of the boys' and their fathers', we determined that the men's stories did not match the boys' versions.

APOSTROPHES TO SHOW POSSESSION		
SINGULAR NOUNS (ADD 'S)	**PLURAL NOUNS ENDING IN S (ADD ')**	**PLURAL NOUNS NOT ENDING IN S**
boy's	boys'	men's
child's	kids'	children's
lady's	ladies'	women's

Verbs

Subject-Verb Agreement

In written language, a subject must agree with its verb in number. In other words, if a subject is singular, the verb must be singular. If the subject is plural, the verb must be plural. If you are unsure whether a verb is singular or plural, apply this simple test. Fill in the blanks in the following two sentences with the matching form of the verb. The verb form that best completes the first sentence is singular. The verb form that best completes the second sentence is plural.

> One person _____. [Singular]
> Two people _____. [Plural]

Look at these examples using the verbs *speak* and *do*. Try it yourself with any verb that confuses you.

> One person *speaks*.   One person *does*.
> Two people *speak*.   Two people *do*.

Pronoun Subjects

Few people have trouble matching noun subjects and verbs, but pronouns are sometimes difficult for even the most sophisticated writers. Some pronouns are always singular, others are always plural, and still others can be either singular or plural, depending on the usage.

These pronouns are always singular:

each	everyone
either	no one
neither	nobody
anybody	one
anyone	somebody
everybody	someone

The indefinite pronouns each, either, and neither are most often misused. You can avoid a mismatch by mentally adding the word one after the pronoun and removing the other words between the pronoun and the verb. Look at the following examples.

> Each **of the officers** wants his own squad car.
> Each **one** wants his own squad car.

> Either **of the suspects** knows where the stolen merchandise is located.
> Either **one** knows where the stolen merchandise is located.

These sentences may sound awkward because many speakers misuse these pronouns, and you are probably used to hearing them used incorrectly. Despite that, the substitution trick (inserting one for the words following the pronoun) will help you avoid this mistake.

Some pronouns are always plural and require a plural verb:

both	many
few	several

Other pronouns can be either singular or plural:

all	none
any	some
most	

The words or prepositional phrases following these pronouns determine whether they are singular or plural. If what follows the pronoun is plural, the verb must be plural. If what follows is singular, the verb must be singular.

> **All** of the **work is** finished.
> All of the jobs are finished.
> **Is any** of the **pizza** left?
> **Are any** of the **pieces** of pizza left?

None of the **time was** wasted.
None of the **minutes were** wasted.

Subjects Joined by and

If two nouns or pronouns are joined by and, they require a plural verb.

He **and** she want to buy a new house.
Jack **and** Jill want to buy a new house.

Subjects Joined by or or nor

If two nouns or pronouns are joined by or or nor, they require a singular verb. Think of them as two separate sentences, and you'll never make a mistake in agreement.

He **or** she wants to buy a new house.
He wants to buy a new house.
She wants to buy a new house.

Neither Jack **nor** Jill is good at basketball.
Jack is not good at basketball.
Jill is not good at basketball.

Practice

Circle the correct verb in each of the following sentences.

10. Every other day either Bert or Ed (takes, take) out the trash.
11. The woman in question (works, work) at the Civic Center box office.
12. A good knowledge of the rules (helps, help) you understand the game.
13. Each of these factors (causes, cause) the crime rate to increase.
14. (Have, Has) either of them ever arrived on time?

Answers

10. takes
11. works
12. helps
13. causes
14. Has

Verb Tense

The tense of a verb tells a reader when the action occurs. Present tense verbs tell the reader to imagine the action happening as it is being read, while past tense verbs tell the reader that the action has already happened. Read the following two paragraphs. The first one is written in the present tense, the second in the past tense. Notice the difference in the verbs. They are highlighted to make them easier to locate.

As Officer Horace **opens** the door, he **glances** around cautiously. He **sees** signs of danger everywhere. The centerpiece and placemats from the dining room table **are scattered** on the floor next to the table. An end table in the living room **is lying** on its side. He **sees** the curtains flapping and **notices** glass on the carpet in front of the window.

As Officer Horace **opened** the door, he **glanced** around cautiously. He **saw** signs of danger everywhere. The centerpiece and placemats from the dining room table **were scattered** on the floor next to the table. An end table in the living room **was lying** on its side. He **saw** the curtains flapping and **noticed** glass on the carpet in front of the window.

You can distinguish present tense from past tense by simply fitting the verb into a sentence.

VERB TENSE	
PRESENT TENSE (TODAY, I __ . . .)	**PAST TENSE (YESTERDAY, I __ . . .)**
drive	drove
think	thought
rise	rose
catch	caught

The important thing to remember about verb tense is to keep it consistent. If a passage begins in the present tense, keep it in the present tense unless there is a specific reason to change—to indicate that some action occurred in the past, for instance. If a passage begins in the past tense, it should remain in the past tense. Verb tense should never be mixed as it is in the following sentence.

Wrong: Officer Terry opens the door and saw the unruly crowd.

Correct: Officer Terry opens the door and sees the unruly crowd.
Officer Terry opened the door and saw the unruly crowd.

However, sometimes it is necessary to use a different verb tense in order to clarify when an action occurred. Read the following sentences and the explanations following them.

The sergeant **sees** the criminal that you **caught**. [The verb sees is in the present tense, indicating that the action is occurring in the present. However, the verb *caught* is in the past tense, indicating that the criminal was caught at some earlier time.]

The prison that **was built** over a century ago **sits** on top of the hill. [The verb phrase *was built* is in the past tense, indicating that the prison was built in the past. However, the verb *sits* is in the present tense, indicating that the action is still occurring.]

Practice
Check yourself with these sample questions. Choose the option that uses verb tense correctly. Answers are at the end of the chapter.

15. a. When I work hard, I always get what I want.
b. When I work hard, I always got what I want.
c. When I worked hard, I always got what I want.
d. When I worked hard, I always get what I wanted.

16. a. It all started after I came home and am in my room studying for a big test.
b. It all started after I came home and was in my room studying for a big test.
c. It all starts after I come home and was in my room studying for a big test.
d. It all starts after I came home and am in my room studying for a big test.

17. a. The suspect became nervous and dashes into the house and slams the door.
b. The suspect becomes nervous and dashed into the house and slammed the door.
c. The suspect becomes nervous and dashes into the house and slammed the door.
d. The suspect became nervous and dashed into the house and slammed the door.

Answers
15. a.
16. b.
17. d.

Pronouns

Pronoun Case
Most of the time, a single pronoun in a sentence is easy to use correctly. In fact, most English speakers would readily identify the mistakes in the following sentences.

Me went to the prison with **he**.
My partner gave **she** a ride to work.

Most people know that Me in the first sentence should be I and that he should be him. They would also know that she in the second sentence should be her. Such errors are easy to spot when the pronouns are used alone in a sentence. The problem occurs when a pronoun is used with a noun or another pronoun. See if you can spot the errors in the following sentences.

> The rookie rode with Jerry and **I**.
> Belle and **him** are going to the courthouse.

The errors in these sentences are not as easy to spot as those in the sentences with a single pronoun. The easiest way to attack this problem is to turn the sentence with two pronouns into two separate sentences. Then the error once again becomes very obvious.

> The rookie rode with Jerry.
> The rookie rode with **me** (not I).

> Belle **is** going to the courthouse. [Notice the singular verb *is* in place of *are*.]
> **He** (not *him*) is going to the courthouse.

Pronoun Agreement

Another common error in using pronouns involves singular and plural pronouns. Like subjects and verbs, pronouns must match the number of the nouns they represent. If the noun a pronoun represents is singular, the pronoun must be singular. On the other hand, if the noun a pronoun represents is plural, the pronoun must be plural. Sometimes a pronoun represents another pronoun. If so, either both pronouns must be singular or both pronouns must be plural. Consult the list of singular and plural pronouns you saw earlier in this chapter.

> The **officer** must take a break when **she** (or **he**) is tired. [singular]
> **Officers** must take breaks when **they** are tired. [plural]

> **One** of the rookies misplaced **her** file. [singular]
> **All** of the rookies misplaced **their** files. [Plural]

If two or more singular nouns or pronouns are joined by and, use a plural pronoun to represent them.

> **Buddha and Muhammad** built religions around **their** philosophies.
> If **he and the sergeant** want to know where I was, **they** should ask me.

If two or more singular nouns or pronouns are joined by or, use a singular pronoun. If a singular and a plural noun or pronoun are joined by or, the pronoun should agree with the closest noun or pronoun it represents.

> **Matthew or Jacob** will loan you **his** extra radio.
> **The elephant or the moose** will furiously protect **its** young.

> Neither **the officers** nor **the sergeant** was sure of **his** location.
> Neither **the sergeant** nor **the officers** was sure of their location.

Practice

Circle the correct pronoun in the following sentences.

18. Andy or Arvin will bring (his, their) camera so (he, they) can take pictures of the party.

19. One of the file folders isn't in (its, their) drawer.

20. The uniform store sent Bob and Ray the shirts (he, they) had ordered.

21. Benny and (he, him) went to the courthouse with Bonnie and (I, me).

22. Neither my cousins nor my uncle knows what (he, they) will do tomorrow.

Answers
18. his, he
19. its
20. they
21. he, me
22. he

Easily Confused Word Pairs

The following word pairs are often misused in written language. By reading the following explanations and looking at the examples, you can learn to use these words correctly every time.

Its/It's

Its is a possessive pronoun that means "belonging to it." *It's* is a contraction for *it is* or *it has*. The only time you will ever use *it's* is when you can also substitute the words *it is* or *it has*.

Who/That

Who refers to people. *That* refers to things.

> There is the officer **who** helped me recover my car.
> The woman **who** invented the copper-bottomed kettle died in 1995.
> This is the house **that** was burglarized.
> The bullets **that** I needed were no longer in stock.

There/Their/They're

Their is a possessive pronoun that shows ownership. *There* is an adverb that tells where an action or item is located. *They're* is a contraction for the words *they are*. Here is an easy way to remember these words.

- *Their* means belonging to them. Of the three words, *their* can be most easily transformed into the word *them*. Extend the *r* on the right side and connect the *i* and the *r* to turn *their*

into *them*. This clue will help you remember that *their* means "belonging to them."
- If you examine the word *there*, you can see that it contains the word *here*. Whenever you use *there*, you should be able to substitute *here*. The sentence should still make sense.
- Imagine that the apostrophe in *they're* is actually a very small letter *a*. Use *they're* in a sentence only when you can substitute *they are*.

Your/You're

Your is a possessive pronoun that means "belonging to you." *You're* is a contraction for the words *you are*. The only time you should use *you're* is when you can substitute the words *you are*.

To/Too/Two

To is a preposition or an infinitive.

- As a preposition: *to* the jail, *to* the bottom, *to* my church, *to* our garage, *to* his school, *to* his hideout, *to* our disadvantage, *to* an open room, *to* a ballad, *to* the precinct
- As an infinitive (*to* followed by a verb, sometimes separated by adverbs): *to* walk, *to* leap, *to* see badly, *to* find, *to* advance, *to* read, *to* build, *to* sorely want, *to* badly misinterpret, *to* carefully peruse

Too means also. Whenever you use the word *too*, substitute the word *also*. The sentence should still make sense.

Two is a number, as in *one*, *two*. If you memorize this, you will never misuse this form.

As you take the portion of the test that assesses your writing skills, apply what you know about the rules of grammar:

- Look for complete sentences.
- Check for periods, commas, and apostrophes.
- Look for subject-verb agreement and consistency in verb tense.
- Check the pronouns to make sure the correct form is used and that the number (singular or plural) is correct.
- Check those easily confused pairs of words.
- When determining which answer is correct to any one question, don't go back and review answer choices that you have already eliminated as being wrong.
- Always read all of the answer choices before selecting one. You may find an even better answer if you keep looking.

Practice

The key is to think consciously about these words when you see them in written language. Circle the correct form of these easily confused words in the following sentences.

23. (Its, It's) (to, too, two) late (to, too, two) remedy the problem now.
24. This is the officer (who, that) gave me the directions I needed.
25. (There, Their, They're) going (to, too, two) begin construction as soon as the plans are finished.
26. We left (there, their, they're) house after the storm subsided.
27. I think (your, you're) going (to, too, two) get at least (to, too, two) extra shifts.
28. The crime syndicate moved (its, it's) home base of operations.

Answers

23. It's, too, to
24. who
25. They're, to
26. their
27. you're, to, two
28. its

Additional Resources

This chapter was a very basic review of only a few aspects of written English. For more help with these aspects and more, consult the following books.

For Nonnative Speakers of English

- *Errors in English and Ways to Correct Them* by Harry Shaw (HarperCollins)
- *Living in English* by Betsy J. Blosser (Passport Books)

For Everyone

- *Grammar Essentials,* 3rd Edition (Learning-Express)
- *Writing Skills Success in 20 Minutes a Day, 3rd Edition* (LearningExpress)
- *501 Grammar and Writing Questions, 3rd Edition* (LearningExpress)
- *Grammar Smart: A Guide To Perfect Usage,* The Princeton Review Series *(Princeton Review)*
- *English Grammar for Dummies* by Geraldine Woods (John Wiley & Sons)

Grammar-Related Websites

- English Grammar Help
  http://owl.english.purdue.edu/owl
- Ask Miss Grammar
  www.protrainco.com/info/writing-editing/grammar.htm
- Grammar Rules and Practice Exercises
  www.chompchomp.com/menu.htm
- Grammar & Style (a complete online grammar guide)
  http://andromeda.rutgers.edu/~jlynch/Writing
- Grammar Slammer
  http://englishplus.com/grammar
- Common Errors In English
  www.wsu.edu/~brians/errors

8 ▶ VOCABULARY AND SPELLING

CHAPTER SUMMARY
Your grasp of the English language will be measured on the written exam in the areas of vocabulary and spelling. This chapter covers both areas, providing useful tips and exercises that can increase your chances of success.

State troopers need the ability to communicate effectively with others. Using good vocabulary and correct spelling is important when writing or speaking. Law enforcement officials need to be able to speak, understand, read, and write the English language efficiently. Use this chapter to improve your vocabulary and spelling skills.

Vocabulary

If your written exam has a section that tests your vocabulary, the questions will most likely deal with synonyms, antonyms, word parts, context, and/or homophones.

- **Synonyms** are words that share the same meaning or nearly the same meaning as other words.
- **Antonyms** are words that are the opposite or nearly the opposite of other words.
- **Word parts** are made up of prefixes, roots, and suffixes.
- **Context** refers to the text surrounding a word.
- **Homophones** are words that sound the same but have different meanings, such as *heard* and *herd*.

Synonym and Antonym Questions

A word is a *synonym* of another word if it has the same or nearly the same meaning as the other word. *Antonyms* are words with opposite meanings. Test questions often ask you to find the synonym or antonym of a word. If you're lucky, the word will be surrounded by a sentence that helps you guess what the word means. If you're less lucky, you will get just the word, and then you have to figure out what the word means without any help.

Questions that ask for synonyms and antonyms can be tricky because they require you to recognize the meanings of several words that may be unfamiliar—not only the words in the questions but also the answer choices. Usually, the best strategy is to look at the structure of the word and to listen for its sound. See if a part of a word—the root—looks familiar. The meaning of a word is located within its root. For instance, the root of *credible* is *cred*, which means to trust or believe. Knowing what common root parts mean can help you understand the meaning of words you don't know. Other words with the root *cred* are *incredible*, *sacred*, and *credit*. Looking for related words that have the same root as the word in question can help you to choose the right answer, even if it is only by process of elimination.

Synonym Practice

Try your hand at identifying the root and other word parts and the related words in these sample synonym questions. Circle the word that means the same or about the same as the underlined word. Answers and explanations appear right after the questions.

1. a set of <u>partial</u> prints
   a. identifiable
   b. incomplete
   c. visible
   d. enhanced

2. <u>substantial</u> evidence
   a. inconclusive
   b. weighty
   c. proven
   d. alleged

3. <u>corroborated</u> the statement
   a. confirmed
   b. negated
   c. denied
   d. challenged

4. <u>ambiguous</u> questions
   a. meaningless
   b. difficult
   c. simple
   d. vague

Answers

The explanations are just as important as the answers, because they show you how to go about choosing a synonym if you don't know the word.

1. **b.** *Partial* means *incomplete*. The root of the word here is *part*. A partial print is only part of the whole.

2. **b.** *Substantial* evidence is *weighty*. The key part of the word here is *substance*. Substance has weight.

3. **a.** *Corroboration* is *confirmation*. Notice the prefix *co-*, which means *with* or *together*. Some related words are *cooperate*, *coworker*, and *collide*. Corroboration means that one statement fits with another.

4. **d.** *Ambiguous* questions are *vague* or uncertain. The key part of this word is *ambi-*, which means *two* or *both*. An ambiguous question can be taken two ways.

Antonym Practice

The main danger in answering questions with antonyms is forgetting that you are looking for opposites rather than synonyms. Most antonym questions will include one or more synonyms as answer choices. The trick is to keep your mind on the fact that you are looking for the opposite of the word. If you're allowed to mark in the books or on the test papers, circle the word *antonym* or *opposite* in the directions to help you remember.

Otherwise, the same tactics that work for synonym questions work for antonyms as well: Try to determine the meaning of part of the word or to remember a context where you've seen the word before.

Circle the word that means the opposite of the underlined word. Answers are immediately after the questions.

5. <u>zealous</u> pursuit
   a. envious
   b. eager
   c. idle
   d. comical

6. <u>inadvertently</u> left
   a. mistakenly
   b. purposely
   c. cautiously
   d. carefully

7. <u>exorbitant</u> prices
   a. expensive
   b. unexpected
   c. reasonable
   d. outrageous

8. <u>compatible</u> partners
   a. comfortable
   b. competitive
   c. harmonious
   d. experienced

9. <u>belligerent</u> attitude
   a. hostile
   b. reasonable
   c. instinctive
   d. ungracious

Answers

Be sure to read the explanations as well as the right answers.

5. **c.** *Zealous* means *eager*, so *idle* is most nearly opposite. Maybe you've heard the word *zeal* before. One trick in this question is not to be misled by the similar sounds of *zealous* and *jealous*. The other trick is not to choose the synonym, *eager*.

6. **b.** *Inadvertently* means *by mistake*, so *purposely* is the antonym. The key element in this word is the prefix *in-*, which usually means *not* or *the opposite of*. Consider related words like *involuntary*, *inappropriate*, and *ineligible*. As usual, one of the answer choices (**a**) is a synonym.

7. **c.** The key element here is *ex-*, which means *out of* or *away from*. *Exorbitant* literally means *out of orbit*. The opposite of an *exorbitant* or *outrageous* price would be a *reasonable* one.

8. **b.** The opposite of *compatible* is *competitive*. Here you have to distinguish among three words that contain the same prefix, *com-*, and to let the process of elimination work for you. The other choices are too much like synonyms.

9. **b.** The key element in this word is the root *belli-*, which means *warlike*. The synonym choices, then, are *hostile* and *ungracious*; the antonym is *reasonable*.

Context Questions

Context is the surrounding text in which a word is used. Most people use context to help them determine the meaning of an unknown word. A vocabulary question that gives you a sentence around the vocabulary word is usually easier to answer than one with little or no context. The surrounding text can help you as you look for synonyms for the specified words in the sentences.

The best way to take meaning from context is to look for key words in sentences or paragraphs that convey the meaning of the text. If nothing else, the context will give you a means to eliminate wrong answer choices that clearly don't fit. The process of elimination will often leave you with the correct answer.

Context Practice

Try these sample questions. Circle the word that best describes the meaning of the underlined word in the sentence.

10. The members of the jury were <u>appalled</u> by the wild and uncontrolled behavior of the witness in the case.
   a. horrified
   b. amused
   c. surprised
   d. dismayed

11. Despite the fact that he appeared to have financial resources, the defendant claimed to be <u>destitute</u>.
   a. wealthy
   b. ambitious
   c. solvent
   d. impoverished

12. Though she was <u>distraught</u> over the disappearance of her child, the woman was calm enough to give the officer her daughter's description.
   a. punished
   b. distracted
   c. composed
   d. anguished

13. The unrepentant criminal expressed no <u>remorse</u> for his actions.
   a. sympathy
   b. regret
   c. reward
   d. complacency

Some tests may ask you to fill in the blank by choosing a word that fits the context. In the following questions, circle the word that best completes the sentence.

14. Professor Washington was a very _____ woman known for her reputation as a scholar.
   a. stubborn
   b. erudite
   c. illiterate
   d. disciplined

15. His _____ was demonstrated by his willingness to donate large amounts of money to worthy causes.
   a. honesty
   b. loyalty
   c. selfishness
   d. altruism

Answers

Check to see whether you were able to pick out the key words that help you define the target word, as well as whether you got the right answer.

10. a. The key words *wild* and *uncontrolled* signify *horror* rather than the milder emotions described by the other choices.

11. d. The key words here are *financial resources,* but this is a clue by contrast. The introductory *Despite the fact* signals that you should look for the opposite of the idea of having financial resources.

12. d. The key words here are *though* and *disappearance of her child,* signalling that you are looking for an opposite of *calm* in describing how the mother spoke to the officer. The only word strong enough to match the situation is *anguished.*

13. b. *Remorse* means *regret for one's actions.* The part of the word here to beware of is the prefix *re-*. It doesn't signify anything in this word, though it often means *again* or *back.* Don't be confused by the two choices that also contain the prefix *re-*. The strategy here is to see which word sounds better in the sentence. The key words are *unrepentant* and *no,* indicating that you're looking for something that shows no repentance.

14. b. The key words here are *professor* and *scholarly.* Even if you don't know the word *erudite,* the other choices don't fit the description of the professor.

15. d. The key phrase here is *large amounts of money to worthy causes.* They give you a definition of the word you're looking for. Again, even if you don't know the word *altruism,* the other choices seem inappropriate to describe someone so generous.

For Nonnative Speakers of English

Be very careful not to be confused by the sound of words that may mislead you. Be sure you look at the word carefully, and pay attention to the structure and appearance of the word as well as its sound. You may be used to hearing English words spoken with an accent. The sounds of those words may be misleading in choosing a correct answer.

Questions about Word Parts

Some tests may ask you to find the meaning of a part of a word: roots, which are the main part of the word; prefixes, which go before the root word; or suffixes, which go after. Any of these elements can carry meaning or change the use of a word in a sentence. For instance, the suffix *-s* or *-es* can change the meaning of a noun from singular to plural: *boy, boys.* The prefix *un-* can change the meaning of a root word to its opposite: *necessary, unnecessary.*

To identify most parts of words, the best strategy is to think of words you already know that carry the same root, suffix, or prefix. Let what you know about those words help you to see the meaning of words that are less familiar.

On the following two pages are some of the word parts that appear most often on vocabulary tests. If you read the following lists of word parts and their meanings for five to ten minutes every day, you will soon have the level of recognition you need to score high on this portion of the exam. You may also wish to create flash cards to carry around with you—write the word part on one side of the card and its meaning and some examples of it on the other.

Word Part Practice

Circle the word or phrase that best describes the meaning of the underlined portion of the word. Answers appear after the questions.

16. <u>pro</u>active
  a. after
  b. forward
  c. toward
  d. behind

17. <u>re</u>cession
  a. against
  b. see
  c. under
  d. back

18. <u>cont</u>emporary
  a. with
  b. over
  c. apart
  d. time

19. etymo<u>logy</u>
  a. state of
  b. prior to
  c. study of
  d. quality of

20. vandal<u>ize</u>
  a. to make happen
  b. to stop
  c. to fill
  d. to continue

Common Prefixes and Their Meanings

a (not, without) *ex*: amoral, apolitical	**ab** (away from, off) *ex*: abnormal, abhor	**bi** (two) *ex*: bifocals, bicentennial
contra (against, opposite) *ex*: contradict, contraceptive	**de** (take away from, down, do the opposite of) *ex*: deflate, derail	**dis** (not, opposite of, exclude) *ex*: disown, disarm
im, in, il (not, negative) *ex*: impossible, inappropriate, illegal	**inter** (between, among) *ex*: interstate, intervene	**mis** (wrong) *ex*: misspell, misplace
non (not, no) *ex*: nonsense, nonconformity	**ob, op** (toward, against, in the way of) *ex*: objection, oppose	**per** (through, very) *ex*: persecute, persuade
port (carry) *ex*: portable, portfolio	**pre** (before) *ex*: precede, predict	**pro** (forward, for) *ex*: protect, propel, provide
re (back, again) *ex*: remember, reply	**term** (end, boundary, limit) *ex*: terminology, termination	**trans** (across, beyond, change) *ex*: transformation, transfer
un (not, against, opposite) *ex*: unstoppable, untrustworthy, unhappy	**voc** (to call) *ex*: vocation, vocal	

Common Root Words and Their Meanings

anim (mind, life, spirit, anger)
ex: animal, animated, animosity

cede, ceed, cess (go, yield)
ex: concede, success, exceed

cred (trust, believe)
ex: credible, sacred, incredible

dic, dict (say, speak)
ex: indication, dictionary, edict

fid (belief, faith)
ex: confide, affidavit, fidelity

flu, flux (to flow, flowing)
ex: fluid, fluctuate

form (shape)
ex: conform, format, formality

ject (throw)
ex: interject, object, intersect

man (by hand, make, do)
ex: manage, craftsmanship, command

oper (work)
ex: operation, cooperate

path (feel)
ex: homeopathic, sympathy, psychopath

pel/pulse (push)
ex: impulse, compel

pict (paint, show, draw)
ex: depiction, picture

rog (ask)
ex: interrogate

rupt (break)
ex: interrupt, corrupt

sent, sens (feel, think)
ex: resentment, sensitive

sist (to withstand, make up)
ex: insist, resist, persist

spir (breath, soul)
ex: inspire, perspire

Common Suffixes and Their Meanings

ance, ence (quality or process)
ex: dominance, dependence

ant, ent (something or someone that performs an action)
ex: client, applicant

ate (office or function)
ex: dedicate, candidate

dom (state of being)
ex: boredom, wisdom

er, or (person or thing that does something)
ex: officer, director

ful (amount or quality that fills)
ex: handful, cheerful

ia (names, diseases)
ex: malaria, anorexia

ian, an (related to, one that is)
ex: custodian, human

ile (capability, aptitude)
ex: fragile, docile

ing (action, result of action)
ex: singing, jumping, clinging

ion (condition or action)
ex: abduction, selection, deduction

ity (expressing state or condition)
ex: sincerity, brevity

ive (condition)
ex: motive, directive

ment (action, product, result)
ex: fragment, ornament, judgment

ness (state, condition, quality)
ex: happiness, goodness, nervousness

or (property, condition)
ex: candor, squalor, splendor

otic (relationship to action, process, or condition)
ex: patriotic, psychotic, hypnotic

ship (status, condition)
ex: partnership, friendship, courtship

ty (quality or state)
ex: unity, civility, anonymity

ure (act, condition, process or function)
ex: exposure, composure, assure

y (inclination, result of an activity)
ex: dreamy, pesky, whiny

Answers

Even if the word in the question was unfamiliar, you might have been able to guess the meaning of the prefix or suffix by thinking of some other word that has the same prefix or suffix.

16. b. Think of a *propeller*. A propeller sends an airplane *forward*.

17. d. Think of *recall*: Manufacturers *recall* or *bring back* cars that are defective; people *recall* or *bring back* past events in memory.

18. a. Think of *congregation*: A group of people gather *with* each other in a house of worship.

19. c. Think of *biology*, the *study of* life.

20. a. Think of *scandalize*: to *make* something shocking *happen*.

How to Answer Vocabulary Questions

- Look for word parts that you know, such as the root, prefix, or suffix, and think of similar words that may give clues to the meaning of the word in question.
- Pay close attention to the directions. Make sure you know when to look for the opposite meaning rather than a similar one.
- Think of how the word makes sense in a sentence.
- Sound out the word inside your head to make sure you aren't reading it wrong.
- Don't be fooled by words that sound the same but have different spellings and meanings.
- Check back over your work if you have time remaining to make sure you haven't made any careless mistakes.

Homophone Questions

Don't be fooled by words that sound alike but have entirely different meanings. The best way to identify these easily confused words is by studying them and quizzing yourself until you have the meanings and spellings memorized. On the next page is a list of homophones that are often found on written exams. Review the list carefully and consult your dictionary to determine the meanings of any words that you are unsure of.

Homophone Practice

Each sentence contains two words in parentheses that are homophones. Circle the word that makes sense in the sentence. Answers and explanations follow the questions.

21. He slammed on his (break, brake) just before the stop sign.

22. The mayor decided to (higher, hire) a few more police officers.

23. His family advised him to seek (council, counsel) before going any further.

24. She told him to get his (facts, fax) straight before speaking to her again.

25. No one (new, knew) exactly what had happened.

26. They wondered if someone would try to (steel, steal) the jewelry.

Answers

Check to see if you selected the correct word in each sentence.

21. brake—a stopping device, such as the brake in a truck or car. (*Break* means to damage something.)

22. hire—to pay for the services of someone. (*Higher* means something or someone is more high than someone or something else.)

23. counsel—advice. (*Council* means a group of people who meet for a purpose.)

24. facts—something that is really true. (*Fax*—short for facsimile—means a document sent or received from a fax machine.)

25. knew—having known something. (*New* is the opposite of old.)

26. steal—taking something that belongs to someone else. (*Steel* is a metal.)

ad, add	hear, here	rap, wrap
affect, effect	heard, herd	right, write
allowed, aloud	higher, hire	road, rode
bare, bear	hoarse, horse	roll, role
bored, board	hole, whole	sale, sail
boulder, bolder	hours, ours	scene, seen
brake, break	incite, insight	see, sea
bred, bread	knew, new	soar, sore
build, billed	know, no	stair, stare
cent, scent	lead, led	steel, steal
cereal, serial	leased, least	sun, son
cite, sight, site	lesson, lessen	sweet, suite
counsel, council	made, maid	tents, tense
course, coarse	marshal, martial	their, there, they're
days, daze	meat, meet	threw, through
died, dyed	morning, mourning	throne, thrown
due, do, dew	one, won	tide, tied
facts, fax	pact, packed	to, too, two
fair, fare	pail, pale	trooper, trouper
feat, feet	passed, past	vary, very
find, fined	patience, patients	wade, weighed
flour, flower	pause, paws	ware, wear, where
for, fore, four	peace, piece	weather, whether
great, grate	plain, plane	weight, wait
groan, grown	poor, pour	wood, would
guessed, guest	rain, reign	your, you're
heal, he'll	raise, rays	

Spelling

Generally, spelling tests are in a multiple-choice format. You will be given several possible spellings for a word and asked to identify the one that is correct. Thus, you must be able to see very fine differences between word spellings. The best way to prepare for a spelling test is to have a good grasp of the spelling fundamentals and be able to recognize when those rules don't apply. Remember that English is full of exceptions in spelling. You have to develop a good eye to spot the errors.

Even though there are so many variant spellings for words in English, state trooper exams generally are looking to make sure that you know and can apply the basic rules. Following are some of those rules to review:

- *i* before *e*, except after *c*, or when *ei* sounds like *a*.

  Examples: piece, receive, neighbor

- *gh* can replace *f* or be silent.

  Examples: enough, night

- Double the consonant when you add an ending.

  Examples: forget/forgettable, shop/shopping

- Drop the *e* when you add -*ing*.

  Example: hope/hoping

- The spelling of prefixes and suffixes generally doesn't change.

  Examples: project, propel, proactive

Spelling Practice

Here are some examples of how spelling questions might appear on a state trooper exam. Choose the word that is spelled correctly in the following sentences.

27. We went to an _____ of early Greek art.
    a. exibition
    b. exhibition
    c. excibition
    d. exebition

28. We will _____ go to the movies tonight.
    a. probly
    b. probbaly
    c. probely
    d. probably

29. We took _____ of pictures on our vacation.
    a. allot
    b. alot
    c. a lot
    d. alott

30. The sharpshooter had the greatest number of _____ target shots.
    a. accurate
    b. acurate
    c. accuret
    d. acccurit

31. He was warned not to use _____ force.
    a. exessive
    b. exccesive
    c. excessive
    d. excesive

Answers

27. b.
28. d.
29. c.
30. a.
31. c.

Using Spelling Lists

Some test makers will give you a list of words to study before you take the test. If you have a list to work with, here are some suggestions.

- Divide the list into groups of three, five, or seven words to study. Consider making flash cards of the words you don't know.
- Highlight or circle the tricky elements in each word.
- Cross out or discard any words that you already know for certain. Don't let them get in the way of the ones you need to study.
- Say the words as you read them. Spell them out in your mind so you can hear the spelling.

- Learn groups of synonyms for words.
- Learn new words in context.
- Memorize common word roots, prefixes, and suffixes.
- Create and use flashcards regularly.

Here's a sample spelling list. These words are typical of the words that appear on exams. If you are not given a list by the agency that's testing you, study this one.

achievement	doubtful	ninety
allege	eligible	noticeable
anxiety	enough	occasionally
appreciate	enthusiasm	occurred
arraignment	equipped	offense
asthma	exception	official
autonomous	fascinate	pamphlet
auxiliary	fatigue	parallel
ballistics	forfeit	personnel
barricade	gauge	physician
beauty	grieve	politics
beige	guarantee	possess
brief	guilt	privilege
bureau	harass	psychology
business	hazard	recidivism
calm	height	recommend
cancel	incident	referral
capacity	indict	salary
cashier	initial	schedule
circuit	innocent	seize
colonel	irreverent	separate
comparatively	jeopardy	specific
courteous	knowledge	statute
criticism	leisure	surveillance
custody	license	suspicious
cyclical	lieutenant	tentative
debt	maintenance	thorough
definitely	mathematics	transferred
descend	mortgage	warrant

How to Answer Spelling Questions

- Sound out the word in your mind. Remember that long vowels inside words usually are followed by single consonants: sofa, total, crime. Short vowels inside words usually are followed by double consonants: dribble, scissors, toddler.
- Give yourself auditory (listening) clues when you learn words. Say Wed-nes-day or lis-ten or bus-i-ness to yourself so that you remember to add the letters you do not hear.
- Look at each part of a word. See if there is a root, prefix, or suffix that will always be spelled the same way. For example, in uninhabitable, un- , in- , and -able are always spelled the same. What's left is habit, a self-contained root word that's pretty easy to spell.

More Practice in Vocabulary and Spelling

Here is a second set of practice exercises with samples of each kind of question covered in this chapter. Answers to all questions are at the end of the test.

Synonyms

Circle the word that means the same or nearly the same as the underlined word.

32. <u>convivial</u> company
  a. lively
  b. dull
  c. tiresome
  d. dreary

33. <u>conspicuous</u> behavior
  a. secret
  b. notable
  c. visible
  d. boorish

34. <u>meticulous</u> record keeping
  a. dishonest
  b. casual
  c. painstaking
  d. careless

35. <u>superficial</u> wounds
  a. life threatening
  b. bloody
  c. severe
  d. shallow

36. <u>impulsive</u> actions
  a. cautious
  b. imprudent
  c. courageous
  d. cowardly

Antonyms

Circle the word that is most nearly opposite in meaning to the underlined word.

37. <u>amateur</u> athlete
  a. professional
  b. successful
  c. unrivaled
  d. former

38. <u>lucid</u> opinions
  a. clear
  b. strong
  c. hazy
  d. heartfelt

39. traveling <u>incognito</u>
  a. unrecognized
  b. alone
  c. by night
  d. publicly

40. <u>incisive</u> reporting
  a. mild
  b. sharp
  c. dangerous
  d. insightful

41. <u>tactful</u> comments
  a. rude
  b. pleasant
  c. complimentary
  d. sociable

Synonyms

Using the context, choose the word that means the same or nearly the same as the underlined word.

42. Though he had little time, the student took <u>copious</u> notes in preparation for the test.
   a. limited
   b. plentiful
   c. illegible
   d. careless

43. Although she was flexible about homework, the teacher was <u>adamant</u> that papers be in on time.
   a. liberal
   b. casual
   c. strict
   d. pliable

44. The suspect's living conditions were <u>deplorable</u>.
   a. regrettable
   b. pristine
   c. festive
   d. tidy

Complete the Sentences

Choose the word that best completes the following sentences.

45. Her position as a(n) _____ teacher took her all over the city.
   a. primary
   b. secondary
   c. itinerant
   d. permanent

46. Despite the witness's promise to stay in town, she remained _____ and difficult to locate.
   a. steadfast
   b. stubborn
   c. dishonest
   d. elusive

Word Roots, Prefixes, and Suffixes

Choose the word or phrase closest in meaning to the underlined part of the word.

47. <u>uni</u>verse
   a. one
   b. three
   c. under
   d. opposite

48. <u>re</u>entry
   a. back
   b. push
   c. against
   d. forward

49. <u>bene</u>fit
   a. bad
   b. suitable
   c. beauty
   d. good

50. educat<u>ion</u>
   a. something like
   b. state of
   c. to increase
   d. unlike

51. urban<u>ite</u>
  a. resident of
  b. relating to
  c. that which is
  d. possessing

Spelling
Circle the correct spelling of the word that fits in the blank.

52. The information was _____ to the action.
  a. irelevent
  b. irrevelent
  c. irrelevant
  d. irelevant

53. She made no _____ to take the job.
  a. comittment
  b. commitment
  c. comitment
  d. comittmint

54. He made an income _____ to meet his needs.
  a. adaquate
  b. adequate
  c. adiquate
  d. adequet

55. We were assigned to stake out the _____.
  a. restarant
  b. restaraunt
  c. restaurant
  d. resteraunt

56. The vote was _____ to elect the chairperson.
  a. unannimous
  b. unanimous
  c. unanimus
  d. unaminous

Answers

32. a.	44. a.
33. c.	45. c.
34. c.	46. d.
35. d.	47. a.
36. b.	48. a.
37. a.	49. d.
38. c.	50. b.
39. d.	51. a.
40. a.	52. c.
41. a.	53. b.
42. b.	54. b.
43. c.	55. c.
	56. b.

9 ▶ MATH

CHAPTER SUMMARY

A basic understanding of math will be tested on some state trooper exams. This chapter reviews the common types of math questions found on these tests and provides tips and exercises to improve your skills in this area.

As a law enforcement officer, it is not likely that you will be doing complex mathematical formulas, but some basic math skills will most certainly be needed. Adding up the value of stolen property and computing the price of street drugs are just a couple of examples of the type of math problems you will need to be able to solve on the job. Use this chapter to brush up on your basic math skills, especially if it has been a while since you have taken a math course or if you suffer from math anxiety.

Math Strategies

- **Don't work in your head! Use your test book or scratch paper to take notes, draw pictures, and calculate.** Although you might think that you can solve math questions more quickly in your head, that's a good way to make mistakes. Write out each step.
- **Read a math question in chunks rather than straight through from beginning to end.** As you read each chunk, stop to think about what it means and make notes or draw a picture to represent that chunk.
- **When you get to the actual question, circle it.** This will keep you more focused as you solve the problem.
- **Glance at the answer choices for clues.** For example, if they're all fractions, you probably should do your work in fractions; if they're decimals, you should probably work in decimals.
- **Make a plan of attack** to help you solve the problem.
- **If a question stumps you, try one of the backdoor approaches** explained in the next section. These are particularly useful for solving word problems.
- **When you get your answer, reread the circled question to make sure you've answered it.** This helps avoid the careless mistake of answering the wrong question.
- **Check your work after you get an answer.** Test takers get a false sense of security when they get an answer that matches one of the multiple-choice answers. Here are some good ways to check your work if you have time:
  - Ask yourself if your answer is reasonable. Does it make sense?
  - Plug your answer back into the problem to make sure the problem holds together.
  - Do the question a second time, but use a different method.
- **Approximate when appropriate.** For example:
  - $5.98 + $8.97 is a little less than $15. (Add: $6 + $9)
  - 0.9876 × 5.0342 is close to 5. (Multiply: 1 × 5)
- **Skip hard questions and come back to them later.** Mark them in your test book so you can find them quickly.

Backdoor Approaches for Answering Questions that Puzzle You

Remember those word problems you dreaded in high school? Many of them are actually easier to solve by backdoor approaches. The two techniques that follow are terrific ways to solve multiple-choice word problems that you don't know how to solve with a straightforward approach. The first technique, *nice numbers*, is useful when there are unknowns (like x) in the text of the word problem, making the problem too abstract for you. The second technique, *working backward*, presents a quick way to substitute numeric answer choices back into the problem to see which one works.

Nice Numbers

1. When a question contains unknowns, like x, plug nice numbers in for the unknowns. A nice number is easy to calculate with and makes sense in the problem.
2. Read the question with the nice numbers in place. Then solve it.
3. If the answer choices are all numbers, the choice that matches your answer is the correct one.

4. If the answer choices contain unknowns, substitute the same nice numbers into *all* the answer choices. The choice that matches your answer is the right one. If more than one answer matches, do the problem again with different nice numbers. You'll have to check only the answer choices that have already matched.

Example: Judi went shopping with *p* dollars in her pocket. If the price of shirts was *s* shirts for *d* dollars, what is the maximum number of shirts Judi could buy with the money in her pocket?

    a. psd **b.** $\frac{ps}{d}$ **c.** $\frac{pd}{s}$ **d.** $\frac{ds}{p}$

To solve this problem, let's try these nice numbers: $p = \$100$, $s = 2$, $d = \$25$. Now reread it with the numbers in place:

Judi went shopping with **$100** in her pocket. If the price of shirts was **2** shirts for **$25**, what is the maximum number of shirts Judi could buy with the money in her pocket?

Since 2 shirts cost $25, that means that 4 shirts cost $50, and 8 shirts cost $100. So our answer is **8**. Let's substitute the nice numbers into all 4 answers:

    a. $100 \times 2 \times 25 = 5{,}000$ **b.** $\frac{100 \times 2}{25} = 8$ **c.** $\frac{100 \times 2}{2} = 1{,}250$ **d.** $\frac{25 \times 2}{100} = \frac{1}{2}$

The answer is choice **b** because it is the only one that matches our answer of **8**.

Working Backward

You can frequently solve a word problem by plugging the answer choices back into the text of the problem to see which one fits all the facts stated in the problem. The process is faster than you think because you will probably only have to substitute one or two answers to find the right one.

    This approach works only when

- all of the answer choices are numbers, and
- you're asked to find a simple number, not a sum, product, difference, or ratio.

    Here's what to do:

1. Look at all the answer choices and begin with the one in the middle of the range. For example, if the answers are 14, 8, 2, 20, and 25, begin by plugging 14 into the problem.
2. If your choice doesn't work, eliminate it. Determine whether you need a bigger or a smaller answer.
3. Plug in one of the remaining choices.
4. If none of the answers work, you may have made a careless error. Begin again or look for your mistake.

Example: Juan ate $\frac{1}{3}$ of the jelly beans. Maria then ate $\frac{3}{4}$ of the remaining jelly beans, which left 10 jelly beans. How many jelly beans were there to begin with?

    a. 60   **b.** 80   **c.** 90   **d.** 120   **e.** 140

Starting with the middle answer, let's assume there were **90** jelly beans to begin with:

Since Juan ate $\frac{1}{3}$ of them, that means he ate 30 ($\frac{1}{3} \times 90 = 30$), leaving 60 of them (90 − 30 = 60). Maria then ate $\frac{3}{4}$ of the 60 jelly beans, or 45 of them ($\frac{3}{4} \times 60 = 45$). That leaves 15 jelly beans (60 − 45 = 15).

The problem states that there were **10** jelly beans left, and we wound up with **15** of them. That indicates that we started with too big a number. Thus, 90, 120, and 140 are all wrong. With only two choices left, let's use common sense to decide which one to try. The next lower answer is only a little smaller than 90 and may not be small enough. So, let's try **60**:

Since Juan ate $\frac{1}{3}$ of them, that means he ate 20 ($\frac{1}{3} \times 60 = 20$), leaving 40 of them (60 − 20 = 40). Maria then ate $\frac{3}{4}$ of the 40 jelly beans, or 30 of them ($\frac{3}{4} \times 40 = 30$). That leaves 10 jelly beans (40 − 30 = 10).

Because this result of **10** jelly beans agrees with the problem, the right answer is choice **a**.

Glossary of Terms

Denominator	The bottom number in a fraction. **Example:** 2 is the denominator in $\frac{1}{2}$.
Difference	Subtract. The difference of two numbers means subtract one number from the other.
Divisible by	A number is divisible by a second number if that second number divides *evenly* into the original number. **Example:** 10 is divisible by 5 (10 ÷ 5 = 2, with no remainder). However, 10 is not divisible by 3. (See *multiple of*)
Even integer	Integers that are divisible by 2, like . . . −4, −2, 0, 2, 4. . . . (See *integer*)
Integer	Numbers along the number line, like . . . −3, −2, −1, 0, 1, 2, 3. . . . Integers include the whole numbers and their opposites. (See *whole number*)
Multiple of	A number is a multiple of a second number if that second number can be multiplied by an integer to get the original number. **Example:** 10 is a multiple of 5 (10 = 5 × 2); however, 10 is not a multiple of 3. (See *divisible by*)
Negative number	A number that is less than zero, like −1, −18.6, −$\frac{3}{4}$.
Numerator	The top part of a fraction. **Example:** 1 is the numerator of $\frac{1}{2}$.
Odd integer	Integers that aren't divisible by 2, like . . . −5, −3, −1, 1, 3. . . .
Positive number	A number that is greater than zero, like 2, 42, $\frac{1}{2}$, 4.63.
Prime number	Integers that are divisible only by 1 and themselves, like 2, 3, 5, 7, 11. . . . All prime numbers are odd, except for 2. The number 1 is not considered prime.
Product	The product of 2 numbers means the numbers are multiplied together.
Quotient	The answer you get when you divide. **Example:** 10 divided by 5 is 2; the quotient is 2.
Real number	All the numbers you can think of, like 17, −5,$\frac{1}{2}$, −23.6, 3.4329, 0. Real numbers include integers, fractions, and decimals. (See *integer*)
Remainder	The number left over after division. **Example:** 11 divided by 2 is 5, with a remainder of 1.
Sum	The sum of two numbers means the numbers are added together.
Whole number	Numbers you can count on your fingers, like 1, 2, 3. . . . All whole numbers are positive.

Word Problems

Many of the math problems on tests are word problems. A word problem can include any kind of math, including simple arithmetic, fractions, decimals, percentages, and even algebra and geometry.

The hardest part of any word problem is translating English into math. When you read a problem, you can frequently translate it word for word from English statements into mathematical statements. At other times, however, a key word in the word problem hints at the mathematical operation to be performed. Here are the translation rules:

EQUALS   key words: is, are, has

English	Math
The rookie **is** 20 years old.	$R = 20$
There **are** 7 hats.	$H = 7$
Officer Judi **has** 5 commendations.	$J = 5$

ADDITION   key words: sum; more, greater, or older than; total; all together

English	Math
The **sum** of two numbers is 10.	$X + Y = 10$
Karen has $5 **more than** Sam.	$K = 5 + S$
The base is 3″ **greater than** the height.	$B = 3 + H$
Judi is 2 years **older than** Tony.	$J = 2 + T$
The **total** of three numbers is 25.	$A + B + C = 25$
How much do Joan and Tom have **all together**?	$J + T = ?$

SUBTRACTION   key words: difference, less or younger than, fewer, remain, left over

English	Math
The **difference** between two numbers is 17.	$X - Y = 17$
Mike has 5 **fewer** cats **than** twice the number Jan has.	$M = 2J - 5$
Jay is 2 years **younger than** Brett.	$J = B - 2$
After Carol ate 3 apples, R apples **remained**.	$R = A - 3$

MULTIPLICATION   key words: of, product, times

English	Math
20% **of** the stolen radios	$.20 \times R$
Half **of** the recruits	$\frac{1}{2} \times R$
The **product** of two numbers is 12.	$A \times B = 12$

DIVISION   key word: per

English	Math
15 drops **per** teaspoon	$\frac{15 \text{ drops}}{\text{teaspoon}}$
22 miles **per** gallon	$\frac{22 \text{ miles}}{\text{gallon}}$

Distance Formula: Distance = Rate × Time

The key words are movement words like *plane, train, boat, car, walk, run, climb, travel,* and *swim.*

- How far did the **plane travel** in 4 hours if it averaged 300 miles per hour?

  $D = 300 \times 4$

  $D = 1{,}200$ miles

- Ben **walked** 20 miles in 4 hours. What was his average speed?

  $20 = r \times 4$

  5 miles per hour $= r$

Solving a Word Problem Using the Translation Table

Remember the problem at the beginning of this chapter about the jelly beans?

Juan ate $\frac{1}{3}$ of the jelly beans. Maria then ate $\frac{3}{4}$ of the remaining jelly beans, which left 10 jelly beans. How many jelly beans were there to begin with?

  a. 60   **b.** 80   **c.** 90   **d.** 120   **e.** 140

We solved it by *working backward*. Now let's solve it using our translation rules.

Assume Juan started with J jelly beans. Eating $\frac{1}{3}$ **of** them means eating $\frac{1}{3} \times J$ jelly beans. Maria ate a fraction of the **remaining** jelly beans, which means we must **subtract** to find out how many are left: $J - \frac{1}{3} \times J = \frac{2}{3} \times J$. Maria then ate $\frac{3}{4}$, leaving $\frac{1}{4}$ **of** the $\frac{2}{3} \times J$ jelly beans, or $\frac{1}{4} \times \frac{2}{3} \times J$ jelly beans. Multiplying out $\frac{1}{4} \times \frac{2}{3} \times J$ gives $\frac{1}{6}J$ as the number of jelly beans left. The problem states that there were **10 jelly beans left**, meaning that we set $\frac{1}{6} \times J$ **equal** to 10:

$$\frac{1}{6} \times J = 10$$

Solving this equation for J gives $J = 60$. Thus, the correct answer is choice **a** (the same answer we got when we *worked backward*). As you can see, both methods—working backward and translating from English to math—work. You should use whichever method is more comfortable for you.

Practice Word Problems

You will find word problems using fractions, decimals, and percentages in those sections of this chapter. For now, practice using the translation table on problems that just require you to work with basic arithmetic.

_____ **1.** Officer Miller pledged three dollars for every mile his son walked in the Police Athletic League walk-a-thon. His son walked nine miles. How much does Officer Miller owe?

  a. $3.00   **b.** $12.00   **c.** $18.00   **d.** $27.00   **e.** $36.00

_____ **2.** Officer Brown writes six speeding tickets every week. At this rate, how long will it take for her to write 21 citations?

  a. 3 weeks   **b.** 4 weeks   **c.** 3.5 weeks   **d.** 4.75 weeks   **e.** 5.5 weeks

_____ **3.** The precinct clerk can type 80 words per minute. How many minutes will it take him to type a report containing 760 words?

      a. 8   **b.** $8\frac{1}{2}$ **c.** 9   **d.** $9\frac{1}{2}$ **e.** 10

_____ **4.** Chief Wallace is writing a budget request to upgrade his personal computer system. He wants to purchase 4gb of RAM, which will cost $100, two new software programs at $350 each, an external hard drive for $249, and printer ink for $25. What is the total amount Chief Wallace should write on his budget request?

      a. $724   **b.** $974   **c.** $1,049   **d.** $1,064   **e.** $1,074

Answers
1. d.
2. c.
3. d.
4. e.

Fraction Review

Problems involving fractions may be straightforward calculation questions, or they may be word problems. Typically, they ask you to add, subtract, multiply, divide, or compare fractions.

Working with Fractions
A fraction is a part of something.

    Example: Let's say that a pizza was cut into 8 equal slices and you ate 3 of them. The fraction $\frac{3}{8}$ tells you what part of the pizza you ate. The following pizza shows this: 3 of the 8 pieces (the ones you ate) are shaded.

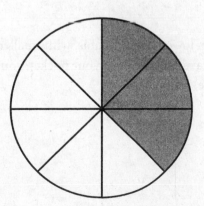

Three Kinds of Fractions

Proper fraction: The top number is less than the bottom number:
$\frac{1}{2}$; $\frac{2}{3}$; $\frac{4}{9}$; $\frac{8}{13}$
The value of a proper fraction is less than 1.

Improper fraction: The top number is greater than or equal to the bottom number:
$\frac{3}{2}$; $\frac{5}{3}$; $\frac{14}{9}$; $\frac{12}{12}$
The value of an improper fraction is 1 or more.

Mixed number: A fraction is written to the right of a whole number:
$3\frac{1}{2}$; $4\frac{2}{3}$; $12\frac{3}{4}$; $24\frac{3}{4}$
The value of a mixed number is more than 1: It is the sum of the whole number plus the fraction.

Changing Improper Fractions into Mixed or Whole Numbers

It's easier to add and subtract fractions that are mixed numbers than those in the form of improper fractions. To change an improper fraction, say $\frac{13}{2}$, into a mixed number, follow these steps:

1. Divide the bottom number (2) into the top number (13) to get the whole number portion (6) of the mixed number:
2. Write the remainder of the division (1) over the old bottom number (2): $6\frac{1}{2}$
3. Check: Change the mixed number back into an improper fraction. (See the following steps.)

$$2\overline{)13} \quad \begin{array}{r} 6 \\ -12 \\ \hline 1 \end{array}$$

Changing Mixed Numbers into Improper Fractions

It's easier to multiply and divide fractions when you are working with improper fractions than with mixed numbers. To change a mixed number, say $2\frac{3}{4}$, into an improper fraction, follow these steps:

1. Multiply the whole number (2) by the bottom number (4): $2 \times 4 = 8$
2. Add the result (8) to the top number (3): $8 + 3 = 11$
3. Put the total (11) over the bottom number (4): $\frac{11}{4}$
4. Check: Reverse the process by changing the improper fraction into a mixed number. If you get back the number you started with, your answer is correct.

Reducing Fractions

Reducing a fraction means writing it in lowest terms, that is, with smaller numbers. For instance, 50¢ is $\frac{50}{100}$ of a dollar, or $\frac{1}{2}$ of a dollar. In fact, if you have a 50¢ piece in your pocket, you say that you have a half dollar. Reducing a fraction does not change its value.

Follow these steps to reduce a fraction:

1. Find a whole number that divides *evenly* into both numbers that make up the fraction (the numerator and the denominator).
2. Divide that number into the top of the fraction, and replace the top of the fraction with the quotient (the answer you got when you divided).
3. Do the same thing to the bottom number.
4. Repeat the first 3 steps until you can't find a number that divides evenly into both numbers of the fraction.

For example, let's reduce $\frac{8}{24}$. We could do it in 2 steps: $\frac{8 \div 4}{24 \div 4} = \frac{2}{6}$; then $\frac{2 \div 2}{6 \div 2} = \frac{1}{3}$. Or we could do it in a single step: $\frac{8 \div 8}{24 \div 8} = \frac{1}{3}$.

Shortcut: When the top and bottom numbers both end in zeros, cross out the same number of zeros in both numbers to begin the reducing process. For example, $\frac{300}{4,000}$ reduces to $\frac{3}{40}$ when you cross out 2 zeros in both numbers.

Whenever you do arithmetic with fractions, reduce your answer. On a multiple-choice test, don't panic if your answer isn't listed. It may mean that you need to reduce it. So try to reduce it and then compare it to the choices.

Reduce the following fractions to lowest terms.

_____ **5.** $\frac{6}{36}$ _____ **8.** $\frac{9}{54}$

_____ **6.** $\frac{18}{33}$ _____ **9.** $\frac{16}{24}$

_____ **7.** $\frac{35}{50}$ _____ **10.** $\frac{58}{66}$

Raising Fractions to Higher Terms

Before you can add and subtract fractions, you have to know how to raise a fraction to higher terms. This is actually the opposite of reducing a fraction.

Follow these steps to raise $\frac{2}{3}$ to 24ths:

1. Divide the old bottom number (3) into the new one (24): $3\overline{)24} = 8$
2. Multiply the answer (8) by the old top number (2): $2 \times 8 = 16$
3. Put the answer (16) over the new bottom number (24): $\frac{16}{24}$
4. Check: Reduce the new fraction to see if you get the original one: $\frac{16 \div 8}{24 \div 8}$

Raise these fractions to higher terms:

_____ **11.** $\frac{3}{8} = \frac{}{32}$

_____ **12.** $\frac{1}{5} = \frac{}{25}$

_____ **13.** $\frac{7}{9} = \frac{}{36}$

_____ **14.** $\frac{5}{13} = \frac{}{39}$

_____ **15.** $\frac{7}{26} = \frac{}{130}$

_____ **16.** $\frac{7}{37} = \frac{}{296}$

Adding Fractions

If the fractions have the same bottom numbers, just add the top numbers together and write the total over the bottom number.

Examples: $\frac{2}{9} + \frac{4}{9} = \frac{2+4}{9} = \frac{6}{9}$ Reduce the sum: $\frac{2}{3}$

$\frac{5}{8} + \frac{7}{8} = \frac{12}{8}$ Change the sum to a mixed number: $1\frac{4}{8}$; then reduce: $1\frac{1}{2}$.

There are a few extra steps to add mixed numbers with the same bottom numbers, say $2\frac{3}{5} + 1\frac{4}{5}$:

1. Add the fractions: $\quad\frac{3}{5} + \frac{4}{5} = \frac{7}{5}$
2. Change the improper fraction into a mixed number: $\frac{7}{5} = 1\frac{2}{5}$
3. Add the whole numbers: $\quad 2 + 1 = 3$
4. Add the results of steps 2 and 3: $\quad 1\frac{2}{5} + 3 = 4\frac{2}{5}$

Finding the Least Common Denominator

If the fractions you want to add don't have the same bottom number, you will have to raise some or all of the fractions to higher terms so that they all have the same bottom number, called the **common denominator**. All of the original bottom numbers divide evenly into the common denominator. If it is the smallest number that they all divide evenly into, it is called the **least common denominator (LCD)**.

Here are a few tips for finding the LCD, the smallest number that all the bottom numbers evenly divide into:

- See if all the bottom numbers divide evenly into the biggest bottom number.
- Check out the multiplication table of the largest bottom number until you find a number that all the other bottom numbers evenly divide into.
- When all else fails, multiply all the bottom numbers together.

Example: $\frac{2}{3} + \frac{4}{5}$

1. Find the LCD. Multiply the bottom numbers: $\qquad 3 \times 5 = 15$
2. Raise each fraction to 15ths: $\qquad \frac{2}{3} = \frac{10}{15}$
$\qquad + \frac{4}{5} = \frac{12}{15}$
3. Add as usual: $\qquad \frac{22}{15}$

Try these addition problems:

_____ **17.** $\frac{1}{4} + \frac{1}{3} =$

_____ **18.** $\frac{1}{3} + \frac{1}{6} =$

_____ **19.** $\frac{1}{4} + \frac{1}{5} + \frac{1}{20} =$

_____ **20.** $3\frac{4}{5} + 2\frac{7}{8} =$

_____ **21.** $5\frac{2}{7} + 3\frac{5}{8} =$

_____ **22.** $3\frac{1}{7} + 5\frac{2}{3} =$

Subtracting Fractions

If the fractions have the same bottom numbers, just subtract the top numbers and write the difference over the bottom number.

Example: $\frac{4}{9} - \frac{3}{9} = \frac{4-3}{9} = \frac{1}{9}$

If the fractions you want to subtract don't have the same bottom number, you will have to raise some or all of the fractions to higher terms so that they all have the same bottom number, or LCD. If you forgot how to find the LCD, just read the section on adding fractions with different bottom numbers.

Example: $\frac{5}{6} - \frac{3}{4}$

1. Raise each fraction to 12ths because 12 is the LCD, the smallest number that 6 and 4 both divide into evenly:

$$\frac{5}{6} = \frac{10}{12}$$

2. Subtract as usual:

$$-\frac{3}{4} = \frac{9}{12}$$
$$\frac{1}{12}$$

Subtracting mixed numbers with the same bottom number is similar to adding mixed numbers.

Example: $4\frac{3}{5} - 1\frac{2}{5}$

1. Subtract the fractions: $\frac{3}{5} - \frac{2}{5} = \frac{1}{5}$
2. Subtract the whole numbers: $4 - 1 = 3$
3. Add the results of steps 1 and 2: $\frac{1}{5} + 3 = 3\frac{1}{5}$

Sometimes, there is an extra borrowing step when you subtract mixed numbers with the same bottom numbers, say $7\frac{3}{5} - 2\frac{4}{5}$:

1. You can't subtract the fractions the way they are because $\frac{4}{5}$ is bigger than $\frac{3}{5}$. So you borrow 1 from the 7, making it 6, and change that 1 to $\frac{5}{5}$ because 5 is the bottom number: $7\frac{3}{5} = 6\frac{5}{5} + \frac{3}{5}$
2. Add the numbers from step 1: $6\frac{5}{5} + \frac{3}{5} = 6\frac{8}{5}$
3. Now you have a different version of the original problem: $6\frac{8}{5} - 2\frac{4}{5}$
4. Subtract the fractional parts of the two mixed numbers: $\frac{8}{5} - \frac{4}{5} = \frac{4}{5}$
5. Subtract the whole number parts of the two mixed numbers: $6 - 2 = 4$
6. Add the results of the last two steps together: $4 + \frac{4}{5} = 4\frac{4}{5}$

Try these subtraction problems:

_____ **23.** $\frac{1}{4} - \frac{1}{8} =$

_____ **24.** $\frac{1}{3} - \frac{1}{9} =$

_____ **25.** $\frac{1}{2} - \frac{1}{5} =$

_____ **26.** $3\frac{1}{3} - 1\frac{5}{8} =$

_____ **27.** $5\frac{4}{9} - 2\frac{2}{3} =$

_____ **28.** $4\frac{3}{5} - 2\frac{3}{8} =$

Now let's put what you've learned about adding and subtracting fractions to work in some real-life problems.

_____ **29.** To train for her physical ability test, Lori ran $5\frac{1}{2}$ miles on Monday, $6\frac{1}{4}$ miles on Tuesday, $4\frac{1}{2}$ miles on Wednesday, and $2\frac{3}{4}$ miles on Thursday. What is the average number of miles Lori ran each day?

    a. 5   **b.** $4\frac{1}{2}$ **c.** 4   **d.** $4\frac{3}{4}$ **e.** $5\frac{1}{4}$

_____ **30.** Officers Perez and Staub are transporting a prisoner from the courthouse to the county jail. The total trip is $54\frac{2}{3}$ miles. If they have completed $23\frac{1}{5}$ miles, how many miles do they have to go?

    a. $31\frac{7}{15}$ **b.** $31\frac{13}{15}$ **c.** $21\frac{4}{15}$ **d.** $31\frac{1}{2}$ **e.** $31\frac{4}{15}$

_____ **31.** The precinct is on $1\frac{3}{4}$ acres of land. To expand the precinct, the county plans to buy the adjoining property, which is $2\frac{3}{4}$ acres. How many acres will the precinct sit on after the purchase?

    a. $5\frac{1}{4}$ **b.** $3\frac{3}{4}$ **c.** $3\frac{1}{2}$ **d.** $4\frac{1}{2}$ **e.** $5\frac{1}{2}$

_____ **32.** Officer DeRosa kept track of how many overtime hours she worked during the month of August. The first week she worked $4\frac{1}{2}$ hours, the second week $3\frac{3}{4}$ hours, the third week $8\frac{1}{5}$ hours, and the fourth week $1\frac{1}{3}$ hours. How many hours of overtime did she work altogether in the month of August?

    a. $17\frac{47}{60}$ **b.** 16   **c.** $16\frac{1}{8}$ **d.** $18\frac{2}{15}$ **e.** $20\frac{1}{4}$

Multiplying Fractions

Multiplying fractions is actually easier than adding them. All you do is multiply the top numbers and then multiply the bottom numbers.

Examples: $\frac{2}{3} \times \frac{5}{7} = \frac{2 \times 5}{3 \times 7} = \frac{10}{21}$ $\frac{1}{2} \times \frac{3}{5} \times \frac{7}{4} = \frac{1 \times 3 \times 7}{2 \times 5 \times 4} = \frac{21}{40}$

Shortcut: Sometimes you can *cancel* before multiplying. Cancelling is a shortcut that makes the multiplication go faster because you're multiplying with smaller numbers. It's very similar to reducing: If there is a number that divides evenly into both a top number and a bottom number, do that division before multiplying. If you forget to cancel, you will still get the right answer, but you will have to reduce it.

Example: $\frac{5}{6} \times \frac{9}{20}$

1. Cancel the 6 and the 9 by dividing 3 into both of them: $6 \div 3 = 2$ and $9 \div 3 = 3$. Cross out the 6 and the 9:

$$\frac{5}{\overset{}{\underset{2}{6}}} \times \frac{\overset{3}{9}}{20}$$

2. Cancel the 5 and the 20 by dividing 5 into both of them: $5 \div 5 = 1$ and $20 \div 5 = 4$. Cross out the 5 and the 20:

$$\frac{\overset{1}{5}}{\underset{2}{6}} \times \frac{\overset{3}{9}}{\underset{4}{20}}$$

3. Multiply across the new top numbers and the new bottom numbers:

$$\frac{1 \times 3}{2 \times 4} = \frac{3}{8}$$

Try these multiplication problems:

_____ **33.** $\frac{4}{5} \times \frac{1}{2} =$ _____ **36.** $\frac{8}{9} \times \frac{3}{4} =$

_____ **34.** $\frac{9}{10} \times \frac{1}{8} =$ _____ **37.** $\frac{5}{6} \times \frac{4}{5} =$

_____ **35.** $\frac{5}{7} \times \frac{2}{3} =$ _____ **38.** $\frac{3}{8} \times \frac{4}{9} =$

To multiply a fraction by a whole number, first rewrite the whole number as a fraction with a bottom number of 1:

Example: $5 \times \frac{2}{3} = \frac{5}{1} \times \frac{2}{3} = \frac{10}{3}$ (Optional: convert $\frac{10}{3}$ to a mixed number: $3\frac{1}{3}$)

To multiply with mixed numbers, it's easier to change them to improper fractions before multiplying.

Example: $4\frac{2}{3} \times 5\frac{1}{2}$

1. Convert $4\frac{2}{3}$ to an improper fraction: $4\frac{2}{3} = \frac{4 \times 3 + 2}{3} = \frac{14}{3}$

2. Convert $5\frac{1}{2}$ to an improper fraction: $5\frac{1}{2} = \frac{5 \times 2 + 1}{2} = \frac{11}{2}$

3. Cancel and multiply the fractions: $\frac{\overset{7}{14}}{3} \times \frac{11}{\underset{1}{2}} = \frac{77}{3}$

4. Optional: Convert the improper fraction to a mixed number: $\frac{77}{3} = 25\frac{2}{3}$

Now try these multiplication problems with mixed numbers and whole numbers:

_____ **39.** $4\frac{1}{3} \times \frac{2}{5} =$

_____ **40.** $2\frac{1}{2} \times 6 =$

_____ **41.** $3\frac{3}{4} \times 4\frac{2}{5} =$

_____ **42.** $3\frac{4}{5} \times 3 =$

_____ **43.** $5\frac{1}{7} \times 3\frac{2}{5} =$

_____ **44.** $6\frac{1}{4} \times \frac{2}{7} =$

Here are a few more real-life problems to test your skills:

_____ **45.** After driving $\frac{1}{4}$ of the 27 miles to work, Officer Hamm stopped to get a cup of coffee. How many miles had she driven when she stopped?

    a. $6\frac{3}{4}$ **b.** $6\frac{1}{2}$ **c.** $5\frac{3}{4}$ **d.** 7   **e.** $7\frac{1}{4}$

_____ **46.** Officer Henry worked a 66-hour work week, of which $\frac{1}{3}$ of the hours were overtime. How many hours of overtime did Officer Henry work?

    a. 6   **b.** 11   **c.** 20   **d.** $20\frac{1}{2}$ **e.** 22

_____ **47.** In 2004, there were 715 auto thefts in Rose County. In 2005, there were only $\frac{2}{5}$ as many. How many auto thefts were there in Rose County in 2005?

    a. 143   **b.** 286   **c.** 385   **d.** 429   **e.** 485

_____ **48.** Officer Amis worked $\frac{4}{5}$ of the days last year. How many days did he work? (1 year = 365 days)

    a. 273   **b.** 281   **c.** 292   **d.** 300   **e.** 312

Dividing Fractions

To divide one fraction by a second fraction, invert the second fraction (that is, flip the top and bottom numbers) and then multiply. That's all there is to it!

    Example: $\frac{1}{2} \div \frac{3}{5}$

1. Invert the second fraction ($\frac{3}{5}$): $\frac{5}{3}$
2. Change the division sign ($\div$) to a multiplication sign ($\times$): $\frac{1}{2} \times \frac{5}{3}$
3. Multiply the first fraction by the new second fraction: $\frac{1}{2} \times \frac{5}{3} = \frac{1 \times 5}{2 \times 3} = \frac{5}{6}$

To divide a fraction by a whole number, first change the whole number to a fraction by putting it over 1. Then follow the previous division steps.

    Example: $\frac{3}{5} \div 2 = \frac{3}{5} \div \frac{2}{1} = \frac{3}{5} \times \frac{1}{2} = \frac{3 \times 1}{5 \times 2} = \frac{3}{10}$

When the division problem has a mixed number, convert it to an improper fraction and then divide as usual.

Example: $2\frac{3}{4} \div \frac{1}{6}$

1. Convert $2\frac{3}{4}$ to an improper fraction:

2. Divide $\frac{11}{4}$ by $\frac{1}{6}$:

3. Flip $\frac{1}{6}$ to $\frac{6}{1}$, change $\div$ to $\times$, cancel, and multiply:

$$2\frac{3}{4} = \frac{2 \times 4 + 3}{4} = \frac{11}{4}$$

$$\frac{11}{4} \div \frac{1}{6} = \frac{11}{4} \times \frac{6}{1}$$

$$\frac{11}{\underset{2}{4}} \times \frac{\overset{3}{6}}{1} = \frac{11 \times 3}{2 \times 1} = \frac{33}{2}$$

Here are some division problems to try:

_____ **49.** $\frac{3}{4} \div \frac{2}{3} =$

_____ **50.** $4\frac{1}{4} \div \frac{1}{3} =$

_____ **51.** $\frac{2}{3} \div 5 =$

_____ **52.** $6\frac{6}{11} \div 1\frac{1}{5} =$

_____ **53.** $\frac{5}{8} \div \frac{5}{8} =$

_____ **54.** $5\frac{1}{6} \div \frac{2}{3} =$

Let's wrap this up with some real-life problems.

_____ **55.** Lucy worked $32\frac{1}{2}$ hours last week and earned $195. What is her hourly wage?

    a. $5.00   **b.** $6.00   **c.** $6.09   **d.** $7.00   **e.** $7.35

_____ **56.** Officers Feliciano and Wolny arrested George Rodney for possession of 28 ounces of marijuana, separated into a number of $3\frac{1}{2}$-ounce packages. How many packages of marijuana were in Rodney's possession?

    a. 2   **b.** 4   **c.** 6   **d.** 8   **e.** 10

_____ **57.** Officer Talis has the flu. If four officers evenly split his $6\frac{1}{2}$ hours of work to cover for him, how many extra hours must each officer work?

    a. $\frac{8}{13}$ **b.** $1\frac{5}{8}$ **c.** $1\frac{1}{2}$ **d.** $1\frac{5}{13}$ **e.** 4

_____ **58.** The Police Athletic League is hosting a bingo night fundraiser and will give away $2,400 in prize money. The first winner of the night will receive $\frac{1}{3}$ of the money. The next ten winners will each receive $\frac{1}{10}$ of the remaining amount. How much prize money will each of the ten winners receive?

    a. $160   **b.** $200   **c.** $240   **d.** $700   **e.** $800

Answers

5. $\frac{1}{6}$

6. $\frac{6}{11}$

7. $\frac{7}{10}$

8. $\frac{1}{6}$

9. $\frac{2}{3}$

10. $\frac{29}{33}$

11. 12

12. 5

13. 28

14. 15

15. 35

16. 56

17. $\frac{7}{12}$

18. $\frac{1}{2}$

19. $\frac{1}{2}$

20. $6\frac{27}{40}$

21. $8\frac{51}{56}$

22. $8\frac{17}{21}$

23. $\frac{1}{8}$

24. $\frac{2}{9}$

25. $\frac{3}{10}$

26. $1\frac{17}{24}$

27. $2\frac{7}{9}$

28. $2\frac{9}{40}$

29. d.

30. a.

31. d.

32. a.

33. $\frac{2}{5}$

34. $\frac{9}{80}$

35. $\frac{10}{21}$

36. $\frac{2}{3}$

37. $\frac{2}{3}$

38. $\frac{1}{6}$

39. $\frac{26}{15}$ or $1\frac{11}{15}$

40. 15

41. $\frac{33}{2}$ or $16\frac{1}{2}$

42. $\frac{57}{5}$ or $11\frac{2}{5}$

43. $\frac{612}{35}$ or $17\frac{17}{35}$

44. $\frac{25}{14}$ or $1\frac{11}{14}$

45. a.

46. e.

47. b.

48. c.

49. $\frac{9}{8}$ or $1\frac{1}{8}$

50. $\frac{51}{4}$ or $12\frac{3}{4}$

51. $\frac{2}{15}$

52. $\frac{60}{11}$ or $5\frac{5}{11}$

53. $\frac{1}{1}$ or 1

54. $\frac{31}{4}$ or $7\frac{3}{4}$

55. b.

56. d.

57. b.

58. a.

Decimals

What Is a Decimal?

A decimal is a special kind of fraction. You use decimals every day when you deal with money—$10.35 is a decimal that represents 10 dollars and 35 cents. The decimal point separates the dollars from the cents. Because there are 100 cents in one dollar, 1¢ is $\frac{1}{100}$ of a dollar, or $.01.

Each decimal place to the right of the decimal point has a name:

Example: .1 = 1 tenth = $\frac{1}{10}$

.02 = 2 hundredths = $\frac{2}{100}$

.003 = 3 thousandths = $\frac{3}{1,000}$

.0004 = 4 ten-thousandths = $\frac{4}{10,000}$

When you add zeros after the rightmost decimal place, you don't change the value of the decimal. For example, 6.17 is the same as all of these:

6.170

6.1700

6.17000000000000000

If there are digits on both sides of the decimal point (such as 10.35), the number is called a *mixed decimal*. If there are digits only to the right of the decimal point (such as .53), the number is simply called a *decimal*. A whole number (such as 15) is understood to have a decimal point at its right (15.). Thus, 15 is the same as 15.0, 15.00, 15.000, and so on.

Changing Fractions to Decimals

To change a fraction to a decimal, divide the bottom number into the top number after you put a decimal point and a few zeros on the right of the top number. When you divide, bring the decimal point up into your answer.

Example: Change $\frac{3}{4}$ to a decimal.

1. Add a decimal point and 2 zeros to the top number (3): 3.00

2. Divide the bottom number (4) into 3.00:

$$\begin{array}{r} .75 \\ 4\overline{)3\ 00} \\ \underline{2\ 8} \\ 20 \\ \underline{20} \\ 0 \end{array}$$

   Bring the decimal point up into the answer:

3. The quotient (result of the division) is the answer: .75

Some fractions may require you to add many decimal zeros in order for the division to come out evenly. In fact, when you convert a fraction like $\frac{2}{3}$ to a decimal, you can keep adding decimal zeros to the top number forever because the division will never come out evenly. As you divide 3 into 2, you will keep getting 6's:

$$2 \div 3 = .6666666666\ldots$$

This is called a **repeating decimal** and it can be written as $.66\overline{6}$ or as $.66\frac{2}{3}$. You can approximate it as .67, .667, .6667, and so on.

Changing Decimals to Fractions

To change a decimal to a fraction, write the digits of the decimal as the top number of a fraction and write the decimal's name as the bottom number of the fraction. Then reduce the fraction, if possible.

Example: .018

1. Write 18 as the top of the fraction: $\frac{18}{}$

2. Three places to the right of the decimal means *thousandths*, so write 1,000 as the bottom number: $\frac{18}{1,000}$

3. Reduce by dividing 2 into the top and bottom numbers: $\frac{18 \div 2}{1,000 \div 2} = \frac{9}{500}$

Change the following decimals or mixed decimals to fractions. The answers can be found at the end of this section on page 134.

_____ **59.** .008   _____ **62.** .090

_____ **60.** 2.58   _____ **63.** .0006

_____ **61.** 127.586
                              _____ **64.** 1.00

Comparing Decimals

Because decimals are easier to compare when they have the same number of digits after the decimal point, tack zeros onto the end of the shorter decimals. Then all you have to do is compare the numbers as if the decimal points weren't there.

   Example: Compare .08 and .1

1. Tack one zero at the end of .1:   .10
2. To compare .10 to .08, just compare 10 to 8.
3. Since 10 is larger than 8, .1 is larger than .08.

Adding and Subtracting Decimals

To add or subtract decimals, line them up so their decimal points are aligned. You may want to tack on zeros at the ends of shorter decimals so you can keep all your digits evenly lined up. Remember, if a number doesn't have a decimal point, then put one at the end of the number.

   Example: 1.23 + 57 + .038

1. Line up the numbers like this:
$$\begin{array}{r} 1.230 \\ 57.000 \\ +.038 \\ \hline \end{array}$$
2. Add: 58.268

   Example: 1.23 − .038

1. Line up the numbers like this:
$$\begin{array}{r} 1.230 \\ -.038 \\ \hline \end{array}$$
2. Subtract: 1.192

Try these addition and subtraction problems:

_____ **65.** .326 + .57 + 96.08

_____ **66.** .009 + 15 + .7

_____ **67.** .015 + 3.49 + 8 + .07

_____ **68.** 4.33 – 2.56

_____ **69.** 30.41 – 19.73

_____ **70.** 121.06 – 98.34

_____ **71.** Officer Peterson drove 6.3 miles to the state park. He then walked .8 miles around the park to make sure everything was all right. He got back into the car, drove 4.33 miles to check on a broken traffic light, and then drove 3 miles back to the police station. How many miles did he drive in total?

a. 14.03   **b.** 13.63   **c.** 14.43   **d.** 15   **e.** 15.43

_____ **72.** The average number of burglaries in Millbrook fell from 63.7 per week to 59.5 per week. By how many burglaries per week did the average fall?

a. 4.2   **b.** 3.3   **c.** 4.1   **d.** 5.2   **e.** 4.9

Multiplying Decimals

To multiply decimals, ignore the decimal points and just multiply the numbers. Then count the total number of decimal digits (the digits to the right of the decimal point) in the numbers you are multiplying. Count off that number of digits in your answer beginning at the right side, and put the decimal point to the left of those digits.

Example: 215.7×2.4

1. Multiply 2157 times 24:

$$
\begin{array}{r}
2157 \\
\times\ 24 \\
\hline
8628 \\
4314\ \\
\hline
51768
\end{array}
$$

2. Because there are a total of 2 decimal digits in 215.7 and 2.4, count off 2 places from the right in 51768, placing the decimal point to the *left* of the last 2 digits:

517.68

If your answer doesn't have enough digits, tack zeros on to the left of the answer.

Example: .03 × .006

1. Multiply 3 times 6: $3 \times 6 = 18$
2. You need 5 decimal digits in your answer, so tack on 3 zeros: 00018
3. Put the decimal point at the front of the number (which is 5 digits in
   from the right):   .00018

You can practice multiplying decimals with the following problems.

_____ **73** .17 × .39

_____ **74.** 1.4 × 6.92

_____ **75.** 192 × .46

_____ **76.** Officer Joe earns $14.50 per hour. Last week, he worked 37.5 hours. How much money did he
earn that week?

     a. $518.00   **b.** $518.50   **c.** $525.00   **d.** $536.50   **e.** $543.75

_____ **77.** Officer Jay bought 25 $0.39 stamps. How much did he spend?

     a. $7.45   **b.** $7.95   **c.** $8.55   **d.** $9.75   **e.** $10.15

_____ **78.** A full box of bullets costs $7.50. Approximately how much will 5.25 boxes of bullets cost?

     a. $38.00   **b.** $38.50   **c.** $39.00   **d.** $39.38   **e.** $41.00

Dividing Decimals

To divide a decimal by a whole number, set up the division $(8\overline{).256})$ and immediately bring the decimal point
straight up into the answer $8\overline{).256}$. Then divide as you would normally divide whole numbers:

Example:

$$
\begin{array}{r}
.032 \\
8\overline{).256} \\
-0 \\
\hline
25 \\
-24 \\
\hline
16 \\
-16 \\
\hline
0
\end{array}
$$

To divide any number by a decimal, you must perform an extra step before you can divide. Move the decimal point to the very right of the number you are dividing by, counting the number of places you are moving
it. Then move the decimal point the same number of places to the right in the number you are dividing into. In
other words, first change the problem to one in which you are dividing by a whole number.

Example: $.06\overline{)1.218}$

1. Because there are two decimal digits in .06, move the decimal point two places to the right in both numbers and move the decimal point straight up into the answer:

$$.06\overline{)1.21\,8}$$

2. Divide using the new numbers:

$$\begin{array}{r} 20.3 \\ 6\overline{)121.8} \\ -12 \\ \hline 01 \\ -00 \\ \hline 18 \\ -18 \\ \hline 0 \end{array}$$

Under certain conditions, you have to add zeros to the right of the last decimal digit in a number you are dividing into:

- if there aren't enough digits for you to move the decimal point to the right
- if the answer doesn't come out evenly when you do the division
- if you are dividing a whole number by a decimal, you will have to tack on the decimal point as well as some zeros

Try your skills on these division problems:

_____ **79.** $.5\overline{)10}$

_____ **80.** $.19\overline{)3.61}$

_____ **81.** $.06\overline{)0.9636}$

_____ **82.** $.42\overline{)1.3734}$

_____ **83.** $1.03\overline{)3.502}$

_____ **84.** $.88\overline{)9.152}$

_____ **85.** If Officer Worthington drove his patrol car 46.2 miles in 2.1 hours, what was his average speed in miles per hour?

    a. 21   **b.** 22   **c.** 44.1   **d.** 48.3   **e.** 97.02

_____ **86.** While training for her physical ability test, Maria ran a total of 24.5 miles in one week. How many miles did she run each day?

    a. 3.5   **b.** 3.75   **c.** 4.5   **d.** 17.5   **e.** 31.5

Answers

59. $\frac{8}{1,000}$ or $\frac{1}{125}$

60. $2\frac{58}{100}$ or $2\frac{29}{50}$

61. $127\frac{586}{1,000}$ or $127\frac{293}{500}$

62. $\frac{9}{100}$

63. $\frac{6}{10,000}$ or $\frac{3}{5,000}$

64. $\frac{1}{1}$

65. 96.976

66. 15.709

67. 11.575

68. 1.77

69. 10.68

70. 22.72

71. b.

72. a.

73. 0.0663

74. 9.688

75. 88.32

76. e.

77. d.

78. d.

79. 20

80. 19

81. 16.06

82. 3.27

83. 3.4

84. 10.4

85. b.

86. a.

Percents

What Is a Percent?

A percent is a special kind of fraction. The denominator is always 100. For example, 17% is the same as $\frac{17}{100}$. Literally, the word *percent* means *per 100 parts*. The root cent means 100: A century is 100 years, there are 100 cents in a dollar, etc. Thus, 17% means 17 parts out of 100. Because fractions can also be expressed as decimals, 17% is also equivalent to .17, which is 17 hundredths.

You come into contact with percents every day. Sales tax, interest, and discounts are just a few common examples. If you are shaky on fractions, you may want to review the fraction section before reading further.

Changing a Decimal to a Percent and Vice Versa

To change a decimal to a percent, move the decimal point two places to the **right** and add a percent sign (%) at the end. If the decimal point moves to the very right of the number, you don't have to write the decimal point. If there aren't enough places to move the decimal point, add zeros on the **right** before moving the decimal point.

To change a percent to a decimal, drop off the percent sign and move the decimal point two places to the left. If there aren't enough places to move the decimal point, add zeros on the **left** before moving the decimal point.

Try changing the following decimals to percents. The answers can be found at the end of this section on page 139.

_____ **87.** .31

_____ **88.** .005

_____ **89.** $.13\frac{4}{5}$

_____ **90.** 2.25

Now change these percents to decimals:

_____ **91.** 32%

_____ **92.** $53\frac{1}{4}$%

_____ **93.** 420%

_____ **94.** .33%

Changing a Fraction to a Percent and Vice Versa

To change a fraction to a percent, there are two techniques. Each is illustrated by changing the fraction $\frac{1}{4}$ to a percent:

Technique 1: Multiply the fraction by 100%.

Multiply $\frac{1}{4}$ by 100%:

$$\frac{1}{\underset{1}{4}} \times \frac{\overset{25}{100}\%}{1} = 25\%$$

Technique 2: Divide the fraction's bottom number into the top number; then move the decimal point two places to the **right** and tack on a percent sign (%).

Divide 4 into 1 and move the decimal point 2 places to the right:

$$4\overline{)1.00} \quad .25 = 25\%$$

To change a percent to a fraction, remove the percent sign and write the number over 100. Then reduce if possible.

   Example: Change 4% to a fraction.

1. Remove the % and write the fraction 4 over 100: $\frac{4}{100}$

2. Reduce: $\frac{4 \div 4}{100 \div 4} = \frac{1}{25}$

Here's a more complicated example: Change $16\frac{2}{3}$% to a fraction.

1. Remove the % and write the fraction $16\frac{2}{3}$ over 100: $\frac{16\frac{2}{3}}{100}$

2. Since a fraction means "top number divided by bottom number," rewrite the fraction as a division problem: $16\frac{2}{3} \div 100$

3. Change the mixed number ($16\frac{2}{3}$) to an improper fraction ($\frac{50}{3}$): $\frac{50}{3} \div \frac{100}{1}$

4. Flip the second fraction ($\frac{100}{1}$) and multiply: $\frac{\overset{1}{\cancel{50}}}{3} \times \frac{1}{\underset{2}{\cancel{100}}} = \frac{1}{6}$

Try changing these fractions to percents:

_____ **95.** $\frac{6}{50}$

_____ **96.** $\frac{9}{20}$

_____ **97.** $\frac{8}{10}$

_____ **98.** $\frac{3}{25}$

Now change these percents to fractions:

_____ **99.** 47%

_____ **101.** 0.8%

_____ **100.** 10%

_____ **102.** 73.5%

Sometimes, it is more convenient to work with a percentage as a fraction or a decimal. Rather than having to calculate the equivalent fraction or decimal, consider memorizing the following conversion table. Not only will this increase your efficiency on the math section of your written exam, but it will also be practical for real-life situations.

CONVERSION TABLE		
DECIMAL	%	FRACTION
.25	25%	$\frac{1}{4}$
.50	50%	$\frac{1}{2}$
.75	75%	$\frac{3}{4}$
.10	10%	$\frac{1}{10}$
.20	20%	$\frac{1}{5}$
.40	40%	$\frac{2}{5}$
.60	60%	$\frac{3}{5}$
.80	80%	$\frac{4}{5}$
.33$\overline{3}$	33$\frac{1}{3}$%	$\frac{1}{3}$
.66$\overline{6}$	66$\frac{2}{3}$%	$\frac{2}{3}$

Percent Word Problems

Word problems involving percents come in three main varieties:

- Find a percent of a whole.
  Example: What is 30% of 40?
- Find what percent one number is of another number.
  Example: 12 is what percent of 40?
- Find the whole when the percent of it is given.
  Example: 12 is 30% of what number?

While each variety has its own approach, there is a single shortcut formula you can use to solve each of these:

$$\frac{is}{of} = \frac{\%}{100}$$

The *is* is the number that usually follows, or is just before, the word *is* in the question.
The *of* is the number that usually follows the word *of* in the question.
The **%** is the number that is in front of the **%** or *percent* in the question.

Or you may think of the shortcut formula as:

$$\frac{part}{whole} = \frac{\%}{100}$$

To solve each of the three varieties, we are going to use the fact that the **cross products** are equal. The cross products are the products of the numbers diagonally across from each other. Remembering that *product* means *multiply*, here's how to create the cross products for the percent shortcut:

$$\frac{part}{whole} = \frac{\%}{100}$$
$$part \times 100 = whole \times \%$$

Here's how to use the shortcut with cross products:

- Find a percent of a whole.
  What is 30% of 40?
  30 is the % and 40 is the *of* number:
  Cross-multiply and solve for *is*:

  $$\frac{is}{40} = \frac{30}{100}$$
  $is \times 100 = 40 \times 30$
  $is \times 100 = 1,200$
  $\mathbf{12} \times 100 = 1,200$

  Thus, **12 *is*** 30% of 40.

- Find what percent one number is of another number.
  12 is what percent of 40?
  12 is the *is* number and 40 is the *of* number:
  Cross-multiply and solve for %:

  $$\frac{12}{40} = \frac{\%}{100}$$
  $12 \times 100 = 40 \times \%$
  $1,200 = 40 \times \%$
  $1,200 = 40 \times \mathbf{30}$

  Thus, 12 is **30%** of 40.

- Find the whole when the percent of it is given.
  12 is 30% of what number?
  12 is the *is* number and 30 is the %:
  Cross-multiply and solve for the *of* number:

$$\frac{12}{of} = \frac{30}{100}$$
$$12 \times 100 = of \times 30$$
$$1{,}200 = of \times 30$$
$$1{,}200 = \mathbf{40} \times 30$$

Thus, 12 is 30% **of 40**.

You can use the same technique to find the percent increase or decrease. The *is* number is the actual increase or decrease, and the *of* number is the original amount.

Example: If a uniform supply store put its $20 hats on sale for $15, by what percent does the selling price decrease?

1. Calculate the decrease, the *is* number: $20 - $15 = $5
2. The *of* number is the original amount, $20:
3. Set up the equation and solve for *of* by cross-multiplying:

$$\frac{5}{20} = \frac{\%}{100}$$
$$5 \times 100 = 20 \times \%$$
$$500 = 20 \times \%$$
$$500 = 20 \times \mathbf{25}$$

4. Thus, the selling price is decreased by **25%**.
   If the store later raises the price of the hats from $15 back to $20, don't be fooled into thinking that the percent increase is also 25%! It's actually more, because the increase amount of $5 is now based on a lower original price of only $15:

$$\frac{5}{15} = \frac{\%}{100}$$
$$5 \times 100 = 15 \times \%$$
$$500 = 15 \times \%$$
$$500 = 15 \times \mathbf{33\tfrac{1}{3}}$$

Thus, the selling price is increased by $33\tfrac{1}{3}$%.

Find a percent of a whole:

_____ **103.** 1% of 50

_____ **104.** 17% of 150

_____ **105.** $32\tfrac{1}{4}$% of 200

_____ **106.** 78.2% of 1,745

Find what percent one number is of another number:

_____ **107.** 12 is what % of 40?

_____ **108.** 3 is what % of 12?

_____ **109.** 12 is what % of 3?

_____ **110.** 7 is what % of 35?

Find the whole when the percent of it is given:

_____ **111.** 20% of what number is 12?

_____ **112.** $32\frac{1}{2}$% of what number is 19.5?

_____ **113.** 400% of what number is 40?

_____ **114.** 75% of what number is $67\frac{1}{2}$?

Now try your percent skills on some real-life problems.

_____ **115.** Last Monday, 15% of the 200-member police department was absent. How many staff members were absent that day?

   a. 15   **b.** 20   **c.** 30   **d.** 185   **e.** 215

_____ **116.** Thirty percent of Cape Rose's police department employees are women. If there are 90 women in Cape Rose's police department, how many men are employed there?

   a. 27   **b.** 60   **c.** 120   **d.** 210   **e.** 300

_____ **117.** Of the 760 crimes committed last month, 76 involved petty theft. What percent of the crimes involved petty theft?

   a. .01%   **b.** 1%   **c.** 10%   **d.** 76%   **e.** .76%

Answers

87. 31%

88. 0.5%

89. 13.8% or $13\frac{4}{5}$%

90. 225%

91. 0.32

92. 0.5325

93. 4.2

94. .0033

95. 12%

96. 45%

97. 80%

98. 12%

99. $\frac{47}{100}$

100. $\frac{1}{10}$

101. $\frac{1}{125}$

102. $\frac{147}{200}$

103. $\frac{1}{2}$ or .5

104. 25.5

105. 64.5

106. 1,364.59

107. 30%

108. 25%

109. 400%

110. 20%

111. 60

112. 60

113. 10

114. 90

115. c.

116. d.

117. c.

Averages

What Is an Average?

An average, also called an *arithmetic mean*, is a number that typifies a group of numbers, and is a measure of central tendency. You come into contact with averages on a regular basis: your bowling average, the average grade on a test, the average number of hours you work per week.

To calculate an average, add up each item being averaged and divide by the total number of items.

Example: What is the average of 6, 10, and 20?

Solution: Add the three numbers together and divide by 3: $\frac{6 + 10 + 20}{3} = 12$

Shortcut

Here's a neat shortcut for some average problems.

- Look at the numbers being averaged. If they are equally spaced, like 5, 10, 15, 20, and 25, then the average is the number in the middle, or 15 in this case.
- If there are an even number of such numbers, say 10, 20, 30, and 40, then there is no middle number. In this case, the average is halfway between the two middle numbers. In this case, the average is halfway between 20 and 30, or 25.
- If the numbers are almost evenly spaced, you can probably estimate the average without going to the trouble of actually computing it. For example, the average of 10, 20, and 32 is just a little more than 20, the middle number.

Try these average questions:

_____ **118.** The number of arrests in Eden Prairie for each of the last five weeks was 130, 135, 142, 160, and 127. What was the average number of arrests per week?

    a. 127   **b.** 135   **c.** 139   **d.** 140   **e.** 160

_____ **119.** Officer Bellini averaged 45 miles an hour for the three hours she drove in town and 55 miles an hour for the three hours she drove on the highway. What was her average speed in miles per hour?

    a. 30   **b.** 45   **c.** 49   **d.** 50   **e.** 100

_____ **120.** There are 10 females and 20 males in the academy first aid course. If the females achieved an average score of 85 and the males achieved an average score of 95, what was the academy average? (Hint: Don't fall for the trap of taking the average of 85 and 95; there are more 95s being averaged than 85s, so the average is closer to 95.)

a. $90\frac{2}{3}$ b. $91\frac{2}{3}$ c. 92   d. $92\frac{2}{3}$ e. 95

_____ **121.** A national park keeps track of how many people enter the park in each car. Today, 57 cars had 4 people, 61 cars had 2 people, 9 cars had 1 person, and 5 cars had 5 people. What is the average number of people per car? Round to the nearest person.

a. 2   b. 3   c. 4   d. 5   e. 6

Answers
118. c.
119. d.
120. b.
121. b.

10 ▶ SPATIAL AND DIRECTIONAL ORIENTATION

CHAPTER SUMMARY

State troopers must have the ability to orient themselves in spatial and directional contexts in order to carry out their functions efficiently and effectively. They must also have the ability to communicate spatial and directional information to others in order to coordinate their activities. Map reading is essential for determining spatial relationships and for determining the best or shortest routes from one point to another.

When studying for the state trooper exam, you should familiarize yourself with various types of maps. Remember a map is a visual or pictorial representation of a geographic location. An important key to looking at a map is to understand that a map does not have to be read from left to right as though reading a page of written text. A map can be turned to the most convenient position to solve the directional problem. Before answering the questions, study the map carefully to see whether there are directional arrows (north, south, east, or west) and where they are located on the map. This will help you orient yourself and prepare yourself for questions that may be based solely on directions or getting from one point on the map to another. Some maps may also present you with a key. The key, also known as a legend, is typically located in the corner of the map and may be in the form of symbols, words, or colors. The map key/legend helps you to identify major points on the map. Always study the key prior to answering any questions. Also, get a sense of what the map conveys; not all maps contain only highway routes. Does the map show streets and avenues, railroad tracks or routes, or cities and towns in relationship to one another?

The key to answer spatial and directional orientation questions is to take your time. Determine where you need to go, and then try to calculate the shortest distance. Check for map keys and/or directional arrows, and utilize them in planning your route. If you hurry through a question, you may misread the question or the answer choices.

Finding the Shortest Route

Some questions may ask you to identify the shortest legal route on a map. The best approach to this type of question is to study your map and get your bearings. Read the question, then turn the map and figure out what looks like the best route to you. (Do not look at the answer choices before figuring out the route you would take.) Start with the first answer choice and study the route turn by turn. If none of the choices looks like the route you came up with after reading the question first, then you may need to reconsider your route. If this is the case, then you'll also need to start over and consider all the answer choices with a fresh eye.

Finding the Direction

Some questions may ask you to identify the directional relationships of two or more locations. These questions may be based on a map, or they may just be written descriptions. Again, trace your path after reading the question. Then, look through the answer choices until you find the one that matches your decision.

Tips for Map-Reading Questions

1. Read carefully and follow all directions.
2. Feel free to move the map around during the test to face the direction you find comfortable.
3. Trace your path lightly on the map with your pencil. Make sure you erase all marks as you complete each question so that you don't confuse yourself for the next question.

Practice Questions

Directions: Answer questions 1 through 6 based on the following map.

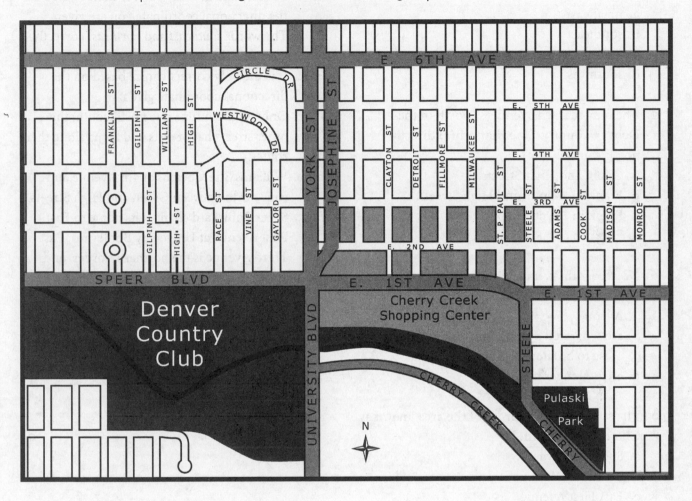

1. Starting from the Denver Country Club, Cherry Creek runs in what direction?
   a. northwest
   b. southeast
   c. northeast
   d. southwest

2. Pulaski Park is located _____ of Cherry Creek Shopping Center and _____ of Cherry Creek.
   a. northwest, northeast
   b. southeast, northeast
   c. northeast, southeast
   d. southwest, southeast

3. Third Avenue intersects with Gilpin Street
_____ of Cherry Creek Shop-
ping Center.
a. northeast
b. southeast
c. northwest
d. southwest

4. The only marked avenue(s) north of the
Denver Country Club that run(s) directly
north/south is (are)
a. Gilpin and High Streets.
b. Franklin, Gilpin, and High Streets.
c. Franklin Street.
d. Franklin and Race Street.

5. North of 4th Avenue, Gilpin and High Streets
a. are closer together than they are south of 4th
Avenue.
b. are separated by Williams Street.
c. cease to be shown on the map.
d. are no longer parallel.

6. The southernmost border of the area known as
Cherry Creek North is
a. Speer Boulevard.
b. East Third Avenue.
c. East First Avenue.
d. Steel Street.

Answers

1. b. Southeast is the only correct choice based on
the directional coordinate you are given.
2. b. The words *southeast* and *northeast* correctly
complete this statement.
3. c. It is the only correct choice based on the
directional coordinate given.
4. c. Only Franklin runs due north/south; the
other streets have twists and turns along their
routes.
5. b. Williams Street begins at 4th Avenue and
runs north between Gilpin and High Streets.
6. c. Speer Boulevard changes its name to East
First Avenue at University Boulevard; East
Third Avenue is the northern border, and
Steel Street is the eastern border, of Cherry
Creek North.

CHAPTER 11 ▶ MEMORY AND OBSERVATION

CHAPTER SUMMARY

Undoubtedly, one of the most essential skills for a state trooper is to be able to commit to memory the details of an observation. During an incident, an officer must have keen observation skills and must be able to store and utilize information to effectively handle problems. Moreover, reports prepared after an incident must be as accurate as possible, and to achieve this, an officer must have the ability to make accurate observations and to correctly recall the observed information.

In court and in other situations requiring testimony, it is imperative that an officer can remember accurately what he or she observed before, during, and after the incident. If an officer demonstrates poor observation and memory abilities, cases may be lost, criminals may unjustly escape proper justice, and the reputation and credibility of the officer and his or her department may be impugned.

Exam questions use a variety of methods to test your observation and memory skills. You may be shown drawings or photographs of street scenes for a brief period of time, and then answer questions about what you observed. Often, exams will utilize wanted posters of suspects with their pedigree information. You will be asked to recall the suspect's description and the pedigree information.

Some questions test your memory skills by having you read a lengthy, detailed block of text within a set amount of time (five to ten minutes is common). You are then asked to answer multiple-choice questions on the material without being able to refer back to the passage.

Memory is a very complicated process. In fact, it is so complicated that researchers cannot agree on how memory works or where memory is actually stored. We tend to have two types of memory: short term and long term. You will be honing your skills to increase your short term memory for the exam. Try to remember as much as you can about the picture or reading you are asked to study, but do not overwhelm yourself. Humans can only hold a certain number of items in their short term memory. If you try to retain too much information, the initial information you obtained will be replaced by the newer information. You can increase your memory storage capacity by practicing your observation skills daily. Skills practice, coupled with confidence, can go a long way in improving your test score on this part of the exam.

Memorizing and Applying Police Information

Questions Based on Written Passages

We've all watched police dramas on television where the gruff sergeant tells the assembled troops which criminals are running amock in the city and then hands out paperwork that our heroes, more often than not, leave on their desks on their way out the door. That scenario is not too far removed from reality. Police officers receive a lot of information in a short length of time and are expected to remember most of it. And of course someone has come up with a way to test your ability to accomplish this task.

You will be given a set time to read one or more written passages and study several drawings of people or places, sometimes with accompanying text. Then you will have to answer questions based on what you learned and observed, without being able to refer back to the material.

The written passages are not usually more than 500–600 words long. The subject matter will have something to do with criminal law, police procedures, or police techniques. The passage will not assume you have any previous knowledge about police techniques, but it will assume that you can read to learn information and then apply that knowledge. Because you don't have much time to absorb the material, it's best

to focus on what you feel will be the most important facts. The questions will most likely ask you to recall the details your common sense will lead you to believe to be most important. For example, here's a short piece on handcuffing techniques. Read it and then answer the questions that follow *without* looking back at the text.

Proper handcuffing technique is an essential part of officer safety. A suspect cannot easily pick up a weapon or hit an officer when his or her hands are firmly secured. When an officer makes the decision to place handcuffs on an individual, departmental policy states that the officer must always handcuff the individual's hands behind his or her back. The only exception to this rule is when the individual has a physical disability that makes this position impossible. A broken arm set in a cast is an example of such a situation.

Officers will handcuff suspects using the following technique:

1. Instruct the suspect to turn around, putting his or her back to you.
2. Instruct the suspect to place both hands behind his or her back.
3. Grab the suspect's wrist firmly with one hand and secure one ring of the handcuff around the wrist.
4. Grab the remaining wrist firmly and secure the other ring of the handcuff to that wrist.
5. Make sure the handcuffs are loose enough to allow for normal circulation.
6. Lock each side of the handcuff to prevent them from tightening accidentally.
7. Place the suspect inside the patrol car.

Answer the following questions without referring back to the handcuffing piece.

1. The passage on proper handcuffing technique says the suspect's hands should always be handcuffed
   a. behind the suspect.
   b. in front of the suspect.
   c. to the officer.
   d. to a hook in the patrol car.

2. The passage on proper handcuffing technique says the first step the officer should take when the decision to handcuff a suspect has been made is to
   a. allow the suspect to telephone a lawyer.
   b. instruct the suspect to place both hands behind his or her back.
   c. instruct the suspect to turn around, placing his or her back to the officer.
   d. lock the handcuffs firmly in place.

Remember, all you have to do to answer questions like this successfully is to remember and apply what you've learned. In the case of question 1, you're applying what you learned about handcuffing if you picked choice **a** as the right answer. In question 2, your common sense should tell you that now is not the time to have the suspect call a lawyer, so choice **a** is not likely to be the answer. Combine your reasoning skills with your ability to remember what you've read, and you should come up with choice **c** as the right answer.

It's also important to pay attention to hints from the author—and this applies both to learning and to memorization. If you see a phrase such as "The most important point to remember," pay attention. The test questions are going to pick up on that kind of hint, so your chances of seeing that material again are really good.

What to Do

1. Visualize as you read. Keeping a movie of sorts running through your mind as you read is a helpful way to remember details. If you have a visual image of what the passage is describing, you are more likely to remember it.
2. Pay special attention to the first and last steps in a list of procedures.
3. Rely on your common sense and ability to reason to supplement your memorization skills. Sometimes, you will instinctively know which answer is right even though you cannot specifically recall the exact words in the passage.
4. When applicable, attach parts of the passage to a personal experience you have had. For example, let's say you once witnessed a person with a physical disability being handcuffed. This experience would help you remember the part of the passage that mentions the one exception to the handcuffing rule.

The passage on handcuffing techniques is approximately 200 words long. On the actual test, you should expect longer passages, perhaps more than one of them, and therefore you should expect more questions on the passages than the two previously given.

If all this seems daunting, think about the times you've read a news article on, say, a grisly murder. You're talking to a friend later that evening and you say, "Did you read in the paper this morning about that guy who got stabbed with an ice pick? Yeah, some guy in a trench coat stabbed him right in the forehead with an ice pick while they were on the ferry to Martha's Vineyard. He jumped overboard right after that." This example may be a little dramatic, but you get the point. It probably takes only a minute or so to read a news article, but the information stays with you much longer than a minute. Face the memory portion of your exam with the expectation that you will remember what you read.

What Not to Do

- **Do not** draw conclusions or waste time thinking of ways a procedure really should be done. For instance, while reading the article about handcuffing techniques, don't waste time thinking of alternative methods of handcuffing. You're being tested on your ability to remember what you've read, not on your knowledge of the subject matter or your creativity.

- **Do not** add elements to the written passage that weren't originally there. If the author didn't mention the advantages of using hinge cuffs over chain cuffs, then there's no reason for you to add this information to the situation.

- **Do not** spend too much of your allotted time on one written passage if your test also includes more passages or drawings. Be sure to leave time for all of the memory material.

Questions Based on Wanted Posters

Many police departments use mock wanted posters to test memorization skills. Some departments send this material out in study guides to be memorized weeks in advance, and some ask you to memorize the material right then and there during the test, within a set period of time. Either way, you will be asking yourself the same question, "How am I going to remember all of this?" The answer is, the same way you'll one day recognize and remember facts about the criminals in your jurisdiction when you've become an officer. The technique you will learn here works in real life as well as in test situations.

Memorization, as you know by now, relies heavily on solid reading comprehension and observation skills. The wanted poster sets you are given to memorize will most likely contain line drawings of adult males, females, and juveniles. Next to the drawings, you will see the text that tells each person's story.

For example, suppose you have a drawing of an adult white male with shoulder-length hair parted down the middle. He is clean-shaven, has large eyes, and has a mole in the middle of his chin. Next to it, you see the following text.

WANTED
Rodney Jones Walker

ALIASES: Rod Jones

WANTED BY: Los Angeles Police Department

CHARGES: Assault

DESCRIPTION:

> **Age:** 37
>
> **Race:** White
>
> **Height:** 5′8″
>
> **Weight:** 190
>
> **Hair:** Black
>
> **Eyes:** Green

REMARKS: Has relatives in the Fresno area and is believed to be headed for San Diego. Was last seen with a white cast on his left wrist.

CAUTION: Switchblade hidden in the suspect's left boot. Known to carry brass knuckles.

Your task is to remember enough details about this person to correctly answer questions about him on the exam. This isn't much to ask until you consider that you will see more than one poster with accompanying text *and* be asked to remember information from written passages. Don't panic, though. Just take the posters one at a time, and remember that there are tricks you can use to improve your memory skills.

Which Comes First, Drawing or Text?

If you're like most people, your eyes will gravitate to the drawing first. That's fine, because you want to make this work as easy on your brain as possible. Start with the top of the head and work your way down. Try holding a conversation in your head to help you memorize the person's features. For example, if you were looking at a drawing of our suspect, you might think to yourself, "Oh, his hair touches his shoulders just the way my Aunt Joan's does. In fact, he has beady eyes like Aunt Joan's. His nose is sort of crooked like hers, and his head is shaped the same way. She doesn't have a mole on her chin like he does, but if she did they'd look like twins." Of course this is outlandish, but when you see the name Rodney Jones Walker, you'll remember exactly what he looks like. What you are doing is creating links between your long-term memory and your short-term memory. This is one of the best ways to improve your short-term memory skills.

While you look at each face, look for jewelry, scars, facial hair (or lack of it), facial shape, size of facial features, and teeth, if the subject is shown smiling. When you eventually get to the text, you will want to tie in such details. For example, suppose Walker is shown wearing a cross on a chain around his neck. After you read the text, you could tie lots of information together by thinking, "Now what is a guy named Rodney Jones Walker, who looks like Aunt Joan and keeps a switchblade in his boot, doing wearing a cross? I wear a cross, and I would not even think about assaulting another person." Your brain has locked in the suspect's name, his weapon, what he looks like, what he's charged with, and a distinctive piece of jewelry all in one thought.

Once you are ready to study the text, you will be using the same technique you used for studying the drawing. Read slowly from top to bottom. As you read, carry on your mental conversation. It may sound something like this: "Rodney James Walker. I used to watch the TV show *Walker, Texas Ranger* with my old college buddy Rodney Jones. Bet I don't forget the name Rodney Jones Walker. And he uses Rod Jones as an alias. My friend Rodney *hates* the nickname 'Rod' because he says it reminds him of the 1980s. Hmm. He's wanted by LAPD for assault. Hey, the actor who

plays Walker probably actually lives in Los Angeles. This guy is 37? That's how old Aunt Joan is. This is getting spooky. Hmm, he's white, just like the actor on *Walker, Texas Ranger,* and he's my height and I weigh 190 also. He's ugly, but he's strong."

You get the picture. Your goal is to find a way to make the information you see mean something to you. Your mental conversation may not turn out to be as elaborate or outlandish as the one previously described, but you will be far more likely to remember the details when you make them come alive and relate them to something or someone familiar.

Look at the information on the previous page again, make up your own mental conversation, and then see how easy it is to answer the following questions.

3. What is Walker wanted for?
   a. homicide
   b. burglary
   c. assault
   d. theft

4. How old is Walker?
   a. 30
   b. 33
   c. 37
   d. 27

5. What kind of weapon is Walker known to carry?
   a. boot knife
   b. diving knife
   c. brass knuckles
   d. boot razor blade

Check your answers by glancing back at the description. These questions should have seemed pretty simple. However, because this isn't a perfect world for the test taker, keep in mind that you'll be seeing questions containing information from other wanted posters. You may be asked to look at six or more posters and memorize them all. For example, in question 3, the right answer is choice **c**, but choices **a**, **b**, and **d** are likely to be crimes committed by some of the other suspects you've memorized for the same test. In other words, don't count on picking the most familiar answer—chances are, the choices will *all* look familiar. Instead, rely on the little conversation you had with yourself about a given suspect; that way you're less likely to confuse the various criminals.

This technique of associating the new and unfamiliar with something old and familiar works well for almost any type of memorization. Practice this technique for the test, and then use it again when you get your patrol car.

What to Do

1. Divide the number of minutes you have for memorizing the wanted posters by the number of posters, and then spend only that number of minutes on each poster.

2. Proceed methodically, top to bottom, with both the picture and the text.

3. Have a conversation with yourself; tell yourself a story about the suspect. Associate the unfamiliar picture and description with people you know.

What Not to Do

- **Do not** choose an answer just because it looks familiar. It might be related to the wrong suspect.

- **Do not** try to memorize all the wanted posters at once. Work on one at a time.

Questions Based on Street Scenes

Another way police departments test your memory skills is to let you study a drawing or photograph of a scene for a certain amount of time—either as part of a packet that include passages and wanted posters or by itself—and then ask you questions about the scene.

The picture will usually be a scene of a busy city street with plenty of details for you to memorize: store names, buses, taxis, people, clothing, action scenes (a mugging or maybe someone changing a flat tire on a car), and street signs.

At the end of this chapter, you will find a street scene and several related questions that you can use to practice.

What to Do

Use a methodical approach to study what you see. When you read sentences on a page, you read from left to right. This skill is as automatic as breathing for most English-language readers. Approach memorizing a picture the same way you read, taking in the information from left to right. Instead of staring at the street scene with the whole picture in focus, make yourself start at the left and work your way across the page until you get to the right.

What Not to Do

- **Do not** let yourself get overwhelmed when you first see the busy street scene. Take a deep breath and decide to be methodical.

- **Do not** try to start memorizing with a shotgun approach, letting your eyes roam all over the page without really taking in the details.

Questions Based on a Video

Some departments will show you a video and then have you answer questions about what you have observed. This test is not widely used, but it is a method you may encounter. Your best bet is to relax, study the situation on the screen carefully and with confidence that you will remember what you see, and then tackle the questions.

Using a Study Guide

Instead of making you memorize material right there during the test, some departments send out a study booklet a few weeks in advance of the test. The booklet contains detailed instructions on what you will be expected to know for the test. The expectation is that you will have plenty of time to memorize the information and that you will be able to answer questions based on what you have memorized.

For example, you may see several pictures of items stolen in a burglary—maybe a wristwatch or a crown inlaid with six rubies. On test day, you may see a question like this:

6. In the study booklet provided to you, there are several drawings of items taken in a burglary. One of the items was a crown. How many jewels did you see on the crown?
   a. three
   b. four
   c. none
   d. six

The questions are simple. No tricks here. You just have to be able to recall details.

What to Do

If you get material to study in advance, study it *in advance*. Don't start the day before the test. Spend a little time on your study booklet every day from the day you get it until the day before the test.

What Not to Do

Do not read the questions too quickly. If you're having trouble remembering the details, going with what initially feels like the correct answer is usually a good idea—but you must make sure you're answering the right question. If you were reading quickly and didn't

look at the last sentence in the previous example, you might anticipate that the question asks you how many crowns you saw in the drawing, not how many jewels were on the crown. Haste can produce easily avoidable errors.

Memorization Tips

Memorization is much easier if you approach the task with the expectation that you *will* remember what you see. Call it positive thinking, self-hypnosis, or concentration—it doesn't really matter as long as you get results. When you run through the practice questions in this book, prepare your mind before you start. Tell yourself over and over that you will remember what you see as you study the images. Your performance level will rise to meet your expectations.

Yes, it's easy for your brain to freeze up when you see a drawing filled with details, a test section full of questions, and a test proctor standing above you with a stopwatch in one hand intoning, "You have five minutes to study this drawing. You may begin." But if you've programmed yourself to stay calm, stay alert, and execute your plan, you will be much more likely to remember the details when you need them.

Plan? Yes, you need a plan. If you have a method for memorizing, say, a busy urban street scene—like the left-to-right scheme we just outlined—then you will be more likely to relax and allow yourself to retain what you've seen long enough to answer the test questions. Keep in mind that you aren't trying to memorize the scene forever; you are merely doing it to retain the information long enough to answer the test questions.

Observation Tips

It's almost impossible to talk about memorization without bringing up observation. Some people are naturally observant. Some drift off frequently and have no awareness of the world around them. Whatever category you think you are in, it's never too late to sharpen, or to acquire, strong observation skills. How? Practice, of course.

Newspaper photos make great practice tools. News photos are action-oriented and usually have more than one person in the scenes. Sit down in a quiet place, clear your mind, remind yourself for several minutes that you will retain all the details you need when you study the picture, and then turn to a picture and study it for about five minutes. At the end of the time, turn the picture over, get a piece of paper and a pencil, then write down all the details you can think of in the picture. Make yourself do this as often as possible before the test.

You can practice your observation skills on the way to work or school, too. Instead of sitting in your car waiting for the light to change with a blank stare on your face, look around you and say out loud what you see. "I'm at the corner of 12th and Walnut. I see a man in a black, full-length raincoat standing on the northeast corner looking in the display window of Hank's Motorcycle Shop. There's a black Subaru station wagon parked at a meter near the motorcycle shop. The license plate is . . ." (If you ride to work on a bus or train, you can say these things silently to yourself.) Not only are you practicing a basic skill that you will need to become an excellent police officer, you are training your mind to succeed at whatever memory questions the test maker throws your way.

Memory and Observation Practice

On pages 154 and 155 is a street scene like those found on some police exams. Following are several questions about details of the scene. Use this scene to practice your memory skills. Take exactly five minutes to study the picture, and then answer the questions that follow without looking back at the picture.

Check your answers by looking back at the scene. If you get all the questions right, you know you're well prepared for memory questions. If you miss a few, you know you need to spend more time practicing, using the tips previously outlined. Remember, you *can* improve your memory with practice.

7. What type of sale is advertised at Howard Jeweler?
   a. 50% off
   b. 2 for 1
   c. going out of business
   d. 20% to 60% off

8. Which of the following is true about the man wearing the Artie's Deli shirt?
   a. His sunglasses are black.
   b. He has a shaved head.
   c. He has a tattoo on his right arm.
   d. He wears an earring in his right ear.

9. What is the complete name of the store located directly to the left of Howard Jeweler?
   a. Photo by Joe
   b. Photo Discount
   c. Joe's Photo
   d. Joe's Discount Photo

- Use a methodical approach to memorization.
- Find ways to create links between your long-term memory and short-term memory.
- For questions based on pictures, "read" the picture from top to bottom or left to right.
- For questions based on materials you receive in advance, study the materials for a few minutes every day before the test.
- Visualize as you read passages, forming the words into a moving picture in your mind.
- Read the questions carefully; make sure you're answering the question that's being asked.
- Practice your memory and observation skills in your daily routine.

10. What is Howard Jeweler's address?
   a. 2 Cortlandt
   b. 2A Cortlandt
   c. 3 Cortlandt
   d. 3A Cortlandt

11. What is Salon & Spa's phone number?
   a. 212-555-1605
   b. 212-555-1606
   c. 212-555-1506
   d. 212-555-1505

12. How many bicycles are there in the photograph?
   a. 0
   b. 1
   c. 2
   d. 3

13. There are two young women talking to each other in the photo. Where are they standing?
   a. at a payphone kiosk
   b. next to a rack of sunglasses
   c. near a bicycle rack
   d. outside the Salon & Spa entrance

14. What phrase is written on Sushi-Time's awning?
   a. Sushi & Noodle Restaurant
   b. Sushi & Noodle
   c. Sushi
   d. Sushi Restaurant

15. What is the man wearing the backpack doing in the photograph?
   a. talking on a cell phone
   b. looking at the Howard Jeweler window display
   c. crossing the street
   d. exiting from Salon & Spa

Additional Resources

To help you improve your memory and observation skills, take advantage of one or more of the following resources.

Books

- *The Memory Book* by Harry Lorayne and Jerry Lucas (Ballantine Books)
- *Learn to Remember: Practical Techniques and Exercises to Improve Your Memory* by Dominic O'Brien (Chronicle Books)
- *Improve Your Memory* by Ron Fry (Career Press)
- *The Complete Idiot's Guide to Improving Your Memory* by Michael Kurland (Alpha Books)

Websites

- www.memoryzine.com/games.html
  If you'd like to get some practice and help improving your memory skills, this site has some memory games developed by the Practical Memory Institute (PMI) that are designed to improve spatial memory and focus.
- www.mindtools.com/memory.html
  This website's explanations are particularly helpful in studying for exams or in situations in which you need to remember detailed, structured information. They also make things like learning foreign languages and remembering people's names much easier.

12 ▶ PROBLEM SOLVING

CHAPTER SUMMARY

State troopers are called to solve problems that other people cannot. In fact, many times when people call the police, they are in distress and unsure of what to do. They rely on the police to solve their problems for them. The variety and types of situations police officers may confront are unlimited, and most often, there are no books or training manuals that can instruct them as to what exact steps they should take in the unique situation they face. Training, practice, and experience can all help you to develop good problem-solving skills, but natural common sense is the indispensable ingredient.

To succeed as a state trooper, you must possess common sense, problem-solving skills, good reasoning ability, good judgment, and sensitivity to human and cultural conditions. Most problem-solving questions on the state trooper exam involve reasoning, judgment, and sensitivity. Major portions of state police exams are devoted to testing a candidate's abilities in these areas.

Safety First

In every action an officer takes, the safety and well-being of everyone involved is priority number one. Protecting life is an officer's first responsibility.

When you look at a test question, remember that troopers have the importance of safety drilled into them from day one at the academy. Is it safer to have the man stand in the street to explain how an accident happened, or is it better to have him move to the sidewalk? Is it safer for you to stand in front of a door or to the side of a door before knocking? Is it safer for bystanders if you pursue the speeder through downtown traffic or let her go?

The safety issue may not surface in every question, but when it does, be aware that safety is a state trooper's highest priority.

Use of Force

The smallest amount possible is the right amount of force. Common sense is important in this area. Expect to see questions asking you what the proper amount of force is for an officer to use when physical control is necessary, and what kind of force is appropriate out of the choices you see.

Improving Your Problem-Solving Skills

In times of stress, people are more likely to carry out a task if they've practiced it—mentally or physically. If you've thought about a situation and you've arrived at a conclusion about what you would do under the given circumstances, then you've given your brain a plan for the situation if it actually comes up. Maybe you've heard someone say, "I didn't know what to do. I just froze." Most likely, he or she didn't have a plan to follow.

Train yourself to play the game "what if." Do it in various public places. Ask yourself, "If I were a state trooper, what would I do if . . ." This simple game could program your brain to respond promptly to these types of problem-solving questions.

Tips for Answering Problem-Solving Questions

- Read carefully, but don't read anything into the situation that isn't there.
- Read through all the options before you choose an answer.
- Find information that supports your answer, if possible.
- Think like a state trooper. Safety first: Use the least possible force.
- Use your common sense.
- Stay calm and work methodically.

Practice Questions

For practice with problem-solving questions, answer the following questions.

Use the following passage to answer practice questions 1 through 3.

Officers who use pepper spray to disperse a crowd should do the following:

1. Warn other officers that pepper spray is about to be deployed.

2. Order the crowd to disperse.

3. Take a position upwind of the crowd.

4. Direct the spray into the crowd while continuing to order them to disperse.

5. Provide first aid to anyone who is overcome by the spray.

1. Officers Brady, Dion, and Rodriguez are called to the scene of a large fight in front of Omar's Grill. When they arrive, they see a group of approximately 15 adult males bunched up in the parking lot, punching each other. Officer Dion pulls out his canister of pepper spray. What should he do next?
   a. Order the crowd to stop fighting.
   b. Warn the other two officers that he's about to spray the crowd.
   c. Warn the crowd that he has pepper spray.
   d. Stand downwind of the crowd before spraying.

2. Officers Perez and Navarro arrive at City Hall to find a mob rocking Mayor Dickson's car back and forth in the street. Officer Navarro shouts to Officer Perez that she is going to use her pepper spray. What should she do next?
   a. Stand downwind of the crowd.
   b. Shout to the crowd to disperse.
   c. Warn the crowd that pepper spray is about to be deployed.
   d. Stand upwind of the crowd before using the spray.

3. A large crowd has formed at the city council chambers to protest a new city ordinance against sleeping in public. The crowd is angry and has begun to throw rocks at the building. Officers Jenson and Morin arrive, followed by Officer Jacobs, who is shouting for them to look out because he is about to spray. He orders the crowd to disperse. What should he do next?
   a. Stand downwind of the other two officers.
   b. Warn the crowd he is about to spray.
   c. Position himself upwind of the crowd.
   d. Spray the crowd.

4. Officer Yang has noticed an increase in gang graffiti in his area. Store owners are complaining about the damage and have asked him to keep a closer eye out for this problem. Which situation below should Officer Yang investigate?
   a. Two teenagers are leaning against a park wall completely covered with gang-related graffiti.
   b. Four teenagers are leaning against the clean white wall of a neighborhood grocery store. One teenager has a spray paint can hanging out of the rear pocket of his baggy pants.
   c. Three teenagers are riding bicycles in a grocery store parking lot late at night.
   d. Six teenagers are walking along the sidewalk bouncing a basketball and yelling at passing cars while making gang signs with their hands.

5. Officer Cartman arrived at the protest on Euclid Avenue first, followed by Officers Scalzo and Lincoln. Officer Scalzo warned her fellow two officers she was going to use pepper spray. Officers Cartman and Lincoln ordered the crowd to disperse while Officer Scalzo dispensed the spray. What mistake did the officers make?
   a. Officer Scalzo should have been providing first aid to those overcome by the spray.
   b. The officers did not take position upwind of the crowd prior to Officer Scalzo spraying.
   c. Officer Lincoln should have called for additional officers to assist.
   d. Officer Cartman did not radio in their location on Euclid Avenue.

6. A group of five males, who have reportedly been drinking alcohol, are fighting outside Tioga's Bar & Grill. Officer Peters arrives on the scene and orders the men to stop fighting. When they do not, he warns that he is going to deploy his pepper spray. Officer Malik arrives to provide support to Officer Peters, who has taken a position upward of the crowd. Officer Peters then directs the spray into the crowd. What mistake was made?

a. Officer Malik should have warned the crowd that he was deploying pepper spray.

b. Officers Peters and Malik should have tried to break up the fight without using pepper spray.

c. Officer Peters should have warned Officer Malik that he was deploying pepper spray.

d. No mistakes were made during this call.

7. Officers Taylor, Hudson, Xavier, and Muller are on the security detail for the governor's visit. Taylor is in front of the stage, Hudson is behind the stage, Xavier is near the exit door, and Muller is at the back of the auditorium. If Hudson switches places with Xavier and Xavier then switches places with Muller, where is Muller?

a. near the exit

b. in front of the stage

c. behind the stage

d. at the back of the auditorium

8. Officials at Saw Mill Road Elementary School are concerned about a man they have seen walking by himself past the door where the kindergarteners are released each day at noon. Which person should appear suspicious to Officer Aon?

a. Two teenagers loudly making their way down the block.

b. A woman riding her bicycle past the school's doors at dismal time.

c. Two men sitting in a convertible car eating lunch at the end of the block.

d. A man with a baseball hat and sunglasses leaning against a van parked directly in front of the doors where the children are released.

9. The neighborhood watch group has complained they see young men standing on the street corners all day and night. The young men walk up to passing cars that pull over, talk at the driver's window for a few seconds, and make an exchange. They also see these men shake hands with others who approach them on the street. Which situation should Officer Alburtus investigate?

a. A group of three men standing in front of a local bar. When a car parks on the street nearby, one of the men walks over to the car and talks to the driver through the side window.

b. Two young women who are sitting on the curb texting and calling friends on their phones.

c. A lone female standing on the corner, looking around, who gets in a car that drives away and does not return.

d. Two older men who are sitting at a table playing cards in front of the local pizza place.

10. Officers Drew, Enoch, Freidrich, and Grovers are assigned to the protest march. Drew is on the northeast corner of 68th Street, Enoch is on the southwest corner of 68th Street, and Friedrich is on the northwest corner. Officer Grovers should therefore be posted at which corner of 68 Street?
a. northeast
b. southeast
c. northwest
d. southwest

Answers

1. b. According to Step 1, the officer should warn the other officers before he takes further action. The officer does want the crowd to stop fighting and will order them to do so (choice **a**), but he must first warn the other two officers that he plans to use his pepper spray. Choice **c** is not listed as a step, and choice **d** is not a good answer because the officer will always want to be upwind of pepper spray, not downwind.

2. b. The officer has already warned her partner that she is about to use the spray. Her next step will be to order the crowd to disperse.

3. c. Officer Jacobs's next step after ordering the crowd to disperse is to position himself upwind of the crowd so that the spray will not come back on him or his partners.

4. b. Seeing a teenager with a spray paint can is the most suspicious of the incidents described since Officer Yang is looking for graffiti artists. Spray paint is not an item most people carry around with them and is suspicious given the circumstances.

5. b. The officer warned her fellow officers she was going to spray, the other two officers ordered the crowd to disperse, but before spraying or providing first aid to anyone in the crowd, the officers should be positioned upwind of the crowd.

6. c. Since he arrived at the scene after Officer Peters, Officer Malik needed to be warned that Officer Peters was going to deploy his pepper spray.

7. c. After all the switches are made, Muller is behind the stage, Hudson is near the exit, Xavier is at the back of the auditorium, and Taylor is in front of the stage.

8. d. Officer Aon should watch the man by himself, who looks like he may be trying to disguise his face.

9. a. The man approaching the car matches the description of the scenario the neighborhood watch group reported.

10. b. The southeast corner is the only one without an officer posted.

13 ▶ STATE TROOPER PRACTICE TEST 2

CHAPTER SUMMARY
This is the second practice exam in this book based on the most commonly tested areas on the state trooper exam.

The practice test consists of 100 multiple-choice questions in the following areas: reading comprehension, writing and information ordering, mathematics, spatial and directional orientation, memory and observation, and problem solving. Give yourself two hours to take this practice test.

State Trooper Practice Test 2

1.	ⓐ	ⓑ	ⓒ	ⓓ
2.	ⓐ	ⓑ	ⓒ	ⓓ
3.	ⓐ	ⓑ	ⓒ	ⓓ
4.	ⓐ	ⓑ	ⓒ	ⓓ
5.	ⓐ	ⓑ	ⓒ	ⓓ
6.	ⓐ	ⓑ	ⓒ	ⓓ
7.	ⓐ	ⓑ	ⓒ	ⓓ
8.	ⓐ	ⓑ	ⓒ	ⓓ
9.	ⓐ	ⓑ	ⓒ	ⓓ
10.	ⓐ	ⓑ	ⓒ	ⓓ
11.	ⓐ	ⓑ	ⓒ	ⓓ
12.	ⓐ	ⓑ	ⓒ	ⓓ
13.	ⓐ	ⓑ	ⓒ	ⓓ
14.	ⓐ	ⓑ	ⓒ	ⓓ
15.	ⓐ	ⓑ	ⓒ	ⓓ
16.	ⓐ	ⓑ	ⓒ	ⓓ
17.	ⓐ	ⓑ	ⓒ	ⓓ
18.	ⓐ	ⓑ	ⓒ	ⓓ
19.	ⓐ	ⓑ	ⓒ	ⓓ
20.	ⓐ	ⓑ	ⓒ	ⓓ
21.	ⓐ	ⓑ	ⓒ	ⓓ
22.	ⓐ	ⓑ	ⓒ	ⓓ
23.	ⓐ	ⓑ	ⓒ	ⓓ
24.	ⓐ	ⓑ	ⓒ	ⓓ
25.	ⓐ	ⓑ	ⓒ	ⓓ
26.	ⓐ	ⓑ	ⓒ	ⓓ
27.	ⓐ	ⓑ	ⓒ	ⓓ
28.	ⓐ	ⓑ	ⓒ	ⓓ
29.	ⓐ	ⓑ	ⓒ	ⓓ
30.	ⓐ	ⓑ	ⓒ	ⓓ
31.	ⓐ	ⓑ	ⓒ	ⓓ
32.	ⓐ	ⓑ	ⓒ	ⓓ
33.	ⓐ	ⓑ	ⓒ	ⓓ
34.	ⓐ	ⓑ	ⓒ	ⓓ
35.	ⓐ	ⓑ	ⓒ	ⓓ

36.	ⓐ	ⓑ	ⓒ	ⓓ
37.	ⓐ	ⓑ	ⓒ	ⓓ
38.	ⓐ	ⓑ	ⓒ	ⓓ
39.	ⓐ	ⓑ	ⓒ	ⓓ
40.	ⓐ	ⓑ	ⓒ	ⓓ
41.	ⓐ	ⓑ	ⓒ	ⓓ
42.	ⓐ	ⓑ	ⓒ	ⓓ
43.	ⓐ	ⓑ	ⓒ	ⓓ
44.	ⓐ	ⓑ	ⓒ	ⓓ
45.	ⓐ	ⓑ	ⓒ	ⓓ
46.	ⓐ	ⓑ	ⓒ	ⓓ
47.	ⓐ	ⓑ	ⓒ	ⓓ
48.	ⓐ	ⓑ	ⓒ	ⓓ
49.	ⓐ	ⓑ	ⓒ	ⓓ
50.	ⓐ	ⓑ	ⓒ	ⓓ
51.	ⓐ	ⓑ	ⓒ	ⓓ
52.	ⓐ	ⓑ	ⓒ	ⓓ
53.	ⓐ	ⓑ	ⓒ	ⓓ
54.	ⓐ	ⓑ	ⓒ	ⓓ
55.	ⓐ	ⓑ	ⓒ	ⓓ
56.	ⓐ	ⓑ	ⓒ	ⓓ
57.	ⓐ	ⓑ	ⓒ	ⓓ
58.	ⓐ	ⓑ	ⓒ	ⓓ
59.	ⓐ	ⓑ	ⓒ	ⓓ
60.	ⓐ	ⓑ	ⓒ	ⓓ
61.	ⓐ	ⓑ	ⓒ	ⓓ
62.	ⓐ	ⓑ	ⓒ	ⓓ
63.	ⓐ	ⓑ	ⓒ	ⓓ
64.	ⓐ	ⓑ	ⓒ	ⓓ
65.	ⓐ	ⓑ	ⓒ	ⓓ
66.	ⓐ	ⓑ	ⓒ	ⓓ
67.	ⓐ	ⓑ	ⓒ	ⓓ
68.	ⓐ	ⓑ	ⓒ	ⓓ
69.	ⓐ	ⓑ	ⓒ	ⓓ
70.	ⓐ	ⓑ	ⓒ	ⓓ

71.	ⓐ	ⓑ	ⓒ	ⓓ
72.	ⓐ	ⓑ	ⓒ	ⓓ
73.	ⓐ	ⓑ	ⓒ	ⓓ
74.	ⓐ	ⓑ	ⓒ	ⓓ
75.	ⓐ	ⓑ	ⓒ	ⓓ
76.	ⓐ	ⓑ	ⓒ	ⓓ
77.	ⓐ	ⓑ	ⓒ	ⓓ
78.	ⓐ	ⓑ	ⓒ	ⓓ
79.	ⓐ	ⓑ	ⓒ	ⓓ
80.	ⓐ	ⓑ	ⓒ	ⓓ
81.	ⓐ	ⓑ	ⓒ	ⓓ
82.	ⓐ	ⓑ	ⓒ	ⓓ
83.	ⓐ	ⓑ	ⓒ	ⓓ
84.	ⓐ	ⓑ	ⓒ	ⓓ
85.	ⓐ	ⓑ	ⓒ	ⓓ
86.	ⓐ	ⓑ	ⓒ	ⓓ
87.	ⓐ	ⓑ	ⓒ	ⓓ
88.	ⓐ	ⓑ	ⓒ	ⓓ
89.	ⓐ	ⓑ	ⓒ	ⓓ
90.	ⓐ	ⓑ	ⓒ	ⓓ
91.	ⓐ	ⓑ	ⓒ	ⓓ
92.	ⓐ	ⓑ	ⓒ	ⓓ
93.	ⓐ	ⓑ	ⓒ	ⓓ
94.	ⓐ	ⓑ	ⓒ	ⓓ
95.	ⓐ	ⓑ	ⓒ	ⓓ
96.	ⓐ	ⓑ	ⓒ	ⓓ
97.	ⓐ	ⓑ	ⓒ	ⓓ
98.	ⓐ	ⓑ	ⓒ	ⓓ
99.	ⓐ	ⓑ	ⓒ	ⓓ
100.	ⓐ	ⓑ	ⓒ	ⓓ

State Trooper Practice Test 2

Directions: Read the following passage, then answer questions 1 through 4.

Chief Justice Warren Burger was the longest serving in the twentieth century. Having been nominated by President Richard Nixon in 1969, he replaced Chief Justice Earl Warren. He restricted or reversed many of the civil liberties granted by the Warren Court during the 1950s and 1960s. He helped develop the "good faith exception" to the exclusionary rule. In law enforcement, in good faith believes if a warrant is legal and valid, and a search produces incriminating evidence, that evidence is admissible in court to be used against the defendant.

While Burger was regarded as a strict constructionist, he did look to other countries for models of more efficient systems of justice. Judges who are strict constructionists believe the U.S. Constitution should be read as it was originally intended or written, not as a document that evolves with society. When deciding cases, they are not concerned with the norms of other countries—our forefathers were creating a new and unique republic different from all other countries. However, in his public comments about the American judicial system, Burger often compared it to those of Scandinavian countries such Norway and Sweden. Off the bench, Warren was more outspoken than most justices today. He made known his opinion of what he regarded as the U.S. criminal justice system's slow and cumbersome nature.

1. What is the primary purpose of the passage?
   a. The exclusionary rule applies to the good faith exception when law enforcement is executing a warrant.
   b. Chief Justice Burger created the exclusionary rule.
   c. Chief Justice Burger, while a traditional justice in some aspects, was also unlike most traditional justices.
   d. Chief Justice Burger is the longest serving justice.

2. When law enforcement knowingly enters a person's home without a warrant and finds incriminating evidence, that evidence is subject to which of the following?
   a. the exclusionary rule
   b. the good faith exception
   c. strict constructionist
   d. Scandinavian norms

3. A strict constructionist
   a. interprets the U.S. Constitution according to modern day standards.
   b. interprets the U.S. Constitution according to Scandinavian standards.
   c. interprets the U.S. Constitution according to its original meaning.
   d. interprets the U.S. Constitution according to 1950s and 1960s standards.

4. According to the passage, what is one of the ways in which Chief Justice Burger was considered nontraditional?
   a. He believed in the exclusionary rule.
   b. He stayed on the bench for a long period of time.
   c. He expanded rights created by the Warren Court.
   d. He looked at other countries for ideas about how to improve the U.S. criminal justice system.

Directions: Read the following passage, then answer questions 5 through 10.

At 8:16 A.M., a police operator received a report of a car accident on Morton Avenue near Farley Street from Helen Moreno of 1523 Morton Avenue. The caller said she had just arrived home when she heard the collision from her living room. Officer Rayburn arrived on the scene at 8:19. He saw that three vehicles, including an armored truck, were involved and that the driver of the green sedan was unconscious. He called for an ambulance and backup. He then checked the injured driver, saw that he was not bleeding, and covered him with a blanket provided by Mrs. Moreno. Martin Wilcox, of 1526 Morton, who was a passenger in the green sedan, identified the driver as Henry Woolf, also of 1526 Morton. Mrs. Moreno identified the third vehicle involved in the accident, a blue convertible, as her car.

The ambulance arrived at 8:24. At 8:25, four officers, including Lieutenant Watts, arrived. Lieutenant Watts assigned Officers Rayburn and Stein to block off both streets and control traffic, Officer Washington to security on the armored truck, and Officer Parisi to examine the skid marks on Farley Street. Mr. Wilcox told Lieutenant Watts that Woolf had stopped at the "T" intersection, then turned left onto Morton. Wilcox said the driver's side was struck almost immediately by the truck, which was skidding down Morton. The impact caused the Woolf vehicle to strike Mrs. Moreno's convertible. Frank Burroughs, the driver of the armored truck, told Officer Washington that he was due at Security Bank at 8:10 and that his brakes had failed. After checking with Lieutenant Watts and Officer Parisi, Officer Washington cited Burroughs for speeding, failing to obey a stop sign, and giving false information.

5. Who was the first person to view the accident scene?
   a. Lieutenant Watts
   b. Officer Washington
   c. Officer Rayburn
   d. the police operator

6. Which of the following can be concluded about the Morton Avenue-Farley Street intersection?
   a. There were at least two stop signs there.
   b. Farley Street is a one-way street.
   c. Morton Avenue runs north and south.
   d. No cars were parked near the intersection.

7. Which of the following best represents the order in which the accident occurred?
   a. The Woolf vehicle struck the Moreno vehicle, which struck the armored vehicle.
   b. The armored vehicle struck the Woolf vehicle, which struck the Moreno vehicle.
   c. The Moreno vehicle struck the armored vehicle, which struck the Woolf vehicle.
   d. The armored vehicle struck the Moreno vehicle, which struck the Woolf vehicle.

8. Who examined evidence relating to Frank Burroughs's claim that his brakes failed?
   a. Officer Rayburn
   b. Officer Stein
   c. Officer Washington
   d. Officer Parisi

9. Which vehicle had been traveling on Farley Street?
   a. the green sedan
   b. the blue convertible
   c. the armored truck
   d. the ambulance

10. Which of the following can be concluded about Helen Moreno's vehicle?
   a. It was parked on a steep incline.
   b. It was parked across the street from the Moreno residence.
   c. It was unoccupied at the time of the accident.
   d. It was struck by the armored truck.

Directions: Read the following passage, then answer questions 11 through 13.

Detectives who routinely investigate violent crimes can't help but become somewhat jaded. Paradoxically, the victims and witnesses with whom they work closely are often in a highly vulnerable and emotional state. The emotional fallout from a sexual assault, for example, can be complex and long lasting. Detectives must be trained to handle people in emotional distress and must be sensitive to the fact that for the victim, the crime is not routine. At the same time, detectives must recognize the limits of their role and resist the temptation to act as therapists or social workers, instead referring victims to the proper agencies.

11. What is the main idea of the passage?
   a. The best detectives do not become emotionally hardened by their jobs.
   b. Victims of violent crime should be referred to therapists and social workers.
   c. Detectives should be sensitive to the emotional state of victims of violent crime.
   d. Detectives should be particularly careful in dealing with victims of sexual assault.

12. According to the passage, what is *paradoxical* about the detective's relationship to the victim?
   a. Detectives know less about the experience of violent crime than do victims.
   b. What for the detective is routine is a unique and profound experience for the victim.
   c. Detectives must be sensitive to victims' needs but can't be social workers or psychologists.
   d. Not only must detectives solve crimes, but they must also handle the victims with care.

13. According to the passage, detectives who investigate violent crimes should NOT
   a. refer victims to appropriate support services.
   b. be aware of the psychological consequences of being victimized.
   c. become jaded.
   d. become too personally involved with the victims' problems.

Directions: Read the following passage, then answer questions 14 through 16.

Following a recent series of arson fires in public-housing buildings, the mayor of a large U.S. city has decided to expand the city's Community Patrol, made up of 18- to 21-year-olds, to about 400 people. The Community Patrol is an important part of the city's efforts to at least reduce the number of these crimes.

In addition to the expanded patrol, the city also plans to reduce the seriousness of these fires, which are most often started in stairwells, by stripping the paint from the stairwell walls. Fed by the thick layers of oil-based paint, these arson fires race up the stairwells at an alarming speed.

Although the city attempted to control the speed of these fires by covering walls with a flame retardant, it is now clear that the retardant failed to work in almost all cases. In the most recent fire, the flames raced up ten stories after the old paint under the newly applied fire retardant ignited. Because the retardant failed to stop the flames, the city decided to stop applying it and will now strip the stairwells down to the bare walls.

14. One of the main points of the passage is that flame retardants
   a. reduce the number of arson fires in large cities.
   b. are being stripped from walls by the Community Patrol.
   c. have not prevented stairwell fires from spreading.
   d. have increased the speed of flames in stairwell fires.

he passage indicates stairwell fires spread extremely rapidly because
  a. the stairwells have no ventilation from the outdoors.
  b. arsonists set the fires in several locations at once.
  c. the stairwell walls are old and often bare.
  d. the flames are fed by the oil-based paint on the walls.

16. The city has decided to stop using flame retardants because the retardants
  a. have failed to control the speed of stairwell fires.
  b. send toxic fumes and gases into the buildings.
  c. are thick and have a flammable oil base.
  d. increase the speed at which flames travel up stairs.

Directions: Read the following passage, then answer questions 17 through 20.

At 1:30 A.M., while parked at 917 Crescent, Police Officers Lin and Lawton were asked to respond to a call from Tucker's Tavern at 714 Clarinda. At 1:42 A.M., when the officers arrived, they found paramedics attempting to revive 18-year-old Brent Morrow, who lay unconscious on the floor. A patron of the tavern, Edward Pickens, stated that at around 12:10 A.M., Mr. Morrow's two companions had playfully challenged Mr. Morrow to "chug" a pint of whiskey and that Mr. Morrow had done so in approximately 15 minutes. Mr. Pickens thought the two should be arrested. Mr. Morrow's companions, Jeremy Roland and Casey Edwards, denied Mr. Pickens's statement. The bartender, Raymond Evans, stated that he had not served Mr. Morrow and that Tucker's Tavern does not sell whiskey by the pint. At 1:50 A.M., paramedics took Mr. Morrow to University Hospital, where he remains unconscious. No arrests were made. An investigation is pending.

17. Which of the following persons most likely called police to Tucker's Tavern?
  a. Raymond Evans
  b. Brent Morrow
  c. Jeremy Roland
  d. Edward Pickens

18. What was the main reason Brent Morrow was removed from Tucker's Tavern?
  a. He was drunk.
  b. He was underage.
  c. He was ill.
  d. He was a university student.

19. At about what time did Brent Morrow finish chugging the pint of whiskey?
  a. 12:25 A.M.
  b. 1:30 A.M.
  c. 1:42 A.M.
  d. 1:50 A.M.

20. According to the passage, which of the following statements is accurate?
  a. Jeremy Roland and Casey Edwards were arrested.
  b. Brent Morrow was treated and released from University Hospital.
  c. Police Officers Lin and Lawton were parked at 917 Crescent at 1:30 A.M.
  d. Paramedics did not attempt to revive Brent Morrow until after 2:00 A.M.

Directions: For questions 21 through 25, choose the answer choice that best rephrases the underlined portion of the given sentence.

21. <u>Upon being asked</u> we all went to Eddie's favorite Japanese restaurant to celebrate his 40th birthday.
  a. Although he asked,
  b. Despite his asking,
  c. Because he asked,
  d. No one asked so

22. A corporation created by the federal government during the Great Depression, the Tennessee Valley Authority (TVA) is responsible for <u>flood control must generate electric power, and soil conservation.</u>
  a. flood control, must generate electric power, and soil conservation.
  b. flood control, generating electric power, and for soil conservation.
  c. controlling floods, generating electric power, and soil conservation.
  d. flood control, the generation of electric power, and soil conservation.

23. With her book *Coming of Age in Samoa*, anthropologist Margaret Mead emphasized the role of culture, <u>in shaping human behavior over biology.</u>
  a. rather than biology, in shaping human behavior.
  b. rather than biology with shaping human behavior.
  c. somewhat better than biology to shape human behavior.
  d. in shaping human behavior, and not biology.

24. Students <u>and teachers, they all often complain</u> that summer seems to go by too fast.
  a. and teachers alike often complain
  b. but not teachers seem to complain
  c. while not teachers, often complain
  d. while their teachers do not complain,

25. The news reporter who <u>covers the story, suddenly became ill, and they called me</u> to take her place.
  a. had been covering the story suddenly became ill, and I was called
  b. was covering the story suddenly becomes ill, and they called me
  c. is covering the story suddenly becomes ill, and I was called
  d. would have been covering the story suddenly became ill, and I am called

26. Three of the sentences below contain one or more grammatical or spelling errors. Select the answer choice that is correct as is.
  a. After renting him the room, Alvin discovered Mr. Morris owned a cat.
  b. After renting him the room, a cat was discovered to belong to Mr. Morris.
  c. A cat belonging to Mr. Morris was discovered by Alvin after renting him a room.
  d. After renting him a room, Mr. Morris was discovered by Alvin to own a cat.

27. Three of the sentences below contain one or more grammatical or spelling errors. Select the answer choice that is correct as is.
  a. Instead of the local news, Jeremy asked for his favorite movie on TV.
  b. Jeremy's favorite movie was on TV, so he asked if we could watch it instead of the local news.
  c. The local news was on TV, and Jeremy wanted to watch his favorite movie on it.
  d. While the local news was on T.V. Jeremy asked we to watch his favorite movie.

28. Three of the sentences below contain one or more grammatical or spelling errors. Select the answer choice that is correct as is.
  a. Officer DeAngelo phoned his partner every day when he was in the hospital.
  b. When his partner was in the hospital, Officer DeAngelo phoned him every day.
  c. When in the hospital, a phone call was made every day by Officer DeAngelo to his partner.
  d. His partner received a phone call from Officer DeAngelo every day while he was in the hospital.

29. Three of the sentences below contain one or more grammatical or spelling errors. Select the answer choice that is correct as is.
  a. Some of the case transcripts I have to type are very long, but that doesn't bother one if the cases are interesting.
  b. Some of the case transcripts I have to type are very long, but that doesn't bother you if the cases are interesting.
  c. Some of the case transcripts I have to type are very long, but it doesn't bother a person if the cases are interesting.
  d. Some of the case transcripts I have to type are very long, but that doesn't bother me if the cases are interesting.

30. Three of the sentences below contain one or more grammatical or spelling errors. Select the answer choice that is correct as is.
  a. For three weeks, the Merryville Fire Chief received taunting calls from an arsonist, who would not say where he intended to set the next fire.
  b. The Merryville Fire Chief received taunting calls from an arsonist, but he would not say where he intended to set the next fire, for three weeks.
  c. He would not say where he intended to set the next fire, but for three weeks the Merryville Fire Chief received taunting calls from an arsonist.
  d. The Merryville Police Chief received taunting calls from an arsonist for three weeks, not saying where he intended to set the next fire.

31. Identify the sentence that contains a mistake in capitalization, punctuation, grammar, or spelling. If you find no mistakes, select choice **d**.
  a. Science and math are my two best subjects.
  b. We met senator Moynihan at a conference last June.
  c. Did you see the movie *Babe*?
  d. no mistakes

32. Identify the sentence that contains a mistake in capitalization, punctuation, grammar, or spelling. If you find no mistakes, select choice **d**.
  a. "Why does the weekend seem so short," the child asked?
  b. "I will provide a study guide for the exam," the teacher said.
  c. "He is not qualified," argued the executive.
  d. no mistakes

33. Identify the sentence that contains a mistake in capitalization, punctuation, grammar, or spelling. If you find no mistakes, select choice **d**.
  a. He's the best dancer in the school.
  b. We were planning to go, but the meeting was canceled.
  c. "Okay," she said, I'll go with you."
  d. no mistakes

34. Identify the sentence that contains a mistake in capitalization, punctuation, grammar, or spelling. If you find no mistakes, select choice **d**.
  a. I have learned to appreciate Mozart's music.
  b. My cousin Veronica is studying to be a Veterinarian.
  c. Mr. Shanahan is taller than Professor Martin.
  d. no mistakes

35. Identify the sentence that contains a mistake in capitalization, punctuation, grammar, or spelling. If you find no mistakes, select choice **d**.
  a. The industrial revolution began in Europe.
  b. Is Labor Day a national holiday?
  c. General Patton was a four-star general.
  d. no mistakes

36. Identify the sentence that contains a mistake in capitalization, punctuation, grammar, or spelling. If you find no mistakes, select choice **d**.
  a. Betsy did not understand the math formula.
  b. Allergies to Peanuts are common among children.
  c. My dog likes to sleep on the couch during the day.
  d. no mistakes

37. Look at the three numbered sentences below. Choose the sentence order that would result in the best paragraph.
  (1) From these teenagers, Philip learned compassion for the poor; from him, they learned that a good deed can pay off big-time.
  (2) After the hit man nearly succeeded in killing him, Philip, dazed and gravely injured, wandered into a bad part of town and was rescued by a couple of homeless teenagers.
  (3) Philip Barnes, a wealthy, 60-year-old CEO of a megaconglomerate, was a happy man until he learned that his wife and business partner had hired a hit man to do away with him.
  a. 1, 2, 3
  b. 2, 3, 1
  c. 3, 1, 2
  d. 3, 2, 1

38. Look at the three numbered sentences below. Choose the sentence order that would result in the best paragraph.
  (1) The reason for so many injuries and fatalities is that a vehicle can generate heat of up to 1,500° F.
  (2) Firefighters know that the dangers of motor-vehicle fires are too often overlooked.
  (3) In the United States, one out of five fires involves motor vehicles, resulting each year in 600 deaths, 2,600 civilian injuries, and 1,200 injuries to firefighters.
  a. 1, 2, 3
  b. 1, 3, 2
  c. 2, 3, 1
  d. 3, 2, 1

39. Look at the four numbered sentences below. Choose the sentence order that would result in the best paragraph.

(1) The course titles will be Yoga for Teenagers; Hip Hop Dance: Learning the Latest Moves; and Creative Journaling for Teens: Discovering the Writer Within.

(2) The latter course will not be held at the Allendale Cultural Center.

(3) The Allendale Cultural Center has expanded its arts programming to include classes for young adults.

(4) It will meet at the Allendale Public Library.

a. 2, 4, 1, 3
b. 1, 4, 2, 3
c. 1, 2, 3, 4
d. 3, 1, 2, 4

40. Look at the three numbered sentences below. Choose the sentence order that would result in the best paragraph.

(1) But to keep the Peace Corps dynamic with fresh ideas, no staff member can work for the agency for more than five years.

(2) People who work for the Peace Corps do so because they want to.

(3) One of the missions of the Peace Corps is to help the people of interested countries meet their need for trained men and women.

a. 1, 2, 3
b. 3, 2, 1
c. 2, 3, 1
d. 3, 1, 2

41. If a squad car travels at the speed of 45 mph for 15 minutes, how far will it travel? (Distance = Rate × Time)

a. 11.25 miles
b. 70 miles
c. 725 miles
d. 1,125 miles

42. A train must travel to a certain town in 6 days. The town is 3,450 miles away. How many miles must the train average each day to reach its destination?

a. 500 miles
b. 525 miles
c. 550 miles
d. 575 miles

43. State Trooper Jancieski drives 2,052 miles in 6 days, stopping at two towns each day. How many miles does she average between stops?

a. 170 miles
b. 200 miles
c. 225 miles
d. 300 miles

44. A police car uses 24 gallons of gas to travel 1,824 miles. How many miles per gallon does the car get?

a. 24 miles per gallon
b. 76 miles per gallon
c. 1,848 miles per gallon
d. 43,776 miles per gallon

45. The cost of a list of supplies for a police station is as follows: $19.98, $52.20, $12.64, and $7.79. What is the total cost?

a. $91.30
b. $92.61
c. $93.60
d. $93.61

46. A police station receives an emergency call on August 3 at 10:42 P.M. and another emergency call at 1:19 A.M. on August 4. How much time has elapsed between emergency calls?

a. 1 hour 37 minutes
b. 2 hours 23 minutes
c. 2 hours 37 minutes
d. 3 hours 23 minutes

47. State Trooper Green earns $26,000 a year. If he receives a 4.5% salary increase, how much will he earn?
a. $26,450
b. $27,170
c. $27,260
d. $29,200

48. If it takes four state troopers 1 hour and 45 minutes to perform a particular job, how long would it take one state trooper working at the same rate to perform the same task alone?
a. 4.5 hours
b. 5 hours
c. 7 hours
d. 7.5 hours

49. $91,101 - 71,175 + 1,223 =$
a. 1,187
b. 21,149
c. 121,149
d. 161,132

50. What is the value of $43,254 \div 8$, rounded to the nearest whole number?
a. 5,000
b. 5,400
c. 5,406
d. 5,407

51. Which of the following choices is divisible by both 7 and 8?
a. 42
b. 78
c. 112
d. 128

52. If one gallon of water weighs 8.35 pounds, a 25-gallon container of water would most nearly weigh
a. 173 pounds.
b. 200 pounds.
c. 209 pounds.
d. 215 pounds.

53. $292 \times 50 =$
a. 14,600
b. 14,500
c. 10,500
d. 1,450

54. $7(87 - 3) - (12 \times 12) =$
a. 444
b. 462
c. 486
d. 4,474

55. The state law enforcement agency is ordering new bullet-proof vests for each of its departments. If 17 vests are ordered for each of the 11 departments, how many vests should be ordered all together?
a. 16
b. 178
c. 187
d. 1,187

Directions: Answer questions 56 through 60 based on the following map. The arrows indicate traffic flow. One arrow indicates a one-way street going in the direction of the arrow; two arrows represent a two-way street. You are not allowed to go the wrong way on a one-way street.

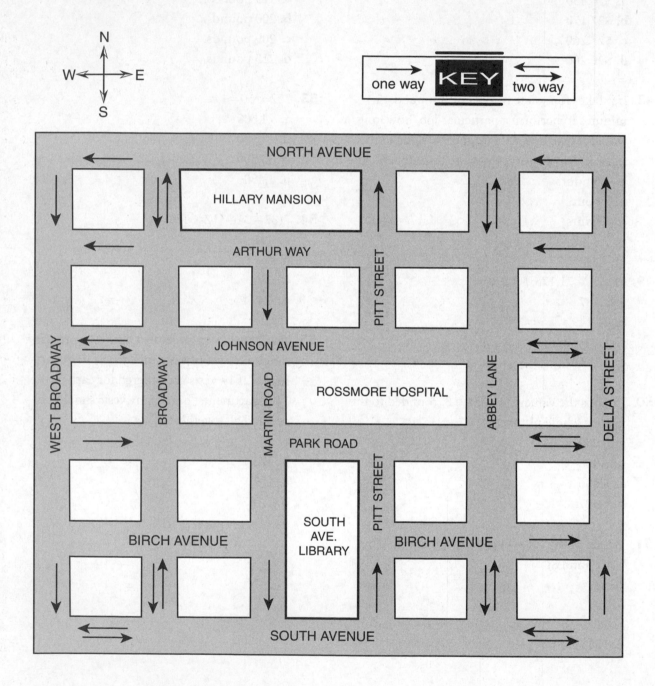

56. Officer Lazere is spending her lunch break at the South Avenue Library, which faces South Avenue. She gets a call of a burglary at the Hillary Mansion, the entrance to which faces North Avenue. What is Officer Lazere's most direct route to the Hillary Mansion?
   a. Go east on South Avenue, then north on Abbey Lane to North Avenue, then west on North Avenue to the Hillary Mansion.
   b. Go east on South Avenue, then north on Pitt Street, then west on North Avenue to the Hillary Mansion.
   c. Go west on South Avenue, then north on West Broadway, then east on North Avenue to the Hillary Mansion.
   d. Go west on South Avenue, then north on Broadway to North Avenue, then east on North Avenue to the Hillary Mansion.

57. Officer Lew is southbound on Martin Road, and has just crossed Park Road. Dispatch assigns a family disturbance call to him and sends him to a residence at the corner of Arthur Way and Della Street. What is Officer Lew's most direct route to the residence?
   a. Make a U-turn on Martin Road, then go north on Martin Road to Arthur Way, and then east on Arthur Way to the residence.
   b. Continue south on Martin Road, then go east on South Avenue, then north on Pitt Street, then east on Park Road, then north on Abbey Lane, and then east on Arthur Way to the residence.
   c. Continue south on Martin Road, then go east on South Avenue, and then north on Della Street to the residence.
   d. Continue south on Martin Road, then go east on Birch Avenue, and then north on Della Street to the residence.

58. Officer Stanley is heading south on Abbey Lane. She makes a left turn on Johnson Avenue, a left on Della Street, a left on Arthur Lane, and finally a left on Martin Road. Which way is Officer Stanley facing?
   a. north
   b. south
   c. east
   d. west

59. There is a report of a driver going the wrong way on Martin Road. If the report is true, which way is this car traveling?
   a. north
   b. south
   c. east
   d. west

60. State Trooper Gurick is heading south on Broadway. At Park Road he makes a left. He drives past Rossmore Hospital and at the corner makes a right. From there he drives two blocks south. Where is he?
   a. northwest corner of Della Street
   b. southwest corner of Della Street
   c. southeast corner of Abbey Lane
   d. southwest corner of Abbey Lane

Directions: Answer questions 61 through 70 based on the following map. The arrows indicate traffic flow. One arrow indicates a one-way street going in the direction of the arrow; no arrows represent a two-way street. You are not allowed to go the wrong way on a one-way street. Smaller boxes within the building outline indicate building entranceways.

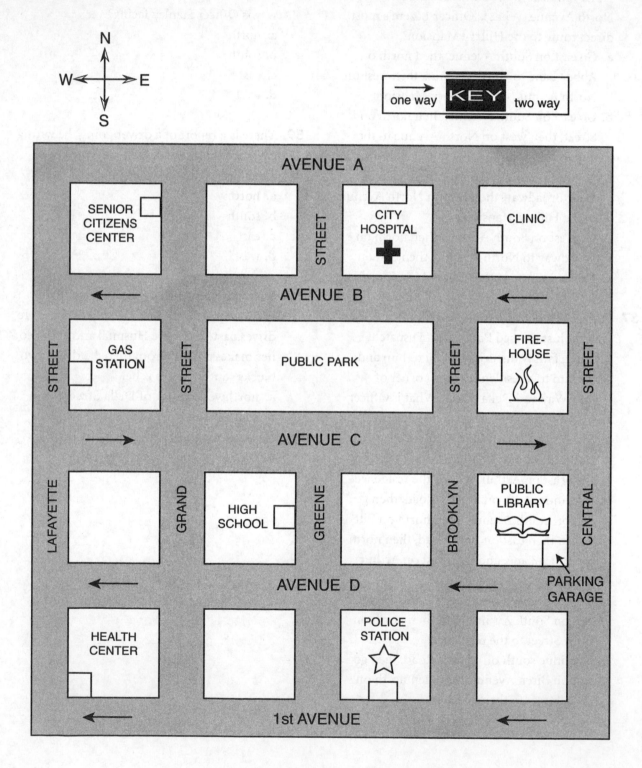

61. While you are on foot patrol, an elderly man stops you in front of the firehouse and asks you to help him find the senior citizens' center. You should tell him to
   a. walk across the street to the senior citizens' center.
   b. walk south to Avenue C, make a right, and walk west on Avenue C, make a right on Grand Street and walk up to the senior citizens' center.
   c. walk north to Avenue B and then west on Avenue B to the end of the park, make a right and go one block.
   d. walk north to Avenue B and then west on Avenue B to Lafayette Street, make a right, and go one block.

62. The head librarian needs gasoline for his automobile. He is leaving the Avenue D garage exit from the library. His quickest legal route is to go
   a. north on Central Street to Avenue C and west on Avenue C to the gas station.
   b. west on Brooklyn Street to Avenue B and north on Avenue B to the gas station.
   c. west on Avenue D to Grand Street and north on Grand Street to the gas station.
   d. west on Avenue D to Lafayette Street and north on Lafayette Street to the gas station.

63. You are dispatched from the police station to an altercation occurring at the northwest corner of the public park. Which is the most direct legal way to drive there?
   a. east to Central Street, north on Central Street to Avenue B, and west on Avenue B to Grand Street
   b. west to Grand Street and north on Grand Street to Avenue B
   c. east to Brooklyn Street, north on Brooklyn Street to Avenue B, and west on Avenue B to Grand Street
   d. west to Greene Street, north on Greene Street to Avenue C, and east on Avenue C to Brooklyn Street

64. Your spouse is a nurse at the health center. When leaving work, she discovers her car battery is dead. She parked near the police station on 1st Avenue. What is the shortest legal route for the tow truck to take to the gas station?
   a. west on 1st Avenue, then north on Lafayette Street to the gas station entrance
   b. east on 1st Avenue, then north on Central Street to the parking garage entrance
   c. north on Greene Street, then west on Avenue C to the gas station entrance
   d. west on 1st Avenue, right on Grand Street, then right on Avenue C to the gas station entrance

65. After responding to a call at the firehouse, you are ready to drive back to the police station for the end of your shift. What is the quickest legal route?
  a. south on Brooklyn Street and west on 1st Avenue to the police station
  b. north on Brooklyn Street, west on Avenue A, south on Lafayette Street, and east on 1st Avenue to the police station
  c. north on Brooklyn Street and east on 1st Avenue to the police station
  d. south on Brooklyn Street, west on Avenue C, south on Grand Street, and east on 1st Avenue to the police station

66. Your unit has been called to the scene of a car accident at the senior citizens' center at the southwest corner of the building. While there, dispatch notifies you of an alarm going off at the high school. What is the quickest route for your unit to take from the center to the high school?
  a. Turn south on Lafayette Street, east on Avenue D, then north on Greene Street.
  b. Turn north on Lafayette Street, east on Avenue A, south on Brooklyn Street, west on Avenue D, then north on Greene Street.
  c. Turn south on Lafayette Street, east on Avenue C, then south on Greene Street.
  d. Turn south on Lafayette Street, east on Avenue D, north on Grand Street, west on Avenue C, then south on Greene Street.

67. State Trooper Park has just come off duty and is driving east on Avenue A. He makes a right on Brooklyn Street, then a left on Avenue C, a right on Central Street, a right on Avenue D, and then another right on Greene Street. What is he facing?
  a. the police station
  b. the firehouse
  c. the public park
  d. the senior citizens' center

68. A woman faints in the public park at the intersection of Greene Street and Avenue C. If she wants to seek medical attention, which route would be the quickest?
  a. east on Avenue C, then north on Central Street, then west on Avenue B, and north on Brooklyn Street to the clinic
  b. east on Avenue C, then north on Brooklyn Street to the clinic
  c. south on Greene Street, then west on Avenue D, then south on Lafayette Street to the health center
  d. west on Avenue C, then south on Lafayette Street to the health center

69. A state trooper is escorting a pregnant woman from the corner of Central Street and Avenue D to the city hospital. What is the most direct legal route for the trooper to take?
  a. north on Central Street, then west on Avenue B, then north on Greene Street, then east on Avenue A
  b. north on Central Street, then west on Avenue B, then north on Grand Street, then east on Avenue A
  c. north on Central Street, then west on Avenue B, then north on Greene Street, then west on Avenue A
  d. north on Central Street, then west on Avenue A, then south on Brooklyn Street

70. A student leaves high school and needs to go to the public library. She will need to park in the parking garage. Taking the most direct route, how many turns will she make?
  a. 1
  b. 2
  c. 3
  d. 4

Directions: You will be given ten minutes to study the following four wanted posters. Try to remember as many details as you can. You may not take any notes at this time. Then, answer questions 71 through 80 without referring back to the wanted posters.

WANTED FOR ASSAULT

NAME:	James Beckham
AGE:	31
HEIGHT:	5'11"
WEIGHT:	215
RACE:	Caucasian
HAIR COLOR:	blonde
EYE COLOR:	green
IDENTIFYING MARKS:	piercing in left ear, tattoo of woman's face on left shoulder
NOTE:	carries a gun and must be considered dangerous; has a heroin habit

WANTED FOR ARMED ROBBERY

NAME:	Manuel Martinez
AGE:	34
HEIGHT:	5'8"
WEIGHT:	198
RACE:	Hispanic
HAIR COLOR:	black
EYE COLOR:	brown
IDENTIFYING MARKS:	tattoo on left shoulder that says "Mother"; scar on right shoulder from previous gunshot wound
NOTE:	has family in the Dominican Republic

WANTED FOR RAPE

NAME:	David Torsiello
AGE:	43
HEIGHT:	5'9"
WEIGHT:	180
RACE:	Caucasian
HAIR COLOR:	brown
EYE COLOR:	brown
IDENTIFYING MARKS:	missing right eye from industrial accident; often wears a patch over right eye
NOTE:	carries a hunting knife; tends to confront victims outside their residences and force them inside

WANTED FOR MURDER

NAME:	Fernando Gomez
AGE:	32
HEIGHT:	5'7"
WEIGHT:	178
RACE:	Hispanic
HAIR COLOR:	brown
EYE COLOR:	brown
IDENTIFYING MARKS:	scar on upper thigh, tattoo of Mexican flag on upper right arm; lost thumb in a car accident
NOTE:	last seen in stolen black 1998 Nissan Altima

71. Which suspect was involved in an industrial accident?

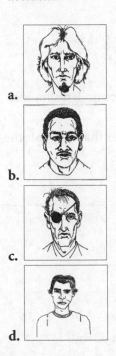

a.

b.

c.

d.

72. Which suspect might flee the country for the Dominican Republic?

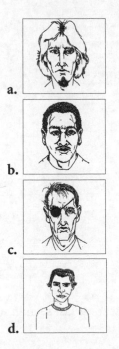

a.

b.

c.

d.

73. Which suspect has green eyes?

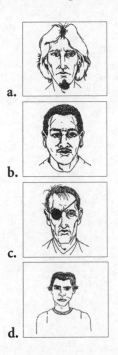

a.

b.

c.

d.

74. An officer observes a suspect lurking outside an apartment building as a woman returns home from her night shift. Which suspect has a history of such behavior?

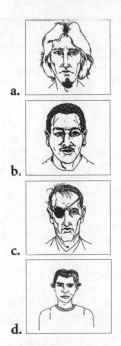

a.

b.

c.

d.

75. Which suspect is not in his thirties?

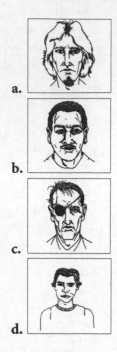

a.

b.

c.

d.

76. Which suspect can you assume is of Mexican heritage?

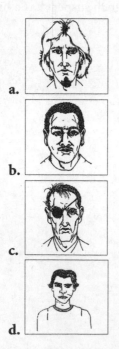

a.

b.

c.

d.

77. What is an identifiable mark of this suspect?

a. tattoo of woman's face on left shoulder
b. scar on upper thigh
c. tattoo on left shoulder that says "Mother"
d. scar on right shoulder

78. The suspect wanted for _____ is missing a finger.
a. rape
b. assault
c. armed robbery
d. murder

79. Which suspect has a drug habit?

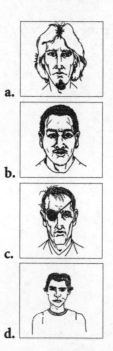

a.

b.

c.

d.

80. Suspect Fernando Gomez was last seen in what kind of stolen car?
a. black 1999 Nissan Altima
b. black 1998 Nissan Altima
c. black 1998 Nissan Pathfinder
d. blue 1998 Nissan Altima

Directions: Read the following passage, then answer questions 81 through 87.

First Bank has recently had a problem with teller drawers coming up short. Banks anticipate a certain amount of this kind of loss, so bank officials were not overly concerned until they began to notice a pattern. Every two or three days, for a period of six months, the cash at teller station 3 would be short; occasionally, another drawer would be short. Vice President Ralph Jensen reported the pattern and authorities were called. There are a total of 12 teller stations, but it is rare that all 12 are open at once. The number of stations that is open depends on the number of tellers working and the amount of business being transacted.

During the course of the investigation, the following statements were made:

1. Vice President Jensen stated that he personally tallied the drawer totals at the end of each business day; on days when he did not work, the tallies were done by Vice President Cruz.
2. Gloria Dennis, the teller supervisor, said that she usually opened teller stations in order; that is, station 1 would be opened first, station 2 second, and so on. Each teller is assigned to a station for the shift, but they cover for each other on breaks.
3. Dennis also stated that there is an average of five stations open at any given time, but sometimes as few as two stations are open.
4. Teller Dave Feller said that the tellers came and went from work at staggered times and that more than half of the tellers only worked part-time.
5. Teller Marilyn Nguyen said that Felicia Ralston, another teller, had recently gotten divorced and complained that her ex-husband was not paying child support.
6. Vice President Enrique Cruz stated that the tallies had never been short on the days he did them.

7. Teller Felicia Ralston said that recently a new customer, John Mitchell, had been coming in every few days and often only wanted change for a large bill. Ralston thought he might be a drug dealer.
8. Teller Mike Richards said that, although tellers were not assigned to particular stations all the time, each teller had a favorite station, and Dennis normally let them work at those stations. Richards said that both Ralston and Nguyen liked station 3.
9. Head of Personnel Heidi Sargent checked the records and said that tellers Nguyen, Ralston, Richards, Ford, Beloit, and Rawlings were all working on days when station 3 came up short. In addition, Gloria Dennis and Ralph Jensen worked all of those days. Teller Feller worked all but two of those days.
10. Teller Sarah Beloit said that she saw Vice President Jensen and Teller Richards have lunch together once or twice a week for the last six months.

81. Which of the following statements could be an attempt by one teller to divert suspicion to another teller?
a. Statements 1 and 4
b. Statements 3 and 6
c. Statements 7 and 10
d. Statements 5 and 8

82. Which of the following statements casts suspicion on Ralph Jensen?
a. Statements 6 and 10
b. Statements 1 and 6
c. Statements 1 and 9
d. Statements 6 and 9

83. Which of the following statements is hearsay?
a. Statement 10
b. Statement 8
c. Statement 7
d. Statement 5

84. Which of the following statements indicates that the drawer shortage might not be a case of employee theft?
a. Statement 7
b. Statement 9
c. Statement 3
d. Statement 5

85. Which of the following statements may offer a motive for the theft?
a. Statement 4
b. Statement 6
c. Statement 5
d. Statement 7

86. Which of the following statements could lead to the conclusion that there is more than one thief?
a. Statement 7
b. Statement 5
c. Statement 8
d. Statement 10

87. Which of the following statements provides the strongest alibi?
a. Statement 7
b. Statement 9
c. Statement 5
d. Statement 3

Directions: Read the following passage, then answer questions 88 through 96.

Wendell March called the local police and said he had evidence that Denise Walker, another student, was spending counterfeit money. Upon questioning, Wendell said he had seen Denise at school carrying several hundred dollars. When he asked her where she got it, she said from her brother, Herb. Later, Wendell heard her tell another student that the money was not real and that there was a great deal more of it. Local police called the Secret Service. During the course of the investigation, the following statements were made:

1. Student Buffy Slater said that Denise had a lot of new clothes lately.
2. Student Todd Carlson said that Wendell asked Denise out three times, but she always turned him down.
3. Margy Adams, cashier at the Sound Wave, said Denise had purchased several new CDs in the past week, always paying cash.
4. Principal Mark Po said that Denise's brother Herb had been a troublemaker who consistently made poor grades, was expelled from school, and had never graduated.
5. Teacher Robert Moss said that Wendell had seemed troubled lately and he heard Wendell's parents were getting divorced.
6. Counselor Rachel Foster said that Herb Walker was a genius, with an IQ over 150, and was an excellent artist.
7. Denise Walker said that her father had recently gotten a promotion at the paper factory where he worked and her mother had just gone back to work as a bookkeeper.
8. Heather Mason, Denise's friend, said that Denise had recently had a lot more money to spend when they went to the mall.
9. Herb Walker said that he suspected Denise might be dealing drugs.
10. April Givins said she was Wendell's girlfriend and had been for two years.

88. Which statement might be an attempt to divert the investigation?
a. Statement 9
b. Statement 10
c. Statement 5
d. Statement 6

89. Which two statements appear to corroborate each other?
- **a.** Statements 2 and 5
- **b.** Statements 4 and 6
- **c.** Statements 3 and 8
- **d.** Statements 7 and 9

90. Which statement along with statement 2 is most damaging to Wendell March?
- **a.** Statement 4
- **b.** Statement 7
- **c.** Statement 10
- **d.** Statement 5

91. Which statement is purely circumstantial evidence?
- **a.** Statement 10
- **b.** Statement 4
- **c.** Statement 1
- **d.** Statement 7

92. Which statement leads one to be suspicious of information given by Herb Walker?
- **a.** Statement 4
- **b.** Statement 6
- **c.** Statement 7
- **d.** Statement 9

93. Which statement indicates the allegations against Denise Walker may not be true?
- **a.** Statement 9
- **b.** Statement 8
- **c.** Statement 5
- **d.** Statement 7

94. Which statement is most damaging to Herb Walker?
- **a.** Statement 3
- **b.** Statement 7
- **c.** Statement 9
- **d.** Statement 6

95. Which statement indicates that Wendell March has a motive to lie?
- **a.** Statement 2
- **b.** Statement 5
- **c.** Statement 7
- **d.** Statement 8

96. Which two statements seem to be contradictory?
- **a.** Statements 1 and 7
- **b.** Statements 4 and 6
- **c.** Statements 7 and 9
- **d.** Statements 5 and 10

97. Abraham has been arrested one more time than Jolson. Kirk has been arrested one less time than Jolson and one more time than Sanchez. Jolson has been arrested seven times. How many times has Sanchez been arrested?
- **a.** six times
- **b.** five times
- **c.** four times
- **d.** eight times

Directions: Read the following passage, then answer question 98.

When a trooper believes a driver who has been stopped is driving under the under the influence of alcohol or narcotics, the trooper should do the following in the given order:

1. Have the driver get out of the vehicle.
2. Demonstrate each field sobriety test and request that the driver perform each of the requested tests.
3. If the driver fails the tests, place the driver under arrest, making sure to explain to the driver why he or she is being arrested.
4. Call the dispatcher to request a vehicle to tow the driver's car to a holding facility.

98. Trooper Jiminez is working at a driving checkpoint where she is obligated to stop every third vehicle. Her third stop involves the ninth car that has travelled through the checkpoint. She informs the driver that he will have to perform a number of tests to prove his sobriety and immediately begins to demonstrate the first test. The driver exits the car, performs the first and subsequent tests satisfactorily, and is allowed by Trooper Jiminez to return to his vehicle and continue on his journey. Under these circumstances, the actions taken by Trooper Jiminez were
- **a.** proper, because she did not arrest a driver who successfully performed the field sobriety tests.
- **b.** improper, because she demonstrated the first test before having the driver exit his vehicle.
- **c.** improper, because she did not stop every third car.
- **d.** proper, because she did stop every third car.

99. The owner of the Sun Times car dealership tells Officer Chervenack that someone is stealing running boards and other parts from the vans he has parked in the south lot sometime after 10:30 P.M. Officer Chervenack decides to patrol the area carefully. Which of the following situations should she investigate?
- **a.** After midnight, a male in his early 20s is walking up and down rows of new pickups parked near the edge of the dealership.
- **b.** After midnight, a panel truck pulls out of the vacant lot next to the dealership near where the vans are lined up.
- **c.** After midnight, two youths in baggy pants and T-shirts are rollerblading in and out of the new cars on the Sun Times lot.
- **d.** After midnight, a station wagon drives into the lot and stops near the door to the main show room. A man gets out and unloads a mop, a bucket, and a broom.

100. Winslow Elementary School is having a criminal mischief problem. Windows are being broken out at the school between 7:00 P.M. and 6:00 A.M. Officer Link has talked to the school principal and is keeping a closer eye on the school. Which of the following situations should he investigate?
- **a.** At 1:00 A.M., Officer Link watches a man carrying a grocery sack cut through the school yard and come out on the other side of the school grounds. The officer can see a loaf of bread protruding out of the sack.
- **b.** At 11:00 P.M., a car pulls up in the school parking lot. Officer Link sees the driver turn on the cabin light and unfold a map.
- **c.** Around 11:30 P.M., Officer Link passes the school and sees two figures come out from behind one of the classroom buildings. They stop when they see him and then start walking, each in a different direction.
- **d.** At 9:00 P.M., several teenagers skateboard into the parking lot, set up a small wooden ramp, and practice skateboarding tricks.

Answers

1. c. The passage describes how Chief Justice Burger was traditional in some regards, but he also demonstrated characteristics considered untraditional.

2. a. The good faith exception only applies if law enforcement believes they have a valid warrant. If they knowingly violate the need for a warrant, any evidence found falls under the exclusionary rule.

3. c. The definition of a strict constructionist is stated in the second sentence of the second paragraph.

4. d. The first three choices are false. The passage indicates he looked to Scandinavian countries such as Norway and Sweden for ideas about how to create an efficient criminal justice system.

5. c. Officer Rayburn was on the scene first. The other officers arrived later, and the police operator was never on the scene.

6. a. The Woolf vehicle had stopped at the "T" intersection before turning on to Morton, so there must have been a stop sign on Farley. Burroughs was cited for failing to obey a stop sign on Morton.

7. b. Mr. Wilcox told Lieutenant Watts that the armored truck struck the car he was riding in, driven by Mr. Woolf, and that the Woolf vehicle subsequently hit Mrs. Moreno's car.

8. d. Officer Parisi examined skid marks, which show that the armored truck was braking.

9. a. The green sedan, with Mr. Woolf driving, had been driving down Farley before turning on to Morton at the "T" intersection.

10. c. Mrs. Moreno was in her house at the time of the accident, so you can conclude that her car was unoccupied.

11. c. This answer encompasses most of the information in the passage. Choice **a** is incorrect because the first sentence suggests that becoming hardened is unavoidable. Choices **b** and **d** are mentioned in the passage but are too narrow to be the main idea.

12. b. See the first two sentences of the passage.

13. c. The passage claims that becoming jaded is inevitable.

14. c. The passage is mainly about how the flame retardant failed to work.

15. d. See the last sentence of the second paragraph.

16. a. See the first sentence of the third paragraph: …*it is now clear that the retardant failed to work in almost all cases.*

17. d. The passage states that Mr. Pickens thought Mr. Morrow's companions should be arrested. Mr. Morrow himself is unconscious. Mr. Evans and Mr. Roland would probably be afraid of being blamed for Mr. Morrow's condition.

18. c. Mr. Morrow chugged a pint of whiskey in 15 minutes and was comatose. He needed medical attention.

19. a. According to Mr. Pickens, Mr. Morrow began to chug the whiskey at 12:10 and did so in about 15 minutes.

20. c. The officers were parked at this location when they were instructed to respond to a call from Tucker's Tavern. All the other choices are inaccurate according to facts in the passage.

21. c. This is the best choice because it is in the positive: *Because he asked, we all went to Eddie's favorite Japanese restaurant to celebrate his 40th birthday.*

22. d. The series of items in the underlined portion of the sentence should be parallel. Only choice **d** has the appropriate parallel construction. Because all three elements in the series follow *is responsible for,* choice **a** is clearly incorrect because the verb *must generate* breaks the parallel flow of the series. In choice **b,** the word *for* breaks the parallel flow. In choice **c,** the series changes and the first two elements, *controlling floods* and *generating electric power*, are parallel, but the third element, *soil conservation*, is not.

23. a. This sentence requires that the comparison between *culture* and *biology* be logical and clear. Choice **b** is wrong because the use of the preposition *with* is confusing and does not observe standard usage conventions. The phrase *somewhat better* in choice **c** makes no sense. Choice **d** results in an unclear comparison.

24. a. This is the only choice that makes a complete and grammatically correct sentence.

25. a. When constructing sentences, unnecessary shifts in verb tenses should be avoided. Choice **a** is best because all three verbs in the sentence indicate that the action occurred in the past (*had been covering, became,* and *was called*). In choice **b**, there is a shift to the present (*becomes*). Choice **c** begins in the present (*is covering, becomes*), then shifts to the past (*called*). Choice **d** makes two tense shifts.

26. a. In choice **b**, the cat seems to be renting the room. In choice **c**, it's unclear whether *he* refers to the cat or to Mr. Morris. Choice **d** implies that Mr. Morris rented a room to himself.

27. b. This is the only grammatically correct sentence with no errors.

28. b. In the other choices, the pronoun reference is ambiguous; it is unclear who is in the hospital.

29. d. The other answers contain unnecessary shifts in person from *I* to *one, you,* and *a person*.

30. a. The other choices are unclear because they are awkwardly constructed, obscuring who intends to set the fire.

31. b. *Senator* should be capitalized because it refers to a particular senator.

32. a. The question mark should replace a comma and come before the quotation marks at the end of the question, not the end of the entire sentence.

33. c. To set off the dialogue, there should be quotation marks before the contraction *I'll*.

34. b. *Veterinarian* is not a proper noun and should not be capitalized.

35. a. *Industrial Revolution* is a proper noun and should be capitalized.

36. b. *Peanuts* is not a proper noun and therefore should not be capitalized.

37. d. This is the correct chronological order of the events described in the paragraph.

38. c. Sentence 2 gives an overview of what the paragraph is about. Sentence 3 gives specific reasons why sentence 2 is correct. Sentence 1 gives the reason why sentence 3 is correct.

39. d. Sentence 3 states the main topic about the Allendale Cultural Center. Sentence 1 adds information to the main topic of sentence 3. Sentence 2 states an exception to the first two statements, while sentence 4 adds information to sentence 2.

40. b. Sentence 3 is the topic sentence and states the purpose of the Peace Corps. Sentence 2 describes the kind of people who join the Peace Corps. Sentence 3 gives a stipulation for the people who join.

41. a. Answering this question requires converting 15 minutes to 0.25 hour, which is the time, and then using the formula 45 mph × 0.25 hour = 11.25 miles.

42. d. To find the average, divide the total number of miles, 3,450, by 6 days.

43. a. This is a two-step division problem: 2,052 miles ÷ 6 days = 342 miles per day, and 342 miles per day ÷ 2 stops = 171 miles between stops.

44. b. Take the total number of miles and find the average by dividing: 1,824 ÷ 24 gallons = 76 miles per gallon.

45. b. You need to add all the numbers together to solve this problem.

46. c. Subtraction and addition will solve this problem. From 10:42 to 12:42, two hours have elapsed. From 12:42 to 1:00, another 18 minutes have elapsed (60 − 42 = 18). Then from 1:00 to 1:19, there are another 19 minutes. 2 hours + 18 minutes + 19 minutes = 2 hours and 37 minutes, choice **c.**

47. b. There are three steps involved in solving this problem. First, convert 4.5% to a decimal: 0.045. Multiply that by $26,000 to find out how much the salary increases. Finally, add the result ($1,170) to the original salary of $26,000 to find out the new salary, $27,170.

48. c. To solve the problem, first you have to convert the total time to minutes (105 minutes), then multiply by 4 (420 minutes), then convert the answer back to hours by dividing by 60 minutes to arrive at the final answer (7 hours). Or, you can multiply hours by 4 to arrive at the same answer.

49. b. Do this problem in the order it is presented; first subtract 91,101 − 71,175 = 19,926. Then add 19,926 + 1,223 = 21,149.

50. d. 43,254 ÷ 8 is equal to 5,406.75. Rounded to the nearest whole number, this is equal to 5,407.

51. c. 112 is divisible by both 7 and 8 because each can divide into 112 without a remainder. 112 ÷ 7 = 16 and 112 ÷ 8 = 14. Choice **a** is divisible only by 7, choice **b** is not divisible by either, and choice **d** is divisible only by 8.

52. c. To solve the problem, take the weight of one gallon of water (8.35) and multiply it by the number of gallons (25): 8.35 × 25 = 208.75. Now, round to the nearest unit to get 209 pounds.

53. a. The correct answer to this multiplication problem is 14,600. An incorrect answer is likely an error in computation, particularly in not carrying digits to the next place.

54. a. Perform the operations in the parentheses first: 87 − 3 = 84 from the first set and 12 × 12 = 144 from the second set. The expression is now 7(84) − 144. Multiply 7 by 84 to get 588 and then subtract: 588 − 144 = 444.

55. c. Multiply the number of departments (11) by the number of vests (17); 11 × 17 = 187.

56. a. This the most direct route to the Hillary Mansion and requires the fewest changes in direction. Choice **b** requires the officer to drive through the Rossmore Hospital. Choice **c** takes the officer the wrong way up West Broadway. Choice **d** takes the officer the wrong way on North Avenue.

57. c. This route requires the fewest number of turns. Choice **a** is wrong because Martin Road is a one-way street. Choice **b** requires a number of turns and goes the wrong way on Arthur Way. Choice **d** requires the officer to drive through the South Avenue Library.

58. b. The left on Johnson Avenue turns Officer Stanley east, the left on Della turns her north, the left on Arthur Lane turns her west, and the left on Martin Road turns her south.

59. a. Because Martin Road is one-way going north-south, the car must be headed north.

60. d. If Officer Gurick makes a left on Park Road, he is heading east. If he drives past Rossmore Hospital and makes a right onto Abbey Lane, he is headed south. Two more blocks south brings him to the southwest corner of Abbey Lane.

61. c. Choice **a** takes the man to the park, not to the senior citizens' center. Choice **b** takes the man too far south. Choice **d** takes him to Lafayette Street, but the entrance to the senior citizens' center is on Grand Street.

62. d. Choice **a** takes the librarian the wrong way on Avenue C. Choice **b** shows the wrong directions for the streets—Brooklyn Street runs north-south, and Avenue B runs east-west. Choice **c** leaves the librarian one block east of the gas station.

63. b. Choices **a** and **c** take you the wrong way on 1st Avenue. Choice **d** will get you to the

southeast, not the northwest, corner of
the park.

64. a. Choice **b** involves going in the wrong direction
on 1st Avenue. Choice **c** involves going in the
wrong direction on Avenue C. Choice **d** takes
you east, away from the gas station.

65. a. Choice **b** is less direct and involves going the
wrong way on 1st Avenue. Choice **c** will lead
you away from 1st Avenue, not toward it.
Choice **d** takes you the wrong way on Avenue
C and 1st Avenue.

66. c. Choices **a** and **d** direct your unit to turn the
wrong way down a one-way street. Choice **b**
requires too much backtracking because Barcelona Boulevard is a one-way street going
east. Choice **b** requires too many turns and is
the least direct route.

67. c. The final right onto Greene Street turns
Trooper Park toward the public park.

68. b. Choice **a** is not the most direct route. Choice
c is incorrect, because the clinic is closer
than the health center. Choice **d** goes down a
one-way street in the wrong direction.

69. a. Choice **b** is not the shortest route to take.
Choices **c** and **d** do not take the trooper to
the city hospital.

70. b. The student can leave the high school
entrance, make a right on Avenue C, and a
right onto Central Street.

71. c. This suspect lost his eye in an industrial accident. Another suspect lost his thumb, but
that was the result of a car accident.

72. b. Manuel Martinez has family in the Dominican Republic.

73. a. Only James Beckham has green eyes.

74. c. David Torsiello is wanted for rape and has
confronted victims outside their residences
before forcing them inside.

75. c. Suspect David Torsiello is 43 years old.

76. d. Fernando Gomez has a tattoo of the Mexican
flag, so you can assume that he is of Mexican
heritage.

77. a. James Beckham has a tattoo of a woman's
face on his left shoulder.

78. d. Fernando Gomez, who is wanted for murder,
is missing his thumb from a car accident.

79. a. James Beckham has a heroin habit.

80. b. Fernando Gomez was last seen in a stolen
black 1998 Nissan Altima.

81. d. Statements 5 and 8 contain information
provided by tellers that indicates motive or
opportunity for other tellers to have embez-
zled the money.

82. b. The fact that only Jensen and Cruz ever tally
the drawer totals, coupled with the fact that
the drawers were never short when Cruz performed the tally, casts suspicion on Jensen.

83. d. Statement 5 is a statement made without personal knowledge, simply repeating what others said.

84. a. Statement 7 presents the possibility that a
bank customer had been coming in every few
days and often he wanted only change for a
large bill.

85. c. Statement 5 indicates an employee is having
financial problems, and that is a motive for
theft. Even though a statement is hearsay, it
can still be helpful to an investigation.

86. d. Statement 10 notes that a person who is a
suspect, Jensen, is meeting regularly with a
person who has access to the teller drawers,
Teller Richards. This may indicate that the
two are involved in the theft together.

87. b. Statement 9 lists the tellers who worked on
days the drawers were short. Any teller who
worked none or only some of those days
would have a strong alibi.

88. a. Statement 9 is an attempt by Herb Walker to
divert the investigation from counterfeiting
to drugs, as well as from himself to his sister,
by alleging his sister is a drug dealer.

89. c. Statements 3 and 8 are statements from different people alleging that Denise has access
to cash.

90. d. Statement 2 indicates both a motive for trying to get Denise in trouble by making a false report and a reason why Wendell might be distraught; Statement 5 presents an additional reason for Wendell's distress and an observation of it.

91. c. Circumstantial evidence is evidence from which the presence of a principle fact of the case can be inferred. From the fact of Denise's new clothes, one can infer she has access to money to buy clothes.

92. a. Statement 4 reports past misbehavior by Herb that could indicate that he might not tell the truth.

93. d. Statement 7 provides an explanation for why Denise may have more money than usual.

94. d. Statement 6 tells investigators that Herb Walker has the ability to be a counterfeiter.

95. a. Denise's rejection of Wendell might be a motive for his calling the police and lying about her.

96. b. Statements 4 and 6 seem to be contradictory. One does not normally expect high school students with high IQs to be troublemakers who drop out (or are expelled) from school.

97. b. Sanchez has been arrested five times. Jolson has been arrested seven times, and Kirk has been arrested one less time (six). Sanchez has been arrested one less time than Kirk.

98. b. The procedure specifically states that the trooper's first action should be to have the driver exit the vehicle.

99. b. A panel truck pulling out of a vacant lot near a car dealership that has suffered a rash of theft of auto parts is suspicious. The truck would be able to hold plenty of auto parts. The two rollerbladers in choice **c** aren't likely to be able to carry off a new running board without attracting attention. The male in his early 20s in choice **a** appears to be doing what a lot of people do late at night, which is look at new cars without having to worry about sales personnel. It is not unusual for cleanup crews to arrive late at night after everyone has gone, as in choice **d**.

100. c. The odd behavior and the location of the two figures should cause the officer to investigate, given the problems the school has been having.

14 ▶ STATE TROOPER PRACTICE TEST 3

CHAPTER SUMMARY
This is the third practice test in this book based on the most commonly tested areas on the state trooper exam.

T he practice test consists of 100 multiple-choice questions in the following areas: reading comprehension, writing and information ordering, mathematics, spatial and directional orientation, memory and observation, and problem solving. You should give yourself two hours to take this practice test.

State Trooper Practice Test 3

1.	ⓐ	ⓑ	ⓒ	ⓓ
2.	ⓐ	ⓑ	ⓒ	ⓓ
3.	ⓐ	ⓑ	ⓒ	ⓓ
4.	ⓐ	ⓑ	ⓒ	ⓓ
5.	ⓐ	ⓑ	ⓒ	ⓓ
6.	ⓐ	ⓑ	ⓒ	ⓓ
7.	ⓐ	ⓑ	ⓒ	ⓓ
8.	ⓐ	ⓑ	ⓒ	ⓓ
9.	ⓐ	ⓑ	ⓒ	ⓓ
10.	ⓐ	ⓑ	ⓒ	ⓓ
11.	ⓐ	ⓑ	ⓒ	ⓓ
12.	ⓐ	ⓑ	ⓒ	ⓓ
13.	ⓐ	ⓑ	ⓒ	ⓓ
14.	ⓐ	ⓑ	ⓒ	ⓓ
15.	ⓐ	ⓑ	ⓒ	ⓓ
16.	ⓐ	ⓑ	ⓒ	ⓓ
17.	ⓐ	ⓑ	ⓒ	ⓓ
18.	ⓐ	ⓑ	ⓒ	ⓓ
19.	ⓐ	ⓑ	ⓒ	ⓓ
20.	ⓐ	ⓑ	ⓒ	ⓓ
21.	ⓐ	ⓑ	ⓒ	ⓓ
22.	ⓐ	ⓑ	ⓒ	ⓓ
23.	ⓐ	ⓑ	ⓒ	ⓓ
24.	ⓐ	ⓑ	ⓒ	ⓓ
25.	ⓐ	ⓑ	ⓒ	ⓓ
26.	ⓐ	ⓑ	ⓒ	ⓓ
27.	ⓐ	ⓑ	ⓒ	ⓓ
28.	ⓐ	ⓑ	ⓒ	ⓓ
29.	ⓐ	ⓑ	ⓒ	ⓓ
30.	ⓐ	ⓑ	ⓒ	ⓓ
31.	ⓐ	ⓑ	ⓒ	ⓓ
32.	ⓐ	ⓑ	ⓒ	ⓓ
33.	ⓐ	ⓑ	ⓒ	ⓓ
34.	ⓐ	ⓑ	ⓒ	ⓓ
35.	ⓐ	ⓑ	ⓒ	ⓓ

36.	ⓐ	ⓑ	ⓒ	ⓓ
37.	ⓐ	ⓑ	ⓒ	ⓓ
38.	ⓐ	ⓑ	ⓒ	ⓓ
39.	ⓐ	ⓑ	ⓒ	ⓓ
40.	ⓐ	ⓑ	ⓒ	ⓓ
41.	ⓐ	ⓑ	ⓒ	ⓓ
42.	ⓐ	ⓑ	ⓒ	ⓓ
43.	ⓐ	ⓑ	ⓒ	ⓓ
44.	ⓐ	ⓑ	ⓒ	ⓓ
45.	ⓐ	ⓑ	ⓒ	ⓓ
46.	ⓐ	ⓑ	ⓒ	ⓓ
47.	ⓐ	ⓑ	ⓒ	ⓓ
48.	ⓐ	ⓑ	ⓒ	ⓓ
49.	ⓐ	ⓑ	ⓒ	ⓓ
50.	ⓐ	ⓑ	ⓒ	ⓓ
51.	ⓐ	ⓑ	ⓒ	ⓓ
52.	ⓐ	ⓑ	ⓒ	ⓓ
53.	ⓐ	ⓑ	ⓒ	ⓓ
54.	ⓐ	ⓑ	ⓒ	ⓓ
55.	ⓐ	ⓑ	ⓒ	ⓓ
56.	ⓐ	ⓑ	ⓒ	ⓓ
57.	ⓐ	ⓑ	ⓒ	ⓓ
58.	ⓐ	ⓑ	ⓒ	ⓓ
59.	ⓐ	ⓑ	ⓒ	ⓓ
60.	ⓐ	ⓑ	ⓒ	ⓓ
61.	ⓐ	ⓑ	ⓒ	ⓓ
62.	ⓐ	ⓑ	ⓒ	ⓓ
63.	ⓐ	ⓑ	ⓒ	ⓓ
64.	ⓐ	ⓑ	ⓒ	ⓓ
65.	ⓐ	ⓑ	ⓒ	ⓓ
66.	ⓐ	ⓑ	ⓒ	ⓓ
67.	ⓐ	ⓑ	ⓒ	ⓓ
68.	ⓐ	ⓑ	ⓒ	ⓓ
69.	ⓐ	ⓑ	ⓒ	ⓓ
70.	ⓐ	ⓑ	ⓒ	ⓓ

71.	ⓐ	ⓑ	ⓒ	ⓓ
72.	ⓐ	ⓑ	ⓒ	ⓓ
73.	ⓐ	ⓑ	ⓒ	ⓓ
74.	ⓐ	ⓑ	ⓒ	ⓓ
75.	ⓐ	ⓑ	ⓒ	ⓓ
76.	ⓐ	ⓑ	ⓒ	ⓓ
77.	ⓐ	ⓑ	ⓒ	ⓓ
78.	ⓐ	ⓑ	ⓒ	ⓓ
79.	ⓐ	ⓑ	ⓒ	ⓓ
80.	ⓐ	ⓑ	ⓒ	ⓓ
81.	ⓐ	ⓑ	ⓒ	ⓓ
82.	ⓐ	ⓑ	ⓒ	ⓓ
83.	ⓐ	ⓑ	ⓒ	ⓓ
84.	ⓐ	ⓑ	ⓒ	ⓓ
85.	ⓐ	ⓑ	ⓒ	ⓓ
86.	ⓐ	ⓑ	ⓒ	ⓓ
87.	ⓐ	ⓑ	ⓒ	ⓓ
88.	ⓐ	ⓑ	ⓒ	ⓓ
89.	ⓐ	ⓑ	ⓒ	ⓓ
90.	ⓐ	ⓑ	ⓒ	ⓓ
91.	ⓐ	ⓑ	ⓒ	ⓓ
92.	ⓐ	ⓑ	ⓒ	ⓓ
93.	ⓐ	ⓑ	ⓒ	ⓓ
94.	ⓐ	ⓑ	ⓒ	ⓓ
95.	ⓐ	ⓑ	ⓒ	ⓓ
96.	ⓐ	ⓑ	ⓒ	ⓓ
97.	ⓐ	ⓑ	ⓒ	ⓓ
98.	ⓐ	ⓑ	ⓒ	ⓓ
99.	ⓐ	ⓑ	ⓒ	ⓓ
100.	ⓐ	ⓑ	ⓒ	ⓓ

State Trooper Practice Test 3

Directions: Read the following passage, then answer questions 1 through 6.

At 2:15 A.M. on September 27, while parked at 365 Fifth Avenue, Officers Gossard and Bastidis were asked to respond to a disturbance at 127 6th Street. When they arrived at the two-story dwelling, the complainant, Morton Greenberger, who resides next door at 125 6th Street, told them that he had been kept awake for hours by the sound of screaming and loud music. He said the occupant of 127 6th Street, a Ms. Elizabeth Grovers, lives alone. The officers approached 127 6th Street and heard yelling and loud music coming from inside. When the officers knocked on the door, Ms. Grovers answered promptly and said, "Thank goodness you're finally here." Inside, broken furniture was strewn about and there was loud music playing in the background. Ms. Grovers said she had been protecting herself from the voices coming from the radio. She went willingly with the officers to Hudson County Hospital at 1175 Palisade Avenue, where she was admitted to the psychiatric unit for observation. No arrests were made.

1. Which of the following is most likely a fact?
   a. Ms. Grovers had been kept awake for hours.
   b. Mr. Greenberger had been making noise yelling.
   c. The officers heard yelling and loud music coming from the house.
   d. Mr. Greenberger often calls the police with complaints about Ms. Grovers.

2. The call to the police was most likely made from which of the following addresses?
   a. 365 Fifth Avenue
   b. 125 6th Street
   c. 127 6th Street
   d. 1175 Palisade Avenue

3. Based on the passage, what was the most likely reason the police were called?
   a. A neighbor was concerned about Mr. Greenberger's safety.
   b. A neighbor was concerned about Ms. Grovers's family.
   c. A neighbor was bothered by the noise coming from Ms. Grovers's house.
   d. A neighbor was curious about Mr. Greenberger's personal life.

4. What was Ms. Grovers's demeanor when the police arrived at her door?
   a. She seemed surprised.
   b. She seemed to have been waiting for them.
   c. She was angered by their presence.
   d. She was frightened by their presence.

5. Based on the passage, what reason would Ms. Grovers herself give for the commotion at her home?
   a. She was mentally ill.
   b. She was cleaning the radio.
   c. She broke some glassware.
   d. She was acting in self-defense.

6. Which of the following statements is accurate according to the passage?
   a. Officers responded to a disturbance at 125 6th Street.
   b. Ms. Grovers was arrested.
   c. Officers responded to a disturbance at 127 6th Street.
   d. Mr. Greenberger went to the hospital with the officers.

Directions: Read the following passage, then answer questions 7 through 11.

It is misleading to consider the activities demanded of inmates in early American prisons rehabilitative. At Eastern State Penitentiary in Philadelphia and Auburn State Prison in New York in the 1820s, generally considered the institutions from which prisons as we know them evolved, incarcerated people were put to work. The competing Pennsylvania and Auburn models, as the approaches came to be known, both included inmate labor in different forms. Under the Pennsylvania model, conceived by Quakers, inmates remained isolated from each other and the world, providing them with time to reflect, or ask for penance, for their wrongs. In solitary cells they were limited to reading the Bible and engaging in small handicraft activities. The earliest programs arose out of these penitentiaries and a need to teach inmates to read the Bible. Because of high rates of illiteracy, literacy programs were developed in order to facilitate inmates' understanding of the religious materials that would lead to their reform. In contrast, at the Auburn or congregate system, inmates worked together in silence in prison shops during the day and returned to single cells to sleep at night.

The Auburn system ultimately became the model of choice for a number of reasons. Complete isolation, as at Eastern State, required more space and staff to oversee inmates spread out over a large facility. Increased space equated increased costs to build and maintain the facilities. And with inmates only able to engage in small handicraft activities, the Auburn model was associated with a greater output of products for the state's profit.

7. According to the passage, early prisons
  a. were concerned with rehabilitation.
  b. were all the same.
  c. were one of two different types.
  d. were expensive to operate.

8. According to the passage,
  a. the demand for inmate labor was high.
  b. many convicts of this time were unable to read.
  c. inmates at Eastern State Penitentiary worked in groups.
  d. inmates at Auburn State Prison did not read the Bible.

9. Which of the following would be a good title for this passage?
  a. "The History of Prisons in America"
  b. "How Inmates Worked in Prison"
  c. "Quakers' Prison Model Loses to New York"
  d. "Literacy Programs Inside Prisons"

10. An inmate incarcerated at Eastern State Penitentiary would most likely spend his day
  a. working outdoors with a large group of other inmates.
  b. alone in his cell.
  c. teaching children to read.
  d. fighting with inmates at Auburn over which model is better.

11. Which is probably true about early prisons?
  a. There was little food or water given out to the inmates.
  b. Males and females were housed together in the same prisons.
  c. Inmates at Auburn State Prison made more money to spend on commissary items than those at Eastern State Penitentiary.
  d. The cost of operating them was considered in designing additional prisons.

Directions: Read the following passage, then answer questions 12 through 16.

At 12:15 A.M., while riding the uptown-bound 12 train, Transit Officers Cobb and Wilson received a report of a disturbance in the fourth car of a downtown-bound 12 train. That train was held at the Fourth Street station until the arrival of the officers, who found complainant Alan Sterns tending his injured eye. Mr. Sterns told Officer Wilson that he had been attacked by Caroline Simpson when he attempted to move her bags, after politely asking her to do so, in order to make room to sit down. He said Ms. Simpson poked him in the eye and then threatened him with a switchblade. Ms. Simpson told Officer Cobb that she had been harassed by Mr. Sterns and struck him in self-defense. The officers asked Mr. Sterns, Ms. Simpson, and witnesses Lisa Walker and Lois Casey to step off the train, and proceeded to question them on the platform. Ms. Walker, whose view of the incident had been partially obstructed by a metal pole, stated that Mr. Sterns had raised his arm only after being struck, but she was not sure whether the gesture was threatening or defensive. Ms. Casey, who sat on the other side of Ms. Simpson, maintained that Mr. Sterns was only protecting himself and had behaved in a polite manner. Ms. Simpson was placed under arrest for carrying a concealed weapon.

12. Where did the assault occur?
a. on a subway platform
b. on the fourth car of the uptown-bound 12 train
c. at the Fourth Street station
d. on the fourth car of the downtown-bound 12 train

13. Which of the following actions caused the arrest?
a. injuring the complainant's eye
b. threatening the complainant
c. carrying a switchblade
d. disturbing the peace

14. The complainant's last name is
a. Sterns.
b. Simpson.
c. Walker.
d. Cobb.

15. Where was Ms. Casey sitting?
a. beside the complainant
b. across the car, behind a metal pole
c. between the complainant and the accused
d. beside the accused

16. According to the complainant, he was struck because
a. he handled the woman's property.
b. he asked the woman to move her bags.
c. he politely asked the woman to move over.
d. he appeared to raise his arm in a threatening manner.

Directions: Read the following passage, then answer questions 17 through 20.

The rules for obtaining evidence, set down in state and federal law, usually come to our attention when they work to the advantage of defendants in court, but these laws were not created with the courtroom in mind. They were formulated with the pragmatic intent of shaping police procedure before the arrest, in order to ensure justice, thoroughness, and the preservation of civil liberties. A good police officer must be as well schooled in the rules for properly obtaining evidence as is a defense lawyer, or risk losing a conviction. When a case is thrown out of court or a defendant is released because of these evidentiary "technicalities," we are often angered and mystified, but we are not always aware of how these rules of evidence shape police procedure in positive ways every day.

17. The main idea of this passage is that
   a. the rules of evidence protect the rights of defendants at trial.
   b. police officers should know the rules of evidence.
   c. the rules of evidence help shape police procedure.
   d. the rules of evidence have more positive than negative effects.

18. According to the passage, rules of evidence are designed to ensure all of the following EXCEPT
   a. meticulousness in gathering evidence.
   b. proof of guilt.
   c. protection of individual rights.
   d. fairness of treatment.

19. According to the passage, why should a police officer know the rules of evidence?
   a. The rules protect the rights of crime victims.
   b. The public does not appreciate the importance of rules.
   c. An officer must follow the rules to obtain a conviction.
   d. Following the rules protects officers from accusations of misconduct.

20. In saying that the intent of rules of evidence is *pragmatic*, the author most likely means that
   a. the focus of the rules is on police procedures in the field rather than on legal maneuvers in court.
   b. the practical nature of the rules enables lawyers to use them in court to protect defendants.
   c. the framers of these rules designed them to maintain idealistic standards of fairness.
   d. the rules are often misused in court because of their limited scope.

Directions: For questions 21 through 25, choose the answer choice that best rephrases the underlined portion of the given sentence.

21. The type of shoe in which people who run wear is important to prevent injury.
   a. which is worn by those who run
   b. worn by people who run
   c. that is worn by those which run
   d. in which people who run, wear

22. The students asked whether I thought there would be a woman president within the next decade?
   a. president within the next decade!
   b. president, within the next decade.
   c. president within the next decade.
   d. president, within the next decade?

23. This is the first time you have ever been to a major league baseball <u>game isn't it?</u>
- **a.** game, isn't it?
- **b.** game, is'nt it?
- **c.** game, isn't it.
- **d.** game isn't it.

24. Chicken <u>pox a virus</u> is very contagious.
- **a.** pox, a virus,
- **b.** pox, a virus
- **c.** pox, a virus—
- **d.** pox a virus,

25. I was born on <u>May 17, 1962 in Corvallis, Oregon.</u>
- **a.** May 17 1962 in Corvallis, Oregon.
- **b.** May 17 1962, in Corvallis Oregon.
- **c.** May 17, 1962 in Corvallis Oregon.
- **d.** May 17, 1962, in Corvallis, Oregon.

26. Look at the four numbered sentences below. Choose the sentence order that would result in the best paragraph.
- (1) Leaving us behind in a bitter cloud of exhaust, the bus would cough and jolt down the narrow main street of Crossland.
- (2) Then, even before the bus got moving, she'd look away, ahead toward her real life.
- (3) But I could always imagine the way it would be once it got out on the open highway, gathered speed, and took Grandma back to a life as exotic to me as the deserts of Egypt.
- (4) When Grandma's visit was over, we'd take her down to the Greyhound station, watch her hand her ticket to the uniformed driver, disappear inside, and reappear to wave good-bye—her expression obscured by the bus's grimy window.
- **a.** 4, 2, 1, 3
- **b.** 4, 1, 3, 2
- **c.** 1, 3, 4, 2
- **d.** 1, 2, 3, 4

27. Look at the four numbered sentences below. Choose the sentence order that would result in the best paragraph.
- (1) The Fifth Amendment of the U.S. Constitution guarantees citizens freedom from double jeopardy in criminal proceedings.
- (2) It also means a person cannot be tried for a crime for which he or she has already been convicted; that is to say, a person convicted by a state court cannot be tried for the same offense in, for example, federal court.
- (3) Finally, a person cannot be punished more than once for the same crime.
- (4) This means that a person cannot be tried for a crime for which he or she has already been acquitted.
- **a.** 1, 4, 2, 3
- **b.** 1, 2, 4, 3
- **c.** 3, 2, 1, 4
- **d.** 3, 4, 2, 1

28. Look at the three numbered sentences below. Choose the sentence order that would result in the best paragraph.
- (1) If this is true, something must have happened to Mars billions of years ago that stripped away the planet's atmosphere.
- (2) These images also implied that Mars once had an atmosphere that was thick enough to trap the sun's heat.
- (3) Close-up images of Mars by the *Mariner* 9 probe indicated networks of valleys that looked like the stream beds on Earth.
- **a.** 2, 3, 1
- **b.** 3, 1, 2
- **c.** 3, 2, 1
- **d.** 1, 3, 2

29. Look at the four numbered sentences below. Choose the sentence order that would result in the best paragraph.

(1) Every spring the softball field became his favorite destination, and he had taken his son Arnie there when he was small to teach him how to pitch.

(2) He walked home, as usual, through the park and, as usual, passed by the softball field.

(3) This memory made him feel sad and guilty.

(4) Arnie hadn't been in the least interested in softball, and so after two or three lessons he had given up the idea.

a. 2, 1, 4, 3
b. 3, 2, 1, 4
c. 4, 3, 1, 2
d. 2, 3, 4, 1

30. Three of the sentences below contain one or more grammatical or spelling errors. Select the answer choice that is correct as is.

a. Bus operators will wait there until the police arrive, will allow passengers off the bus at this point, and no passengers will be allowed on until the situation is resolved.

b. Bus operators will wait there until the police arrive, will allow passengers off the bus at this point, and, until the situation is resolved, no passengers are allowed on.

c. Bus operators will wait there until the police arrive, will allow passengers off the bus at this point, and will not allow passengers on until the situation is resolved.

d. Bus operators will wait there until the police arrive, will allow passengers off the bus at this point, and no passengers will be allowed on until the situation is resolved.

31. Three of the sentences below contain one or more grammatical or spelling errors. Select the answer choice that is correct as is.

a. Herbert was enjoying the cool bright fall afternoon. Walking down the street red and yellow leaves crunched satisfyingly under his new school shoes.

b. Herbert was enjoying the cool, bright fall afternoon. He was walking down the street, red and yellow leaves crunched satisfyingly under his new school shoes.

c. Herbert was enjoying the cool, bright fall afternoon. Walking down the street, he crunched red and yellow leaves satisfyingly under his new school shoes.

d. Herbert was enjoying the cool, bright fall afternoon. Walking down the street, red and yellow leaves were crunched satisfyingly under his new school shoes.

32. Three of the sentences below contain one or more grammatical or spelling errors. Select the answer choice that is correct as is.

a. Research says, people who live, without pets, are not as healthy as people, who live, with pets.

b. Demonstrated by research, people with pets are healthier, than other people, those who live without pets.

c. According to research, pets are better, people stay healthier, and without pets, people are not healthy.

d. Research has demonstrated that people who live with pets are healthier than those without pets.

33. Three of the sentences below contain one or more grammatical or spelling errors. Select the answer choice that is correct as is.

   a. The TV show *Columbo* is said to have been inspired in part of the classic Russian novel *Crime and Punishment*.

   b. The TV show *Columbo* is said to have been inspired in part by the classic Russian novel *Crime and Punishment*.

   c. The TV show *Columbo* is said to have been inspired in part off of the classic Russian novel *Crime and Punishment*.

   d. The TV show *Columbo* is said to have been inspired in part from the classic Russian novel *Crime and Punishment*.

34. Identify the sentence that contains a mistake in capitalization, punctuation, grammar, or spelling. If you find no mistakes, select choice **d**.

   a. My mother likes to make meatballs every Sunday.

   b. Sues leg is healing well after the operation.

   c. We both went to visit him in April.

   d. no mistakes

35. Identify the sentence that contains a mistake in capitalization, punctuation, grammar, or spelling. If you find no mistakes, select choice **d**.

   a. Either Cassie nor I heard the door open.

   b. How many people signed the Declaration of Independence?

   c. Draw up a plan before you make your decision.

   d. no mistakes

36. Identify the sentence that contains a mistake in capitalization, punctuation, grammar, or spelling. If you find no mistakes, select choice **d**.

   a. "Meet me at six o'clock," she said.

   b. Tired of running, she slowed her pace to a fast walk.

   c. Gabriel and me will attend the geography bee.

   d. no mistakes

37. Identify the sentence that contains a mistake in capitalization, punctuation, grammar, or spelling. If you find no mistakes, select choice **d**.

   a. The lost dog wandered sad through the streets.

   b. Frustrated, Boris threw his pencil across the room.

   c. We'll stop at their house first.

   d. no mistakes

38. Identify the sentence that contains a mistake in capitalization, punctuation, grammar, or spelling.

   a. The memo was distributed on Friday.

   b. Although the managers and the support staff had been called.

   c. The company was being acquired by a large corporation.

   d. Be sure to attend the meeting.

39. Identify the sentence that contains a mistake in capitalization, punctuation, grammar, or spelling. If you find no mistakes, select choice **d**.

   a. Eddie went to the movies by himself.

   b. They said their project was ready.

   c. My favorite shoes is only sold at this store.

   d. no mistakes

40. Identify the sentence that contains a mistake in capitalization, punctuation, grammar, or spelling.
  a. Anne will head out first, and Nick will follow her.
  b. Maya Angelou, a famous poet, has directed a movie.
  c. The clerk asked for my address and phone number.
  d. Cod liver oil is the most awfulest drink.

41. Dorothy is standing directly under a plane that is 300 meters above her. She sees another plane flying straight behind the first. It is 500 meters away from her, and she has not moved. How far apart are the planes from each other?
  a. 40 meters
  b. 400 meters
  c. 4,000 meters
  d. 40,000 meters

42. Police confiscated 30,000 kg of cocaine in a drug bust. The cocaine was packaged in 10 kg bags. How many bags of cocaine did the police confiscate?
  a. 300 bags
  b. 3,000 bags
  c. 30,000 bags
  d. 300,000 bags

43. 1 hour 20 minutes + 3 hours 30 minutes =
  a. 4 hours
  b. 4 hours 20 minutes
  c. 4 hours 50 minutes
  d. 5 hours

44. Fire departments commonly use the following formula to find out how far from a wall to place the base of a ladder:

(Length of ladder ÷ 5) + 2 = distance from the wall.

Using this formula, if the base of a ladder is placed 10 feet from a wall, how tall is the ladder?
  a. 48 feet
  b. 72 feet
  c. 40 feet
  d. 100 feet

45. Angel drove to Samson's house at a constant speed of 35 mph. If Samson's house is 180 miles away from Angel's, and Angel wants to get there in exactly 3 hours, how fast should he drive?
  a. 35 mph
  b. 40 mph
  c. 55 mph
  d. 60 mph

46. What is another way to write 2.75×100^2?
  a. 275
  b. 2,750
  c. 27,500
  d. 270,000

47. Which of the following means $5n + 7 = 17$?
  a. 7 more than 5 times a number is 17
  b. 5 more than 7 times a number is 17
  c. 7 less than 5 times a number is 17
  d. 12 times a number is 17

48. A trash container, when empty, weighs 27 pounds. If this container is filled with a load of trash that weighs 108 pounds, what is the total weight of the container and its contents?
a. 81 pounds
b. 135 pounds
c. 145 pounds
d. 185 pounds

49. What is the value of y when $x = 3$ and $y = 5 + 4x$?
a. 6
b. 9
c. 12
d. 17

50. What two numbers should come next in the following series?
9, 12, 15, 18, 21, 24, . . .
a. 28, 32
b. 27, 30
c. 26, 28
d. 27, 29

51. $7 + (-18) =$
a. 25
b. −25
c. 11
d. −11

52. The city's bus system carries 1,200,000 people each day. How many people does the bus system carry each year? (1 year = 365 days)
a. 3,288 people
b. 32,880 people
c. 43,800,000 people
d. 438,000,000 people

53. $24 \times 70 \times 3 =$
a. 4,440
b. 5,040
c. 6,400
d. 6,040

54. Mark's temperature at 9 A.M. was 97.2 degrees. At 4 P.M., his temperature was 99 degrees. By how many degrees did his temperature rise?
a. 0.8 degrees
b. 1.8 degrees
c. 2.2 degrees
d. 2.8 degrees

55. Which of the following expressions is equal to 40,503?
a. 400 + 50 + 3
b. 4,000 + 500 + 3
c. 40,000 + 50 + 3
d. 40,000 + 500 + 3

56. State Trooper Fitzgerald is driving east on Amsterdam Avenue. She makes a U-turn and then turns left. What direction is she now heading?
a. north
b. south
c. east
d. west

57. State Trooper Munoz is pursuing a Honda that was involved in a robbery and is now heading north on Route 80. The Honda notices that it is being followed and quickly makes a left turn, then another left turn. The Honda runs a red light and is hit on its right side by a car entering the intersection. The car that hit the Honda was heading in what direction?
a. north
b. south
c. east
d. west

58. An ambulance is traveling southwest on the parkway. Traffic is merging into the ambulance's lane from the left. The merging traffic is heading in what direction?
  a. north
  b. south
  c. east
  d. west

59. State Trooper Ahmed is driving south on Prospect Avenue during his nightshift. He makes a right turn and notices a late model Ford heading toward him. What direction is the Ford heading?
  a. north
  b. south
  c. east
  d. west

60. State Trooper Troncellito is patrolling a southbound highway when she sees smoke to her left. If she wishes to go investigate the cause of the smoke, she should turn into the next exit to the
  a. north.
  b. south.
  c. east.
  d. west.

61. State Trooper Howard Smith travels west one block on Elm Street. He turns left onto Beaver Street for one block, turns right onto Providence Avenue for one block, then right for one block onto Michigan Avenue. Finally, State Trooper Smith makes a left and is heading
  a. west on Providence Avenue.
  b. north on Beaver Street.
  c. east on Elm Street.
  d. west on Elm Street.

62. An SUV is driving north on route 287. At the junction of route 287 and Smithfield Road, the SUV turns and proceeds west on Smithfield Road. At the first intersection, the SUV yields to a police car crossing Smithfield Road and entering the intersection from the right. The police car is heading in what direction?
  a. north
  b. south
  c. east
  d. west

Directions: Answer questions 63 through 66 based on the following map. The arrows indicate traffic flow. One arrow indicates a one-way street going in the direction of the arrow; two arrows represent a two-way street. You are not allowed to go the wrong way on a one-way street.

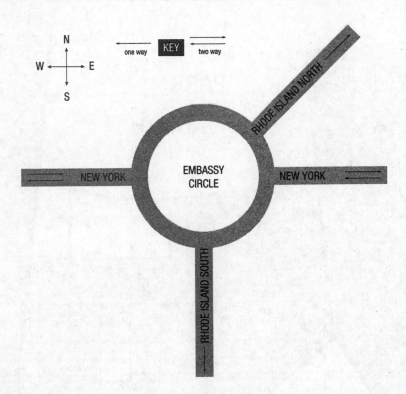

63. If a police vehicle traveling from the east wanted to go west on New York Avenue, it would need to travel around the circle
   a. north and east.
   b. north and west.
   c. south and east.
   d. south and west.

64. Your unit is driving east on New York Avenue and needs to enter Rhode Island Avenue South. You should travel
   a. northeast.
   b. northwest.
   c. southeast.
   d. southwest.

65. If State Trooper William Gates is traveling from east to west in the traffic circle, he must
   a. drive completely around the traffic circle.
   b. drive north around the traffic circle.
   c. drive south around the traffic circle.
   d. none of the above

66. Rhode Island Avenue runs
   a. from north to south.
   b. from south to north.
   c. south and northeast.
   d. south to northeast.

Directions: Answer questions 67 through 70 based on the following map.

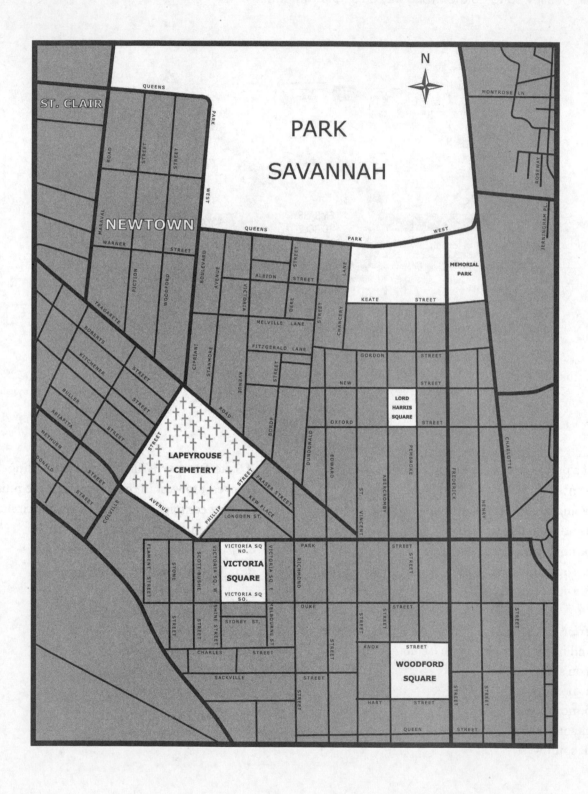

67. Presuming you are at the northeast corner of Woodford Square and want to walk the shortest distance to the closest corner of Victoria Square, your path would be to walk
   a. north to Duke Street and west to the intersection of Victoria Square South and Victoria Square East.
   b. south to Sackville Street and east until you come to Victoria Square.
   c. north to Duke Street and west to the intersection of Victoria Square South and Victoria Square East.
   d. north to Park Street and east to the intersection of Victoria Square North and Park Street.

68. Lapeyrouse Cemetery is in what direction from Victoria Square?
   a. northeast
   b. southeast
   c. southwest
   d. northwest

69. The Newtown section is located in the
   _____ area of Park Savannah.
   a. northeast
   b. southeast
   c. southwest
   d. northwest

70. The streets that provide direct routes from Lapeyrouse Cemetery to Park Savannah are
   a. Cipriani Boulevard, Stanmore Avenue, and Victoria Avenue.
   b. Cipriani Boulevard and Victoria Avenue.
   c. Stanmore Avenue and Dundonald Street.
   d. Stanmore Avenue, Victoria Avenue, and Borde Street.

Directions: You will have ten minutes to read and study the following passage. Then, answer questions 71 through 80 without referring back to the passage.

On Wednesday, January 11, 2006, three defendants were assaulted at the Camden Courthouse. At approximately 1:30 P.M., a blond suspect attacked defendants John Dendler, Erin Finkle, and Fred Gussoni with a knife. Officer Martin Thomas recognized that defendant Dendler appeared to have been stabbed in the thigh. He immediately called 911, and EMT personnel transported Dendler to the St. Joseph's Medical Center, where he was discharged the next day. The two other defendants sustained minor injuries and were treated at the scene of the incident.

At approximately 3:00 P.M., the suspect in the assault was removed from the courthouse by Officer Ryan Morton and Officer Ed Buckworth. During the removal, the suspect, William Dawkins, became unruly and attempted to strike Officer Buckworth in the head with his own head. Dawkins was restrained by Morton.

At 6:30 P.M., Officer Delongo questioned defendant Dendler at St. Joseph's Medical Center regarding the assault. Dendler denied that the incident was drug related and claimed that prior to that afternoon, he had only spoken to Dawkins once before, in passing.

At 9:30 A.M. on Thursday, January 12, 2006, Officer Delongo questioned defendants Finkle and Gussoni at their respective residences. All statements made by defendants Finkle and Gussoni closely corroborated with inmate Dendler's statements regarding the assault.

71. What day of the week did the assault occur?
a. Wednesday
b. Saturday
c. Monday
d. Thursday

72. Which defendant was stabbed in the thigh?
a. Finkle
b. Gussoni
c. Dendler
d. Dawkins

73. In which courthouse were the three defendants assaulted?
a. Camden Courthouse
b. Central Courthouse
c. Central Community Courthouse
d. Camdall Courthouse

74. Who transported the defendant who had been stabbed in the thigh to the medical center?
a. Thomas
b. Buckworth
c. EMT personnel
d. Delongo

75. Which officer did William Dawkins attempt to strike?
a. Thomas
b. Morton
c. Buckworth
d. Bush

76. At approximately what time was the suspect in the assault removed from the courthouse?
a. 1:30 P.M.
b. 3:00 P.M.
c. 6:30 P.M.
d. 9:30 A.M.

77. Where were the two other stabbed defendants treated?
a. at their residences
b. at the courthouse
c. at the medical center
d. in the ambulance

78. What color hair did the attacker have?
a. brown
b. black
c. blond
d. gray

79. Defendant Dendler had spoken to the suspect
a. never.
b. once before in passing.
c. three times in the courtroom.
d. numerous times.

80. Who was treated at the scene of the incident?
a. Gussoni and Dawkins
b. Gussoni and Dendler
c. Finkle and Dendler
d. Gussoni and Finkle

Directions: Read the following passage, then answer questions 81 through 87.

Henry Allen, a fiscally conservative candidate for city council, contacted the Internal Security Division of the Internal Revenue Service and alleged that an IRS employee was giving Allen's tax information to an opponent, Susan Vickers. Vickers was threatening to release information that Allen's business had been operating at a loss the last five years. Molly Hepplewhite, an internal security inspector for the IRS, commenced an investigation.

During the course of the investigation, the following statements were made:

1. Milton Banks, Susan Vickers's neighbor, said that he once caught Vickers going through his trash.

2. Bill Pushman, Henry Allen's campaign manager, said he dated Alice West in college. Alice now works at the IRS.

3. Shelby Gray, Susan Vickers's sister, said Susan would always do whatever she needed to do to get what she wanted.

4. Calvin Morris, Susan Vickers's campaign manager, said that his sister-in-law, Mary Yate, works at the IRS, but they haven't spoken in months.

5. IRS employee Doug Edwards said that Mary Yate and Alice West have lunch together almost every day.

6. Frank Luther, Henry Allen's neighbor, said that Allen has no business running for city council when he can't even keep his dog in his own yard.

7. Felicia Dial said that she plans to vote for Henry Allen because he promises to run the city as efficiently as he runs his business.

8. IRS employee Mary Yate said that Frank Luther and Doug Edwards have been friends since grade school.

9. IRS employee Avery Page said that Alice West makes a lot of personal phone calls and once he heard her say, "He can't treat you like that!"

10. Henry Allen said that current council member Mavis Wright said that Susan Vickers said she'd do anything to win this election.

81. Which statement is most damaging to the Susan Vickers campaign?
    a. Statement 1
    b. Statement 3
    c. Statement 4
    d. Statement 10

82. Which statement is least helpful to the investigation?
    a. Statement 1
    b. Statement 8
    c. Statement 2
    d. Statement 6

83. Which two statements are hearsay?
    a. Statements 1 and 2
    b. Statements 9 and 10
    c. Statements 5 and 6
    d. Statements 3 and 4

84. Which statement represents circumstantial evidence?
    a. Statement 5
    b. Statement 2
    c. Statement 4
    d. Statement 7

85. Which statement indicates that an IRS employee is providing information to the Vickers campaign?
    a. Statement 1
    b. Statement 3
    c. Statement 10
    d. Statement 4

86. Which two statements imply the possibility that the Allen campaign is attempting to make the Vickers campaign appear guilty?
    a. Statements 4 and 8
    b. Statements 1 and 3
    c. Statements 2 and 5
    d. Statements 8 and 10

87. Which two statements tend to implicate Frank Luther?
    a. Statements 6 and 8
    b. Statements 1 and 5
    c. Statements 2 and 9
    d. Statements 4 and 5

Directions: Read the following passage, then answer questions 88 through 94.

Bert Hines was imprisoned in a federal facility for forgery. Hines, along with three other prisoners and two guards, was taken from lock-up to a local optometrist's office on January 17. The four prisoners were secured by handcuffs to an eight-foot length of chain during transport. While sitting in the optometrist's waiting room, Hines was released from the chain and taken to the examination room, where a preliminary eye exam was conducted. He was then escorted back to the waiting room. While another prisoner was being released, Hines, who had not been reshackled, seized a gun from one of the guards and managed to escape. He took Michelle Rogers, the optometrist's receptionist, hostage and fled with her. He released her within 30 minutes, when he stole a car. During the course of the investigation, the following statements were made:

1. Jeff Reynolds, one of the four prisoners, said that Hines's cellmate told him Hines had a girlfriend in town.
2. The optometrist said that Hines acted "weird" during the exam.
3. Jessie Seymour, one of the guards, said that Hines was not reshackled because his exam was not complete.
4. Mary Hobbes, the guard whose gun was stolen, said that the gun was not regulation.
5. Maurice Chang, one of the four prisoners, said Hines made eye contact with a female passerby as the prisoners were led into the office.
6. Martin Steffins, Michelle Rogers's fiancé, said Michelle was always afraid on the days prisoners came to the office.
7. Michelle Rogers said that Hines retrieved a package from the planter in front of the office and later showed her a passport and an envelope containing several thousand dollars.

8. Rachel Firth, the owner of the stolen car, said that one of her husband's suits, which she had picked up at the dry cleaner, was hanging in the car.
9. Michael Jones, Rachel's husband, said the car tended to cut out at speeds over 60 miles per hour.
10. Raymond Diaz, Hines's cellmate, said that Hines spoke French fluently.

88. Which statement is hearsay?
   a. Statement 1
   b. Statement 2
   c. Statement 4
   d. Statement 7

89. Which two statements indicate that Hines may have been planning to leave the country?
   a. Statements 7 and 8
   b. Statements 2 and 10
   c. Statements 8 and 10
   d. Statements 7 and 10

90. Which two statements, along with statement 2, are least likely to be of use in this investigation?
   a. Statements 3 and 5
   b. Statements 4 and 6
   c. Statements 1 and 7
   d. Statements 8 and 10

91. Which two statements indicate the escape was planned, rather than spontaneous?
   a. Statements 2 and 5
   b. Statements 3 and 7
   c. Statements 2 and 3
   d. Statements 5 and 7

92. Which statement indicates an avoidable mistake on the part of prison guards?
   a. Statement 2
   b. Statement 3
   c. Statement 1
   d. Statement 5

93. Assuming law enforcement officers spot Hines driving Firth's car, which statement would lead officers to consider commencing a high-speed chase?
   a. Statement 7
   b. Statement 8
   c. Statement 6
   d. Statement 9

94. Which statement indicates officers should contact security at the local airport?
   a. Statement 7
   b. Statement 8
   c. Statement 9
   d. Statement 10

95. In the K-9 Corps, Officer Thomas is partnered with Ranger, Officer Cain is partnered with Scout, Officer Stern is partnered with Laddie, and Officer Walker is partnered with Astro. If Officer Thomas switches partners with Officer Stern and Officer Stern then switches with Officer Cain, who is Officer Stern's new partner?
   a. Ranger
   b. Scout
   c. Laddie
   d. Astro

96. Officers aren't always required to make a custody arrest that very moment even though the law has been broken. A warrant can always be issued at a later date for the suspect if the person can be identified. Which of the following situations best illustrates this point?
   a. Jeremy is well known in his community for his appearance at political demonstrations. Police are called to the scene of a massive riot where Jeremy has incited over 100 college students to throw rocks and attack the outnumbered police force.
   b. Melody is walking along the street when a man jumps out from the shadows, grabs her purse, and takes off running. Officer Bentley catches him one block later.
   c. Antonio tells Officer DiAngelo that his cousin has been threatening to come burn his house down. While Antonio is telling this story, a gasoline can comes crashing through the living room window.
   d. Rachel walks up to Officer Xavier, dragging a teenager by the jacket. She tells the officer that she caught the young man putting his hand into her coat pocket when she was waiting at the bus stop.

Directions: Read the following passage, then answer questions 97 and 98.

Police officers are required to give out physical descriptions of suspects over police radios for other officers to assist in locating the person. A description should be given out in the following order:

1. race and sex
2. weapons the suspect may be carrying
3. approximate height and weight
4. color and length of hair

5. baseball cap or other headgear
6. coat, jacket, or shirt
7. long or short pants
8. footwear

97. Officer Lundy was on patrol when he saw a man on a sidewalk waving wildly at him. The man told him he'd been robbed about one block away by a white male carrying a lock-blade knife. The suspect has on white tennis shoes, olive drab fatigue pants, a black turtleneck, and a black baseball cap. He's about 6 feet tall and weighs about 180 pounds. What is the first thing Officer Lundy should put out over the radio when he begins describing the suspect?
   a. a description of the suspect's knife
   b. a description of the suspect's race and sex
   c. a description of the suspect's pants
   d. a description of the suspect's speaking voice

98. Officer Scott is taking a report of a purse-snatching at the mall. The victim says the thief was 5′10″ tall, weighed about 160 pounds, had short red hair, and was wearing a New York Yankees baseball cap with gray warm-up pants and a gray sweatshirt. He was wearing black jogging shoes, was a white male, and appeared to be without weapons. Officer Scott begins his description with the race and sex of the suspect, but is interrupted by the victim. When he resumes his description, Officer Scott should begin with the
   a. suspect's footwear.
   b. suspect's headgear.
   c. suspect's height and weight.
   d. suspect's weapon.

99. Officer Mattox is listening to Claude, an angry citizen. Claude is furious with Officer Mattox because he feels that he doesn't deserve a ticket for running a stop sign. At what point should the officer consider physically arresting Claude?
   a. Claude is seated in his automobile shouting, "Why aren't you out catching real crooks?" while the officer opens his ticket book.
   b. Claude is standing beside his car on the sidewalk holding his arms out, with palms up, at passing cars while the officer writes the ticket.
   c. Claude points his pen at Officer Mattox and says, "I want your name and badge number because I'm calling your supervisor."
   d. Claude pokes his forefinger in Officer Mattox's chest and tells him he doesn't know what he's talking about.

100. During the graduation ceremony at the police academy, Cadet Jurgens is standing immediately to Cadet Shirley's left. Cadet Shirley is immediately to the left of Cadet Davis. Cadet Riley is to the right of Cadet Shirley. There are no other cadets in this row. In what order are the cadets standing?
   a. Jurgens, Shirley, Davis, Riley
   b. Riley, Jurgens, Shirley, Davis
   c. Shirley, Davis, Riley, Jurgens
   d. Davis, Riley, Jurgens, Shirley

Answers

1. c. The only statement that can be corroborated by the officers is statement **c.**

2. b. Morton Greenberger most likely made the call from 125 6th Street.

3. c. Mr. Greenberger said he had been kept awake by the noise from Ms. Grovers's house.

4. b. Ms. Grovers said, "Thank goodness you are finally here," which implies she had been waiting for them.

5. d. Ms. Grovers said she was protecting herself from the voices coming from inside the radio.

6. c. Ms. Grovers's address, where the officers heard the noise, is 127 6th Street.

7. c. The passage describes the Auburn versus the Pennsylvania models of prisons.

8. b. The passage states that literacy programs had to be developed for inmates to be able to read the Bible at Eastern State Penitentiary. The passage includes nothing about whether inmates at Auburn State Prison read the Bible.

9. a. The first sentence mentions early American prisons. The second sentence identifies Eastern State Penitentiary in Philadelphia and Auburn State Prison in New York as the early institutions from which prisons as we know them evolved.

10. b. The passage says inmates remained isolated from each other and described the isolation as complete.

11. d. The passage says isolation meant more space was needed, which increased building costs, and since they worked in shops outside of their cells, inmates at Auburn were able to make more products for the state to sell and profit from.

12. d. See the first sentence of the passage. The officers were initially in the uptown-bound train.

The subway platform is where the questioning occurred.

13. c. Although Ms. Simpson allegedly assaulted the complainant and created a disturbance, she was arrested for the concealed weapon.

14. a. Alan Sterns is identified as the complainant in the second sentence of the passage.

15. d. See the next-to-last sentence in the passage.

16. a. According to Mr. Sterns, Ms. Simpson struck him when he attempted to move her bags.

17. d. This idea is stated in the second sentence and discussed throughout the passage.

18. b. Proof of guilt is the whole point of gathering evidence, but this is never referred to in the passage.

19. c. This is stated in the third sentence. Choice **a** is incorrect because, though rules of evidence protect the accused, that is not the reason the passage gives that an officer must know them.

20. a. The pragmatic, or practical, intent the author refers to in the second sentence is the purpose of shaping police procedure before arrest.

21. b. This is the only grammatically correct choice.

22. c. This is a declarative sentence; it asks an indirect question, so a question mark should not be used. Also, the comma is unnecessary.

23. a. The sentence requires a comma before the phrase *isn't it.*

24. a. The phrase *a virus* is a nonessential element in the sentence and needs to be set off with commas.

25. d. Commas separate dates and addresses.

26. a. In this choice, the order is chronological. In sentence 4, they take Grandma to the Greyhound station. In sentence 2, the bus has not yet moved away from the station. In sentence 1, the bus jolts away but is still in town. In sentence 3, the bus (at least in the narrator's mind) is out on the open highway.

27. a. Sentence 1 is the topic sentence. Sentence 4 defines the term *double jeopardy* used in sentence 1; sentence 2 gives another definition, signaled by *also*; sentence 3 begins with the word *Finally* and gives the last definition.

28. c. Sentence 3 is the general topic sentence. Sentence 2 repeats the word *images* to make a link to the topic sentence. Sentence 3 gives the details of the example; sentence 1 offers an explanation for the idea presented in the topic sentence.

29. a. Sentence 2 sets the stage—this is a memory. After that, the order is chronological: In sentence 1, the man tries to teach his son how to pitch. In sentence 4, he wasn't interested, so the man gave up. Sentence 3 logically follows—the memory of giving up makes him feel sad and guilty.

30. c. This choice makes use of parallel structure because the list of the drivers' obligations are all expressed in the same subject/verb grammatical form: Bus drivers *will wait, will allow, will not allow*. In choices **a**, **b**, and **d**, the parallelism of the list is thrown off by the last item in the list, which changes the subject of its verb from *operators* to *passengers*.

31. c. This choice adds the subject *he* in the second sentence, eliminating the dangling modifier *walking down the street*. Otherwise, the sentence reads as if the leaves are walking down the street. All other choices ignore the problem of the dangling modifier and add grammatical mistakes to the sentences.

32. d. The other choices have unnecessary commas.

33. b. The correct preposition is *by*; choices **a**, **c**, and **d** contain the incorrect prepositions *of*, *off of*, and *from*.

34. b. The sentence is missing an apostrophe. It should read: *Sue's leg is healing well after the operation.*

35. a. *Either* is incorrect. Use *either* with *or* and *neither* with *nor*.

36. c. The correct pronoun is *I*, not *me*. *I* is the choice because along with *Gabriel*, it is the compound subject of the sentence (subjective or nominative case).

37. a. The adjective *sad* should be replaced with the adverb *sadly*, which modifies the verb *wandered*.

38. b. This is a sentence fragment; the other answer choices are complete sentences.

39. c. *Shoes* is plural and should be followed by *are*, which is plural, not *is*, which is for singular nouns.

40. d. *Most awfulest* is a double superlative and is, therefore, redundant.

41. b. The first plane is actually the triangle's right vertex. The distance between Dorothy and the second plane is the hypotenuse. Plug the known measurements into the Pythagorean theorem: $300^2 + b^2 = 500^2$. $90,000 + b^2 = 250,000$. $b^2 = 160,000$. $b = 400$. Notice that if you divide each side by 100, this is another 3-4-5 triangle.

42. b. Divide the total amount of cocaine (30,000 kg) by the amount in each bag (10 kg) to get the number of bags (3,000).

43. c. Add the hours first, then the minutes: 1 hour + 3 hours = 4 hours, and 20 minutes + 30 minutes = 50 minutes. Combine the two: 4 hours 50 minutes.

44. c. Because the distance from the wall is known, the formula would be $(x \div 5) + 2 = 10$. To find x, start by subtracting 2 from both sides, so you have $x \div 5 = 8$. Then, multiply both sides by 5, and you end up with $x = 40$.

45. d. Rearrange $D = RT$ to $R = D \div T = 180 \div 3 = 60$ mph.

46. c. $100^2 = (100)(100)$, or 10,000. $(10,000)(2.75) = 27,500$.

47. a. The expression $5n$ means 5 times n. The addition sign before the 7 indicates the phrase *more than*.

48. b. This is a basic addition problem: 108 pounds + 27 pounds = 135 pounds.

49. d. Substitute 3 for *x* in the expression 5 + 4*x* to determine that *y* equals 17.

50. b. The numbers are increasing by three. 24 + 3 = 27 and 27 + 3 = 30.

51. d. You are adding numbers that have different signs; therefore, subtract the smaller number from the larger number. In this case, the larger number is a negative number, so the answer is −11.

52. d. This is a multiplication problem. The simplest way to solve this problem is to temporarily take away the five zeros, then multiply: 365 × 12 = 4,380. Now add back the five zeros for a total of 438,000,000. If you selected choice **a**, you divided when you should have multiplied.

53. b. Do the multiplication in order, so 24 × 70 = 1,680 and 1,680 × 3 = 5,040.

54. b. This is a subtraction problem. Be sure to align the decimal points: 99.0 − 97.2 = 1.8.

55. d. Use the place value of each of the non-zero numbers. The 4 is in the ten-thousands place, so it is equal to 40,000. The 5 is in the hundreds place, so it is equal to 500. The 3 is in the ones place, so it is equal to 3.

56. b. When she made the left turn, State Trooper Fitzgerald was heading south.

57. c. The Honda was heading south, with its right side facing west. The car that hit it was, therefore, heading east.

58. d. If the ambulance is traveling southwest, the merge on the left is a merge from the east and is heading to the west.

59. c. State Trooper Ahmed is heading west after making the right turn, so the Ford is heading east.

60. c. On a southbound highway, east is on the left side, so State Trooper Troncellito should turn into the next exit to the east.

61. d. If Trooper Smith is traveling west on Elm Street and makes a left, he is now heading south on Beaver Street. His right turn will take him west on Providence Avenue, and the next right turn will take him north on Michigan Avenue. The final left turn will put Trooper Smith back on Elm Street heading west.

62. b. The SUV was traveling west, so the police car to the right is traveling south.

63. b. The vehicle would need to go up around the circle (north), then continue west.

64. c. Your unit would need to go down around the circle (south), then continue east.

65. b. State Trooper Gates is entering from the right and must drive north because of the direction of the arrows in the traffic circle.

66. c. Rhode Island Avenue does not run directly north and south, so choices **a** and **b** can be eliminated. Rhode Island Avenue runs south on the bottom of the map, but it runs northeast on the top of the map. Therefore, Rhode Island Avenue runs south *and* northeast, not south *to* northeast.

67. a. It is the most direct route from the northwest corner of Woodford Square to the southeast corner of Victoria Square.

68. d. Using the directional coordinates given to you in the description, the cemetery is northwest of Victoria Square.

69. c. Using the directional coordinates given to you in the description, Newtown is nestled against the southwestern corner of Park Savannah.

70. a. These are the only three streets that provide direct access from the cemetery to the park.

71. a. The assault occurred on a Wednesday. Choice **d**, Thursday, was the day that Officer Delongo questioned defendants Finkle and Gussoni at their respective residences.

72. c. The passage does not state that Finkle or Gussoni, choices **a** and **b**, was stabbed in the thigh. Choice **d**, Dawkins, was the person who assaulted the defendants with the knife.

73. a. The courthouses mentioned in choices **b**, **c**, and **d** are not mentioned in the passage.

74. c. Choice **a** is tricky—Senior Court Officer Thomas called 911, but he did not escort the defendant to the medical center.

75. c. Choices **a** and **b** were not involved in the attempted assault, and choice **d** is not mentioned in the passage.

76. b. The times in the other choices are all mentioned in the passage, but they describe other events.

77. b. The passage states that the defendants were treated *at the scene*: in this case, the Camden Courthouse.

78. c. The second sentence of the passage states that *a blond suspect attacked* the defendants.

79. b. The passage states that Dendler had spoken to Dawkins only once before, in passing.

80. d. Choice **a** is incorrect, because Dawkins was the stabbing suspect, not one of the defendants who was stabbed. Dendler was not treated at the scene, so choices **b** and **c** can be ruled out.

81. c. Statement 4 provides information on the opportunity the Vickers campaign had to receive information from the IRS.

82. d. Statement 6 is not related to the investigation at all.

83. b. Statements 9 and 10 are statements made without personal knowledge, simply repeating what others said.

84. a. Circumstantial evidence is evidence from which the presence of a principal fact of the case can be inferred. The fact that Mary Yate and Alice West frequently have lunch together proves nothing by itself; however, one may infer it means they have a closer relationship than coworkers normally have.

85. d. Statement 4 provides the opportunity for the campaign to receive information from the IRS.

86. c. Statements 2 and 5 indicate a connection from the Allen campaign to the IRS and then to the Vickers campaign.

87. a. Statements 6 and 8 show that Luther holds a grudge against Allen and has access to the IRS through Doug Edwards.

88. a. Statement 1 is a statement made without personal knowledge, simply repeating what others said.

89. d. Statement 7 demonstrates that Hines has the means—a passport and money—to leave the country, and statement 10 contains the information that Hines speaks a foreign language, facilitating Hines going to another country.

90. b. The fact that the guard was carrying a nonregulation firearm has no bearing on the investigation into Hines's disappearance; neither does the fact that Michelle Rogers was not comfortable with the prisoners.

91. d. Statements 5 and 7 indicate that someone left the package outside the office for Hines, requiring prior planning.

92. b. Statement 3 was an entirely avoidable mistake; Hines should have been reshackled when he returned to the waiting room.

93. d. Statement 9 indicates that the car may experience mechanical difficulties at speeds over 60 miles an hour; if the officers can force Hines to drive faster than that, the car might be disabled.

94. a. Statement 7 provides information that Hines is planning to go where he will need a passport. Chances are that this will require him to travel by air.

95. b. After all the switches were made, Officer Stern's partner was Scout. Officer Thomas's partner was Laddie, Officer Cain's was Ranger, and Officer Walker's was Astro.

96. a. Outnumbered officers attempting to control a hostile crowd may not be able to arrest the instigator safely; however, according to the situation, they will likely be able to find him later, because they are aware of his identity. In the other situations, custody arrests are appropriate and more easily accomplished. Although in choice **c** it seems apparent that Antonio knows his cousin's identity, and that a warrant could therefore be issued at a later date, the violence of the situation makes immediate action necessary.

97. b. The first step is to give the race and sex of the suspect. In this case, the victim has provided that information.

98. c. The next information the officer can give out is a height and weight description. Because no weapon was seen, choice **d** is not possible.

99. d. Claude has just assaulted Officer Mattox by poking him in the chest. This is a safety issue for the officer, and he should not allow contact of this nature. Allowing an angry citizen to vent and release a certain amount of frustration, as in the other options, is appropriate in many situations.

100. a. The order of the cadets is Jurgens, Shirley, Davis, and Riley. Jurgens is on Shirley's immediate left, and Davis is on Shirley's immediate right. Riley is therefore on Davis's immediate right.

15 ▶ STATE TROOPER PRACTICE TEST 4

CHAPTER SUMMARY
This is the fourth practice test in this book based on the most commonly tested areas on the state trooper exam.

The practice test consists of 100 multiple-choice questions in the following areas: reading comprehension, writing and information ordering, mathematics, spatial and directional orientation, memory and observation, and problem solving. As with the previous practice tests, you should give yourself two hours to take this practice test.

State Trooper Practice Test 4

#	a	b	c	d		#	a	b	c	d		#	a	b	c	d
1.	ⓐ	ⓑ	ⓒ	ⓓ		36.	ⓐ	ⓑ	ⓒ	ⓓ		71.	ⓐ	ⓑ	ⓒ	ⓓ
2.	ⓐ	ⓑ	ⓒ	ⓓ		37.	ⓐ	ⓑ	ⓒ	ⓓ		72.	ⓐ	ⓑ	ⓒ	ⓓ
3.	ⓐ	ⓑ	ⓒ	ⓓ		38.	ⓐ	ⓑ	ⓒ	ⓓ		73.	ⓐ	ⓑ	ⓒ	ⓓ
4.	ⓐ	ⓑ	ⓒ	ⓓ		39.	ⓐ	ⓑ	ⓒ	ⓓ		74.	ⓐ	ⓑ	ⓒ	ⓓ
5.	ⓐ	ⓑ	ⓒ	ⓓ		40.	ⓐ	ⓑ	ⓒ	ⓓ		75.	ⓐ	ⓑ	ⓒ	ⓓ
6.	ⓐ	ⓑ	ⓒ	ⓓ		41.	ⓐ	ⓑ	ⓒ	ⓓ		76.	ⓐ	ⓑ	ⓒ	ⓓ
7.	ⓐ	ⓑ	ⓒ	ⓓ		42.	ⓐ	ⓑ	ⓒ	ⓓ		77.	ⓐ	ⓑ	ⓒ	ⓓ
8.	ⓐ	ⓑ	ⓒ	ⓓ		43.	ⓐ	ⓑ	ⓒ	ⓓ		78.	ⓐ	ⓑ	ⓒ	ⓓ
9.	ⓐ	ⓑ	ⓒ	ⓓ		44.	ⓐ	ⓑ	ⓒ	ⓓ		79.	ⓐ	ⓑ	ⓒ	ⓓ
10.	ⓐ	ⓑ	ⓒ	ⓓ		45.	ⓐ	ⓑ	ⓒ	ⓓ		80.	ⓐ	ⓑ	ⓒ	ⓓ
11.	ⓐ	ⓑ	ⓒ	ⓓ		46.	ⓐ	ⓑ	ⓒ	ⓓ		81.	ⓐ	ⓑ	ⓒ	ⓓ
12.	ⓐ	ⓑ	ⓒ	ⓓ		47.	ⓐ	ⓑ	ⓒ	ⓓ		82.	ⓐ	ⓑ	ⓒ	ⓓ
13.	ⓐ	ⓑ	ⓒ	ⓓ		48.	ⓐ	ⓑ	ⓒ	ⓓ		83.	ⓐ	ⓑ	ⓒ	ⓓ
14.	ⓐ	ⓑ	ⓒ	ⓓ		49.	ⓐ	ⓑ	ⓒ	ⓓ		84.	ⓐ	ⓑ	ⓒ	ⓓ
15.	ⓐ	ⓑ	ⓒ	ⓓ		50.	ⓐ	ⓑ	ⓒ	ⓓ		85.	ⓐ	ⓑ	ⓒ	ⓓ
16.	ⓐ	ⓑ	ⓒ	ⓓ		51.	ⓐ	ⓑ	ⓒ	ⓓ		86.	ⓐ	ⓑ	ⓒ	ⓓ
17.	ⓐ	ⓑ	ⓒ	ⓓ		52.	ⓐ	ⓑ	ⓒ	ⓓ		87.	ⓐ	ⓑ	ⓒ	ⓓ
18.	ⓐ	ⓑ	ⓒ	ⓓ		53.	ⓐ	ⓑ	ⓒ	ⓓ		88.	ⓐ	ⓑ	ⓒ	ⓓ
19.	ⓐ	ⓑ	ⓒ	ⓓ		54.	ⓐ	ⓑ	ⓒ	ⓓ		89.	ⓐ	ⓑ	ⓒ	ⓓ
20.	ⓐ	ⓑ	ⓒ	ⓓ		55.	ⓐ	ⓑ	ⓒ	ⓓ		90.	ⓐ	ⓑ	ⓒ	ⓓ
21.	ⓐ	ⓑ	ⓒ	ⓓ		56.	ⓐ	ⓑ	ⓒ	ⓓ		91.	ⓐ	ⓑ	ⓒ	ⓓ
22.	ⓐ	ⓑ	ⓒ	ⓓ		57.	ⓐ	ⓑ	ⓒ	ⓓ		92.	ⓐ	ⓑ	ⓒ	ⓓ
23.	ⓐ	ⓑ	ⓒ	ⓓ		58.	ⓐ	ⓑ	ⓒ	ⓓ		93.	ⓐ	ⓑ	ⓒ	ⓓ
24.	ⓐ	ⓑ	ⓒ	ⓓ		59.	ⓐ	ⓑ	ⓒ	ⓓ		94.	ⓐ	ⓑ	ⓒ	ⓓ
25.	ⓐ	ⓑ	ⓒ	ⓓ		60.	ⓐ	ⓑ	ⓒ	ⓓ		95.	ⓐ	ⓑ	ⓒ	ⓓ
26.	ⓐ	ⓑ	ⓒ	ⓓ		61.	ⓐ	ⓑ	ⓒ	ⓓ		96.	ⓐ	ⓑ	ⓒ	ⓓ
27.	ⓐ	ⓑ	ⓒ	ⓓ		62.	ⓐ	ⓑ	ⓒ	ⓓ		97.	ⓐ	ⓑ	ⓒ	ⓓ
28.	ⓐ	ⓑ	ⓒ	ⓓ		63.	ⓐ	ⓑ	ⓒ	ⓓ		98.	ⓐ	ⓑ	ⓒ	ⓓ
29.	ⓐ	ⓑ	ⓒ	ⓓ		64.	ⓐ	ⓑ	ⓒ	ⓓ		99.	ⓐ	ⓑ	ⓒ	ⓓ
30.	ⓐ	ⓑ	ⓒ	ⓓ		65.	ⓐ	ⓑ	ⓒ	ⓓ		100.	ⓐ	ⓑ	ⓒ	ⓓ
31.	ⓐ	ⓑ	ⓒ	ⓓ		66.	ⓐ	ⓑ	ⓒ	ⓓ						
32.	ⓐ	ⓑ	ⓒ	ⓓ		67.	ⓐ	ⓑ	ⓒ	ⓓ						
33.	ⓐ	ⓑ	ⓒ	ⓓ		68.	ⓐ	ⓑ	ⓒ	ⓓ						
34.	ⓐ	ⓑ	ⓒ	ⓓ		69.	ⓐ	ⓑ	ⓒ	ⓓ						
35.	ⓐ	ⓑ	ⓒ	ⓓ		70.	ⓐ	ⓑ	ⓒ	ⓓ						

State Trooper Practice Test 4

Directions: Read the following passage, then answer questions 1 through 10.

The Advisory Committee of the State Police has issued the following guidelines for establishing a roadblock in order to identify and apprehend drunk drivers:

Selecting the location. The roadblock must be established in a location that affords motorists a clear view of the stop. It cannot be established, for example, just over a hill or around a curve. Motorists must be able to see that a roadblock is ahead and that cars are being stopped.

Staffing the location. A roadblock must display visible signs of police authority. Therefore, uniformed officers in marked patrol cars should primarily staff the roadblock. Plainclothes officers may supplement the staff at the roadblock, but the initial stop and questioning of motorists should be conducted by uniformed officers. In addition to the officers conducting the motorist stops, officers should be present to conduct field sobriety tests on suspect drivers. A command observation officer must also be present to coordinate the roadblock.

Operation of the roadblock. All cars passing through the roadblock must be stopped. It should not appear to an approaching motorist that cars are being singled out for some reason while others are not stopped, as this will generate unnecessary fear on the part of the motorist. The observation vehicle that is present at the roadblock will be able to pursue any motorists who refuse to stop.

Questioning the drivers. Each motorist stopped by the roadblock should be questioned only briefly. In most cases, an officer should ask directly if the driver has been drinking. In suspicious cases, an officer may engage in some further questioning to evaluate the driver's sobriety. A driver who appears to have been drinking should be directed to the side of the road, out of the line of traffic, where other officers may conduct a field sobriety test. Each non-suspicious driver should be stopped only briefly, for approximately a minute or less.

Duration of operation. No drunk-driving roadblock should be in operation for more than two hours. Roadblocks in place for longer periods lose their effectiveness as word spreads as to location of the roadblock, and motorists who have been drinking will avoid the area. In addition, on average only about 1% of all the drivers who pass through a roadblock will be arrested for drunk driving, and, after a short period of time, officers can be used more efficiently elsewhere.

Charges other than drunk driving. A roadblock may only be established for a single purpose—in this case, detecting drunk drivers—and should not be seen as an opportunity to check for a variety of motorist offenses. However, officers are not required to ignore what is plainly obvious. For example, motorists and passengers who are not wearing seat belts should be verbally warned that failure to do so is against the law. Detaining and ticketing such drivers is not the purpose of the roadblock and would unduly slow down the stops of other cars. An officer who spots a situation that presents a clear and present danger should follow through by directing the motorist to the side of the road where the officers are conducting field sobriety tests. These officers can then follow through on investigating the driver for crimes other than drunk driving.

1. According to the roadblock guidelines, officers must be sure they set up a drunk-driving roadblock that
   a. can be seen by motorists from a distance.
   b. provides a well hidden place for officers to park their cars.
   c. is near a bar or tavern.
   d. is near a busy street or highway.

2. While questioning motorists at a drunk-driving roadblock, Officer Firth notices that, although the driver of a particular car seems sober, the passenger in that car seems extremely nervous and has bruises on his face. She asks the passenger if he is all right, and after glancing at the driver, the passenger nods "yes." According to the guidelines, Officer Firth should
   a. let the car pass because the driver is not drunk.
   b. question the passenger and the driver further about the passenger's condition.
   c. arrest the driver on suspicion of assault.
   d. direct the driver to pull to the side of the road where other officers can investigate further.

3. Officers have been conducting a drunk-driving roadblock since 7:00 P.M. and have made 35 drunk-driving arrests, which is one-quarter of all cars stopped. It is now 9:00 P.M. According to the guidelines, the officers should
   a. continue the roadblock because they are making a high percentage of arrests.
   b. reestablish the roadblock one-quarter mile down the road.
   c. ask the Advisory Committee for permission to operate the roadblock longer.
   d. dismantle the roadblock, because it has been in operation for two hours.

4. Officers have been directed to operate a drunk-driving roadblock from 6:00 P.M. to 8:00 P.M. at the corner of Greene and First. At 6:45, the unusually heavy traffic begins to back up. According to the guidelines, the officers should NOT
   a. dismantle the roadblock early.
   b. begin stopping only every third car.
   c. move the roadblock to a quieter intersection.
   d. ask for extra officers to help staff the roadblock.

5. According to the guidelines, the officers stopping and questioning motorists at a drunk-driving roadblock should be in uniform so that motorists
   a. will take the roadblock more seriously.
   b. will answer their questions more truthfully.
   c. can identify which agency they are from.
   d. can tell from a distance that this is an official activity.

6. Officer Robb is stopping and questioning eastbound cars at the drunk-driving roadblock on Highway 7. He asks one driver if she has been drinking. The driver says, "No, officer, I haven't," but she slurs her words. According to the guidelines, Officer Robb should
   a. ask the driver a few more questions.
   b. arrest the driver for drunk driving.
   c. ask the driver to take a field sobriety test.
   d. pass the driver through with a warning.

7. A car approaching a drunk-driving roadblock slows downs, then at the last minute speeds up and passes through the roadblock without stopping. According to the guidelines,
   a. officers should note the car's license number and radio headquarters.
   b. the officers should request backup to pursue the car.
   c. the officer in the command observation vehicle should pursue the motorist.
   d. the officers conducting field sobriety tests should pursue the vehicle.

8. Based on the guidelines, which of the following statements is true?
   a. Guidelines for drunk-driving roadblocks are determined by the State Police.
   b. Guidelines for drunk-driving roadblocks are determined by local police departments.
   c. Guidelines for drunk-driving roadblocks are determined by the state legislature.
   d. Guidelines for drunk-driving roadblocks are determined by the county sheriff.

9. According to the guidelines, officers operating a drunk-driving roadblock can expect
   a. cooperation from most drivers.
   b. to arrest only about 1% of the drivers stopped.
   c. to issue several tickets for failure to wear a seat belt.
   d. that many cars will refuse to stop.

10. According to the guidelines, the main role of the command observation officer at a drunk-driving roadblock is to
   a. conduct field sobriety tests.
   b. establish the official police presence.
   c. determine when to dismantle the roadblock.
   d. coordinate the roadblock.

Directions: Read the following passage, then answer questions 11 through 15.

At approximately 10:15 P.M., Mrs. Padilla, who resides at 1023 West Cove Drive, apartment 5C, noticed a man climbing down her neighbor's fire escape. At 10:16 P.M., Mrs. Padilla called to report the incident to the police. Officer Cox and Sergeant Murphy arrived at the home of Ms. Padilla's neighbor, Ms. Mendoza, located at 1024 West Cove Drive, apartment 3A, just as Ms. Mendoza was arriving home from work; the time was approximately 10:25 P.M. Both Officer Cox and Sergeant Murphy informed Mrs. Mendoza of the call from her neighbor, and both of them accompanied Ms. Mendoza up the stairs to her apartment. Upon entering the apartment, it was evident that the window leading to the fire escape was broken. She reported that her large screen TV, her stereo, and her son's Xbox 360 were gone. She also noticed that she was missing some jewelry, including her mother's platinum diamond engagement ring. Ms. Mendoza stated that her son's friend, Joe Smalls, who was addicted to methamphetamines and recently released from prison on a drug charge, came by her house yesterday at 3:15 P.M. to ask her for some money. When she refused, he became irate and said to her, "You'll pay for this. I'll get the money from you one way or another." He then stormed out of the building. Officer Cox and Sergeant Murphy went across the street to question Mrs. Padilla. Because of the time of night, she was unable to obtain a clear description of the perpetrator. She said he was wearing a hooded sweatshirt and a baseball cap, and was of medium build. Officer Cox contacted Mr. Smith's parole officer, Officer Burns. Officer Burns arrived at Mr. Smith's apartment, located at 2030 Jerome Avenue, apartment 2F, at 9:00 A.M. the following morning. Upon entering his apartment, she saw that he had an Xbox in his living room connected to a large screen TV. Officer Burns arrested Mr. Smith on a parole violation. Officer Cox and Sergeant Murphy proceeded with their investigation.

11. Who reported the crime to the police?
   a. Mrs. Padilla
   b. Ms. Mendoza
   c. Officer Cox
   d. Mr. Smith

12. Where did the crime occur?
   a. 1023 West Cove Drive, apartment 5C
   b. 1024 West Cove Drive, apartment 3A
   c. 2030 Jerome Avenue, apartment 2F
   d. 1024 West Cove Drive, apartment 5C

13. Who was responsible for conducting the investigation?

  a. Officer Cox and Sergeant Murphy
  b. Officer Cox, Sergeant Murphy, and Officer Burns
  c. Officer Burns and Officer Cox
  d. Officer Burns and Sergeant Murphy

14. What time did Mr. Smith first come to Ms. Mendoza's apartment?

  a. 9:00 A.M.
  b. 10:16 P.M.
  c. 10:15 P.M.
  d. 3:15 P.M.

15. What was broken in the victim's apartment?

  a. a TV
  b. a stereo
  c. a window
  d. a jewelry box

Directions: Read the following passage, then answer questions 16 through 20.

According to the National Highway and Traffic Safety Administration, more than 40,000 members of the general population of the United States lost their lives in traffic-related fatalities in 2004. The investigation of traffic collisions is an important part of a state trooper's job. Any information obtained during these investigations helps law enforcement, traffic engineering, and driver education personnel in making roadways safer places to travel.

A state trooper should arrive at the collision scene promptly to identify and aid any injured parties and prevent traffic congestion or secondary collisions. In addition, getting to the scene quickly will enable a state trooper to identify witnesses.

Use of emergency signaling equipment while responding is authorized if injuries are known to exist and the extents of the injuries are not known, or if it is unknown if injuries exist (a "no detail" collision).

The collision investigation begins as a state trooper approaches the collision scene. He or she should note any conditions that may have contributed to the collision, such as:

- reduced visibility
- obstructed views
- hazards in the roadway
- malfunctioning traffic control devices
- roadway construction
- weather conditions
- unusually narrow lane widths
- unusual roadway surface conditions

If a hit-and-run collision has occurred, responding state troopers should be alert for suspicious or damaged vehicles leaving the area. If such a vehicle is observed, the state trooper assigned to respond to the scene should continue the response and notify other responding units of the vehicle's description, direction of travel, number of occupants, rate of speed, and any other information that could aid these other officers in stopping that vehicle for questioning.

When en route to any collision scene, a state trooper should obtain the following information from the dispatcher:

- exact location of the collision
- whether medical help has been dispatched
- existence and extent of any injuries

This information is vital to making intelligent decisions governing the response to the scene.

Upon arriving at a collision scene, the state trooper should do the following:

1. Have all drivers move all vehicles not in need of a tow truck out of the roadway.
2. Position the patrol car behind disabled vehicles to keep other traffic from becoming involved.
3. Turn on emergency lights so other traffic is warned of the problem.
4. Call tow trucks if needed.
5. Put on a reflective traffic vest if traffic direction becomes necessary.

6. Have the drivers, passengers, and witnesses step out of the roadway.

7. Collect information from drivers, passengers, and witnesses.

16. According to the passage, which is NOT a reason that a state trooper should arrive at the collision scene in a prompt manner?
   a. to aid any injured people
   b. to prevent involved parties from leaving the scene
   c. to help prevent additional car accidents
   d. to locate witnesses

17. What is a "no detail" collision?
   a. a collision in which it is unknown if injuries exist
   b. a collision in which it is unknown how many parties are involved
   c. a collision in which it is unknown how many vehicles are involved
   d. a collision in which it is unknown where the collision occurred

18. When heading to a collision scene, what information is NOT necessary for a state trooper to obtain from the dispatcher?
   a. that the vehicle driver has a concussion
   b. the cross streets of the accident
   c. that the vehicle driver has a suspended license
   d. that the EMT has been dispatched to the scene

19. According to the passage, as a state trooper approaches a collision scene, he or she should note
   a. local businesses.
   b. functioning traffic control devices.
   c. construction zones.
   d. parked cars.

20. Officer Gallagher has been dispatched to a four-car collision at Maple and Walnut. When he arrives, he notices that all four cars are in the same lane of traffic and have apparently run into each other. What is the first thing he should do?
   a. Call for four tow trucks to be sent to his location.
   b. Have the drivers move all drivable cars into a nearby parking lot.
   c. Put on his reflective vest.
   d. Collect information from all drivers, passengers, and witnesses.

Directions: For questions 21 through 25, choose the answer choice that best rephrases the underlined portion of the given sentence.

21. Civil service exam scores are used to determine promotion even though they may not be a direct reflection of one's ability to perform their job.
   a. promotion, even though, they
   b. promotion, even though they
   c. promotion; even though they
   d. promotion. Even though they

22. Some urban residents possess a negative view of law enforcement nevertheless my experience with law enforcement has always been positive.
   a. law enforcement, nevertheless my
   b. law enforcement, nevertheless, my
   c. law enforcement nevertheless, my
   d. law enforcement; nevertheless, my

23. "Am I crazy," asked Samantha, "Am I the only one who thinks volleyball is a waste of time?"
   a. crazy?" asked Samantha. "Am
   b. crazy?" asked Samantha, "Am
   c. crazy," asked Samantha? "Am
   d. crazy? asked Samantha, "Am

24. Some scientists <u>maintain: that we</u> are born with a fear of snakes.
   a. maintain, that we
   b. maintain that, we
   c. maintain that we
   d. maintain—that we

25. After the cop arrested the <u>suspect the suspects girlfriend</u> came down to the stationhouse to provide him with an alibi.
   a. suspect: the suspects girlfriend
   b. suspect, the suspects' girlfriend
   c. suspect, the suspect's girlfriend
   d. suspect the suspect's girlfriend

26. Look at the four numbered sentences below. Choose the sentence order that would result in the best paragraph.
   (1) The hard work is usually in the beginning and can require months of consistent training.
   (2) Families should consider whether they have time to devote to a dog.
   (3) Although they can be a lot of fun, they also require a lot of hard work.
   (4) Before adopting a dog, a family should give their decision careful consideration.
   a. 4, 3, 2, 1
   b. 4, 2, 3, 1
   c. 4, 2, 1, 3
   d. 2, 4, 1, 3

27. Look at the three numbered sentences below. Choose the sentence order that would result in the best paragraph.
   (1) In some areas, the salt is combined with calcium chloride, which is more effective in below-zero temperatures and melts ice better.
   (2) After a snow- or icefall, city streets are treated with ordinary rock salt.
   (3) This combination of salt and calcium chloride is also less damaging to foliage along the roadways.
   a. 2, 1, 3
   b. 1, 3, 2
   c. 3, 2, 1
   d. 2, 3, 1

28. Look at the four numbered sentences below. Choose the sentence order that would result in the best paragraph.
   (1) If someone expresses a bias toward the case, they may be dismissed from having to serve jury duty.
   (2) In order to qualify as a juror in a criminal or civil case, one has to successfully complete the stage of *voir dire*.
   (3) Once someone is dismissed for bias, *voir dire* must continue until an appropriate number of jurors are selected.
   (4) *Voir dire* is when potential jurors are questioned about their biases; it literally means *to tell the truth*.
   a. 1, 2, 3, 4
   b. 2, 1, 3, 4
   c. 2, 3, 1, 4
   d. 2, 4, 1, 3

29. Look at the four numbered sentences below. Choose the sentence order that would result in the best paragraph.

    (1) Before you begin to compose a business letter, sit down and think about your purpose in writing the letter.
    (2) Do you want to request information, order a product, register a complaint, or apply for something?
    (3) Always keep your objective in mind.
    (4) Do some brainstorming and gather information before you begin writing.

    a. 4, 3, 2, 1
    b. 2, 4, 3, 1
    c. 1, 2, 4, 3
    d. 3, 2, 1, 4

30. Choose the sentence that expresses the idea most clearly and correctly.

    a. Dr. Richard K Brown, CEO of the company, will speak to the scientists at Brookhaven National Laboratory on Wed at 9:00 A.M.
    b. Dr Richard K Brown, CEO of the company, will speak to the scientists at the Brookhaven National Laboratory on Wed. at 9:00 A.M.
    c. Dr. Richard K. Brown, CEO of the company, will speak to the scientists at the Brookhaven National Laboratory on Wed. at 9:00 A.M.
    d. Dr. Richard K. Brown, CEO of the company, will speak to the scientists at the Brookhaven National Laboratory on Wed at 9:00 A.M.

31. Choose the sentence that expresses the idea most clearly and correctly.

    a. As soon she realized that the hurricane was going to strike, the mayor told the residents to evacuate the city.
    b. As soon she realized that the hurricane was going to strike, the city residents were told to evacuate by the mayor.
    c. As soon she realized that the hurricane was going to strike, the mayor tells the city residents of her decision to evacuate.
    d. As soon she realized that the hurricane was going to strike, the residents of the city were told to evacuate by the mayor.

32. Choose the sentence that expresses the idea most clearly and correctly.

    a. A sharpshooter for many years, a pea could be shot off a person's shoulder from 70 yards away by Miles Johnson.
    b. A sharpshooter for many years, Miles Johnson could shoot a pea off a person's shoulder from 70 yards away.
    c. A sharpshooter for many years, from 70 yards away off a person's shoulder Miles Johnson could have shot a pea.
    d. A sharpshooter for many years, Miles Johnson could shoot from 70 yards away off a person's shoulder a pea.

33. Choose the sentence that expresses the idea most clearly and correctly.
   a. By the time they are in the third or fourth grade, the eyes of most children in the United States are tested.
   b. Most children by the time they are in the United States have their eyes tested in the third or fourth grade.
   c. Most children in the United States have their eyes tested by the time they are in the third or fourth grade.
   d. In the United States by the time of third or fourth grade, there is testing of the eyes of most children.

34. Choose the sentence that expresses the idea most clearly and correctly.
   a. Recession, as well as budget cuts, is hard on the cop on the beat.
   b. Recession and budget cuts is hard on the cop on the beat.
   c. Recession, as well as budget cuts, are hard on the cop on the beat.
   d. Budget cuts, as well as the recession, is hard on the cop on the beat.

Directions: For questions 35 through 37, choose the sentence that best combines the two sentences.

35. Recently there have been government cutbacks in funds. Experts foresee steady hiring in the government's future.
   a. Despite recent government cutbacks in funds, experts foresee steady hiring in the government's future.
   b. Whereupon recent government cutbacks in funds, experts foresee steady hiring in the government's future.
   c. So that there have been recent government cutbacks in funds, experts foresee steady hiring in the government's future.
   d. Nonetheless there have been recent government cutbacks in funds, experts foresee steady hiring in the government's future.

36. The federal government has diversity of jobs and geographic locations. The federal government offers flexibility in job opportunities that is unmatched in the private sector.
   a. In spite of its diversity of jobs and geographic locations, the federal government offers flexibility in job opportunities that is unmatched in the private sector.
   b. No matter its diversity of jobs and geographic locations, the federal government offers flexibility in job opportunities that is unmatched in the private sector.
   c. Because of its diversity of jobs and geographic locations, the federal government offers flexibility in job opportunities that is unmatched in the private sector.
   d. The federal government has diversity of jobs and geographic locations, so it offers flexibility in job opportunities that is unmatched in the private sector.

37. There have been great strides in the practical application of quantum physics in the last decade. We are no closer to actually understanding it than were the physicists of the 1920s.

a. Unless there have been great strides in the practical application of quantum physics in the last few decades, we are no closer to actually understanding it than were the physicists of the 1920s.

b. In the last few decades, we are no closer to actually understanding it than were the physicists of the 1920s, until there have been great strides in the practical application of quantum physics.

c. Although there have been great strides in the practical application of quantum physics in the last few decades, we are no closer to actually understanding it than were the physicists of the 1920s.

d. In the last few decades, if there have been great strides in the practical application of quantum physics we are no closer to actually understanding it than were the physicists of the 1920s.

Directions: For questions 38 through 40, fill in the blank with the word that creates the most logical sentence.

38. _____ strip mining is the cheapest method of mining, it is often harmful to the environment.
a. Besides
b. Unless
c. Nevertheless
d. Although

39. Joelle's favorite beverages are herb tea and mineral water. Chelsea, _____, drinks only milk or juice.
a. however
b. therefore
c. then
d. too

40. Sandra Day O'Connor, the first woman to serve on the United States Supreme Court, _____ appointed by President Ronald Reagan in 1981.
a. she
b. and
c. but
d. was

41. During a race, markers will be placed along a roadway at regular 0.2-mile intervals. If the entire roadway is 10,560 feet long, how many such markers will be used?
a. 10
b. 100
c. 20
d. 200

42. If the ratio of union workers to nonunion workers is 2:3 and there are 360 nonunion workers, how many workers are there in all?
a. 240
b. 360
c. 600
d. 720

43. An elevator sign reads "Maximum weight 600 pounds." Which of the following may ride the elevator?
  a. three people: one weighing 198 pounds, one weighing 185 pounds, one weighing 200 pounds
  b. one person weighing 142 pounds with a load weighing 500 pounds
  c. one person weighing 165 pounds with a load weighing 503 pounds
  d. three people: one weighing 210 pounds, one weighing 101 pounds, one weighing 298 pounds

44. Kira's register contains 10 twenty-dollar bills, 3 five-dollar bills, 98 one-dollar bills, 88 quarters, 52 dimes, 200 nickels, and 125 pennies. How much money is in the register?
  a. $351.45
  b. $351.20
  c. $350
  d. $345.51

45. A work crew paves a 120-yard section of road in four hours. If each crew member works at the rate of 10 yards per hour, how many people are working?
  a. 3
  b. 4
  c. 12
  d. 36

46. Two times a number is the result when 7 times a number is taken away from 99. What is the number?
  a. 85
  b. 11
  c. 46
  d. 9

47. When Anthony and Dave work together, they can complete a task in 3 hours. When Anthony works alone, he can complete the same task in 8 hours. How long would it take for Dave to complete the task alone?
  a. $6\frac{1}{2}$ hours
  b. 6 hours
  c. $4\frac{4}{5}$ hours
  d. 4 hours

48. Denise had $120. She gave $\frac{1}{8}$ of this amount to Suzanne. She then gave $\frac{1}{4}$ of the remainder to Darlene. How much money does Denise have left?
  a. $26.25
  b. $30
  c. $78.75
  d. $80

49. Officer Jozwiak has made a vow to jog five days a week for an average of one hour daily. He cut his workout short on Wednesday by 40 minutes but was able to make up 20 minutes on Thursday and 13 minutes on Friday. How many minutes of jogging did Officer Jozwiak lose for the week?
  a. 3 minutes
  b. 7 minutes
  c. 13 minutes
  d. 20 minutes

50. If Martin exchanges 120 quarters, 300 dimes, 600 nickels, and 500 pennies for bills, he may get
  a. 4 twenty-dollar bills, 2 ten-dollar bills, and 1 five-dollar bill.
  b. 3 twenty-dollar bills, 1 ten-dollar bill, and 1 five-dollar bill.
  c. 2 fifty-dollar bills and 1 twenty-dollar bill.
  d. 1 fifty-dollar bill, 2 twenty-dollar bills, and 1 five-dollar bill.

51. Pete made $4,000 in January, $3,500 in February, and $4,500 in March. If he put 30% of his total earnings into his savings account and the rest into his checking account, how much money does he have in his savings account?
  a. $3,600
  b. $4,200
  c. $6,300
  d. $8,400

52. A police precinct is purchasing 5 computer monitors at $175 each, 3 printers at $120 each, and 8 surge suppressors at $18 each. If the precinct receives a 12% discount, what is the final cost (excluding tax)?
  a. $1,379
  b. $1,313.52
  c. $1,213.52
  d. $1,200

53. A map drawn to scale shows that the distance between two towns is 31 inches. If the scale is such that 1 inch equals 1.5 km, how far away are the two towns in kilometers?
  a. 15.5 km
  b. 31 km
  c. 46.5 km
  d. 47 km

54. If Michael runs at a constant rate of 2.5 meters per second, how long will it take him to run 1 kilometer?
  a. 4 minutes
  b. 40 minutes
  c. 400 seconds
  d. 4,000 seconds

55. Amy can run 8 miles at a constant rate in 40 minutes. Sharon can run 12 miles at a constant rate in an hour. Who has a faster rate?
  a. Amy
  b. Sharon
  c. They both run at the same rate.
  d. It cannot be determined by the information given.

56. Your unit is driving west on the interstate and makes a right to turn onto Lake Street. A fallen tree branch on Lake Street forces your unit to make a left onto Littlefield Road. What direction is your unit now traveling?
  a. north
  b. south
  c. east
  d. west

57. State Trooper Rudy Levin is driving north on Main Street when he makes a left turn. If he makes a second left turn, what direction will he be heading?
  a. north
  b. south
  c. east
  d. west

58. Your unit is driving east, makes a left turn, then makes a right turn. What direction is your unit heading now?
  a. north
  b. south
  c. east
  d. west

Directions: Answer questions 59 through 61 based on the following map. The arrows indicate traffic flow. One arrow indicates a one-way street going in the direction of the arrow; two arrows represent a two-way street. You are not allowed to go the wrong way on a one-way street.

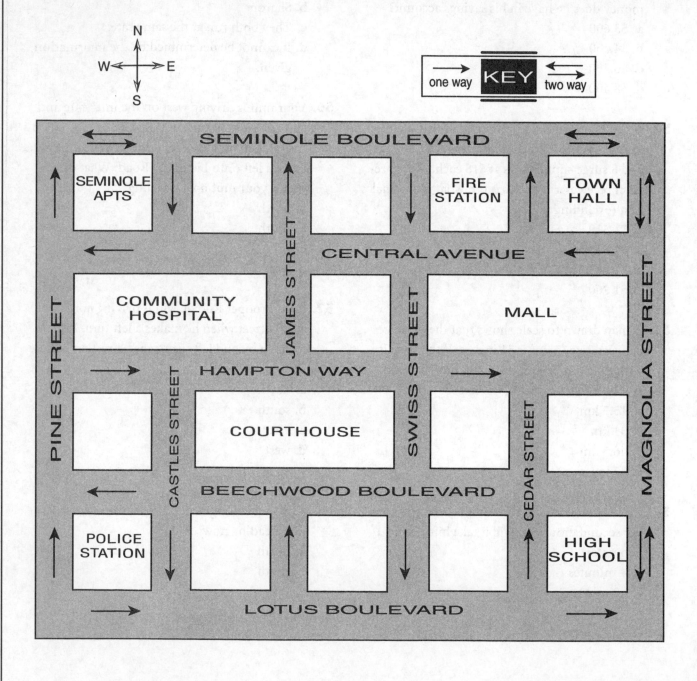

59. You are driving north on Pine Street at Central Avenue and need to pick up a friend at the south entrance of the mall. How many turns will you make, taking the most direct legal route?
- **a.** 3
- **b.** 4
- **c.** 5
- **d.** 6

60. State Trooper DeSiervo has just come off duty and is driving west on Central Avenue. He makes a right onto James Street, then a left onto Seminole Boulevard, then a left onto Castles Street. What direction is he facing?
- **a.** east
- **b.** south
- **c.** west
- **d.** north

61. Your unit is southbound on Magnolia Street and has just crossed Hampton Way, when a call comes in about a domestic disturbance at the Seminole Apartments. What is the quickest route for your unit to take to the incident?
- **a.** Keep driving south, turn west onto Lotus Boulevard, turn north onto Pine Street, and turn east onto Seminole Boulevard.
- **b.** Keep driving south, turn west onto Beechwood Boulevard, turn north onto Pine Street, and turn east onto Seminole Boulevard.
- **c.** Keep driving south, turn west onto Beechwood Boulevard, turn north onto Cedar Street, and west onto Hampton Way.
- **d.** Keep driving south, turn west onto Beechwood Boulevard, turn north onto Swiss Street, and turn west onto Seminole Boulevard.

Directions: Answer questions 62 through 67 based on the following map.

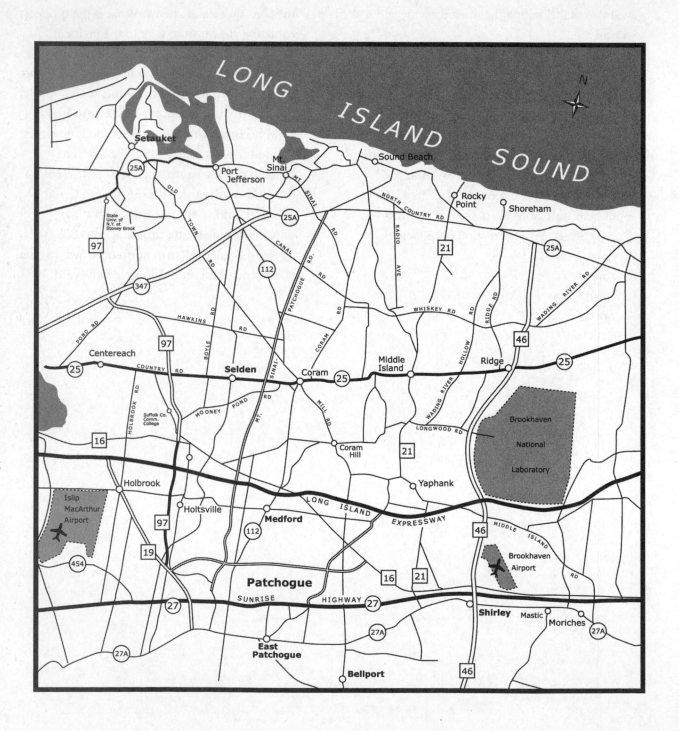

62. The town of Port Jefferson is
_____ of the town of Medford.
  a. northwest
  b. northeast
  c. southwest
  d. southeast

63. Three towns that are located along a major
east/west highway are
  a. Holtsville, Medford, and Selden.
  b. Selden, Coram, and Middle Island.
  c. Coram, Yaphank, and Shirley.
  d. Bellport, Shirley, and Coram.

64. You received instructions to drive from East
Patchogue to Shirley. The roadway that seems
to provide the most direct route is
  a. Route 27.
  b. Route 27A.
  c. the Sunrise Highway.
  d. Route 46.

65. What is the one local roadway that leads into
the Brookhaven National Laboratory?
  a. Ridge Road
  b. Route 25
  c. Route 46
  d. Longwood Road

66. The direction of the drive from Islip MacArthur Airport to Brookhaven National Laboratory is
  a. northwest.
  b. northeast.
  c. southwest.
  d. southeast.

67. The most direct route to travel from the State
University of New York at Stony Brook to Suffolk County Community College is via
  a. Pond Road.
  b. Mooney Pond Road.
  c. Route 97.
  d. Stony Brook Road.

Directions: Answer the following questions based on the map below. The arrows indicate traffic flow. One arrow indicates a one-way street going in the direction of the arrow; two arrows represent a two-way street. You are not allowed to go the wrong way on a one-way street.

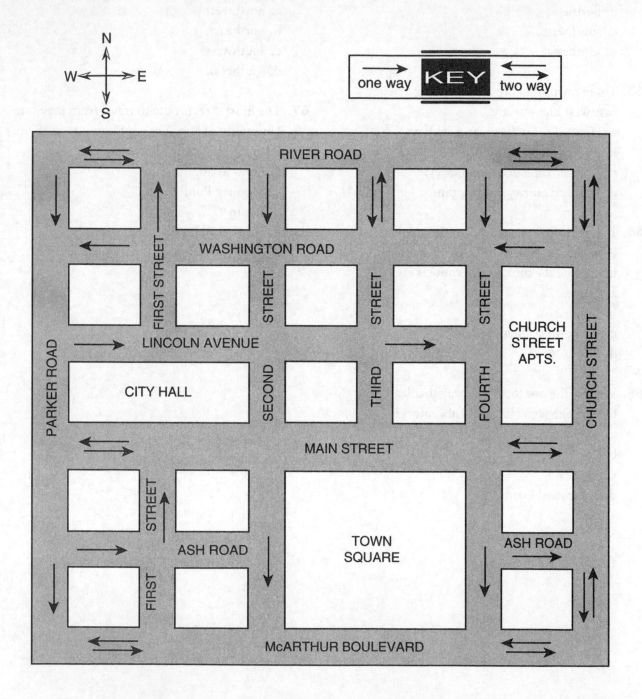

68. Officer Harolds is sitting at a red light at the intersection of Fourth Street and Washington Road facing southbound. The dispatcher sends him on a one-vehicle collision call. A motorist has run into the northwest corner of the City Hall building. What is the quickest route for Officer Harolds to take to City Hall?

    a. Turn west onto Washington Road, then south on Third Street, and then west on Main Street to Parker Road.

    b. Turn west onto Washington Road, then south onto Parker Road.

    c. Turn west onto Washington Road, south onto Second Street, and then east onto Main Street to Parker Road.

    d. Turn west onto Washington Road, then south onto Parker Road, and then east onto Main Street.

69. Officer Watson is driving eastbound on Main Street at Fourth Street. If he makes a U-turn on Main Street, turns onto Third Street, and then makes another U-turn, what direction will he be facing?

    a. east

    b. west

    c. north

    d. south

70. On a rainy night, Officers Epps and Burton are dispatched to a burglar alarm at a business on Ash Road and Church Street. They are driving north on First Street and have just passed Washington Road. What is the quickest route they can take?

    a. North on First Street, then west on River Road, then south on Parker Road, then east on McArthur Boulevard, then north on Church Street to Ash Road.

    b. North on First Street, then east on River Road, then south on Third Street, then east on Main Street, then north on Church Street to Ash Road.

    c. North on First Street, then east on River Road, then south on Church Street to Ash Road.

    d. North on First Street, then west on River Road, then south on Parker Road, then east on Lincoln Avenue, then south on Second Street, then east on McArthur Boulevard, then north on Church Street to Ash Road.

Directions: You will have ten minutes to read and study the following passage. Then, answer questions 71 through 80 without referring back to the passage.

On Tuesday, May 25th at 9:25 A.M., one vehicle (vehicle A) struck another vehicle (vehicle B) from behind at the intersection of 3rd Avenue and 125th Street. Vehicle A was speeding and moving at 55 mph in a 30 mph zone. The streets were wet from rain that fell earlier in the morning. Vehicle A's driver tried to slam on the brakes when the light at the intersection turned red; his wheels locked and his car slid into the bumper of vehicle B. Driver A was not injured, but driver B was complaining of pain in his lower back.

Vehicle A was a light blue sedan that had sustained scratches on the front right passenger door from a previous accident, with a New Jersey license plate. Vehicle B was a dark green SUV, with a bumper sticker on the back bumper. Vehicle B had a New York license plate with the number BK6324. The current accident left scratches on the front of vehicle A's bumper and on the back of vehicle B's bumper. Vehicle A's driver was a 30-year-old white male named Mark. Vehicle B's driver was a 45-year-old white male named Peter.

Officer Cox, with two years on the job, arrived at the scene of the accident at 9:33 A.M. Upon questioning both drivers, in addition to questioning a witness, he concluded that Mark was speeding and unable to completely stop his car when he arrived at the intersection. The witness, walking toward the subway, was a 20-year-old female on her way to class at a nearby college. She was standing at the intersection when the accident occurred. Officer Cox took his blue pen out of his right pocket and began writing the report. The entire investigation was completed at 10:15 A.M. He thanked the witness for her cooperation and told both drivers that they could come to the police station the following day to receive a copy of the police report.

71. What is the name of vehicle A's driver?
   a. Mark
   b. Tim
   c. Cox
   d. Tom

72. How old was the driver of vehicle B?
   a. 35
   b. 30
   c. 45
   d. 20

73. What state was the license plate of vehicle A's car?
   a. New York
   b. New Jersey
   c. Connecticut
   d. Pennsylvania

74. What was the plate number of vehicle B's car?
   a. KB2463
   b. BK6324
   c. BC6324
   d. KC2463

75. How many years did Officer Cox have on the job?
   a. four years
   b. three years
   c. two years
   d. five years

76. Vehicle A's car contained scratches from an earlier accident. Where were these scratches located?
   a. back left passenger door
   b. back right passenger door
   c. front bumper
   d. front right passenger door

77. What kind of car was the driver of vehicle A driving?
   a. light blue sedan
   b. light blue SUV
   c. dark green SUV
   d. dark green sedan

78. At what intersection did the accident occur?
   a. 125th street and 3rd Avenue
   b. 3rd Street and 12th Avenue
   c. 3rd Avenue and 12th Street
   d. 12th street and 5th Avenue

79. What time did the officer arrive at the scene of the accident?
   a. 9:25 A.M.
   b. 10:15 A.M.
   c. 9:33 A.M.
   d. 3:30 P.M.

80. The officer told both drivers that they could come to the stationhouse to pick up the report the following day. Which day of the week would this be?
   a. Monday
   b. Tuesday
   c. Wednesday
   d. Thursday

Directions: Read the following passage, then answer questions 81 through 89.

Customs Inspector Ellen Mitchell noticed several boxes marked "Assorted hand-carved wooden figures from Cameroon," which were being unloaded from a United Express cargo plane. The boxes were sent from Mandara Exports, Ltd. to Freddy Jones Imports. Inspector Mitchell was suspicious of the shipment for several reasons. It was a large shipment, and she had never heard of Freddy Jones Imports before; the boxes were triple-sealed; and Jones himself was there waiting to claim the boxes. Mitchell opened one of the crates and found figures carved of ivory. During the course of the investigation, the following statements were made.

1. Freddy Jones stated that he had ordered wooden figures and he had the invoice to prove it.
2. Margaret Woo, United Express employee, said she picked up this shipment from another plane in Madrid and looked only at the bill of lading, which indicated the crates contained hand-carved wooden figures from Cameroon. Her supervisor happened to be present at the pickup.
3. In Cameroon, Michelle Eseka, president of Mandara Exports, Ltd., stated she obtained carved wooden figurines from several suppliers and cooperatives.
4. William Calabar, head of purchasing for Mandara Exports, said he has recently been dealing mostly with Francis Onitsha, a supplier from eastern Cameroon, for the wooden carvings.
5. Rosemary Ndele, Michelle Eseka's administrative assistant, said that William Calabar was a compulsive gambler.
6. Michelle Eseka said she had told Calabar not to deal with Onitsha, because Onitsha once asked her to send some contraband along with one of her regular shipments.

7. Kenneth Yokadouma, Michelle Eseka's banker, said that Mandara Exports had been losing money lately and that Eseka was in danger of losing the business.
8. A member of Women's Hands, a cooperative that carves figures and makes jewelry, said that Francis Onitsha asked them to do some ivory carvings.
9. Francis Onitsha said that Rosemary Ndele put Freddy Jones in touch with Mandara Exports.
10. Customs officials in Douala, Cameroon, said they had no record of this shipment.

81. Which statement is most damaging to Francis Onitsha?
   a. Statement 6
   b. Statement 8
   c. Statement 2
   d. Statement 4

82. Which statement appears to be an attempt by the speaker to establish innocence?
   a. Statement 7
   b. Statement 9
   c. Statement 10
   d. Statement 6

83. Which statement indicates that United Express employees knew nothing about the illegal shipment?
   a. Statement 4
   b. Statement 6
   c. Statement 2
   d. Statement 10

84. Which statement causes one to be suspicious of the information provided by Rosemary Ndele?
   a. Statement 9
   b. Statement 8
   c. Statement 4
   d. Statement 5

85. Which statement provides a motive for Michelle Eseka to make the illegal shipment?
   a. Statement 6
   b. Statement 8
   c. Statement 9
   d. Statement 7

86. Which two statements cast the greatest suspicion on William Calabar?
   a. Statements 3 and 4
   b. Statements 7 and 10
   c. Statements 5 and 6
   d. Statements 1 and 2

87. Which statement illustrates cooperation between United States and Cameroon law enforcement agencies?
   a. Statement 8
   b. Statement 3
   c. Statement 10
   d. Statement 7

88. Which statement implies Freddy Jones had knowledge of the illegal shipment?
   a. Statement 1
   b. Statement 9
   c. Statement 2
   d. Statement 10

89. Which two statements indicate the bill of lading may have been tampered with?
   a. Statements 2 and 10
   b. Statements 1 and 6
   c. Statements 3 and 9
   d. Statements 2 and 6

Directions: Read the following passage, then answer questions 90 through 96.

The president was scheduled to speak at the Civic Arena. There was no charge to attend the event, but audience members had to obtain a ticket beforehand in order to be admitted to the arena the day of the speech. One week before the event, the Secret Service arrived to finalize security plans. The next day, the box office at the arena received a letter containing a threat on the president's life. During the course of the investigation, the following statements were made.

1. Edna Thurber, box office manager, said that mail was always delivered into a locked box and only she and Bob White, the arena manager, had keys.
2. Randy Shoemaker, a box office employee, said the tickets were all distributed two weeks before the speech.
3. After examining the envelope in which the threat arrived, Police Officer Connie Hall noted that the stamp was not canceled.
4. Rita Lawe, a box office employee, said that several people had tried to obtain tickets in the last week; a short, thin, scruffy man had come to the box office several times.
5. Bob White said he knew for a fact that Edna Thurber had volunteered for a "get out the vote drive" in the last election.
6. Randy Shoemaker said that Rita Lawe was mad at the president because she was being harassed to repay her student loans.
7. Special Agent Maury Thurston said that several members of the public had spoken to him while he was examining the exterior of the arena. He remembered a thin man in a shabby raincoat who asked if there would be bomb-sniffing dogs.

8. Edna Thurber said that Alan Pip, Bob White's assistant, was always talking about how members of the government were also members of a satanic cult.

9. Bob White said that prior to getting the job managing the arena, he was in the military.

10. Alan Pip said that last week when he went out on the loading dock to have a cigarette, he saw a man looking around the area. He said the man was thin and wearing a dirty sweatshirt.

90. Which statements, along with statement 4, indicate the threat was made by someone who does not work at the arena?
   a. Statements 3 and 6
   b. Statements 7 and 10
   c. Statements 1 and 5
   d. Statements 6 and 8

91. Which statement leads one to question the reliability of Alan Pip?
   a. Statement 1
   b. Statement 10
   c. Statement 3
   d. Statement 8

92. Which two statements are most damaging to Bob White?
   a. Statements 1 and 3
   b. Statements 5 and 9
   c. Statements 4 and 8
   d. Statements 2 and 10

93. Which statement is least damaging to Edna Thurber?
   a. Statement 8
   b. Statement 1
   c. Statement 5
   d. Statement 3

94. Which statement represents an idle threat?
   a. Statement 4
   b. Statement 6
   c. Statement 7
   d. Statement 9

95. Which two statements indicate cooperation between the Secret Service and local police?
   a. Statements 5 and 9
   b. Statements 1 and 3
   c. Statements 5 and 7
   d. Statements 3 and 7

96. Which statement is the least helpful in solving the case?
   a. Statement 8
   b. Statement 6
   c. Statement 5
   d. Statement 2

97. When an officer goes to a business to pick up a shoplifter who is already in the custody of private security guards, the officer should take the following steps in the order listed:

1. Check with store security personnel to verify that the circumstances fit the criteria for shoplifting.
2. Have store personnel fill out witness statements and a complaint form for shoplifting.
3. Take a photograph of the evidence, and return the evidence to the store.
4. Search the suspect for weapons or contraband.
5. Place the suspect in the patrol car and secure his or her seat belt.
6. Transport the suspect directly to jail.

Officer O'Brien is dispatched to the Blue Moon Art Gallery to pick up a shoplifter. When she arrives, she talks to Jeffrey, the store security guard, who tells her that he watched a man pick up a five-inch-long statue, stuff it in his coat pocket, and walk out the front door of the shop. He chased the man down and brought him back to the store. Jeffrey takes Officer O'Brien into the back room, where he gives her a photograph of the statue for her to turn in as evidence. Officer O'Brien searches the suspect for weapons and then places him in the patrol car, seat belting him in securely. They drive straight to the jail where O'Brien books the suspect for shoplifting. Officer O'Brien's actions were

a. proper, because the incident was obviously a shoplifting.
b. improper, because she did not take the statue itself in as evidence.
c. proper, because the security guard watched the man carefully before accusing him of anything.
d. improper, because she did not have the guard fill out a witness statement or complaint form.

98. The police department is staking out a warehouse. Officer Walters is stationed north of Officer Smits. Officer Foster is stationed north of Officer Walters. Officer Balboa is stationed south of Officer Foster. Given these facts, which of the following statements is definitely true?

a. Officer Walters is the farthest north of all the officers.
b. Officer Balboa is the farthest south of all the officers.
c. Officer Smits is stationed south of Officer Foster.
d. Officer Balboa is stationed south of Officer Walters.

99. In many smaller police departments, the first officer to arrive at the scene of a homicide is often the same officer who will be responsible for taking photographs to preserve the scene. That officer should take the following steps in the order listed:

1. Make sure the crime scene is secure and assign another officer to be responsible for who comes in and out of the area.
2. Leave the crime scene as it is, not moving any objects or specific items of evidence until photos can be taken of the scene as it first appears to the officer.
3. Take a picture of the overall crime scene area, then take a more specific photo of the area where the body is, and then take photos of specific pieces of evidence.
4. After the first set of photographs is taken, shoot another set and put in an object such as a ruler that will give whoever looks at the pictures a sense of perspective.
5. Place the film in a container and write on the container the case number, the photographer's name and employee number, the date, and the location where the photographs were taken.
6. Take the film to the department photo lab to be developed.

Officer Scales received a call at 8:00 A.M. of a headless body found in a trash bin in an alley behind 4501 W. Thompson St. He arrives on scene and secures the area by having everyone step away from the trash bin and by assigning backup Officer Angel to keep onlookers away from the scene. He reaches inside the trash bin and moves a cardboard box so that he can see the body better. He steps back, takes an over-all shot of the scene, then moves in closer and takes specific shots of the body and then of all items that appear to be potential evidence. He takes a second set of photographs of the scene using a ruler for a marker. He then places the film in an evidence container and writes the case number, his name and employee number, the date, and the location of where the photos were taken. He takes the film to the department photo lab. Based on the information in the passage, Officer Scales's actions were

a. improper, because he needed a flash unit given that the inside of the trash bin is dark.

b. improper, because he didn't witness the development of the film himself to protect the chain of evidence.

c. improper, because he moved the cardboard box before taking photographs of the scene as it first appeared.

d. proper, because he fulfilled all the duties as outlined in the procedures.

100. The police department files information on crimes by date committed. Baker robbed a bank before Mitchell assaulted a police officer, but after Nelson stole a car. Edgar burgled a warehouse before Nelson committed his crime. In what order do these files appear at the police department?

a. Nelson, Baker, Mitchell, Edgar

b. Edgar, Nelson, Baker, Mitchell

c. Baker, Mitchell, Edgar, Nelson

d. Edgar, Mitchell, Nelson, Baker

Answers

1. a. The passage states, *Motorists must be able to see that a roadblock is ahead and that cars are being stopped.*

2. d. The passage states that *an officer who spots a situation that presents a clear and present danger should follow through by directing the motorist to the side of the road where the officers are conducting field sobriety tests. These officers can then follow through on investigating the driver for crimes other than drunk driving.*

3. d. According to the passage, *no drunk-driving roadblock should be in operation for more than two hours.*

4. b. The passage notes that every car passing through a roadblock must be stopped; at no time should motorists feel that certain cars are being singled out.

5. c. The passage states that a roadblock should display visible signs of police authority, such as uniforms and marked patrol cars.

6. a. The passage says that *in suspicious cases, an officer may engage in some further questioning to allow him or her to evaluate the driver's sobriety.*

7. c. The passage states that the observation vehicle *will be able to pursue any motorists who refuse to stop.*

8. a. According to the selection, the guidelines are issued by the Advisory Committee of the State Police.

9. b. The passage notes that *on average only about 1% of all the drivers who pass through a roadblock will be arrested for drunk driving.*

10. d. The passage states that a command observation officer *must ...be present to coordinate the roadblock.*

11. a. Mrs. Padilla was the one who reported the crime after seeing the perpetrator climb down her neighbor's fire escape.

12. b. The crime occurred at the residence of Ms. Mendoza, located at 1024 West Cove Drive, apartment 3A.

13. a. Both Officer Cox and Sergeant Murphy were conducting the investigation. Officer Burns arrested Mr. Smith on a parole violation, but the actual investigation was conducted by Sergeant Murphy and Officer Cox.

14. d. Mr. Smith first went to Ms. Mendoza's apartment the day before the crime occurred at 3:15 P.M. demanding money.

15. c. The window leading to the fire escape was broken.

16. b. The passage never states that an officer should arrive at a collision scene quickly to prevent individuals from fleeing the scene.

17. a. According to the passage, a "no detail" collision is one in which it is unknown if injuries exist.

18. c. A dispatcher does not need to tell a state trooper that the vehicle driver has a suspended license. All the other answer choices contain vital information.

19. c. The state trooper should note any conditions that may have contributed to the collision, including roadway construction. Choice **b** would be correct if it was *malfunctioning* traffic control devices.

20. b. The first step in the procedure is to move all drivable vehicles out of the road.

21. b. The comma separates the long clause—*civil service exam scores are used to determine promotion*—from the subordinate clause—*even though they may not be a direct reflection of one's ability to perform their job.*

22. d. The semicolon is used to separate both main clauses. The clauses are related to one another but could each stand alone as an independent sentence.

23. a. The quotation is a question, and the tag *asked Samantha* ends the sentence.

24. c. No puncuation is needed before or after the word *that* in this sentence.

25. c. The word *suspect's* is singular and possessive and requires an apostrophe. A comma is also needed between the words *suspect* and *the suspect's girlfriend*.

26. b. Sentence 4 introduces the reader to the subject of the paragraph, dog adoption. Sentence 2 leads into sentence 3. Sentence 1 concludes the paragraph.

27. a. Sentence 2 is the topic sentence. Sentence 1 provides reasons for the procedure described in the topic sentence. Sentence 3 gives further definition as a conclusion.

28. d. Sentence 2 introduces the topic of *voir dire*. Sentence 4 provides a description of *voir dire*. Sentence 1 describes what happens if someone has a bias and does not pass *voir dire*. Sentence 3 tells the reader that the next step will be to question additional jurors.

29. c. Sentence 1 is the topic sentence and states the general situation. Sentence 2 poses a question about the situation in the topic sentence. Sentence 4 offers the response. Sentence 3 concludes the paragraph as it gives a reminder about the original goal.

30. c. Periods are correctly placed after all abbreviations in this sentence.

31. a. This choice is clear, has no misplaced modifiers, and has no shifts in verb tense. Choices **b** and **d** have misplaced modifiers and result in unclear sentences; choice **c** has an unnecessary shift from past to present tense.

32. b. This is the only choice that does not have a misplaced modifier. Because Miles Johnson is the sharpshooter, his name should be placed immediately after the introductory phrase, which rules out choices **a** and **c**. Choice **d** is awkwardly constructed and unclear.

33. c. This is the only choice that is clear and logical. Choice **a** reads as though the eyes are in the third or fourth grade. Choices **b** and **d** are unclear.

34. a. The subject *recession* agrees in number with its verb *is*; in the other choices, the subjects and verbs do not agree.

35. a. The word *despite* establishes a logical connection between the main and subordinate clauses. *Whereupon* and *so that* (choices **b** and **c**) make no sense. Choice **d** is both illogical and ungrammatical.

36. c. The subordinator *because* in choice **c** establishes the logical causal relationship between the subordinate and main clauses; choices **a** and **b** do not make sense. Choice **d** has faulty construction.

37. c. The subordinator *although* shows a logical contrasting relationship between the subordinate and main clause. The other choices do not make sense.

38. d. *Although* means "despite the fact that" or "even though." Even though strip mining is cheap, it is harmful. The other choices do not convey this meaning.

39. a. *However* indicates an impending contradiction; it is the best choice because the two clauses compare tastes. In this case, the comparison contrasts Joelle's preference to Chelsea's.

40. d. This is the only choice that results in a complete and logical sentence. Choice **a** is illogical; choices **b** and **c** result in sentence fragments.

41. a. 5,280 feet = 1 mile, so 10,560 feet = 2 miles. To solve, divide the total 2 mile distance by the interval, 0.2 miles: $2 \div 0.2 = 10$.

42. c. Here, you are given a 2:3 ratio. You know one part: There are 360 nonunion workers. You can set up a proportion in order to calculate the unknown part: $\frac{2}{3} = \frac{?}{360}$. Cross multiply to get $360 \times 2 = 3 \times ?$, or $720 = 3 \times ?$. Divide both sides by 3 to get ? = 240. This is the missing part: the number of union workers. Finally, add the number of union workers to nonunion workers to get the whole: 360 + 240 = 600.

43. a. Rounding off the numbers will show that choice **a** is less than 600 pounds and choices **b**, **c**, and **d** are all over 600 pounds.

44. a. First, multiply the amount of coins (or bills) by the value of the coin (or bill):

10 twenty-dollar bills = 10 × $20 = $200

3 five-dollar bills = 3 × $5 = $15

98 one-dollar bills = 98 × $1 = $98

88 quarters = 88 × $.25 = $22

52 dimes = 52 × $.10 = $5.20

200 nickels = 200 × $.05 = $10

125 pennies = 125 × $.01 = $1.25

Next, add up all the money: $200 + $15 + $98 + $22 + $5.20 + $10 + $1.25 = $351.45.

45. a. 120 yards ÷ 4 hours = 30 yards per hour; 30 yards ÷ 10 yards per hour = 3 people.

46. b. Let x = the number sought. Begin by breaking up the problem into smaller pieces: *two times a number* = $2x$, *seven times a number* = $7x$, and *seven times a number is taken away from* $99 = 99 - 7x$. Next, combine the terms, $2x = 99 - 7x$, and simplify, $9x = 99$. Thus, $x = 11$.

47. c. Anthony can complete $\frac{1}{8}$ of the task in 1 hour. You know this because he completes the entire task in 8 hours. Together, Anthony and Dave complete $\frac{1}{3}$ of the task in 1 hour. (Thus, they are done in 3 hours.) Convert both fractions into *twenty-fourths*. $\frac{8}{24}$ per hour (both men) $- \frac{3}{24}$ per hour (just Anthony) $= \frac{5}{24}$ per hour (just Dave). Thus, Dave completes $\frac{5}{24}$ of the task per hour. It will take him $\frac{24}{5}$ hours to complete the entire task; $\frac{24}{5} = 4\frac{4}{5}$ hours.

48. c. $\frac{1}{8}$ of the $120 went to Suzanne: $\frac{1}{8} \times 120 = $15. This means there was $120 - 15 = $105 left. $\frac{1}{4}$ of the $105 went to Darlene: $\frac{1}{4} \times 105 = $26.25. Thus, the amount remaining is $105 - 26.25 = $78.75.

49. b. This is a three-step problem involving multiplication, subtraction, and addition. First find out how many fewer minutes Officer Jozwiak jogged this week than usual: 5 hours × 60 minutes = 300 minutes – 40 minutes missed = 260 minutes jogged. Now add back the number of minutes Officer Jozwiak was able to make up: 260 + 20 + 13 = 293 minutes. Now subtract again: 300 – 293 = 7 minutes jogging time lost.

50. d. Multiply the number of coins by the value of the coin:

120 quarters = 120 × $.25 = $30

300 dimes = 300 × $.10 = $30

600 nickels = 600 × $.05 = $30

500 pennies = 500 × $.01 = $5

Next, add all of the dollar amounts up: $30 + $30 + $30 + $5 = $95. The only choice that represents $95 is **d**: 1 fifty-dollar bill, 2 twenty-dollar bills, and 1 five-dollar bill.

51. a. First, calculate the total amount of money: $4,000 + $3,500 + $4,500 = $12,000. He puts 30% of the $12,000, or 0.30 × $12,000 = $3,600, into the savings account.

52. c. Five monitors will cost $175 × 5 = $875; three printers will cost $120 × 3 = $360; eight surge suppressors will cost $18 × 8 = $144. Before the discount, this adds to: $875 + $360 + $144 = $1,379; 12% of $1,379 = 0.12 × 1,379 = $165.48. Thus, the final cost will be $1,379 – 165.48 = $1,213.52.

53. c. If 1 inch on the map denotes 1.5 km, then 31 inches on the map would represent 46.5 kilometers.

54. c. 1 kilometer = 1,000 meters. Use $D = RT$ with $D = 1,000$, $R = 2.5$ m/sec, and T as the unknown. Rearrange $D = RT$ to $T = \frac{D}{R} = \frac{1000}{2.5} = 400$ seconds.

55. c. Rearrange $D = RT$ into $R = D \div T$ by dividing both sides of the equation by T. Amy's rate is then $R = 8$ mi ÷ 40 min = 0.2 mi/min. Next, calculate Sharon's rate in the same units of miles per minute. This means you need to convert the 1 hour into 60 min. Sharon's rate is then $R = 12$ mi ÷ 60 min = 0.2 mi/min.

56. d. With the left turn, your unit will be heading in the same direction you were originally driving when your unit was on the interstate.

57. b. Two left turns will take State Trooper Levin in the opposite direction as he was originally driving.

58. c. Your unit will be heading in the same direction you were originally driving.

59. b. Taking the most direct legal route, you will be making four turns: right onto Pine Street, right onto Seminole Boulevard, right onto Swiss Street, and left onto Hampton Way.

60. b. If State Trooper DeSiervo turns left onto Castles Street, he will be facing south.

61. b. This is the most direct route because it requires the fewest turns. All the other choices require your unit to go the wrong way on one-way streets.

62. a. It is the only correct choice based on the directional coordinate shown on the map.

63. b. Selden, Coram, and Middle Island are all located along Route 25; in the other answer choices, at least one of the towns named is not located along an east-west highway.

64. b. Both towns are shown directly on Route 27A. Choices **a** and **c** are incorrect; they are the same roadway, which takes you too far away from either town. Choice **d** is incorrect; although Shirley is located on this route, it is nowhere near East Patchogue.

65. d. The easternmost portion of Longwood Road is shown going directly to the laboratory.

66. b. It is the only correct choice based on the directional coordinate shown on the map.

67. c. It is the only roadway that runs adjacent to each campus. The other local roads are near one campus or the other, but are not near both.

68. b. The first turn after heading west on Washington is to turn south onto Parker Road, then east to Lincoln Road, which will put the officer at the scene of the collision.

69. d. Officer Watson is heading east on Main Street and if he makes a U-turn, he will be heading west. If he turns onto Third Street, the only way he can turn will have him heading north. If he makes a second U-turn, he will now be facing south.

70. c. This is the best option to get to Ash Road and Church Street without going the wrong way on any one-way streets.

71. a. Vehicle A's driver, the driver who caused the accident, is named Mark.

72. c. Vehicle B's driver, the victim in the accident, was a 45-year-old white male.

73. b. Vehicle A had a New Jersey plate.

74. b. Vehicle B's New York plate number was BK6324.

75. c. Officer Cox has two years on the job.

76. d. Vehicle A sustained scratches on the front right passenger door from a previous accident.

77. a. Vehicle A was a light blue sedan, while Vehicle B was a dark green SUV.

78. a. The accident occurred at 125th Street and 3rd Avenue.

79. c. Officer Cox arrived at the scene at 9:33 A.M.

80. c. The accident happened on a Tuesday. The following day would be Wednesday.

81. b. Statement 8 indicates a direct link between Francis Onitsha and the making of ivory figurines.

82. d. In statement 6, Michelle Eseka may be trying to focus the investigation away from her and toward Onitsha.

83. c. Margaret Woo referred only to the paperwork and did not actually check the contents of crates. Her story can easily be checked through her supervisor.

84. a. Statement 9 presents the possibility that Rosemary Ndele is working in concert with Freddy Jones. Because Jones is a primary suspect, her association with him makes her information of questionable value.

85. d. Statement 7 indicates that Eseka's business is in financial trouble; that could be a motive for engaging in a lucrative smuggling scheme.

86. c. Statements 5 and 6 provide a possible motive for William Calabar (a gambling debt) and indicate that he disregarded a direct order from his boss.

87. c. Statement 10 states that Cameroon officials provided U.S. investigators with information from official records.

88. b. Statement 9 indicates the possibility that Jones sought out Mandara Exports and that he knows an employee there. This is a deviation from the normal course of business.

89. a. Statement 2 states that the bill of lading contains what is now known to be inaccurate information about the shipment. Statement 10 indicates that Cameroon customs was avoided, because officials there might check the shipment against the bill of lading.

90. b. Statements 7 and 10 both provide information about a member of the public, who may be the person mentioned in statement 4.

91. d. Statement 8 indicates that Alan Pip may be somewhat unstable.

92. a. Statements 1 and 3 provide information about White's ability to access a locked postal box, along with the information that the envelope may not have gone through the U.S. Postal Service, but may instead have simply been placed with the mail.

93. c. Merely doing work to get more people to vote does not cast suspicion on a volunteer. Statements 1 and 3 might cast a little suspicion on Edna, and statement 8 could be an attempt by Edna to divert attention from herself.

94. b. Even if Lawe had been making angry comments about the president and her student loans, it is doubtful that would be a serious threat.

95. d. Statements 3 and 7 taken together refer to the involvement of local police and Secret Service in preparations for the president's visit and the threat investigation.

96. d. Statement 2 provides no information that would further the investigation.

97. d. Step 2 says the officer should have asked the security guard to fill out a witness statement and a complaint form.

98. c. Officer Smits is stationed south of Officer Foster. Officer Walters cannot be farthest north, because Foster is north of Walters. Balboa is south of Foster, but may or may not be south of Walters; therefore, Balboa may not be farthest south, nor south of Walters.

99. c. Step 2 instructs the officer not to move any objects until photos are taken of them as they first appeared when the officer arrived.

100. b. Edgar burgled a warehouse before Nelson stole a car. Baker robbed a bank after Nelson stole a car; Mitchell assaulted a police officer after Baker robbed a bank and Nelson stole a car.

16 ▶ STATE TROOPER PRACTICE TEST 5

CHAPTER SUMMARY
This is the fifth practice test in this book based on the most commonly tested areas on the state trooper exam.

The practice test consists of 100 multiple-choice questions in the following areas: reading comprehension, writing and information ordering, mathematics, spatial and directional orientation, memory and observation, and problem solving. Allot two hours to take this practice test.

This practice test is available through the LearningExpress online link, if you prefer to take it on the computer.

State Trooper Practice Test 5

1. (a) (b) (c) (d)
2. (a) (b) (c) (d)
3. (a) (b) (c) (d)
4. (a) (b) (c) (d)
5. (a) (b) (c) (d)
6. (a) (b) (c) (d)
7. (a) (b) (c) (d)
8. (a) (b) (c) (d)
9. (a) (b) (c) (d)
10. (a) (b) (c) (d)
11. (a) (b) (c) (d)
12. (a) (b) (c) (d)
13. (a) (b) (c) (d)
14. (a) (b) (c) (d)
15. (a) (b) (c) (d)
16. (a) (b) (c) (d)
17. (a) (b) (c) (d)
18. (a) (b) (c) (d)
19. (a) (b) (c) (d)
20. (a) (b) (c) (d)
21. (a) (b) (c) (d)
22. (a) (b) (c) (d)
23. (a) (b) (c) (d)
24. (a) (b) (c) (d)
25. (a) (b) (c) (d)
26. (a) (b) (c) (d)
27. (a) (b) (c) (d)
28. (a) (b) (c) (d)
29. (a) (b) (c) (d)
30. (a) (b) (c) (d)
31. (a) (b) (c) (d)
32. (a) (b) (c) (d)
33. (a) (b) (c) (d)
34. (a) (b) (c) (d)
35. (a) (b) (c) (d)

36. (a) (b) (c) (d)
37. (a) (b) (c) (d)
38. (a) (b) (c) (d)
39. (a) (b) (c) (d)
40. (a) (b) (c) (d)
41. (a) (b) (c) (d)
42. (a) (b) (c) (d)
43. (a) (b) (c) (d)
44. (a) (b) (c) (d)
45. (a) (b) (c) (d)
46. (a) (b) (c) (d)
47. (a) (b) (c) (d)
48. (a) (b) (c) (d)
49. (a) (b) (c) (d)
50. (a) (b) (c) (d)
51. (a) (b) (c) (d)
52. (a) (b) (c) (d)
53. (a) (b) (c) (d)
54. (a) (b) (c) (d)
55. (a) (b) (c) (d)
56. (a) (b) (c) (d)
57. (a) (b) (c) (d)
58. (a) (b) (c) (d)
59. (a) (b) (c) (d)
60. (a) (b) (c) (d)
61. (a) (b) (c) (d)
62. (a) (b) (c) (d)
63. (a) (b) (c) (d)
64. (a) (b) (c) (d)
65. (a) (b) (c) (d)
66. (a) (b) (c) (d)
67. (a) (b) (c) (d)
68. (a) (b) (c) (d)
69. (a) (b) (c) (d)
70. (a) (b) (c) (d)

71. (a) (b) (c) (d)
72. (a) (b) (c) (d)
73. (a) (b) (c) (d)
74. (a) (b) (c) (d)
75. (a) (b) (c) (d)
76. (a) (b) (c) (d)
77. (a) (b) (c) (d)
78. (a) (b) (c) (d)
79. (a) (b) (c) (d)
80. (a) (b) (c) (d)
81. (a) (b) (c) (d)
82. (a) (b) (c) (d)
83. (a) (b) (c) (d)
84. (a) (b) (c) (d)
85. (a) (b) (c) (d)
86. (a) (b) (c) (d)
87. (a) (b) (c) (d)
88. (a) (b) (c) (d)
89. (a) (b) (c) (d)
90. (a) (b) (c) (d)
91. (a) (b) (c) (d)
92. (a) (b) (c) (d)
93. (a) (b) (c) (d)
94. (a) (b) (c) (d)
95. (a) (b) (c) (d)
96. (a) (b) (c) (d)
97. (a) (b) (c) (d)
98. (a) (b) (c) (d)
99. (a) (b) (c) (d)
100. (a) (b) (c) (d)

State Trooper Practice Test 5

Directions: Read the following passage, then answer questions 1 through 3.

From the time of death, the temperature of a dead body decreases at the rate of one degree per hour until it reaches the surrounding environmental temperature. Normal body temperature is 98° F. Rigor mortis (the stiffening of muscles and joints) commences approximately four hours after death, progresses slowly for 16 hours, and gradually subsides for an additional 16 hours until it has completely dissipated.

1. Detective Ellis and Medical Examiner Slate respond to the scene of a homicide and examine the body of the victim. They note that the room temperature is 70°, the body's temperature is 88°, and the body is in partial rigor mortis. Which of the following would be the most reasonable inference?
   a. The time of death was about two hours before the examination.
   b. The time of death was about ten hours before the examination.
   c. The time of death was about 24 hours before the examination.
   d. The time of death was more than 48 hours before the examination.

2. Detective Ellis and Medical Examiner Slate respond to the scene of a homicide and examine the body of the victim. They note that the room temperature is 38°, the body's temperature is 60°, and the body has no rigor mortis. Which of the following would be the most reasonable inference?
   a. The time of death was about two hours before the examination.
   b. The time of death was about ten hours before the examination.
   c. The time of death was about 38 hours before the examination.
   d. The time of death was about 48 hours before the examination.

3. Detective Ellis and Medical Examiner Slate respond to the scene of a homicide and examine the body of the victim. They note that the room temperature is 90°, the body's temperature is 90°, and the body has no rigor mortis. Which of the following would be the most reasonable inference?
   a. The time of death was about eight hours before the examination.
   b. The time of death was about two hours before the examination.
   c. The time of death was about 24 hours before the examination.
   d. The time of death was more than 36 hours before the examination.

Directions: Read the following passage, then answer questions 4 and 5.

A lawful arrest must be based on probable cause, which is defined as facts and circumstances based on apparently reliable information that would lead a person of reasonable intelligence, experience, and common sense to conclude that an offense has been, is being, or will be committed by a particular person. Reasonable suspicion about a crime may be enough to stop and question a person, but without probable cause it is not enough to make a lawful arrest.

4. A trooper could make a lawful arrest based on which of the following?
    a. A bank manager approaches the trooper, points to a man sitting in a car across the street from the bank, and tells the officer that the man appears to have been watching the entrance to the bank for more than an hour.
    b. A trooper observes a man walk quickly out of a bank, enter a double-parked car, and drive away rapidly.
    c. An obviously intoxicated person approaches the trooper, points to a bank located across the street, and tells the officer to arrest the bank manager for stealing all the money out of his savings account.
    d. A bank manager approaches the trooper, points to an obviously intoxicated person, and tells the officer that the person reached over the bank counter and stole money from the bank teller.

5. A trooper could make a lawful arrest based on which of the following?
    a. reasonable suspicion by a trained trooper that a crime may have been committed
    b. an anonymous letter alleging a crime and who committed it
    c. hearsay information about a person with a reputation for criminal conduct
    d. the observation of a person who begins to run from the scene of crime as he sees the police approaching

Directions: Read the following passage, then answer questions 6 through 8.

A person is guilty of criminal trespass when he or she knowingly enters or remains unlawfully in a building. He or she enters or remains unlawfully when he or she does so without permission, license, or privilege. A person is guilty of burglary when he or she knowingly enters or remains unlawfully in a building with intent to commit a crime therein. A person is guilty of assault when, with intent to cause physical injury to another person, he or she causes such physical injury.

6. Charlotte Cooper received a call from her son's teacher, Mrs. Stoker, who told her that her son was going to fail his courses. Ms. Cooper immediately went to the school and entered the building through the front door, passing under the signs that say "No Trespassing" and "All Persons Must Stop at Security." She passed the security desk without stopping and proceeded to Mrs. Stoker's classroom. Cooper asked for an explanation from Stoker, but a heated argument developed and Cooper grabbed Stoker by the neck, choked her for a few seconds, and pushed her into a chair. Stoker was not injured. The school principal filed a complaint, and Trooper Cook arrested Cooper. Regarding charges against Cooper, which of the following is correct?
    a. She is guilty of criminal trespass for unlawfully entering the building, because she did not stop at the security desk.
    b. She is not guilty of criminal trespass because she was the parent of a student and had legitimate business in the school.
    c. She is guilty of assault because she choked Stoker.
    d. She is guilty of burglary for unlawfully entering the school with intent to commit a crime therein.

7. Assume the same facts as question 6, but, in addition, as Cooper was leaving the classroom, she noticed the teacher's grade book on the desk. She went into the women's bathroom and hid there, waiting for Stoker to leave so that she could take the grade book and destroy it. When Stoker left, Cooper entered the classroom, took the grade book, ripped out the pages, and threw them into a trash can. Regarding charges against Cooper, which of the following is incorrect?

a. She is guilty of criminal trespass for unlawfully entering or remaining in the building without license or privilege.

b. She is not guilty of burglary because she did not have the intent to commit a crime when she first entered the school, and the intent to steal and destroy the grade book was formulated after she entered.

c. She is guilty of burglary for unlawfully entering or remaining in the school with intent to commit a crime therein, i.e., the larceny and destruction of the grade book.

d. She is guilty of both criminal trespass and burglary.

8. Assume the same facts as in questions 6 and 7, but, in addition, as Cooper left her house to go to the school, she told her neighbor that she was going to beat the heck out of her son's teacher. Regarding charges against Cooper, which of the following is NOT true?

a. She is guilty of criminal trespass for unlawfully entering or remaining in the school without license or privilege.

b. She is guilty of assault because she entered the school with the intent to assault Mrs. Stoker.

c. She is guilty of burglary for unlawfully entering or remaining in the school with intent to commit a crime therein, i.e., assault.

d. She is guilty of both criminal trespass and burglary.

Directions: Read the following passage, then answer questions 9 and 10.

Traffic laws are enacted to enhance the orderly flow of traffic, to regulate motor vehicles and drivers, and to promote public safety. The number of vehicles, drivers, and roads far exceeds the number of law enforcement personnel available for regulatory duties.

9. To achieve the goals of traffic law, it is most effective for a police agency to enforce traffic laws in a manner to

a. ensure that summonses are issued for all violations.

b. concentrate only on the most serious violations.

c. encourage the public's voluntary compliance with the traffic laws.

d. raise as much revenue as possible.

10. A trooper observes a motorist pass a steady red light. The trooper should issue a summons in all of the following circumstances, except when the

a. motorist did not intentionally drive through the light.

b. motorist appears to be an upstanding, law-abiding citizen.

c. motorist intentionally drove through the light but had looked both ways before proceeding.

d. motorist carefully drove through the light because of an exteme emcrgency.

Directions: Read the following passage, then answer questions 11 through 15.

In order for a murder to be justified under the law of self-defense, it must satisfy the following conditions: 1) the defendant must believe that he or she is in imminent danger of death or serious bodily harm, 2) the force used to counter an attack must be proportionate to the unlawful force, and 3) this belief must be reasonable. If the fact finder does not believe that an individual's response was reasonable under his or her circumstances, they will not be successful in their claim for self-defense. Other jurisdictions may impose additional conditions. The "retreat rule" maintains that force is unreasonable if one can retreat in complete safety. Approximately one-half of states follow this rule and one-third follow the "true man" or "no retreat rule" (i.e. a man is allowed to stand his ground during a confrontation). The exception to the retreat rule is the "castle exception." Most states abide by the castle exception, which maintains that one does not have to retreat from their home during a confrontation even if they can retreat in complete safety. Furthermore, most states hold that a defendant cannot claim self-defense if they are the initial aggressor.

11. Which of the following circumstances would allow Carol to have a reasonable claim for self-defense?
   a. Ivette attacks Carol with a knife in an alleyway, and Carol hits Ivette with a lead pipe, causing Ivette to have permanent brain damage.
   b. Ivette runs toward Carol in a crowded street, with no visible weapon. Carol is scared for her life, takes out a gun, and shoots Ivette.
   c. Ivette calls Carol and makes threatening remarks. Carol sees Ivette on the street the next day and shoots her.
   d. Ivette is standing in front of Carol's house stating that she has a gun and will kill her. Carol points her gun out of the window, shoots, and wounds Ivette in the leg.

12. In which of the following scenarios would the force used to counter an attack be considered unreasonable?
   a. A 230-pound man comes toward a 100-pound woman with a baseball bat. She takes out a knife and stabs him.
   b. A 230-pound man is approached in a threatening manner by a 175-pound man. The 230-pound man stabs him.
   c. A 230-pound man is approached by a 100-pound woman with a gun. The two ensue in a struggle, the gun goes off, and the 100-pound woman is killed.
   d. A 230-pound man wakes up to find a 135-pound man standing over him with a knife. He reaches under his pillow, takes out his gun, and shoots him.

13. In domestic violence cases, if a woman who is battered kills her abuser, which of the following claims would most likely result in a successful self-defense claim?
   a. A woman is being hit repeatedly by her husband in the kitchen. She takes out a knife and kills him.
   b. A woman has been brutally physically and sexually abused by her husband for over ten years. One night, after he beats her, she waits until he falls asleep and stabs him.
   c. A woman has been brutally physically and sexually abused by her husband for over 20 years. She decides to hire a hit-man to kill him.
   d. A woman has been brutally physically and sexually abused by her husband for over ten years. One hour after a horrible beating, he begins yelling at her again. She fears he might get up and hit her. She reaches for a gun and shoots him.

STATE TROOPER PRACTICE TEST 5

14. In which of the following situations would a claim of self-defense be unreasonable?
  a. Man A approaches man B with a knife. Man B hits man A with a glass bottle causing serious injury. Man B claims self-defense.
  b. Man A approaches man B with a knife, threatening to kill him. Man B takes out a gun and shoots man A, killing him. Man B claims self-defense.
  c. Man A approaches man B with a broken bottle. Man B takes another bottle and hits man A repeatedly. Man A takes a gun out of his pocket and shoots man B, killing him. Man A claims self-defense.
  d. Man A, while yelling and screaming, approaches man B with a lead pipe. Man B takes a box cutter and slices man A several times in the face, causing permanent scarring. Man B claims self-defense.

15. In a state that does not have a "Castle Exception," which of the following would constitute a self-defense claim?
  a. A homeowner, who is just opening his front door to enter his house, sees a strange man standing in his living room. The homeowner takes out a gun and shoots him.
  b. A homeowner hears a noise in the basement. As he is walking down the stairs, he is confronted by a stranger. The homeowner takes out a gun and shoots him.
  c. A homeowner hears a noise and jumps out of bed to find a stranger running across his lawn, toward the street. The homeowner takes out his gun and shoots him.
  d. A homeowner hears a noise. As he runs down the stairs, he sees a stranger climbing out of his window. The homeowner takes out his gun and shoots him.

Directions: Read the following passage, then answer questions 16 and 17.

When performing a line-up for identification purposes, officers should remember that witnesses, particularly victims of crime, can be highly vulnerable. Because of their desire to please the officer, they may pick anyone in the line-up (usually the person who looks most like the perpetrator), in order to make the officer happy and help the case. Hence, an innocent person may go to jail. Therefore, officers should be very careful not to say anything suggestive or display any body language that appears suggestive in order to elicit the most objective identification.

16. Of the following, which would be allowable for a state trooper to say during or after a line-up?
  a. You picked the wrong guy.
  b. That is the same person everyone else picked.
  c. You did a great job.
  d. Thanks for your help.

17. Of the following, which body language would not be considered suggestive during or after a witness identification in a line-up?
  a. The officer laughs.
  b. The officer stares at the suspect through the one-way mirror.
  c. The officer looks directly at the witness, without facial expression.
  d. The officer sighs and frowns.

18. Grand larceny from the person is a less serious crime than grand larceny by extortion. Robbery is more serious than grand larceny from the person, but less serious than kidnapping. Kidnapping is more serious than grand larceny by extortion. Which crime is the most serious?
  a. grand larceny from the person
  b. grand larceny by extortion
  c. robbery
  d. kidnapping

19. Grand larceny by extortion is a more serious crime than grand larceny from the person. Robbery is less serious than kidnapping, but more serious than grand larceny from the person. Kidnapping is more serious than grand larceny by extortion. Which crime is the least serious?
   a. grand larceny by extortion
   b. grand larceny from the person
   c. robbery
   d. kidnapping

20. A trooper assigned as a station house watch officer receives an anonymous telephone call. The caller states that he has information about a serious crime that had been recently reported in the newspapers. The caller states that he does not want to be identified, and he does not give any information regarding his motive or reliability. Of the following, the best way for the trooper to handle the call would be to
   a. insist that the caller identify himself before continuing the conversation.
   b. put the caller on hold while attempting to contact the detectives assigned to the case.
   c. note the information given and attempt to get more details by pointing out the discrepancies between the caller's story and other available information.
   d. get all the details possible from the caller without providing the caller with any other available information.

21. Three of the sentences below contain one or more grammatical or spelling errors. Select the answer choice that is correct as is.
   a. There was a time when cops could beat a suspect to obtain a confession; this was an acceptable practice.
   b. There were a time when cops could beat a suspect to obtain a confession; this was an acceptable practice.
   c. There was a time when cops could beat a suspect to obtain a confession; this is an acceptable practice.
   d. There was a time when cops could beat a suspect to obtain a confession, this was an acceptable practice.

22. Three of the sentences below contain one or more grammatical or spelling errors. Select the answer choice that is correct as is.
   a. Robert and Robin wanted to become troopers because they wanted to be a part of a well-respected organization.
   b. Robert and Robin wanted to become a trooper because they wanted to be a part of a well-respected organization.
   c. Robert and Robin wanted to become troopers because they wanted to be apart of a well-respected organization.
   d. Robert and Robin wanted to become Troopers because he/she wanted to be part of a well-respected organization.

23. Three of the sentences below contain one or more grammatical or spelling errors. Select the answer choice that is correct as is.
  a. In many cities in the United States, the tenor of a mayor is four years before they must run for reelection.
  b. In many city's in the United States, the tenure of a mayor is four years before he or she must run for reelection.
  c. In many cities in the United States, the tenure of a mayor is four years before he or she must run for reelection.
  d. In many citys in the united states, the tenure of a mayor is four years before he or she must run for reelection.

24. Three of the sentences below contain one or more grammatical or spelling errors. Select the answer choice that is correct as is.
  a. Yesterday. Sergeant Thomas asked Officer Josephs if he wants to patrol Highway 5.
  b. Yesterday, Sergeant Thomas asks Officer Josephs if he wanted to patrol Highway 5.
  c. Yesterday, Sergeant Thomas asked Officer Josephs if he wanted to patrol Highway 5.
  d. Yesterday, Sergeant Thomas asks Officer Josephs if he wants to patrol Highway 5.

25. Three of the sentences below contain one or more grammatical or spelling errors. Select the answer choice that is correct as is.
  a. The amount of summons that Trooper Busby wrote in March was 42.
  b. The amount of summonses that Trooper Busby wrote in March were 42.
  c. The number of summons that Trooper Busby wrote in March was 42
  d. The number of summonses that Trooper Busby wrote in March was 42.

26. Three of the sentences below contain one or more grammatical or spelling errors. Select the answer choice that is correct as is.
  a. The severity of Trooper Prentiss's injury was not known.
  b. The severeness of Trooper Prentisses injury was not known.
  c. The severity of Trooper Prentise's injury was not known.
  d. The severness of Trooper Prentiss's injury was not known.

27. Three of the sentences below contain one or more grammatical or spelling errors. Select the answer choice that is correct as is.
  a. Trooper Allen and Trooper Biaz likes his/her job.
  b. Trooper Allen and Trooper Biaz like their job.
  c. Trooper Allen and Trooper Biaz like his and her jobs.
  d. Trooper Allen and Trooper Biaz like their jobs.

28. One of the sentences below contains one or more grammatical or spelling errors. Select the answer choice that contains an error.
  a. Although state police patrol methods have remained similar over the years regardless of some people's call for changes.
  b. State police patrol methods have remained similar over the years regardless of some people's call for changes.
  c. Although state police patrol methods have remained similar over the years, some people have called for changes.
  d. State police patrol methods have remained similar over the years despite some politicians' calls for changes.

29. One of the sentences below contains one or more grammatical or spelling errors. Select the answer choice that contains an error.
  a. Troopers need to keep their strength up during training.
  b. Troopers need to keep their strengths up during training.
  c. A trooper needs to keep his or her strength up during training.
  d. Each trooper needs to keep his or her strength up during training.

Directions: For questions 30 through 35, choose the word or phrase that best fills the blank to properly complete the sentence.

30. Officer Taylor forgot to read the suspect his rights before asking him about his involvement in the crime; _____, the entire confession was held inadmissible at trial.
  a. therefore
  b. however
  c. conversely
  d. nevertheless

31. There are _____ troopers who are dedicated to their positions as protectors of the public.
  a. more
  b. many
  c. much
  d. most

32. Officer Cox was running everyday at the track for two months in preparation for a special unit in the department. None of the other officers trained for the physical portion of the exam. _____, he was the only one that passed.
  a. Accordingly
  b. Conversely
  c. Yet
  d. Still

33. The training sergeant gave each trooper considerable _____ attention.
  a. personnel
  b. personal
  c. personable
  d. personnell

34. The Sergeant told everyone that they would be _____ responsible for their own mistakes if they did not pay attention to his instructions.
  a. singularly
  b. singlairly
  c. singinlary
  d. sinulary

35. When making a traffic stop, a trooper should always remember to ask the driver for his or her _____.
  a. lysence
  b. lesence
  c. license
  d. licence

36. Identify the sentence that contains a mistake in capitalization, punctuation, grammar, or spelling. If you find no mistakes, select choice **d.**
  a. John Jones has always wanted to be a Trooper.
  b. My uncle took me to Yankee Stadium.
  c. Suzanne took her dog Princess to see Dr. Doogie.
  d. no mistakes

37. Identify the sentence that contains a mistake in capitalization, punctuation, grammar, or spelling. If you find no mistakes, select choice **d.**
  a. Juan was elected vice president of his academy class.
  b. Suzanne's nickname is Frenchie because she was born in Martinique.
  c. Trooper Goodcup issued two Summonses to a Motorist.
  d. no mistakes

Directions: Read the following paragraph and answer questions 38 through 40.

When a trooper provides physical descriptions of suspects for a dispatcher to broadcast, some information is more important than other portions of the description. Items that should be given out include:

1. Color and length of hair
2. Headgear (hat, cap, scarf, etc.) the suspect might have been wearing
3. Race and sex
4. Weapons the suspect displayed or may be carrying
5. Approximate height and weight
6. Upper body clothing such as coat, jacket, or shirt
7. Lower body clothing (long or short pants, skirt, etc.)
8. Footwear

38. Select the most appropriate order for providing information to be broadcast.
   a. 3, 4, 5, 7
   b. 6, 5, 1, 3
   c. 8, 1, 6, 2
   d. 3, 2, 6, 7

39. Select the least appropriate order for providing information to be broadcast.
   a. 8, 1, 6, 4
   b. 2, 6, 1, 7
   c. 4, 3, 5, 7
   d. 3, 4, 7, 8

40. Trooper Pitty is taking a report of a chain-snatch from a teenager at the bus terminal. The teen says the person who snatched his chain from around his neck was a chubby white male wearing a red bandana, white sneakers, and a dark-colored windbreaker, and was the same height as the teen (5′9″). He also recalled that the snatcher was wearing blue jeans, and had in his hand something that looked like a knife but might have been a box cutter.

What is the first thing Trooper Pitty should mention in his description?
   a. The suspect was wearing a red bandana.
   b. The suspect was chubby.
   c. the suspect's race and sex
   d. the suspect's height

Directions: Read the following paragraph and answer questions 41 through 43.

A trooper is told to respond to a burglary in a rural part of town. Upon entering the dwelling, the victim tells the trooper that her house was burglarized while she was at work. She worked unusually late this evening and said it could have happened anytime between 8:00 A.M. and 7:00 P.M. The victim manages an electronic store and is often asked to bring items home for testing. According to the victim, several items of significant value from the electronic store were stolen, such as two digital cameras, three multimedia home theater projectors, five laptop computers, and one plasma TV.

The items are valued at:

- Digital cameras: $1,525 each
- Laptop computers: $2,550 each
- 60" plasma HDTV: $6,670 each
- Multimedia projector: $4,549 each

41. What is the total value of the multimedia projectors that were stolen?
   a. $9,098
   b. $4,549
   c. $13,467
   d. $13,647

42. What is the total value of all the laptops that were stolen?
   a. $12,750
   b. $2,550
   c. $10,200
   d. $12,755

43. What is the total value of everything that was stolen?
   a. $15,294
   b. $36,117
   c. $25,917
   d. $33,567

Directions: Read the following paragraph and answer questions 44 through 46.

Trooper Suki is sent on a three-day training exercise that requires her to travel to the state's capital city. She will take her personal car and receive mileage reimbursement of 49.5 cents a mile. She will also receive reimbursement of expenses for meals at the per diem rate of $49 per day, with 75% reimbursement for her two travel days. The total mileage Trooper Suki put on her vehicle was 250 miles.

44. Trooper Suki's reimbursement for mileage is
   a. $12.37.
   b. $123.75.
   c. $122.50.
   d. $12.50.

45. Trooper Suki's reimbursement for meals is
   a. $220.50.
   b. $245.
   c. $183.75.
   d. none of the above

46. Trooper Suki's total reimbursement for the training trip is
   a. $257.37.
   b. $353.
   c. $344.25.
   d. none of the above

47. Trooper Acton drives his marked car 80 miles on Sunday, 50 miles on Monday, 50 miles on Tuesday, 80 miles on Wednesday, and 60 miles on Thursday. What is the average number of miles driven?
   a. 80 miles
   b. 50 miles
   c. 58 miles
   d. 64 miles

48. Seventy-five percent of the summonses issued by the officers in Troop X were for speeding. If 460 summonses were issued in the month of April, how many were NOT for speeding?
   a. 100
   b. 115
   c. 230
   d. There is not enough information to answer the question.

49. Trooper Rosen is taking the train from his headquarters to a meeting at the state capitol. The train trip takes three hours; his meeting is at 2 P.M., and it takes about 30 minutes to get from headquarters to the train station. To be sure to get to his meeting on time but not more than 30 minutes early, Trooper Rosen should plan to take a train that leaves at what time?
  a. 11:30 A.M.
  b. 11:00 A.M.
  c. 10:30 A.M.
  d. 10:00 A.M.

Directions: Read the following paragraph and answer questions 50 through 52.

Trooper Addison responds to take a report of a burglary at Bette's Beauty Supply Store. According to Bette, both personal items and beauty supply items were missing when she opened the store on Saturday morning. Among the personal items were her portable CD player, valued at $57; four compact disks (CDs), valued at $12.99 each; her leather jacket, valued at $450; and $125 in cash. Store items that were missing included:

- 10 boxes of combs and hair ornaments, each box valued at $112
- 9 boxes of hair color, each box valued at $90
- 6 boxes of sunscreen, each box valued at $80
- 5 boxes of lipsticks, each box valued at $55

50. What is the total value of the personal items reported missing by Bette?
  a. $626.96
  b. $632
  c. $683.96
  d. $783.96

51. What is the total value of all the store items reported missing by Bette?
  a. $2,685
  b. $1,565
  c. $1,875
  d. $1,975

52. What is the total value of Bette's personal items and store items that were reported missing?
  a. $2,197
  b. $2,601.96
  c. $3,368.96
  d. $3,468.96

Directions: Read the following paragraph and answer questions 53 through 55.

Many police departments use military time to ensure that officers are not confused when reporting for duty or writing reports. Military time uses a 24-hour clock. One minute after midnight is 0001 hours; one minute after noon is 1201 hours, 1:00 P.M. is 1300 hours, 2:00 P.M. is 1400 hours, and so on until the clock strikes midnight (2400 hours).

53. Trooper Oliver works an eight-hour shift that begins at 1500 hours. In nonmilitary time, this means that she works from
  a. 5 P.M. to 1 A.M.
  b. 3 P.M. to 11 P.M.
  c. 1:50 P.M. to 9:50 P.M.
  d. 1:30 A.M. to 9:30 A.M.

54. Trooper Padilla works a seven-hour shift from 1500 hours to 2300 hours. Trooper Torres works the same hours, but his shift is from 1400 hours to 2100 hours. Trooper Padilla was given overtime and left work at 0130 hours, and Trooper Torres left work early at 2100 hours. How many more hours did Trooper Padilla work than Trooper Torres?

a. 3 hours and 30 minutes

b. 4 hours

c. 4 hours and 30 minutes

d. 1 hour

55. Trooper Mendoza is supposed to report to work at 0700 hours and work until 1500 hours. Officer Mendoza was given four hours of overtime. At what time did he leave work?

a. 6:00 A.M.

b. 7:00 A.M.

c. 7:00 P.M.

d. 8:00 P.M.

Directions: Use the following map to answer questions 56 through 60.

Center City is laying out the route of its new light rail system. The map legend shows you the proposed route (called *alignment* on the map), and uses an X to show where streets will be closed and an O to show where the tracks will cross a street that will also be open to vehicle traffic. For these questions, you may ignore whether the route will be grade separated with the light rail train (LRT) going over or under the street crossing.

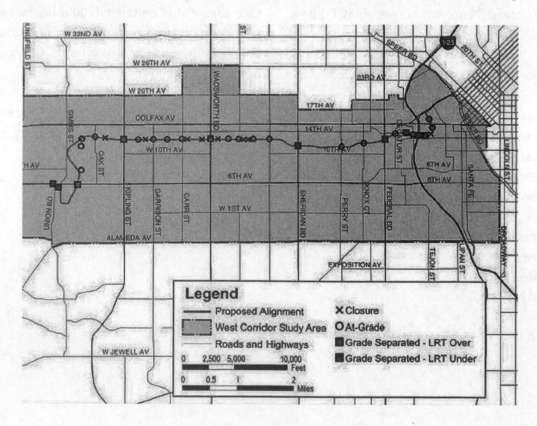

56. The total number of *grade separated crossings* from Federal Bd to Kipling St is
a. two.
b. three.
c. four.
d. five.

57. W. Jewell Av intersects the proposed rail route at which point?
a. Alameda Av
b. Exposition Av
c. Kipling St
d. It does not intersect the proposed rail route at all.

58. The total number of grade separated crossings on 6th Av is
a. one.
b. two.
c. three.
d. four.

59. How many times will a vehicle traveling on Federal Bd from Exposition Av to 23rd Av cross the alignment?
a. one
b. two
c. three
d. zero

60. According to the map, the alignment will affect I-25 in what way?
a. by creating a grade separation somewhere between 10th Av and 8th Av
b. by creating a grade separation somewhere between Colfax Av and 8th Av
c. by creating a grade crossing somewhere between 8th Av and 6th Av
d. I-25 will not be affected by the alignment.

Directions: Read the following paragraph and answer questions 61 through 70.

At about 5:00 A.M., a trooper driving on a two-way north-south road is directed by the radio dispatcher to respond forthwith to the town of Middletown, New York. He knows that Middletown is west of Bear Mountain, which is east of the trooper's location and on the same approximate latitude as Middletown. He also knows that the road on which he is currently driving is east of Middletown. On all roads that the trooper might travel on, the speed limit is 60 miles per hour.

61. If the trooper is driving north and reaches a two-way east-west road that leads to Middletown, he should
a. keep going straight.
b. turn right.
c. turn left.
d. turn around and head south.

62. If the trooper is driving south and reaches an east-west road that leads to Middletown, he should
a. keep going straight.
b. turn right.
c. turn left.
d. turn around and head north.

63. If the trooper is driving north and he is located north of Middletown and Bear Mountain when he receives the call, he should
a. keep going straight.
b. turn right at the next intersection.
c. turn left at the next intersection.
d. turn around and head south.

64. If the trooper is driving south and he is located south of Middletown and Bear Mountain when he receives the call, he should
  a. keep going straight.
  b. turn right at the next intersection.
  c. turn left at the next intersection.
  d. turn around and head north.

65. If the trooper makes a turn on the two-way east-west road and sees a sign that Bear Mountain is ahead, he should
  a. keep going straight.
  b. turn around, return to the north-south road, and head north.
  c. turn around, return to the north-south road, and head south.
  d. turn around and continue past the north-south road.

66. If Middletown is 20 miles west of the north-south road and the trooper is 20 miles south of the east-west road when he receives the call, traveling at the speed limit, he could correctly estimate that he could reach Middletown in
  a. 20 minutes.
  b. 30 minutes.
  c. 40 minutes.
  d. 60 minutes.

67. If Middletown is 20 miles west of the north-south road and the trooper is 40 miles north of the east-west road when he receives the call, traveling at the speed limit, he could correctly estimate that he could reach Middletown in
  a. 20 minutes.
  b. 40 minutes.
  c. 60 minutes.
  d. 80 minutes.

68. If Middletown is 20 miles west of the north-south road and the trooper is 30 miles north of the east-west road, heading north when he receives the call, he could correctly estimate that he could reach Middletown in
  a. 30 minutes.
  b. 40 minutes.
  c. 50 minutes.
  d. 70 minutes.

69. If Middletown is 20 miles west of the north-south road and the trooper is 20 miles south of the east-west road, heading north when he receives the call, traveling at 30 miles per hour, he could correctly estimate that he could reach Middletown in
  a. 20 minutes.
  b. 40 minutes.
  c. 60 minutes.
  d. 80 minutes.

70. Middletown is 20 miles west of the north-south road. The trooper is driving north on the north-south road and is 40 miles south of the east-west road when he receives the call. He turns right at the east-west road and drives for 5 miles before realizing he is going in the wrong direction, then turns around and proceeds to Middletown. Traveling at the speed limit, approximately how long did it take him to reach Middletown?
  a. 50 minutes
  b. 60 minutes
  c. 70 minutes
  d. 80 minutes

Directions: Study the following photo, then answer questions 71 through 76 without looking back at the photo.

71. Based on the photo, the number of people crossing the street in front of the train is
  a. one.
  b. two.
  c. three.
  d. undeterminable from the photo.

72. Based on the photo, the number of people who are crossing the street while wearing a personal music device is
  a. one.
  b. two.
  c. three.
  d. undeterminable from the photo.

73. Other than those seen crossing the street in front of the train, how many other people or non-transit vehicles can be observed in the photo?
  a. one person and no vehicles
  b. one person and one vehicle
  c. two people and no vehicle
  d. two people and one vehicle

74. What is the total number of people who are seen in the photo?
  a. three
  b. four
  c. five
  d. six

75. The two people coming toward the photographer appear to be
  a. women dressed casually.
  b. men dressed in jeans.
  c. in conversation with each other.
  d. women in business attire.

76. Based on the photo, how many sets of tracks do the pedestrians appear to be crossing?
  a. one
  b. two
  c. three
  d. undeterminable from the photo

77. Compare the sets and select the answer from the choices below.
  94726179   j94726179   94726179
  a. All three names or numbers are exactly alike.
  b. Only the first and second names or numbers are exactly alike.
  c. Only the first and third names or numbers are exactly alike.
  d. Only the second and third names or numbers are exactly alike.

78. Compare the sets below.
  94726179   j94726179   94726179
  The difference between the sets would best be described as which of the following?
  a. The middle combination begins with a letter and the others do not.
  b. The last two digits of all three are different.
  c. The first two numbers of all three are different.
  d. None of the statements is correct.

79. Compare the sets and select the answer from the choices below.
  Rodriquez24
  Rodriquez24
  Rodrigues24
  Rodriques24
  a. All four names or numbers are exactly alike.
  b. Only the first and second names or numbers are exactly alike.
  c. Only the first and fourth names or numbers are exactly alike.
  d. Only the second and third names or numbers are exactly alike.

80. There are four more people that submitted their name for the state trooper exam. The proctor must alphabetize the name cards before the applicants arrive. The four names in front of her are:

Collica, Annie
Collica, Anne
Callico, Ann
Callico, Antoinette

Where would *Ann Callico*'s card be placed?
a. before all the other names
b. between *Antoinette Callico* and *Anne Collica*
c. between *Anne Collica* and *Annie Collica*
d. after *Annie Collica*

Directions: Read the following passage and answer questions 81 through 84.

To properly perform their police duties, troopers need to understand the fundamental rules of evidence. They need to understand the hearsay rule and the exceptions to it.

Unless an exception applies, hearsay evidence will not be admissible at trial. Hearsay is a statement made out of court that is offered in court for the truth of the fact asserted in the statement. Consequently, to prove a defendant committed a crime, a police officer could not testify at trial that a witness told him or her the defendant had committed the crime. To avoid the hearsay rule, the witness would have to take the stand and testify to his or her direct observations.

When an out-of-court statement is offered in court not for the truth of its content but for another purpose such as impeaching a witness by showing prior inconsistent statements, it is not hearsay and may be admitted.

Several exceptions to the hearsay rule apply, such as spontaneous declarations and excited utterances. Spontaneous declarations and excited utterances are statements made close in time to a startling event, while the person making the statement is under the stress of excitement caused by the event, and before there is an opportunity for the person to reflect or to contrive a self-serving statement. Under some circumstances in which these exceptions apply, a trooper may testify about a statement made out of court to prove the fact asserted in the statement.

81. A trooper is called to a family dispute. When he arrives, a woman runs toward him, screaming, "My husband tried to choke me to death." The trooper notices red marks around the woman's throat. After a brief investigation, the trooper arrests the husband. Later, at the police station while the trooper is filling out paperwork, the woman calls the trooper over and makes a second statement to him, "I pretended to be dead so he would stop." The husband is charged with attempted murder and assault. However, at the trial, the woman refuses to testify against her husband, and the trooper is called to the stand. Regarding the trooper's testimony, which of the following would be correct?
a. The trooper would be allowed to testify only about his observation of the red marks on the woman's throat.
b. He would be allowed to testify about both statements the woman made, because she was under extreme emotional stress when she made the statements.
c. He would be allowed to testify about his observation of the red marks and about the first statement the woman made but not the second statement.
d. He would be allowed to testify about his observation of the red marks and about the second statement the woman made, because the woman had calmed down by the time she made that statement.

82. When the trooper investigated the woman's complaint, he found the husband sitting in a chair, smoking a cigarette, and watching a football game. The trooper asked the husband what had happened, and the husband answered, "I didn't choke her. She was choking me." During the trial, the husband claimed self-defense, and his lawyer questioned the trooper. Regarding the trooper's testimony, which of the following would be correct?

   a. The trooper would be allowed to testify about the husband's statement because it was a spontaneous statement.

   b. The trooper would be allowed to testify about the husband's statement because it was an excited utterance.

   c. The trooper would not be allowed to testify about the husband's statement because it was in response to a question.

   d. The trooper would not be allowed to testify about the husband's statement because it was made after the husband had an opportunity to reflect or to contrive.

83. During the trial, the husband testified in his own defense. He testified that he and his wife had had an argument but that no physical contact had occurred between them. He testified that she accused him because she was jealous of his relationship with another woman. After the husband's testimony, the trooper was recalled to the witness stand as a rebuttal witness. Regarding the trooper's testimony, which of the following would be correct?

   a. The trooper would be allowed to testify about the husband's statement because it was a spontaneous statement.

   b. The trooper would be allowed to testify about the husband's statement because it was an excited utterance.

   c. The trooper would be allowed to testify about the husband's statement because the wife had refused to testify.

   d. The trooper would be allowed to testify about the husband's statement because the testimony was offered not for the truth of the fact asserted in the statement, but to impeach the husband's credibility by showing that he had made a prior inconsistent statement.

84. Which of the following statements most likely would NOT be admissible as a spontaneous declaration or excited utterance exception to the hearsay rule?

   a. Immediately after an automobile accident, one of the drivers stated, "I'm sorry, I should have been paying more attention."

   b. Immediately after an automobile accident, a bystander said to one of the drivers, "You idiot. Why did you go through the light?"

   c. A half-hour after an automobile accident, one of the drivers stated, "I had the right of way. The other guy went through the stop sign."

   d. When a stabbing victim fell to the ground and was asked what was wrong, he answered, "Mildred stabbed me."

Directions: Read the following paragraph and answer questions 85 through 95.

In many state police agencies, the first trooper to arrive at the scene of a serious crime is often the same trooper who will be responsible for taking photographs to preserve the scene and for collecting evidence. The trooper should take the following steps in the order listed:

1. Make sure the crime scene is secure and assign another trooper to be responsible for who comes in and out of the area.
2. Leave the crime scene as it is, not moving any objects or specific items of evidence until photographs can be taken of the scene.
3. Take a photograph of the overall crime scene area, and then take more specific photos of all pertinent pieces of potential evidence.
4. After the first set of photographs is taken, take another set that includes a ruler to provide a sense of scale.
5. Place the film in a container and mark the container with the case number, the date and location, and the trooper's identity.
6. Collect pertinent pieces of evidence. The trooper should mark the evidence pieces directly by scratching his or her initials into the object, or place the pieces into containers and mark the container with the case number, the date and location, and the officer identification.
7. Preserve a chain of custody for all evidence and limit the custodians to as few persons as possible.
8. Deliver the photographs and evidence to the department laboratory.

Trooper Fitzpatrick and Trooper Hanson respond to a past burglary at a private residence. Trooper Fitzpatrick has been trained as an evidence technician. Trooper Hanson is a rookie and has not received such training yet. They are met at the residence by the owner, a distraught woman, who tells them that her home has been ransacked and many of her personal items have been destroyed. Hanson listens while Fitzpatrick asks the woman questions. Fitzpatrick tells Hanson to wait by the front door. The woman leads Fitzpatrick through the house and shows him her china dishes that were broken, old photographs that were ripped up, and food in her kitchen that was partially eaten and thrown about the floor. She tells him that her jewelry has been stolen, and opens her jewelry boxes to show him that they are empty. They find a back window that was pried open, and they see several smoked cigarette stubs on the floor.

As Fitzpatrick begins to take photographs of the residence, Hanson comes in and asks whether he needs any help. Fitzpatrick takes first a set of overall photos of each room, and then takes a set of photos of specific, pertinent items. He takes specific photographs of the pried-open window, the jewelry boxes, the broken dishes, and the torn photographs. While he does this, Trooper Hanson checks out the rest of the house with the owner. As Fitzpatrick finishes the second set of photographs, Hanson approaches him and says, "Look what I found. This was in the backyard." She is holding a small crowbar. She places the crowbar on the marks where the window had been pried open to see whether the crowbar fits with the marks. She says, "Yeah. It's about the right size. Should we take this as evidence?" Hanson puts the crowbar on the windowsill, and Fitzpatrick takes a photograph of it.

After a few minutes, the woman's relatives arrive, and they begin cleaning up the mess in the kitchen. The woman says, "Look, they ate half of my apple," and she throws the apple in the garbage. Trooper Fitzpatrick asks the relatives to stop cleaning up because he wants to see whether any fingerprints have been left.

Trooper Fitzpatrick attempts to find fingerprints in the kitchen and where the back window was pried open, but he does not find any useable prints. He takes the crowbar as evidence, taping a note to it with the date and his name. Then, Trooper Fitzpatrick goes off duty, and sends Trooper Hanson to deliver the photographs and the crowbar to the department laboratory.

85. Which action or actions of Trooper Fitzpatrick were improper?
   a. telling Trooper Hanson to wait by the front door
   b. allowing the woman into the house with him
   c. allowing the woman to lead him through the house
   d. allowing the woman to open the jewelry boxes to show him they were empty

86. Which action or actions of Trooper Fitzpatrick were improper?
   a. taking overall photographs of each room before taking specific photographs
   b. taking photographs of the pried-open window
   c. taking a photograph of the crowbar on the windowsill
   d. taking photographs of the broken china and torn photographs

87. Which action or actions of Trooper Hanson were proper?
   a. offering to help Trooper Fitzpatrick
   b. checking out the rest of the house with the owner
   c. picking up the crowbar
   d. listening as Fitzpatrick questioned the woman

88. Which action or actions of Trooper Hanson were improper?
   a. picking up the crowbar before it was photographed where it was found
   b. placing the crowbar on the marks where the window had been pried
   c. placing the crowbar on the windowsill to be photographed
   d. all of the above

89. Which action or actions of Trooper Hanson most seriously impaired the evidence gathering process?
   a. finding the crowbar
   b. picking up the crowbar before a photograph was taken
   c. placing the crowbar on the marks where the window had been pried
   d. placing the crowbar on the windowsill to be photographed

90. Considering that Trooper Fitzpatrick was the senior officer and had been trained as an evidence technician, which of his actions was improper?
   a. his failure to clearly instruct Hanson to stay at the front door and to prevent unauthorized persons from entering the crime scene
   b. his failure to stop Hanson from placing the crowbar on the marks, which could have destroyed or marred the evidentiary value of the marks
   c. photographing the crowbar on the windowsill when it was found at a different location
   d. all of the above

91. Considering that Trooper Fitzpatrick was the senior officer and had been trained as an evidence technician, which of his actions was improper?
   a. his failure to take a second set of photographs with a ruler included in the photos
   b. his failure to take photographs of the cigarette stubs
   c. his failure to take photographs of the partially eaten food, including the apple
   d. all of the above

92. Considering that Trooper Fitzpatrick was the senior officer and had been trained as an evidence technician, which of his actions was improper?
- **a.** asking the relatives not to clean up the food in the kitchen
- **b.** attempting to find fingerprints in the kitchen
- **c.** attempting to find fingerprints on the back window
- **d.** allowing the woman to throw the apple in the garbage

93. Regarding the apple, Trooper Fitzpatrick's best action would have been to
- **a.** allow the woman to throw the apple in the garbage, because it was perishable.
- **b.** photograph the apple before disposing of it.
- **c.** take a sample of it to the laboratory.
- **d.** collect, preserve, and deliver it to the laboratory for possible DNA recovery or possible bite mark comparisons.

94. Considering that Trooper Fitzpatrick was the senior officer and had been trained as an evidence technician, which of his actions was proper?
- **a.** taking the crowbar as evidence
- **b.** marking the crowbar as evidence by taping a note to it with the date and his name
- **c.** not instructing Hanson to initial the crowbar
- **d.** sending Hanson to deliver his photographs to the department laboratory

95. Regarding the crowbar, Trooper Fitzpatrick's best action would have been to
- **a.** put the crowbar back where it was found in the backyard and photograph it there.
- **b.** place the crowbar on the marks on the window and take close photographs of the match.
- **c.** mark the crowbar as evidence by taping a note to it with the date and his name.
- **d.** instruct Trooper Hanson to scratch her initials into the crowbar because she found it.

Directions: Read the following paragraph and answer questions 96 through 100.

A trooper responding to a robbery in progress must act in accordance with the public safety purposes of protecting life and property, avoiding unnecessary injury to the public, apprehending criminals, and collecting and preserving evidence.

While patrolling in his radio patrol car, Trooper Evans was notified of a silent alarm indicating that a robbery was taking place at the National Bank located at Broad and Main Streets. Trooper Evans was approximately one mile from the bank. He turned on his overhead lights and constant siren and sped to the bank, slowing to approximately 20 miles per hour as he proceeded through red lights at intersections. When he arrived at the bank, he angle-parked the radio car in front of the entrance, leaving on the turret light and siren, drew his gun, and rushed in the front door of the bank. Inside, he found that the robbers had already fled. Evans questioned the bank manager, and the following exchange occurred:

Evans: "Which way did they go?"
Manager: "They left by the front door."
Evans: "How many were there?
Manager: "Three."
Evans: "Were they white or black?"

Manager: "I'm not sure. I think they were Hispanic."
Evans: "What kind of guns did they have?"
Manager: "I'm not sure."

Trooper Evans went to his car and radioed the following message to the radio dispatcher: "Be on the lookout for three Hispanic males, armed with guns, who fled the National Bank at Broad and Main Streets, approximately two minutes ago."

Trooper Evans returned to the bank, sat at the bank manager's desk, and asked the bank manager to describe what happened. The bank manager told him that she had been sitting at her desk when a male and a female came into his office and sat down. They asked about a loan. Shortly thereafter, a very tall Hispanic male joined them, saying he was a relative. After a minute, the taller male moved behind the bank manager, and the shorter male stood up, leaned on the desk, and put a knife against the manager's neck. The shorter male told the manager to take them behind the tellers' counter or he would cut her throat. The manager agreed and escorted them behind the tellers' counter. The tall male filled a tan canvas bag with money, and the three robbers left. At that point, one of the tellers pressed the silent alarm button.

96. Which of the following actions taken by Trooper Evans was proper and in accordance with the purposes of public safety?
   a. speeding with his overhead lights and siren on directly to the front of the bank
   b. slowing down to approximately 20 miles per hour as he proceeded through red lights at intersections
   c. angle parking in front of the bank entrance and leaving on his overhead lights and siren
   d. drawing his gun as he entered the bank

97. During Trooper Evans's initial questions to the bank manager, what was the most improper, leading, and suggestive question that he asked?
   a. Which way did they go?
   b. How many were there?
   c. Were they white or black?
   d. What kind of guns did they have?

98. Which part of the message that Trooper Evans transmitted to the radio dispatcher was supported by the information he had received from the bank manager?
   a. three Hispanic males
   b. armed with guns
   c. fled the National Bank at Broad and Main Streets
   d. about two minutes ago

99. What information would have been important to give to the radio dispatcher?
   a. One robber was a very tall Hispanic male.
   b. The robbers were carrying a canvas bag filled with money.
   c. One robber was a female, and one robber had a knife.
   d. all of the above

100. Regarding the collection and preservation of evidence, for which action could Trooper Evans be most criticized?
   a. transmitting an inaccurate description of the robbers
   b. asking leading and suggestive questions before letting the bank manager describe what had occurred
   c. sitting in the bank manager's chair
   d. failing to immediately set up a crime scene

Answers

1. b. The body temperature dropped 10°, corresponding to ten hours, during the progress of rigor mortis. Choices **a**, **c**, and **d** do not correctly apply the formula of body temperature loss and the time factors involved.

2. c. The body temperature dropped 38°, corresponding to 38 hours, after rigor mortis dissipated. Choices **a**, **b**, and **d** do not correctly apply the formula of body temperature loss and the time factors involved.

3. d. No rigor mortis was present; therefore, the correct answer must be either less than four hours or more than 36 hours. Choices **a**, **b**, and **c** are incorrect. Because the body temperature dropped 8°, corresponding to eight hours, the answer could not be less than four hours and must be more than 36 hours.

4. d. The bank manager appears to be a reliable complainant with credible information about the crime. Choices **a** and **b** are incorrect because, though the conduct could raise a reasonable suspicion, the people involved more than likely had innocent explanations. Choice **c** is incorrect because the intoxicated person's complaint, without further information, appears farfetched.

5. d. Running from the police under these circumstances satisfies the standards of probable cause to make an arrest. Choice **a** is incorrect because reasonable suspicion alone is not enough to make a lawful arrest. Choice **b** in itself is not reliable. Choice **c** is incorrect because a reputation for criminal conduct does not amount to a crime.

6. a. Cooper entered the school unlawfully because she was not licensed or privileged to enter the school. Choice **b** is incorrect because parents must stop at the security desk. Choice **c** is incorrect because Stoker was not physically injured. Choice **d** is incorrect because Cooper did not have the intent to commit a crime when she entered the school.

7. b. This is the only choice that provides an incorrect charge, because Cooper remained in the school with intent to commit a crime therein. Choices **a**, **c**, and **d** are correct answers because she unlawfully entered and she unlawfully remained with the intent to commit a crime therein.

8. b. This is the only choice that provides an untrue charge; Cooper is not guilty of assault because Stoker was not physically injured. Choice **c** is true because Cooper entered the building with the intent to commit a crime therein. Choices **a** and **d** are also true.

9. c. The traffic system can work only with the public's cooperation and voluntary compliance. Not enough troopers are available to issue summonses for every violation, so choice **a** is incorrect. Choice **b** is incorrect because troopers should not ignore the less serious violations when they are committed in their presence. Choice **d** is incorrect because revenue is not the primary consideration.

10. d. This is the best answer because all laws are qualified by the need to act in genuine emergencies. Choice **a** is incorrect because traffic laws are designed not only for intentional violators, but also for negligent or careless violators. Choice **b** is incorrect because traffic laws are enforced against all citizens to encourage them to drive carefully. Choice **c** is incorrect because looking both ways does not excuse the violation.

11. a. This choice is correct because Carol used proportionate force in protecting herself, and it appeared as if she was in imminent danger. Choices **b** and **c** are incorrect; Carol is not in imminent danger and could have retreated safely. Choice **d** is incorrect; Carol could have stayed (retreated) safely into her home and called the police.

12. b. The larger man is approached by the smaller man in a threatening manner. There is no weapon present, and the larger man could have retreated. Choice **a** is incorrect; the man was much larger than the woman and the baseball bat could be considered a deadly weapon. Choice **c** is incorrect; even though the man is much larger than the woman, she came toward him with a deadly weapon. Choice **d** is incorrect; the larger man is in his "castle" and even if his state follows the retreat rule, the smaller man was standing over him with a deadly weapon, making a safe retreat highly unlikely.

13. a. The woman killed her abuser during a confrontation where her safety was in imminent danger. Choice **b** is incorrect; the woman's abuser was sleeping at the time of the incident. She was not in imminent danger and could have retreated safely. Choice **c** is incorrect; hiring a hit-man would actually increase the penalty for the murder because it illustrates premeditation and deliberation. Choice **d** is incorrect; although she may be afraid, based on the account, she is not in imminent danger, according to the law.

14. c. Man A cannot claim self-defense because he was the initial aggressor. Choice **a** is incorrect; man B has a claim for self-defense. Choice **b** is incorrect; man B used proportional force in defending himself. Choice **d** is incorrect; again, man B was lawfully defending himself.

15. b. The homeowner was confronted on his stairs. There was no way he could retreat safely, and he had good reason to believe that his life was in danger. Choice **a** is incorrect; if the homeowner was in the doorway and not yet in the house, he could have retreated safely. Choice **c** is incorrect; the homeowner was not in danger if the stranger was running away from the house. Choice **d** is incorrect; the stranger was crawling out of the window, hence, he was not in any danger.

16. d. The officer thanks the witness for coming but does not say anything suggestive. Choices **a**, **b**, and **c** are all suggestive and give the witness the impression that they picked the right or the wrong person. This could later affect their ability to make a correct identification in court if the case goes to trial.

17. c. The officer looked directly at the witness and did not show any expression of emotion. Choices **a**, **b**, and **d** are all suggestive and again, give the witness the impression that they chose the right person. Once an identification is reinforced by a person in power, such as an officer, it is unlikely that the witness will recant the identification, even if they have some doubts.

18. d. Kidnapping is more serious than robbery and also more serious than grand larceny by extortion, which is more serious than grand larceny from the person.

19. b. Grand larceny from the person is less serious than grand larceny by extortion and robbery, both of which are less serious than kidnapping.

20. d. The details obtained may be helpful to the investigation. Choices **a** and **b** are incorrect because both actions could cause the caller to hang up. Choice **c** is incorrect because the officer should not provide information to the caller about the case that the caller may not know.

21. a. Choice **a** is the only answer that is grammatically correct. Choice **b** uses the word *were* instead of *was*. Choice **c** uses *is* instead of *was*. All verbs should be in the same tense. Choice **d** uses a comma, which makes the sentence a run-on sentence.

22. a. The words that pertain to *Robert and Robin* are all plural to agree with the plural subject.

23. c. In choice **a**, *a mayor* does not agree in number with *they*. Choices **b** and **d** spell *cities* incorrectly for this sentence's intended meaning. Choice **d** also incorrectly lowercases *United States*.

24. c. Choice **c** is the only answer that is grammatically correct because it is the only one that consistently uses verbs in the past tense. Choice **a** uses the word *wants* instead of *wanted*. Choices **b** and **d** use *asks* instead of *asked*.

25. d. Use *number* with nouns that can be counted: number of summonses, number of cars. Also, *summonses* is the correct plural of the noun *summons*. In addition, *was* is the proper verb to use with the singular number.

26. a. The correct word is *severity*; *severeness* and *severness* are not words. *Trooper Prentiss's* is the proper possessive form; *Prentisses* is not a possessive.

27. d. The compound noun requires a plural verb and plural object.

28. a. This is a sentence fragment. Choices **b**, **c**, and **d** are grammatically correct sentences.

29. b. *Troopers* is a plural subject and should have a plural verb. Choices **a**, **c**, and **d** all have subject and verb agreement.

30. a. *Therefore* implies that Officer Taylor's mistake resulted in inadmissible evidence.

31. b. *Many* is a countable noun and the only choice that is grammatically correct. Use *many* with countable nouns and *much* with uncountable nouns. Words such as *more* and *most* can be used for either.

32. a. *Accordingly* implies that Officer Cox's coworkers did not pass the test because they were not training for the run.

33. b. Choices **a** and **d** are incorrect; *personnel* is spelled with one *l* and is not a synonym for *personal*. Choice **c** is incorrect because *personable* is an adjective that is appropriately used to modify only a person's personality or character traits.

34. a. *Singularly* is the correct spelling.

35. c. *License* is the correct spelling.

36. a. *Trooper* is not a proper noun and, therefore, should not be capitalized.

37. c. Both *summonses* and *motorist* are common nouns; there is no need to capitalize either.

38. a. This includes personal descriptors that a suspect is not likely to be able to alter and provides safety information as to whether the suspect may have been armed.

39. b. This includes descriptors that the suspect may most easily alter within a short period of time. Headgear and upper body outerwear may be easily discarded. The suspect may have been wearing a wig. Lower body outerwear is not so easily discarded but is often very general (e.g., blue jeans, black slacks).

40. c. Although the description is very general, it is the most important piece of information, followed by choices **d** and **b**. Choice **a** provides the least useful information because the suspect can easily discard the bandana, but it may be useful in conjunction with the other information.

41. d. The price of one home theater projector was $4,549. The victim had three projectors stolen. Take $4,549 and multiply by three, and your answer is $13,647.

42. a. The price of one laptop is $2,550. The victim has five laptops. Take $2,550 and multiply by five, and your answer is $12,750.

43. b. The price of all the items is $36,117. There are two cameras at $1,525 ($3,050), five laptop computers at $2,550 each ($12,750), three projectors at $4,549 each ($13,647), and one TV at $6,670. Add all of the totals together and you have $36,117.

44. b. $123.75 is determined by solving 0.495 × 250 miles. Choices **a**, **c**, and **d** are arrived at by incorrectly placing the decimal point or rounding up or down the 49.5 cents a mile.

45. a. Choice **a** is determined by solving $49 × 3 for the days of travel, which totals $147.

You must then determine that 75% of $49 is $36.75, which is the reimbursement for each of the two travel days. The total reimbursement is $147 + $73.50, which totals $220.50. Choice **b** is based on Trooper Suki receiving $49 for all five days. Choice **c** is based on Trooper Suki receiving $36.75 for all five days, and choice **d** is incorrect because a correct answer is available.

46. c. Choice **c** is determined by adding the correct mileage reimbursement to the correct meal reimbursement ($123.75 + $220.50 = $344.25). Choices **a** and **b** are derived from earlier incorrect calculations.

47. d. This is a two-step problem. First, add the five numbers: 80 + 50 + 50 + 80 + 60 = 320. Now, divide the sum by 5 (the number of days) to find the average: 320 ÷ 5 = 64.

48. b. First, determine what percent of the summonses were not for speeding by subtracting: 100% − 75% = 25%. Change 25% to a decimal (0.25) and solve 0.25 × 460.

49. d. Trooper Rosen's decision is based on a three-hour train ride, about 30 minutes to get from the station to his meeting site, and another 30 minutes of extra time, for a total of four hours. If he is on the 10 A.M. train, he will have four hours to reach his destination.

50. c. You must multiply the value of the CDs by four and then correctly add the other items to derive the total.

51. a. Choice **a** is the sum of all the values. (10 × $112) + (9 × $90) + (6 × $80) + (5 × $55) = $2,685.

52. c. Choice **c** is the sum of Bette's personal items plus the value of the store's items ($683.96 + $2,685 = $3,368.96).

53. b. 1500 hours is 3 P.M.; an eight-hour shift that begins at 3 P.M. would end at 11 P.M.

54. c. Trooper Padilla worked until 1:30 A.M. or 0130 hours, while Trooper Torres worked until 9:00 P.M. or 2100 hours. If Torres worked until 9:00 P.M. and Padilla stayed until 1:30 A.M., she worked four hours and 30 minutes more than Torres.

55. c. If Trooper Mendoza works 0700 hours (7:00 A.M.) to 1500 hours (3:00 P.M.) and received four hours of overtime, he left work at 1900 hours or 7:00 P.M.

56. c. The map legend shows grade-separated crossings at Federal Bd, Sheridan Bd, Wadsworth Bd, and Kipling St.

57. d. The map shows that part of W Jewell Av runs parallel to the proposed rail route, but it does not intersect it anywhere along the route.

58. c. The map shows three separated crossings, one at Union Bd, one at Simms St, and one between Simms and Oak Streets.

59. a. The vehicle traveling on Federal Bd from Exposition Av to 23rd Av will cross the alignment at the intersection of 10th Av and Federal Bd.

60. b. Although the map does not indicate the name of every avenue, these can be identified in the area of the I-25 grade crossing. Choice **a** is incorrect because 10th Av is shown as ending at Federal Bd. Choice **c** is incorrect because neither 8th Av nor 6th Av shows a crossing planned for the places at which they intersect with I-25. Choice **d** is incorrect because the map shows that I-25 will be affected by the alignment.

61. c. Turning left would be turning west, and Middletown is west of the road. Choice **a** is incorrect because continuing north would not bring him west. Choice **b** is incorrect because turning right would be turning to the east. Choice **d** is incorrect because heading south would not bring him west.

62. b. Turning right would be turning west, and Middletown is west of the road. Choice **a** is incorrect because continuing south would not bring him west. Choice **c** is incorrect because turning left would be turning to the east. Choice **d** is incorrect because heading north would not bring him west.

63. d. He must head south to the east-west road before turning west. Choice **a** is incorrect because continuing north would not bring him west. Choice **b** is incorrect because turning right would be turning to the east. Choice **c** is incorrect because although he would be heading west, he would be north of Middletown, and this would not be as efficient as proceeding to the east-west road on the same latitude as Middletown.

64. d. He must head north to the east-west road before turning west. Choice **a** is incorrect because continuing south would not bring him west. Choice **b** is incorrect because although he would be heading west, he would be south of Middletown, and this would not be as efficient as proceeding to the east-west road on the same latitude as Middletown. Choice **c** is incorrect because turning left would be turning to the east.

65. d. Because Bear Mountain was east of his location, he must turn around and head west to Middletown. Choice **a** is incorrect because going straight would be continuing east and Middletown is west. Choice **b** is incorrect because heading north would not bring him west. Choice **c** is incorrect because heading south would not bring him west.

66. c. The trooper is 20 + 20 = 40 miles from Middletown when he receives the call. Traveling at 60 mph, which is one mile per minute, he could reach Middletown in 40 minutes.

67. c. 20 + 40 = 60. 60 miles at 60 mph = 60 minutes.

68. c. 20 + 30 = 50. 50 miles at 60 mph = 50 minutes.

69. d. 20 + 20 = 40 miles. 30 mph = one-half mile per minute. 40 miles at one-half mile per minute = 80 minutes to travel 40 miles.

70. c. 20 + 40 + 5 + 5 = 70. 70 at 60 mph = 70 minutes.

71. c. Three people are seen crossing the street in the photo.

72. a. The woman in the center of the photo closest to the viewer is wearing headphones that appear to be connected to a personal music device.

73. d. On the right-hand side of the photo, two people are in the corner of the photo, one partially hidden by a wall and the other crouched in front of the wall. One vehicle can be seen in the background moving in the direction opposite the train.

74. c. Three people are seen crossing the tracks, and two people are visible in the left-hand portion of the photo.

75. a. The two people coming toward the photographer appear to both be women who are dressed casually.

76. b. The train is on one set of tracks and another set can be seen where the woman with the personal music device is walking.

77. c. The first and third numbers are exactly alike.

78. a. All the numbers are the same; the difference is that the middle combination is preceded by the letter *j*.

79. b. The first and second names and numbers are exactly alike.

80. a. *Anne Callico* would be the first name, followed by *Antoinette Callico*, *Anne Collica*, and *Annie Collica*. When the last names are the same, look to the first name and each succeeding letter to discern which name would go first.

81. c. The woman's first statement appears to have been an excited utterance because it was made while she was running and screaming after she had just been choked. The choking was evidenced by the red marks. Choice **a** is incorrect because the trooper would be allowed to testify to the first statement. Choices **b** and **d** are incorrect; the trooper would not be allowed to testify to the second statement, because it was made after considerable time had passed and the woman had had time to calm down and reflect.

82. d. The husband made the statement after considerable time had passed; he apparently was calm and had had time to reflect and to contrive a self-serving answer. Choices **a**, **b**, and **c** are incorrect because the statement was neither a spontaneous declaration nor an excited utterance.

83. d. Out-of-court statements may be admissible when they are not offered for the truth of the fact asserted in the statement. Here it was offered to attack the husband's credibility by showing his prior inconsistent statement. Choices **a**, **b**, and **c** are incorrect because the statement was neither a spontaneous declaration nor an excited utterance.

84. c. It would not be admissible because considerable time had passed and the driver had had time to reflect and to contrive a self-serving answer. Choices **a**, **b**, and **d** are incorrect because they may be admissible, because they were made in response to and immediately after startling events.

85. d. This is improper because nothing should be touched until photographs are taken and the item is examined for fingerprints. Choices **a**, **b**, and **c** were proper.

86. c. This is improper because they did not find the crowbar on the windowsill but in the backyard. Choices **a**, **b**, and **d** were proper.

87. d. Because Trooper Hanson is a rookie, it was proper for her to let Fitzpatrick take the lead. Choices **a** and **b** were improper; she should have remained at the front door as instructed. Choice **c** was improper; she picked up evidence and moved it before it was photographed.

88. d. Choices **a**, **b**, and **c** were all improper handling of evidence.

89. c. This is the most serious impairment because by placing the crowbar on the marks, she may have destroyed or marred the evidentiary value of the initial marks. Choice **a** is not a serious impairment, though finding the crowbar without picking it up would have been beneficial. Choices **b** and **d** are impairments, but not as serious as choice **c**.

90. d. Choices **a**, **b**, and **c** were all improper.

91. d. Choices **a**, **b**, and **c** were all improper.

92. d. The apple could be evidence to identify the perpetrator. It could be possible to recover DNA evidence from the perpetrator's saliva on the apple. It could also be possible to photograph and preserve the apple to match the bite with a suspect's teeth. Choices **a**, **b**, and **c** were all proper actions.

93. d. This is the best action. Choices **a**, **b**, and **c** were all improper because potential evidence was destroyed.

94. a. The crowbar is potential evidence. Choice **b** is improper because a note can be lost; he should have scratched his initials into the crowbar. Choice **c** is improper because Hanson found the crowbar and should have been the one to initial it for identification. Choice **d** is improper because he should have delivered the photographs himself to preserve and limit the chain of evidence.

95. d. Because Hanson found the crowbar and will have to be the one to identify it in court, she will need to identify it with her initials. Choice **a** is incorrect because the crowbar has already been moved from its initial crime scene placement. Choice **b** is incorrect because placing the crowbar could damage the existing marks and/or create new marks. Choice **c** is incorrect because a taped note can be easily lost.

96. d. Because the trooper decided to enter the bank, it was reasonable for him to draw his gun as he approached the potentially dangerous situation. Choices **a** and **c** are incorrect because approaching the bank with the siren on would alert the robbers that the police were coming. Choice **b** is incorrect because going through red lights at 20 miles per hour recklessly endangers the public. A trooper should come to a full stop before proceeding through a red light.

97. **d.** This is the most improper because the question assumed the fact that the robbers had guns. Choice **c** was improper but less so than choice **d**. Choices **a** and **b** were proper questions.

98. **c.** It is the only choice with correct information. Choices **a**, **b**, and **d** contain erroneous information.

99. **d.** Choices **a**, **b**, and **c** each provided useful descriptive information.

100.c. By sitting in the bank manager's chair where part of the crime occurred, the trooper may have destroyed fingerprints or other evidence. Choice **d** is not the best answer because although the trooper failed to set up a crime scene, it was not as severe an error as **c**. Choices **a** and **b** are not the best answers because they do not directly relate to the preservation of evidence.

17 ▶ STATE TROOPER PRACTICE TEST 6

CHAPTER SUMMARY
This is the sixth and final practice test in this book based on the most commonly tested areas on the state trooper exam.

The practice test consists of 100 multiple-choice questions in the following areas: reading comprehension, writing and information ordering, mathematics, spatial and directional orientation, memory and observation, and problem solving. Set aside two hours to take this practice test.

This practice test is available through the LearningExpress online link, if you prefer to take it on the computer.

State Trooper Practice Test 6

1.	ⓐ	ⓑ	ⓒ	ⓓ
2.	ⓐ	ⓑ	ⓒ	ⓓ
3.	ⓐ	ⓑ	ⓒ	ⓓ
4.	ⓐ	ⓑ	ⓒ	ⓓ
5.	ⓐ	ⓑ	ⓒ	ⓓ
6.	ⓐ	ⓑ	ⓒ	ⓓ
7.	ⓐ	ⓑ	ⓒ	ⓓ
8.	ⓐ	ⓑ	ⓒ	ⓓ
9.	ⓐ	ⓑ	ⓒ	ⓓ
10.	ⓐ	ⓑ	ⓒ	ⓓ
11.	ⓐ	ⓑ	ⓒ	ⓓ
12.	ⓐ	ⓑ	ⓒ	ⓓ
13.	ⓐ	ⓑ	ⓒ	ⓓ
14.	ⓐ	ⓑ	ⓒ	ⓓ
15.	ⓐ	ⓑ	ⓒ	ⓓ
16.	ⓐ	ⓑ	ⓒ	ⓓ
17.	ⓐ	ⓑ	ⓒ	ⓓ
18.	ⓐ	ⓑ	ⓒ	ⓓ
19.	ⓐ	ⓑ	ⓒ	ⓓ
20.	ⓐ	ⓑ	ⓒ	ⓓ
21.	ⓐ	ⓑ	ⓒ	ⓓ
22.	ⓐ	ⓑ	ⓒ	ⓓ
23.	ⓐ	ⓑ	ⓒ	ⓓ
24.	ⓐ	ⓑ	ⓒ	ⓓ
25.	ⓐ	ⓑ	ⓒ	ⓓ
26.	ⓐ	ⓑ	ⓒ	ⓓ
27.	ⓐ	ⓑ	ⓒ	ⓓ
28.	ⓐ	ⓑ	ⓒ	ⓓ
29.	ⓐ	ⓑ	ⓒ	ⓓ
30.	ⓐ	ⓑ	ⓒ	ⓓ
31.	ⓐ	ⓑ	ⓒ	ⓓ
32.	ⓐ	ⓑ	ⓒ	ⓓ
33.	ⓐ	ⓑ	ⓒ	ⓓ
34.	ⓐ	ⓑ	ⓒ	ⓓ
35.	ⓐ	ⓑ	ⓒ	ⓓ

36.	ⓐ	ⓑ	ⓒ	ⓓ
37.	ⓐ	ⓑ	ⓒ	ⓓ
38.	ⓐ	ⓑ	ⓒ	ⓓ
39.	ⓐ	ⓑ	ⓒ	ⓓ
40.	ⓐ	ⓑ	ⓒ	ⓓ
41.	ⓐ	ⓑ	ⓒ	ⓓ
42.	ⓐ	ⓑ	ⓒ	ⓓ
43.	ⓐ	ⓑ	ⓒ	ⓓ
44.	ⓐ	ⓑ	ⓒ	ⓓ
45.	ⓐ	ⓑ	ⓒ	ⓓ
46.	ⓐ	ⓑ	ⓒ	ⓓ
47.	ⓐ	ⓑ	ⓒ	ⓓ
48.	ⓐ	ⓑ	ⓒ	ⓓ
49.	ⓐ	ⓑ	ⓒ	ⓓ
50.	ⓐ	ⓑ	ⓒ	ⓓ
51.	ⓐ	ⓑ	ⓒ	ⓓ
52.	ⓐ	ⓑ	ⓒ	ⓓ
53.	ⓐ	ⓑ	ⓒ	ⓓ
54.	ⓐ	ⓑ	ⓒ	ⓓ
55.	ⓐ	ⓑ	ⓒ	ⓓ
56.	ⓐ	ⓑ	ⓒ	ⓓ
57.	ⓐ	ⓑ	ⓒ	ⓓ
58.	ⓐ	ⓑ	ⓒ	ⓓ
59.	ⓐ	ⓑ	ⓒ	ⓓ
60.	ⓐ	ⓑ	ⓒ	ⓓ
61.	ⓐ	ⓑ	ⓒ	ⓓ
62.	ⓐ	ⓑ	ⓒ	ⓓ
63.	ⓐ	ⓑ	ⓒ	ⓓ
64.	ⓐ	ⓑ	ⓒ	ⓓ
65.	ⓐ	ⓑ	ⓒ	ⓓ
66.	ⓐ	ⓑ	ⓒ	ⓓ
67.	ⓐ	ⓑ	ⓒ	ⓓ
68.	ⓐ	ⓑ	ⓒ	ⓓ
69.	ⓐ	ⓑ	ⓒ	ⓓ
70.	ⓐ	ⓑ	ⓒ	ⓓ

71.	ⓐ	ⓑ	ⓒ	ⓓ
72.	ⓐ	ⓑ	ⓒ	ⓓ
73.	ⓐ	ⓑ	ⓒ	ⓓ
74.	ⓐ	ⓑ	ⓒ	ⓓ
75.	ⓐ	ⓑ	ⓒ	ⓓ
76.	ⓐ	ⓑ	ⓒ	ⓓ
77.	ⓐ	ⓑ	ⓒ	ⓓ
78.	ⓐ	ⓑ	ⓒ	ⓓ
79.	ⓐ	ⓑ	ⓒ	ⓓ
80.	ⓐ	ⓑ	ⓒ	ⓓ
81.	ⓐ	ⓑ	ⓒ	ⓓ
82.	ⓐ	ⓑ	ⓒ	ⓓ
83.	ⓐ	ⓑ	ⓒ	ⓓ
84.	ⓐ	ⓑ	ⓒ	ⓓ
85.	ⓐ	ⓑ	ⓒ	ⓓ
86.	ⓐ	ⓑ	ⓒ	ⓓ
87.	ⓐ	ⓑ	ⓒ	ⓓ
88.	ⓐ	ⓑ	ⓒ	ⓓ
89.	ⓐ	ⓑ	ⓒ	ⓓ
90.	ⓐ	ⓑ	ⓒ	ⓓ
91.	ⓐ	ⓑ	ⓒ	ⓓ
92.	ⓐ	ⓑ	ⓒ	ⓓ
93.	ⓐ	ⓑ	ⓒ	ⓓ
94.	ⓐ	ⓑ	ⓒ	ⓓ
95.	ⓐ	ⓑ	ⓒ	ⓓ
96.	ⓐ	ⓑ	ⓒ	ⓓ
97.	ⓐ	ⓑ	ⓒ	ⓓ
98.	ⓐ	ⓑ	ⓒ	ⓓ
99.	ⓐ	ⓑ	ⓒ	ⓓ
100.	ⓐ	ⓑ	ⓒ	ⓓ

State Trooper Practice Test 6

Directions: Read the following passage, then answer questions 1 and 2.

All law enforcement officers in the United States can apply for membership with the Fraternal Order of Police (FOP). The FOP provides support for all law enforcement agents and strives to improve working conditions in departments all over the country. The FOP was created in 1915 when officers were often forced to work 12 hours a day, 365 days a year. They received little in terms of benefits, such as a pension, vacation time, or sick time. Police officers had little in regard to job security and were treated unfairly in the workplace. Two officers from Pittsburgh organized the first meeting to tackle law enforcement labor issues. Despite its humble beginnings, it is currently the largest police organization in the country with over 325,000 members. It has always remained an organization that has officers representing the interests of other officers.

1. The paragraph best supports the statement that the FOP
   a. will continue to consistently increase its membership numbers.
   b. is dedicated to having law enforcement officers serve in FOP positions.
   c. offers educational and employment services to its members.
   d. will work to increase the pensions of law enforcement agents.

2. From the paragraph, you can infer that
   a. the FOP will eventually offer membership to non-law enforcement members.
   b. the FOP has members from every police department in the country.
   c. the FOP holds weekly labor meetings.
   d. none of the above

Directions: Read the following passage, then answer questions 3 through 14.

According to law, a trooper, in the course of effecting an arrest or preventing the escape from custody of a person whom he or she reasonably believes to have committed a crime, may use deadly physical force to effect the arrest or prevent the escape when and to the extent he or she reasonably believes such to be necessary only when he or she reasonably believes the crime was:

   1. A felony or attempt to commit a felony involving the use or attempted use or threatened imminent use of physical force against a person; or
   2. Kidnapping, arson, escape in the first degree, burglary in the first degree or any attempt to commit such a crime; or
   3. A felony, and in the course of resisting arrest or attempting to escape from custody, the person who committed the felony is armed with a firearm or deadly weapon.

Regardless of the particular offense which is the subject of the arrest or attempted escape, the use of deadly physical force is necessary to defend the police officer or another person from what the trooper reasonably believes to be the use or imminent use of deadly physical force.

State police department policies emphasize that troopers use deadly physical force only as a last resort and only when reasonable and necessary.

3. Robbery is a crime involving the use or attempted use or threatened imminent use of physical force against a person. A trooper on patrol near a school has observed a 16-year-old youth threaten a smaller youth. The 16-year-old yelled that he would punch the younger boy in the face if the boy did not give him his lunch money. When the trooper approaches, the 16-year-old runs. The trooper tries to catch him, but cannot. What action should the trooper NOT take?

   a. Use deadly physical force to effect the arrest.
   b. Ask the smaller youth whether he knows the name of the 16-year-old.
   c. Transmit a radio description of the 16-year-old.
   d. Prepare a report and refer the case to the detective division for further investigation.

4. Felonious assault is a crime involving the use or attempted use or threatened imminent use of physical force against a person. A trooper responds to a 911 call of a family fight in a private house. When he enters the house, a woman tells him that her husband severely beat her. She is bruised and bleeding. She tells the trooper her husband is in the kitchen, and she wants him arrested. As the trooper enters the kitchen, the husband runs out a back door. The trooper chases him, but the husband jumps in his car and starts to drive away. As the husband passes the trooper, the trooper should

   a. shoot at him before the car picks up speed.
   b. shoot the windshield so the husband will not be able to drive away.
   c. shoot one of the tires to disable the car.
   d. get the plate number of the car and transmit a radio description of the car and the husband.

5. Murder is a crime involving the use of physical force against a person. A trooper responds to a 911 call of a family fight in a private house. When she enters the house, she finds the body of a recently deceased woman. The deceased has stab wounds to her torso. The trooper determines that the woman's husband is still in the house and is carrying a knife. The trooper finds the husband sitting on a chair in a bedroom. The husband refuses to surrender and refuses to drop the knife. The trooper should

   a. call for backup and try to keep the husband contained until assistance arrives.
   b. shoot the husband if he starts to get out of the chair.
   c. try to shoot the knife out of his hand.
   d. shoot him if he tries to jump out of the bedroom window.

6. A trooper responds to a 911 call outside an apartment building regarding a past rape. When he arrives, the parents of a 13-year-old female complain to the trooper that their daughter had sexual intercourse with a 20-year-old male who lives in a different apartment in the same building. The trooper enters the building to arrest the male, but the male flees. The trooper chases the male, but the male outruns him and is about to get away. What action should the trooper take?

   a. The trooper should shoot the male in the legs to prevent his escape.
   b. The trooper should shoot only if he cannot radio for the assistance of other troopers.
   c. The trooper should let the male get away rather than shoot at him.
   d. The trooper should fire warning shots over the head of the male.

7. A trooper responds to a 911 call regarding a suspicious man at a playground. As the trooper arrives, several women run toward her, shouting that a man just dragged a little girl into a parking lot. The man threatened the women with a knife. He was wearing a gray sweatshirt. The trooper runs into the parking lot and sees a man wearing a gray and white sweatshirt slam the trunk of a car closed. The man hurries to the driver's door and begins to open the door with car keys. The trooper shouts to the man to stop, but the man turns the key in the door. What action would be improper for the trooper to take?

a. to refrain from shooting, because she cannot be sure that it is the same man the women described or that the girl is in the trunk

b. to run to the man and attempt to prevent him from getting in the car

c. to immediately shoot the man if she does not believe that by using other means, she can prevent the man from driving away

d. to take the plate number and transmit a radio description of the car and the man

8. Burglary first degree is a crime involving the use or attempted use or threatened imminent use of physical force against a person. In which of the following circumstances might a trooper be justified in using deadly physical force if reasonable and necessary to arrest or prevent escape from custody?

a. when a person has committed burglary third degree

b. when a person has committed burglary second degree

c. when a person has committed burglary first or second degree

d. when a person has committed burglary first degree

9. In which of the following circumstances might a trooper be justified in using deadly physical force if reasonable and necessary to arrest or prevent escape from custody?

a. when a person has committed escape third or second degree

b. when a person has committed escape second degree

c. when a person has committed escape first or second degree

d. when a person has committed escape first degree

10. It would be most accurate to state that a trooper might be justified in using deadly physical force if reasonable and necessary to arrest or prevent escape from custody of a person who committed

a. arson third or second degree.

b. arson second degree.

c. arson first degree.

d. arson first, second, or third degree.

11. It would be most accurate to state that a trooper might be justified in using deadly physical force if reasonable and necessary to arrest or prevent escape from custody in which of the following circumstances?

a. to arrest a person who committed a felony

b. to arrest a person who committed a felony and who resists arrest by running away

c. to arrest a person who committed a felony and who resists arrest by threatening to use physical force

d. to arrest a person who committed a misdemeanor and who resists arrest by threatening to use deadly physical force

12. It would be most accurate to state that a trooper might be justified in using deadly physical force if reasonable and necessary to arrest or prevent escape from custody in which of the following circumstances?

a. to arrest a person who committed a felony

b. to arrest a person who committed a felony and who resists arrest by running away

c. to arrest a person who committed a misdemeanor and who, while resisting arrest, is armed with a deadly weapon

d. none of the above

13. It would be most accurate to state that a trooper might be justified in using deadly physical force if reasonable and necessary to arrest or prevent escape from custody in which of the following circumstances?

a. to arrest a person who committed the felony of burglary third degree and who resists arrest by running away

b. to arrest a person who committed the felony of burglary third degree and who, while resisting arrest, is armed with a deadly weapon

c. to arrest a person who committed the felony of burglary second degree and who resists arrest by running away

d. to arrest a person who committed the felony of burglary second degree and who resists arrest by threatening to use physical force

14. It would be most accurate to state that a trooper might be justified in using deadly physical force if reasonable and necessary to arrest or prevent escape from custody in which of the following circumstances?

a. to arrest a person for an offense when the person threatens to punch the officer in the face

b. to arrest a person for an offense when the person refuses to put his or her hands behind his or her back to be handcuffed

c. to arrest a person for an offense when the person backs away from the officer while holding a knife

d. to arrest a person for an offense when the person refuses to comply with the officer's directions to freeze, takes a combat stance, reaches into his or her waistband, and removes an object that appears to be a weapon

Directions: Read the following passage, then answer questions 15 through 20.

Many troopers are eager to prevent crime, often at the expense of their own safety. State police departments, on the other hand, often prefer that troopers take less dangerous actions and rather observe and report possible criminal behavior and even, sometimes, allow a possible suspect to leave the scene to assure the protection of life first, whether the trooper's or someone else's.

15. At ten minutes to midnight, Trooper Gold observes two men standing outside a liquor store. He has not seen these men in the neighborhood before, and Gold knows that the liquor-store owner usually closes at midnight and takes the day's receipts home with him. Which of the following would be the most appropriate action for Gold to take?
   a. Immediately stop and frisk the men for weapons.
   b. Chase the two men away from the store.
   c. Pay no more attention to them since they may have a perfectly innocent explanation for standing outside the store.
   d. Observe the men until the store owner closes the store and leaves safely.

16. Assume in connection with the previous question that Trooper Gold had decided the two men outside the liquor store were probably there for innocent purposes, and Gold drove away because he was off duty at midnight. Assume further that at ten minutes after midnight, as Gold was parking his patrol car at the station house, a report of a robbery at the liquor store was broadcast over the police radio. Which of the following would be the best action for Gold to take?
   a. Park the car, sign out, and go home.
   b. Prepare a report regarding what he had seen and leave it for the next shift.
   c. Immediately call the sergeant and tell her what he had done.
   d. Contact the radio dispatcher to ascertain what had happened at the robbery scene and, if appropriate, advise the dispatcher of the description of the two men he had observed.

17. A trooper is aware of several vicious robberies that have occurred in her area of responsibility. She is dispatched to a reported robbery in a liquor store, and when she arrives she finds the store manager bleeding profusely from a stab wound to the upper arm. The manager tells her that the robber stabbed him and just ran out the back door that leads to an alleyway. The trooper should immediately
   a. run after the robber before he or she gets too far away.
   b. get a description from the manager and transmit it over the police radio.
   c. because the manager is cut only in the upper arm, run after the robber, but transmit a request for an ambulance as she runs.
   d. render medical aid to the manager.

18. In a busy commercial area, a trooper stops two men who fit the description of two robbers who had robbed a fast-food store at gunpoint. The trooper draws her weapon and directs the men to place their hands against the wall in a spread-eagle fashion. One man, who is on the left, complies, placing his hands far apart and keeping his legs spread apart. However, the other man, who is on the right, keeps moving about, pushing off the wall, and bringing his legs together. In considering issues of safety, what is the best course of action for the trooper to take?

a. The trooper, keeping her gun trained on the men, should take cover and not attempt to frisk the men until backup arrives.

b. The trooper, with her gun in her right hand, should approach the man on the right and attempt to frisk him with her left hand.

c. The trooper, with her gun in her right hand, should approach the man on the left and attempt to frisk him with her left hand.

d. The trooper should direct the man on the right to turn around so she can see whether the man is armed or not.

19. Trooper Green encounters two intoxicated men fighting on the street. Each of the men has a broken beer bottle in his hand. The trooper orders them to drop the beer bottles and to stop fighting, but they continue to circle each other and continue to swing the beer bottles at each other. What should Trooper Green do next?

a. Get between the two men so that cannot strike each other.

b. Stay away from the men, call for help, and wait for backup to arrive.

c. Take out his gun and threaten to shoot the men if they do not stop.

d. Do not get in between the men, but wait for an opportunity to safely disarm them.

20. Considering her own and the public's safety, which of the following would be the most appropriate circumstances for a trooper to respond to a radio call, using the overhead lights and siren of her vehicle to bypass traffic signals?

a. responding to a robbery in progress

b. responding to a burglary in progress

c. responding to a fight among high school students

d. responding to a past murder

21. Three of the sentences below contain one or more grammatical or spelling errors. Select the answer choice that is correct as is.

a. Trooper Rasheed responded to a report from the dispatcher that someone had tripped and fallen in Newtown Mall, and discovered a 10-year-old boy who was hurt bad.

b. Trooper Rasheed responded to a report from the dispatcher that someone had tripped and had fell in Newtown Mall, and discovered a 10-year-old boy who was hurt bad.

c. Trooper Rasheed responded to a report from the dispatcher that someone had tripped and had fell in Newtown Mall, and discovered a 10-year-old boy that was badly hurt.

d. Trooper Rasheed responded to a report from the dispatcher that someone had tripped and fallen in Newtown Mall, and discovered a 10-year-old boy who was badly hurt.

22. Three of the sentences below contain one or more grammatical or spelling errors. Select the answer choice that is correct as is.
   a. Troopers are expected to have his/her uniforms neat, clean, and pressed whenever he/she are on duty.
   b. Troopers are expected to have their uniforms neat, clean, and pressed whenever they are on duty.
   c. A trooper is expected to have their uniform neat, clean and pressed whenever they are on duty.
   d. Troopers are expected to have one's uniforms neat, clean, and pressed whenever one is on duty.

23. Three of the sentences below contain one or more grammatical or spelling errors. Select the answer choice that is correct as is.
   a. Each morning during training, Sergeant Hardy leaded the rookies in a one-mile run at the academy.
   b. Each morning during training, Sergeant Hardy lead the rookies in a one-mile run at the academy.
   c. Each morning during training, Sergeant Hardy led the rookies in a one-mile run at the academy.
   d. Each morning during training, Sergeant Hardy leded the rookies in a one-mile run at the academy.

24. Three of the sentences below contain one or more grammatical or spelling errors. Select the answer choice that is correct as is.
   a. Trooper Alonzo had a better assignment then Trooper Berra.
   b. Trooper Alonzo has a better assignment then Trooper Berra.
   c. Trooper Alonzo has a better assignment than Trooper Berra.
   d. Trooper Alonzo had a betterer assignment than Trooper Berra.

25. Three of the sentences below contain one or more grammatical or spelling errors. Select the answer choice that is correct as is.
   a. Each week, the training sergeant gave the award to the trooper that had the best test scores.
   b. Each week, the Training Sergeant gave the award to the Trooper who had the best test scores.
   c. Each week, the training sergeant gave the award to the trooper who had the best test scores.
   d. Each week, the training sergeant gave the award to the trooper which had the best test scores.

26. Three of the sentences below contain one or more grammatical or spelling errors. Select the answer choice that is correct as is.
   a. Many people believe the community center should be run like a business.
   b. Many people believe the community center should be ran like a business.
   c. Many people believe the community center should be run as a business.
   d. Many people believe the community center should be ran as a business.

27. Three of the sentences below contain one or more grammatical or spelling errors. Select the answer choice that is correct as is.
   a. Sergeant Senior was impressed by the way they do their job.
   b. Sergeant Senior was impressed by the way they did their jobs.
   c. Sergeant Senior was impressed by the way they did their job.
   d. Sergeant Senior was impressed by the way they done their jobs.

28. One of the sentences below contains one or more grammatical or spelling errors. Select the answer choice that contains an error.
   a. The media has a major role in how society portrays women in police forces.
   b. The media have a major role in how women are viewed as police officers.
   c. The media play a major role in how the public views women police officers.
   d. The media have a major role in how women police officers are viewed by members of a community.

29. One of the sentences below contains one or more grammatical or spelling errors. Select the answer choice that contains an error.
   a. The two troopers and two sergeants was sick yesterday.
   b. Two troopers and two sergeants were sick yesterday.
   c. Two troopers and the two sergeants were sick yesterday.
   d. Two troopers and two sergeants reported sick yesterday.

Directions: For questions 30 through 33, choose the word or phrase that best fills the blank to properly complete the sentences.

30. To combat economic difficulties, departments are offering _____ overtime opportunities.
   a. fewer
   b. a lots less
   c. decreased
   d. less

31. Despite economic problems, most departments are looking to hire _____ troopers to enhance community safety.
   a. increased
   b. lots more
   c. tons more
   d. many more

32. When you _____ troopers together as partners, you want to make sure that they will be able to work well with one another.
   a. pare too
   b. pair two
   c. pair to
   d. pare two

33. When you interrogate a suspect, it is sometimes helpful to remain _____ about his or her involvement with the crime rather than ask direct questions.
   a. vague
   b. clear
   c. apparent
   d. unambiguous

34. Identify the sentence that contains a mistake in capitalization, punctuation, grammar, or spelling.
   a. Officer Cox always dresses neatly for work.
   b. Officer Cox is happy. Even though he had a bad day.
   c. Officer Cox cannot understand why it is raining; the weather station predicted sun for the rest of the afternoon.
   d. Office Cox is sleepy, but will accept the offer for a few overtime hours.

35. Identify the sentence that contains a mistake in capitalization, punctuation, grammar, or spelling. If you find no mistakes, select choice **d**.

a. Its so sad that Officer Torres retired.

b. It's so sad that Officer Torres retired.

c. It is so sad that Officer Torres retired.

d. no mistakes

36. Identify the sentence that contains a mistake in capitalization, punctuation, grammar, or spelling. If you find no mistakes, select choice **d**.

a. There Boss was so strict, they were never allowed to listen to music.

b. By the time the officer arrived at the scene, the suspect had escaped.

c. Boston, a city in Massachusetts, is credited for having the first formalized police department.

d. no mistakes

37. Identify the sentence that contains a mistake in capitalization, punctuation, grammar, or spelling. If you find no mistakes, select choice **d**.

a. Each trooper should know if his or her gun has a magazine safety disconnect. Without one, the gun will fire one chambered round when the trigger is pulled.

b. After completing the training, each officer must pass a test.

c. Don't bring that coffee into the patrol car if your going to spill it.

d. no mistakes

Directions: Read the following paragraph and answer questions 38 through 40.

Troopers Chen and Vann were directed by the dispatcher to respond to a private house to take a report of a past burglary. At the scene, the homeowner informed them that she was gone all day on Monday, May 8, that the address for her house was 200 Vee Lane, that her name was Suzie Katzie, and that she had no idea who could have entered her home in the time she left in the morning and returned that evening. She said the intruder took her laptop computer, which was in the house when she left, but is now the only item she has so far determined to be missing.

38. Trooper Chen, the senior officer, is writing up the crime report. Select the answer that expresses the facts reported to her most clearly and accurately.

a. Suzie Katzie reported that her home at 200 Vee Lane was broken into on May 8 and that her laptop computer is now missing.

b. Susanne Katz reported that she wasn't home on May 8 and that she lost her laptop computer sometime during her travels that day.

c. Suzanne Katze reported that her home at 200 V Lane was broken into on May 8 and that her laptop computer is now missing.

d. Suzie Katzie reported that she went to the mall to buy a dress and that when she came home after stopping along the way for groceries she entered her home at 200 Vee Lane and discovered that her computer wasn't there any more.

39. In the same incident, Troopers Chen and Vann also learn from Suzie Katzie that she had left her front door unlocked because she was expecting a guest, Annie Martin, from out of town, but that Annie had not arrived. Based on this additional information, Trooper Chen decides that her next best action is to do what?

a. not to take a report because it is obvious that Annie Martin arrived and borrowed the laptop

b. request a description of Annie Martin and inform the dispatcher that Martin is wanted in connection with a house burglary

c. lecture Suzie Katzie about the perils of leaving her front door unlocked

d. none of the above

40. In the same incident, later that night, Trooper Vann explains to her friend that she responded to a call involving a robbery in which a woman named Annie Martin living at 20 Vee Lane reported her laptop was taken. How many facts of the case did Trooper Vann confuse?
  a. one
  b. two
  c. three
  d. four

Directions: Read the following paragraph and answer questions 41 through 45.

Troopers must be very careful when asking a witness and/or victim to identify a suspect. Certain behaviors exhibited by the law enforcement agent, if deemed suggestive, could make the identification inadmissible at trial. Suggestive procedures can include verbal cues (i.e., you picked the right person) or non-verbal cues (i.e., smiling and nodding one's head). Any cues from the agent could affect the witness's ability to make an objective identification. Furthermore, the witness may identify the suspect based solely on the agent's cues. During a line-up or photo array, all suspects should resemble one another as much as possible. If the alleged perpetrator has a physical characteristic that is drastically different from the other suspects, it could taint the identification. Nonetheless, not all suggestive procedures automatically make an identification inadmissible at trial.

The Supreme Court ruled that highly suggestive procedures are not reasons for exclusion per se; they do not necessarily undermine the reliability of the identification. They have stressed five criteria:

1. The opportunity of the eyewitness to view the offender at the time of the crime
2. The witness's degree of attention
3. The accuracy of the witness's prior description of the offender
4. The level of certainty displayed by the witness at the identification procedure

5. The length of time between the crime and the identification procedure

These criteria have been criticized by researchers. Accuracy of description was found to be a poor predictor of accuracy in identification. Biased line-ups can actually lead eyewitnesses to overestimate how good of a view they had of the perpetrators, and it gives them a false sense of confidence, especially when they testify during the suspect's trial. As a result, many departments will have agents that are not associated with the case manage the identification procedure. This does not entirely eliminate law enforcement bias, but it decreases it substantially.

41. Trooper Padilla just finished interviewing Ms. Mendoza about her victimization. Ms. Mendoza was held captive for three days by the alleged offender before she was able to escape. Ms. Mendoza was tired and unable to continue looking at offender photographs to make a positive identification. As Officer Padilla was ready to escort Ms. Mendoza to the elevator, the alleged offender was escorted in handcuffs to the interrogation room. Ms. Mendoza saw him and screamed, "That's him! That's the man who kidnapped me!" The defendant's attorney filed a motion against the admissibility of the identification; he claimed that the identification of his client was highly suggestive, especially since he was in handcuffs. Based on the criteria set forth by the court, this identification
  a. would be admissible at trial because of Ms. Mendoza's certainty in identifying him as the perpetrator.
  b. would be admissible at trial because Ms. Mendoza had the opportunity to see the perpetrator over the course of three days while she was held captive.
  c. would be admissible at trial because of **a** and **b**.
  d. would not be admissible at trial regardless of **a** and **b**.

42. Carol was robbed on her way home from work. She described the suspect as a white male, in his 30s, about 5'2", and 150 pounds. Officer Padilla wanted Carol to identify the suspect in a line-up. Carol picked suspect three as the man who robbed her. The defense attorney filed a motion against the inadmissibility of the identification, claiming the line-up was highly prejudicial. Which of the following would most likely result in approval of the defense's motion?

   a. Out of the five men in the line-up, the suspect was the only one that was 5'2" inches. Line-up members one and two were 5'1" and line-up members four and five were 5'3".

   b. Out of the five men in the line-up, line-up member five had a tattoo on his right arm. Carol never mentioned whether she saw a tattoo on the man that robbed her.

   c. Out of the five men in the line-up, suspect three had very short hair but line-up members one, two, four, and five all had hair past their shoulders.

   d. none of the above

43. During a line-up, Carol picks line-up member three as the man who robbed her. What should Officer Padilla do next?

   a. smile and nod her head

   b. say, "Good job, you picked the right guy."

   c. say, "We will let you know if we need anything further."

   d. give her the thumbs-up sign

44. According to the paragraph, the best way to avoid law enforcement influence on a victim's identification of the suspect is to

   a. provide encouragement to the victim.

   b. never smile at the victim.

   c. never speak to the victim during the line-up.

   d. hand the identification procedure over to another officer that is not involved with the case.

45. Edwin was kidnapped and held captive as a child by Mr. Bowman for six months. After five years, the police were finally able to catch Mr. Bowman and bring him for a line-up. After several minutes, Edwin finally identified Mr. Bowman as his kidnapper. Edwin was certain of his identification. Mr. Bowman's attorney filed a motion against the admissibility of the identification; he claimed that too many years had passed for a valid identification. Based on the criteria set forth by the court, this identification

   a. would not be admissible at trial because Edwin took several minutes to identify Mr. Bowman.

   b. would most likely be admissible at trial.

   c. would not be admissible at trial because five years passed.

   d. would be a difficult issue for the court to decide.

46. Police must be careful when interrogating suspects. A confession could be excluded as evidence during trial if it was elicited by:

   1. Brute force
   2. Prolonged isolation
   3. Prolonged deprivation of food or sleep
   4. Threats of harm or punishment
   5. Promises of immunity or leniency
   6. Not notifying a suspect of their constitutional rights (i.e. Miranda) (barring exceptional circumstances)

According to this paragraph, under which of the following circumstances would a suspect's confession be legal?
a. The suspect was denied water for one hour.
b. The suspect was physically threatened by the officer, even though the officer never planned on touching the suspect.
c. The suspect was not read his Miranda rights.
d. The suspect was left alone in the interrogation room without food for over 24 hours.

Directions: Read the following paragraph and answer questions 47 and 48.

Troopers Allen and Reedy have been advised by the dispatcher to respond to an apparent burglary at the Experts Are Us computer store. When they arrive, they interview the owner, Mr. Smithfield, who says he locked up on Sunday afternoon and arrived on Monday morning to find the following items missing:

- 3 telephone sets, each valued at $150
- 3 laptop computers, each valued at $2,000
- 2 desktop computers, each valued at $960
- 2 monitors, each valued at $500
- 10 flash drives, each valued at $45

47. What is the total value of all the items reported by Mr. Smithfield?
a. $3,820
b. $8,820
c. $9,370
d. $9,820

48. On Tuesday, Mr. Smithfield calls the troopers and reports that the telephone sets were not stolen; he found them in a trash can behind the store and believes the thieves left them behind because the other items were more valuable. When Troopers Allen and Reedy file their follow-up report, the total value of items reported missing should be reduced by
a. $150.
b. $300.
c. $450.
d. nothing, because the sets were removed from the store.

49. Trooper Doyle has been assigned to work with the local elementary school students on arts and crafts projects during antidrug week activities. She spent some of her own money for supplies, and the captain has given her permission to request reimbursement. She spent $10 on crayons, $12 on drawing paper, $12.50 on pens, and $26.80 on cutouts and puppets for the students' presentations. What is the total amount that Trooper Doyle is entitled to receive?
a. $49
b. $49.30
c. $61.30
d. $73.80

50. According to the *Casper Star-Tribune*, in 2005, the Wyoming Highway Patrol issued about 55,000 speeding tickets, 73% of which were issued to men. Assuming the number to have been exactly 55,000 speeding tickets, how many of the speeding tickets were issued to men?
a. 40,000
b. 40,150
c. 40,300
d. 40,450

Directions: Read the following paragraph and answer questions 51 through 53.

Officer Gonzales was dispatched to the gift shop parking lot to take a report from Linda Opheimer, who reported that when she was placing a number of small items she had purchased into her vehicle's trunk, a young man reached into the trunk, grabbed a shopping bag that had already been in the trunk and fled toward the park's exit. She was unable to provide a description of the man, but provided the officer with a list of the contents of her shopping bag:

- 1 sweater valued at $260.00
- 3 gold-colored bracelets with charms attached, each valued at $365.00
- 1 computer game valued at $78.00
- 1 lizard-shaped pin with ruby eye valued at $130.00

51. What is the total value of the items reported stolen by Linda Opheimer?
a. $833
b. $1,485
c. $1,563
d. $1,653

52. What is the value of the jewelry items reported stolen by Linda Opheimer?
a. $495
b. $860
c. $938
d. $1,225

53. A day after the report, Linda Opheimer called Officer Gonzales and reported that the receipt for her sweater showed it was actually valued at $360.00 and that she had located the lizard-shaped pin in her jewelry box. The value of the stolen items should be recalculated to
a. $1,426.
b. $1,462.
c. $1,533.
d. $1,952.

Directions: Read the following paragraph and answer questions 54 and 55.

The average starting salary for troopers is $38,000. Rookie troopers spend their first six months in the academy, during which time they earn no overtime pay. Troopers are generally able to earn about 10% over their salary once they are on patrol. In addition, they receive a 4.5% increase at the end of their first full year as troopers.

54. Trooper Alticri should probably expect to earn _____ during her first year.
a. $38,000
b. $39,000
c. $39,900
d. $41,000

55. The base salary for Trooper Altieri will be _____ during her second year as a trooper.
a. $39,100
b. $39,710
c. $42,000
d. $55,100

Directions: The city of Pittsburgh is laying out the route for an extension of its existing transit system. The map legend shows you which portions of the new lines will be underground, which will be above ground, and the locations of existing and new stations. A number of major sections of the city and major attractions within those sections are also indicated on the map. Use this map to answer questions 56 through 58.

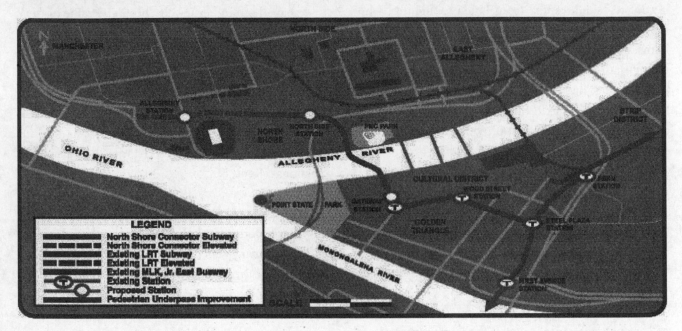

56. East Allegheny is in what direction in relationship to the existing Gateway Station?
  a. northeast
  b. northwest
  c. southeast
  d. southwest

57. The closest station to PNC Park will be
  a. Allegheny Station.
  b. North Side Station.
  c. Gateway Station.
  d. none of the above.

58. The rivers that meet at Point State Park are the
  a. Ohio and Allegheny rivers.
  b. Allegheny and Monongahela rivers.
  c. Ohio and Monongahela rivers.
  d. Ohio, Allegheny, and Monongahela rivers.

Directions: Use the following photo to answer questions 59 through 61.

59. From the photo, it is most logical to presume that the Broadway Station intersects with highway
- **a.** D 18.
- **b.** C Union.
- **c.** 30th Route.
- **d.** I-25.

60. The number of destinations other than Broadway Station that are shown in the photo is
- **a.** one.
- **b.** two.
- **c.** three.
- **d.** zero.

61. Based on the directional arrows on the signage at Broadway Station, a rail rider could correctly assume that the train will be heading _____ from Broadway Station to Union Station.
- **a.** south
- **b.** north
- **c.** east
- **d.** west

Directions: The map provides you with locations and routes in south Florida. Lauderdale by the Sea is the northernmost town on the coast; Hallendale Beach is the southernmost; Sunrise is the westernmost. Use this map to answer questions 62 through 66.

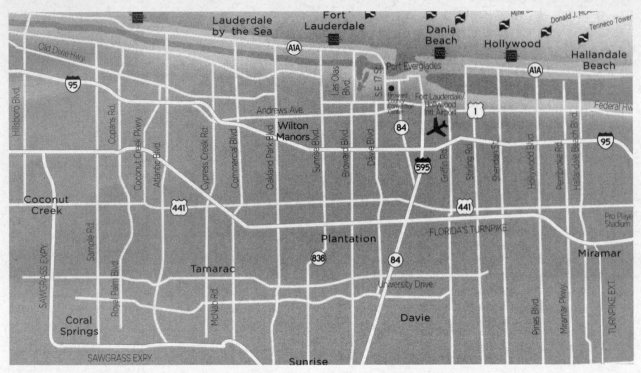

62. To travel from the Broward County Convention Center to Fort Lauderdale/Hollywood International Airport, you would need to go in which direction?
  a. northeast
  b. southwest
  c. southeast
  d. northwest

63. The Florida Turnpike runs roughly parallel to U.S. 441 between
  a. Coconut Creek Parkway and Pembroke Road.
  b. Cypress Creek Road and Hollywood Boulevard.
  c. Oakland Park Boulevard and Hollywood Boulevard.
  d. Oakland Park Boulevard and Pembroke Road.

64. Old Dixie Highway crosses Interstate 95 at
  a. Copans Road.
  b. Coconut Creed Parkway.
  c. Atlantic Boulevard.
  d. no point.

65. The local road that appears to take you closest to Fort Lauderdale/Hollywood International Airport is
  a. Griffin Road.
  b. Stirling Road.
  c. Davie Boulevard.
  d. S.E. 15th Street.

66. To travel south from Tamarac to Miramar with a minimum of route changes, a driver would be advised to travel on
  a. University Drive.
  b. the Florida Turnpike.
  c. Interstate 95.
  d. US 441.

Directions: Use the following map to answer questions 67 through 70.

67. Martin Luther King Blvd. intersects with I-70 at which of the following intersections?
  a. Peoria
  b. Havana
  c. Colfax
  d. none of the above

68. The most direct way to get from Arapahoe Rd. to Hampden and University Blvd. is to take
  a. Colorado Blvd. to County Line Rd., turn onto University Blvd., and proceed to Hampden.
  b. Arapahoe Rd. to University Blvd. and proceed to Hampden.
  c. Arapahoe Rd. to I-25, take I-25 to I-225, and proceed to Hampden and University Blvd.
  d. Arapahoe Rd. to Broadway, take Broadway to Hampden, and proceed on Hampden to University Blvd.

69. For the portion of the two routes shown on the map, I-70 runs _____ to Colfax.
  a. perpendicular
  b. on a 90-degree angle
  c. parallel
  d. on a 70-degree angle

70. At no point on the map does I-225 appear to cross
  a. Colfax.
  b. Martin Luther King Blvd.
  c. Yosemite St.
  d. Leetsdale Parker Rd.

Directions: Study the following scene and answer questions 71 through 75 without referring back to the picture.

71. How many people can you see in the karate school through the window?
   a. five
   b. three
   c. one
   d. two

72. How many adults are currently crossing the street?
   a. five
   b. two
   c. one
   d. three

73. How many police officers are at the scene?
   a. two
   b. three
   c. none
   d. one

74. How many vehicles are involved in the accident?
   a. one
   b. two
   c. three
   d. four

75. What business is directly above the 23rd Bakery?
   a. National Bank
   b. Bait Shop
   c. Karate
   d. none

Directions: Use the following paragraph to answer questions 76 and 77.

In response to complaints by merchants of thefts from cars parked in a strip mall of fewer than eight stores, Trooper Sassoon has been assigned to patrol the area. He hears and sees the following:

1. Two well-dressed women exit a minivan, pick up dry cleaning from one of the shops, reenter the minivan, and drive away.
2. A man honks his car horn continuously until a teenager comes out of the video store, tosses a small package into the car, and enters the car. The man then drives away.
3. A man leaves the corner sporting goods store carrying a bulky item and runs toward a car parked along the mall but not in the parking area.
4. A woman pushing an empty baby carriage engages in conversation with a shabbily dressed man who has been standing in front of the mall liquor store for approximately an hour.

76. Sergeant Eng later asked Trooper Sassoon to list what he observed during his patrol in the order of most suspicious to least suspicious. Select the most appropriate order for Trooper Sassoon's list.
   a. 1, 2, 3, 4
   b. 2, 3, 4, 1
   c. 4, 3, 2, 1
   d. 3, 4, 2, 1

77. After Trooper Sassoon filed his report, he and Sergeant Eng double-checked earlier reports and learned that some merchants had reported that items were missing from their stores after women shoppers had departed. Had Trooper Sassoon known that, he might have altered his previous report to give
   a. higher priority to the two well-dressed women.
   b. higher priority to the woman pushing an empty baby carriage.
   c. lower priority to the man leaving the sporting goods store.
   d. all of the above

Directions: Read the following paragraph and answer questions 78 through 80.

Trooper Gallagher broke her wrist and has been assigned to perform clerical work in the Records Section. Sergeant Torelli has asked her to alphabetize some contact cards. She must place the name in capital letters in the correct place in the files.

SARGANT, SUSAN

Names already in the file are:
Saegent, Suzie
Sergent, Susie
Sergent, Suzanne
Sugant, Sally

78. Where in the card file will Trooper Gallagher place *Sargant, Susan*?
   a. after *Saegent, Suzie* but before *Sergent, Susie*
   b. after *Sergent, Susie* but before *Sergent, Suzanne*
   c. after *Sergent, Suzanne* but before *Sugant, Sally*
   d. after *Sugant, Sally*

79. When Trooper Gallagher begins to actually file the cards she has alphabetized, she learns that Sargant, Susan is an incorrect name and that the name of the contact is actually Sargante, Susan. Based on this new information, where will she now file the card?
   a. before *Saegent, Suzie*
   b. before *Sergent, Susie*
   c. after *Sergent, Suzanne*
   d. after *Sugant, Sally*

80. Trooper Gallagher has discovered yet another error. The correct spelling of Sargant, Susan is actually Sargante, Susan. Based on this even newer information, where will she finally file the card?
   a. before *Saegent, Suzie*
   b. before *Sergent, Susie*
   c. after *Sergent, Suzanne*
   d. after *Sugant, Sally*

Directions: Read the following paragraphs and answer questions 81 through 83.

Many state police departments deploy a portion of their personnel to plainclothes anticrime patrol. Being dressed in plainclothes, rather than in uniform, allows these officers a better opportunity to observe criminal activity and to apprehend criminals before or immediately after a criminal act. Plainclothes patrol requires certain adjustments in police procedures, and rules for communicating with uniformed officers have been developed.

An elderly man hurriedly approaches a uniformed trooper and reports that he was mugged by a young man wearing a blue sweatshirt, blue jeans, and sneakers who just ran around the corner. The mugger took the elderly man's watch and wallet. The uniformed trooper runs around the corner, and from a distance, he believes he sees someone enter an abandoned building. He transmits over his portable radio a description of the mugger and the address of the abandoned building. Two anticrime officers in plainclothes respond and meet the uniformed trooper at the building, which is a three-story building with boarded-up windows. The first anticrime officer says that she will cover the back, and she immediately runs down an alleyway along the side of the building. The second anticrime officer says to the uniformed trooper, "Let's go," and they enter the building to search for the suspect, both taking out their firearms. The plainclothes officer attaches his police badge to his left breast pocket where it can be seen.

The building is dark inside except for dim light coming through some of the broken, boarded-up windows. The uniformed trooper has a large flashlight, but the anticrime officer has only a small penlike flashlight. The uniformed trooper goes up the stairs to search the upper two floors while the anticrime officer waits at the bottom of the stairs. As the anticrime officer waits at the bottom of the stairs, he hears something that he believes is coming from under the stairs. With his small flashlight he steps around behind the staircase and finds a trap door to the basement. He lifts the trap door, but it is heavy, and he drops it. Just as he drops it, two backup uniformed troopers enter the building. They hear the trap door drop and see the anticrime officer jump away with his gun in his hand. They shout to him to drop the gun. He is surprised and turns toward them. They shoot at him 12 times, striking him twice.

81. Which of the following is the most serious mistake made by the first uniformed trooper?
a. transmitting a description of the mugger before he obtained complete information from the victim
b. transmitting the address of the abandoned building based on only his belief that he saw someone enter it
c. entering the abandoned building with the plainclothes officer
d. leaving the plainclothes officer alone in the abandoned building

82. Which of the following is the most serious mistake made by the second anticrime officer?
a. entering the building with the uniformed trooper
b. entering the building with only a small penlike flashlight
c. attaching his badge to his breast pocket rather than holding it up in his hand
d. failing to transmit to the radio dispatcher that a plainclothes officer was entering the abandoned building

83. Which of the following is the most accurate statement regarding the actions of the two backup uniformed troopers?
a. It was a mistake to enter the building.
b. It was a mistake to fire at the plainclothes officer before identifying him.
c. It was a mistake to fire so many bullets at the plainclothes officer.
d. Based on the available information, it would be unfair to criticize their actions.

Directions: Read the following paragraph and answer questions 84 and 85.

Line-up procedures can have an impact on the accuracy of identifications made. Line-up procedures include the structural properties of line-ups (i.e., appearance characteristics of line-up members are similar to those of the alleged perpetrator) and the procedural properties (i.e., instructions given to eyewitnesses prior to viewing are objective and not suggestive). Research shows that certain methods of conducting line-ups are particularly likely to promote false identifications. Mistaken eyewitness identification is responsible for more wrongful convictions than all other cases combined.

84. To improve line-up identifications, law enforcement must make sure
   a. all line-up member characteristics are analogous to the suspect.
   b. they encourage the witness to choose at least one suspect in the line-up.
   c. they tell the victim if they picked the right or wrong person.
   d. none of the above

85. According to the paragraph, wrongful convictions are the result of
   a. structural properties of a line-up.
   b. procedural properties of the line-up.
   c. a scared and confused witness.
   d. mistaken eyewitness identification.

Directions: Read the following paragraphs and answer questions 86 through 91.

Criminally negligent homicide occurs when a person causes the death of another person through criminal negligence. Manslaughter occurs when a person recklessly causes the death of another person. Murder occurs when a person, under circumstances evincing a depraved indifference to human life, recklessly engages in conduct that creates a grave risk of death to another person and thereby causes the death of another person.

Assault third degree occurs when a person, through criminal negligence, causes physical injury to another person by means of a deadly weapon or dangerous instrument. Assault second degree occurs when a person recklessly causes serious physical injury to another person by means of a deadly weapon or dangerous instrument. Assault first degree occurs when a person, under circumstances evincing a depraved indifference to human life, recklessly engages in conduct that creates a grave risk of death to another person and thereby causes serious physical injury to another person.

A person acts with criminal negligence with respect to a result defined as an offense when he fails to perceive a substantial and unjustifiable risk that such result will occur. The risk must be of such nature and degree that the failure to perceive it constitutes a gross deviation from the standard of care that a reasonable person would observe in the situation.

A person acts recklessly with respect to a result defined as an offense when he or she is aware of and consciously disregards a substantial and unjustifiable risk that such result will occur.

86. Danny Donovan is 25 years old. He buys a new .22 caliber rifle and takes it to the countryside to test-fire it. He drives to an apparently uninhabited area, parks his car on the side of a country road, and walks deep into the woods. Surrounded by trees, he fires the gun at tree trunks and branches. He does not know that a hundred yards beyond the woods is the soccer field of an elementary school. One of the bullets he fires travels out of the woods and strikes a child playing soccer. The child suffers a minor grazing wound to his leg. Donovan is unaware of this, and as he returns to his car, he is arrested for shooting the child. The most serious and appropriate charge of which Donovan would be guilty is

a. criminally negligent homicide.
b. assault third degree.
c. assault second degree.
d. none of the above

87. Danny Donovan is 25 years old. He buys a new .22 caliber rifle and takes it to the countryside to test-fire it. Driving to the countryside, he notices a few houses scattered in the heavily wooded area. He parks his car on the side of a country road and walks into a wooded area. Surrounded by trees, he fires the gun at tree trunks and branches. He does not know that a hundred yards beyond the wooded area is the soccer field of an elementary school. One of the bullets he fires travels out of the woods and strikes a child playing soccer. The child suffers a minor grazing wound to his leg. Donovan is unaware of this, and as he returns to his car, he is arrested for shooting the child. The most serious and appropriate charge of which Donovan would be guilty is

a. criminally negligent homicide.
b. assault third degree.
c. assault second degree.
d. none of the above

88. Danny Donovan is 25 years old. He buys a new .22 caliber rifle and takes it to the countryside to test-fire it. Driving to the countryside, he notices houses and residential developments scattered in the area. He parks his car on the side of a road and walks into a wooded area. He considers that there might be houses or buildings in the area, but he assumes that they are far enough away to test-fire his gun. Surrounded by trees, he fires the gun at tree trunks and branches. A hundred yards beyond the wooded area is the soccer field of an elementary school. One of the bullets he fires travels out of the woods and strikes a child playing soccer. The child suffers a serious injury to his leg. Donovan is unaware of this, and as he returns to his car, he is arrested for shooting the child. The most serious and appropriate charge of which Donovan would be guilty is

a. criminally negligent homicide.
b. assault third degree.
c. assault second degree.
d. assault first degree.

89. Danny Donovan is 25 years old. He buys a new .22 caliber rifle and takes it to the countryside to test-fire it. Driving to the countryside, he notices houses and residential developments scattered in the area. He parks his car on the side of a road and walks into a wooded area. He considers that there might be houses or buildings in the area, but he assumes that they are far enough away to test-fire his gun. Surrounded by trees, he fires the gun at tree trunks and branches. A hundred yards beyond the wooded area is the soccer field of an elementary school. One of the bullets he fires travels out of the woods and strikes a child playing soccer. The child is struck between the eyes and dies. Donovan is unaware of this, and as he returns to his car, he is arrested for shooting the child. The most serious and appropriate charge of which Donovan would be guilty is
a. assault first degree.
b. criminally negligent homicide.
c. manslaughter.
d. murder.

90. Danny Donovan is 25 years old. He buys a new .22 caliber rifle and takes it to the countryside to test-fire it. Driving to the countryside, he notices houses and residential developments scattered in the area. He parks his car on the side of a road and walks into a wooded area. Surrounded by trees, he fires the gun at tree trunks and branches. Not satisfied with testing the gun in the enclosed wooded area, Donovan walks to the end of the woods and sees the soccer field of an elementary school. A few kids are practicing on the soccer field. To see how far his bullets will travel and to see whether the kids can hear where the shots were coming from, Donovan fires at the goal post near where the kids are playing. One of the bullets travels past the goal post and strikes a child. The child suffers a serious injury to his leg. Donovan is unaware of this, and as he returns to his car, he is arrested for shooting the child. The most serious and appropriate charge of which Donovan would be guilty is
a. criminally negligent homicide.
b. assault third degree.
c. assault second degree.
d. assault first degree.

91. Danny Donovan is 25 years old. He buys a new .22 caliber rifle and takes it to the countryside to test-fire it. Driving to the countryside, he notices houses and residential developments scattered in the area. He parks his car on the side of a road and walks into a wooded area. Surrounded by trees, he fires the gun at tree trunks and branches. Not satisfied with testing the gun in the enclosed wooded area, Donovan walks to the end of the woods and sees the soccer field of an elementary school. A few kids are practicing on the soccer field. To see how far his bullets will travel and to see whether the kids can hear where the shots were coming from, Donovan fires at the goal post near where the kids are playing. One of the bullets travels past the goal post and strikes a child. The child is struck between the eyes and dies. Donovan is unaware of this, and as he returns to his car, he is arrested for shooting the child. The most serious and appropriate charge of which Donovan would be guilty is
a. assault first degree.
b. criminally negligent homicide.
c. manslaughter.
d. murder.

Directions: Read the following paragraphs and answer questions 92 through 98.

Trooper Acosta responds to the scene of a robbery at a convenience store. The store clerk tells the officer that a man came in with a gun and robbed her of all the money in the cash register. The robber had threatened her with the gun, saying that he would blow the clerk's head off if she did not give him the money. Three customers saw the robber leave.

The witnesses each described what they saw of the gun. The store clerk said she only saw a barrel pointed at her and that is all she can remember. The first witness said it was a silver automatic pistol. The second witness said it was a revolver. The third witness said he saw only that it was black.

The store clerk said the robber was a black male about 30 years old, about six feet tall and 160 pounds, wearing blue pants and a gray sweatshirt with a hood. The first witness said the robber was a Hispanic male, dark skinned, between 5′8″ and 5′10″ and 170 pounds, about 25 years old, wearing blue pants and a blue sweatshirt with a hood. The second witness said the robber was a Hispanic male about 20 years old, between 5′8″ and 5′10″ and 160 pounds, wearing black pants and a gray jacket. The third witness said the robber was a Hispanic male, dark skinned, about 6′2″ and 180 pounds, between 20 and 30 years old, wearing blue jeans and a gray sweatshirt.

92. The store clerk and the three customers each gave descriptions of the robber. Which description of the robber is most likely correct?
a. He wore blue pants and a gray sweatshirt with a hood.
b. He wore blue pants and a blue sweatshirt with a hood.
c. He wore black pants and a gray jacket.
d. He wore blue jeans and a gray sweatshirt.

93. The store clerk and the three customers each gave descriptions of the robber. Which description of the robber is most likely correct?
a. He was a black male about 30 years old.
b. He was a Hispanic male, dark skinned, about 25 years old.
c. He was a Hispanic male about 20 years old.
d. He was a Hispanic male, dark skinned, between 20 and 30 years old.

94. The store clerk and the three customers each gave descriptions of the robber. Which description of the robber is most likely correct?
- **a.** He was about six feet tall and 160 pounds.
- **b.** He was between 5′8″ and 5′10″ and 170 pounds.
- **c.** He was between 5′8″ and 5′10″ and 160 pounds.
- **d.** He was about 6′2″ and 180 pounds.

95. The witnesses each described what they saw of the gun. Which description of the gun is most likely correct?
- **a.** It was an automatic pistol.
- **b.** It was a revolver.
- **c.** It was black.
- **d.** It was a handgun of unknown type and color.

96. Trooper Acosta should transmit which of the following as the most accurate be-on-the-lookout (BOLO) report?
- **a.** BOLO for a Hispanic male, approximately 30 years old, six feet tall, 160 pounds, wearing blue pants and a gray sweatshirt with a hood—and armed with a gun.
- **b.** BOLO for a Hispanic male, dark skin, approximately 30 years old, six feet tall, 160 pounds, wearing blue pants and a gray sweatshirt with a hood—and armed with a gun.
- **c.** BOLO for a Hispanic male, dark skin, approximately 20 years old, between 5′8″ and 5′10″ tall, 160 pounds, wearing a gray sweatshirt—and armed with a handgun.
- **d.** BOLO for a Hispanic male, dark skin, approximately 30 years old, between 5′8″ and 5′10″ tall, 160 pounds, wearing blue pants and a gray sweatshirt with a hood—and armed with a handgun.

97. Trooper Acosta was aware of four other store robberies that occurred in the past year. He returned to the station house and reviewed the reports for those robberies to see whether the description of the convenience store robber matched the description of any of the suspects in the prior robberies.

Suspect in Robbery #1: Black male, 35 years old, six feet tall, 200 pounds, wearing a white T-shirt—and armed with a black automatic pistol.

Suspect in Robbery #2: Hispanic male, 25 years old, 5′10″ tall, 160 pounds, wearing a gray sweatshirt—and armed with an automatic pistol.

Suspect in Robbery #3: Hispanic male, dark skin, between 20 and 25 years old, between 5′8″ and 5′10″ tall, between 160 and 180 pounds, wearing blue pants and a gray sweatshirt with a hood—and armed with a handgun.

Suspect in Robbery #4: White or Hispanic male, approximately 20 years old, six feet tall, 140 pounds, wearing a black shirt and black pants—and armed with a knife.

Of the following choices, which descriptions of the prior robbery suspects most closely match the description of the suspect in the robbery of the convenience store?
- **a.** #1 and #2
- **b.** #2 and #3
- **c.** #3 and #4
- **d.** only #2

98. Trooper Acosta also reviewed the prior robbery reports to see what language the suspects used when confronting the robbery victim.

Suspect in Robbery #1 said: "Hand me all the money before I use this."

Suspect in Robbery #2 said: "I don't want to hurt you. Just give me the money."

Suspect in Robbery #3 said: "Gimme the money or I'll blow your head off."

Suspect in Robbery #4 said: "I'm gonna cut you if you don't give it up."

Of the following choices, which language of the prior robbery suspects most closely matches the language of the suspect in the robbery of the convenience store?
- **a.** #1 and #2
- **b.** #2 and #3
- **c.** #3 and #4
- **d.** only #3

Directions: Read the following paragraph and answer questions 99 and 100.

At 2:00 A.M., a trooper responds to several noise complaints in an apartment complex. Upon arriving to the complex, the trooper sees what appears to be a party in progress. The trooper knocks on the door, and a man claiming to be the resident steps into the hallway. The resident, a 30-year-old white male, is obviously drunk but cooperative.

99. The best action the trooper should take is to
- **a.** ask the resident to keep the noise down and leave.
- **b.** draw his weapon and tell the resident that he will be arrested if he does not comply.
- **c.** call for backup.
- **d.** push the door open and go inside.

100. If the resident becomes belligerent and physically aggressive, the officer should
- **a.** just walk away to avoid an incident.
- **b.** barge in the resident's home to see if there is just cause for arrest.
- **c.** tell the individual to clam down, and if he fails to comply, arrest him.
- **d.** curse and yell at the resident in return.

Answers

1. b. The paragraph states that the FOP has always been an organization that has officers representing the interests of other officers. Choices **a**, **c**, and **d** are incorrect; they are not specifically mentioned as current FOP goals in the paragraph.

2. d. None of these options can be inferred from the paragraph. Choice **a** is never mentioned. Choice **b** is incorrect; although they have a large membership, they do not claim to have members from every department. Choice **c** could be true, however, there is no mention of how often labor meetings take place.

3. a. It would *not* be reasonable and necessary to use deadly physical force to arrest the youth under these circumstances. Choices **b**, **c**, and **d** are all proper actions for the trooper to take.

4. d. The husband's identity is known and other police units will most likely be able to stop his car or locate him. It is unreasonable and unnecessary to shoot him. Choices **a**, **b**, and **c** would each be dangerous, unreasonable, and ineffective.

5. a. Nothing has been shown that would necessitate shooting the husband. Choices **b** and **d** are incorrect; unless the husband attacks the trooper, nothing has happened that would necessitate shooting him. Choice **c** is incorrect because it is an unreasonable action.

6. c. This is a statutory rape without any indication of the use or threatened use of physical force. Therefore, the trooper is unauthorized to use deadly physical force. Choices **a** and **b** are incorrect because this situation does not warrant shooting. Choice **d** is incorrect because warning shots are dangerous, unnecessary, and unjustified.

7. c. It would be improper to immediately shoot the man without first attempting to stop him and investigate further. Choices **a**, **b**, and **d** are incorrect because they are all proper courses of action to take under the circumstances.

8. d. Burglary first degree is one of the offenses for which the use of deadly physical force can be justified. Choices **a**, **b**, and **c** are incorrect; they are not among the offenses for which the use of deadly physical force can be justified.

9. d. Escape first degree is one of the offenses for which the use of deadly physical force can be justified. Choices **a**, **b**, and **c** are incorrect; they are not among the offenses for which the use of deadly physical force can be justified.

10. d. All of the degrees of arson are among the offenses for which the use of deadly physical force can be justified.

11. d. A trooper can defend himself or herself against the threat of deadly physical force. Choice **c** is incorrect because the threat was of physical force, but not deadly physical force. Choices **a** and **b** are incorrect because they would require the person to be armed with a deadly weapon while resisting in order to justify the use of deadly physical force.

12. d. Choices **a** and **b** are incorrect because they would require the person to be armed with a deadly weapon while resisting in order to justify the use of deadly physical force. Choice **c** is incorrect because, though the person is armed with a deadly weapon, the underlying crime is only a misdemeanor, not a felony.

13. b. Deadly physical force can be justified when the person committed a felony and is armed with a deadly weapon when he resists arrest. Choices **a** and **c** are incorrect because burglary second or third degree does not involve the use of physical force, and deadly physical force is authorized only for burglary first degree. Choice **d** is incorrect because the threat was of only physical force, not deadly physical force.

14. d. The trooper could reasonably believe the person was going to shoot at him or her.

Choice **a** is incorrect because without more information, this is a threat of only physical force, not deadly physical force. Choice **b** is incorrect; a trooper could use physical force to make the person comply, but not deadly physical force. Choice **c** is incorrect because the person may potentially use deadly physical force, but while he or she is backing away, it is not imminent. If he or she moved toward the trooper, the trooper may be justified to use deadly physical force.

15. d. It is the most reasonable, prudent, and lawful action to take. Choices **a** and **b** are incorrect. Based on the circumstances, the trooper did not have lawful authority to frisk or chase the men. Choice **c** is incorrect because the trooper would be derelict in his duties were the men in fact contemplating a crime.

16. d. The trooper's information and description of the possible suspects may be helpful in apprehending the suspects. Choice **a** is incorrect because the trooper would be derelict in his duties if he did not ascertain whether the two men he observed were possible suspects. Choice **b** is incorrect because time is of the essence in attempting to apprehend the perpetrators of a robbery. Choice **c** is incorrect because it is more important to broadcast a description of the men, and he could tell the sergeant at the first practicable opportunity.

17. d. A trooper's first duty is to protect life. The manager was bleeding profusely and could have been bleeding from an artery. Choices **a**, **b**, and **c** are incorrect because they are of secondary importance to saving life.

18. a. This is the safest course of action; it would be too risky for one trooper to attempt to frisk these potentially dangerous and armed criminals. Choices **b** and **c** are not safe courses of action for the trooper. Choice **d** is incorrect because it is a better and safer tactic to keep the suspect facing away from the trooper.

19. d. This maintains the trooper's safety while he remains close enough to resolve the situation when the opportunity arises. Choice **a** is a poor tactic that exposes the trooper to injury. Choice **b** is incorrect. Although the trooper must be cautious, he cannot ignore the situation. Choice **c** is incorrect; unless the trooper is personally threatened or one of the men is clearly assaulting the other, the trooper should not shoot or threaten to shoot.

20. c. Upon hearing the sirens, the students might stop fighting. Choices **a** and **b** are incorrect because each would warn a criminal that the police were on the way and would prevent the police from apprehending the criminal. Choice **d** is incorrect. The murder was in the past, so the circumstances do not warrant the use of these emergency devices.

21. d. Choice **a** needs the adverb *badly* instead of the word *bad*. Choices **b** and **c** each contain a verb tense error. *Fell* should be *fallen*.

22. b. Choices **a**, **c**, and **d** each contain number agreement errors.

23. c. Choices **a** and **b** use the wrong verb tense of *to lead*. Choice **d** uses *leded*, which is not a form of *to lead*.

24. c. Choices **a** and **b** are incorrect. The comparative is *than*, not *then*. In choice **d**, *betterer* is not a word.

25. c. The word *trooper* describes a person and requires the use of *who* or *whom* rather than *that* or *which*. Choices **a**, **b**, and **d** each have one or more grammatical or usage errors.

26. a. The sentence calls for use of the present verb tense. It also calls for the word *like* rather than *as*.

27. b. The sentence requires a past tense, so choices **a** and **d** can be ruled out. Choice **c** is wrong; the word *jobs* should be plural because *their* is plural.

28. a. This choice presumes the word *media* is singular, which is incorrect. It also says that society portrays women, not that the media do. Choices **b**, **c**, and **d** are grammatically correct sentences.

29. **a.** The subject of the sentence is plural and, therefore, requires a plural verb.

30. **a.** This is the only grammatically correct statement. Fewer is used with count nouns.

31. **a.** This is the only grammatically correct statement.

32. **b.** *Pair* means to put two items together, whereas *pear* is a fruit. *Two* is the amount found in a pair.

33. **a.** *Vague* questioning would be the opposite of direct questioning.

34. **b.** *Even though he had a bad day* is not a complete sentence.

35. **a.** *Its* is incorrect. The sentence should start with *it is* or the conjunction *it's*.

36. **a.** The word there should be *their*, and the comma makes it a run-on sentence.

37. **c.** *Your* should be *you're*.

38. **a.** This choice provides all the correct information in a concise report. Choice **b** is incorrect because the victim's name is changed and because the report implies that her laptop computer was not in the house at the time of the burglary. Choice **c** is incorrect because the victim's name is changed and the address is incorrectly reported. Choice **d** is incorrect because it provides information that is not relevant to the incident.

39. **d.** Choice **a** is incorrect because Trooper Chen must take the report even if she suspects the laptop was borrowed and will eventually be located. Choice **b** is incorrect because if Martin has the laptop as Trooper Chen suspects, based on what the trooper was told, there is a good chance Martin is not a burglar. Choice **c** is incorrect because, though Trooper Chen might mention that leaving one's door unlocked is unwise, it is not her role to lecture citizens who are reporting what they believe to be crimes.

40. **d.** Four elements of the situation were not properly recalled: the name of the victim, the type of crime reported, the address, and whose laptop was missing.

41. **c.** The answers are both **a** and **b**. Two of the five criteria stated that courts must look at the certainty of the witness when making the identification and the amount of time the victim had with the suspect.

42. **c.** The fact that the suspect was the only one in the line-up without long hair is enough to taint the identification.

43. **c.** This is the only response that is not suggestive.

44. **d.** The paragraph clearly states that many departments utilize this procedure to prevent law enforcement bias.

45. **b.** Even though five years passed, Edwin saw this man every day for a six month period. It may have taken him several minutes to make an identification, but he was certain of his choice.

46. **a.** Denying the suspect water for one hour would not constitute prolonged deprivation.

47. **d.** This is the sum of the total value of all the items Mr. Smithfield reported. You must multiply the value of each item by the number reported missing, and then add the subtotals. Choices **a**, **b**, and **c** each leave out some of the items that Mr. Smithfield reported missing.

48. **c.** The three telephone sets, with a total value of $450, were no longer missing. Therefore, they should not be included in the value of the missing property.

49. **c.** Add all the expenses to determine Trooper Doyle's reimbursement.

50. **b.** To calculate 73% of 55,000, multiply 0.73 by 55,000.

51. **c.** This is a problem in multiplication and addition. You must remember to multiply the value of the bracelets ($365 × 3) before adding it to the other figures.

52. d. This is also a problem in multiplication and addition. You must remember the number of bracelets and you must be sure to include only the jewelry (choice **c** also includes the computer game).

53. c. You must recalculate the figures by adding the additional value of the sweater ($100) and subtracting the value of the pin ($130), remembering not to transpose any numbers in your calculations.

54. c. There are three steps involved in solving this calculation. First, convert 10% to a decimal: 0.10. Multiply $19,000 (one-half the annual salary) by 0.10 (the percent to be earned). Then, add this amount ($1,900) to the annual salary.

55. b. There are three steps involved in solving this calculation. First, convert 4.5% to a decimal: 0.045. Multiply that by $38,000 to find the salary increase. Then, add the result ($1,710) to the original salary ($38,000).

56. a. The indicator in the upper left-hand corner orients you to north, from which you must determine that east is right, west is left, and south would be in the opposite direction that the arrow is pointing.

57. b. PNC Park is located on the north side of the Allegheny River, and North Side Station will be the closest station to it once it opens.

58. d. All three rivers meet at Point State Park.

59. d. I-25 is prominent in the station name and is designated in the style common for the Interstate Highway System.

60. c. Three other station names are shown: 18th and California, 30th and Downing, and Union Station.

61. b. The arrow in the photograph indicates the train will be traveling north from the Broadway Station to Union Station.

62. b. Using the coordinates given to you in the description, the airport is southwest of the Convention Center.

63. c. This is the section of the Florida Turnpike that runs almost perfectly parallel to U.S. 441.

64. d. Old Dixie Highway and Interstate 95 follow a similar route, but they do not cross at any point shown on the map.

65. a. Griffin Road and U.S. 595 are shown closest to the airport. Of the two, Griffin Road is a local road, and U.S. 595 is the interstate bypass.

66. b. Choice **a** is incorrect because University Drive does not go far enough south. Choice **c** is incorrect because it takes you out too far east. Choice **d** is incorrect because it takes you farther east than choice **b**.

67. d. Martin Luther King Blvd. is shown as a relatively short street that runs parallel to I-70.

68. b. It is the most direct route, requiring the least number of road changes.

69. c. I-70 can be seen at the top of the map; Colfax is below Martin Luther King Blvd. running parallel to I-70.

70. b. Martin Luther King Blvd. is a short street between I-70 and Colfax that does not intersect at any point on the map with I-225.

71. d. Two people are shown in the school's window.

72. b. Two people are shown crossing the street with a baby carriage. A man across the street appears to be looking at the accident, not crossing the street.

73. a. There is one police officer taking notes and another directing traffic.

74. b. There are two vehicles involved in the accident. The other vehicles—a police car, an ambulance, and a tow truck—are responding to the accident, but you may presume that they were not part of the accident.

75. d. The four windows above the 23rd Bakery do not have any commercial sign; it appears to be a residential property.

76. d. This places first the most suspicious action, namely the man leaving the store carrying a bulky item and not entering a car parked in the mall. Choices **a** and **b** list first activities that without further investigation appear to be normal mall behavior. Choice **c** lists first a behavior that is less common than those in choices **a** and **b**, but not as suspicious as the behavior listed first in choice **d**.

77. d. With additional information, Trooper Sassoon might have viewed the situations differently, particularly the activities involving the women.

78. a. When the first letter is the same, names are alphabetized based on each succeeding letter. In this example, the first names are not relevant.

79. b. When the first letter is the same, names are alphabetized based on each succeeding letter. The *e* added to *Sargente* does not change the name's place in the alphabetical listing.

80. b. When the first letter is the same, names are alphabetized based on each succeeding letter. The *e* added in the middle to create *Saregente* does not change the name's place in the alphabetical listing.

81. d. This is the most serious mistake, because the uniformed trooper left the plainclothes officer alone in the dimly lit building, where he could easily be mistaken for the suspect. Choice **c** is a mistake but not as serious as choice **d**. Choices **a** and **b** were proper actions.

82. d. This is the most serious mistake. The officer should have foreseen that uniformed troopers would respond to the building and should have warned them of his presence inside the building. Choices **a** and **b** were mistakes, but were not as serious as choice **d**. Choice **c** was a proper action.

83. d. The troopers were unaware that a plainclothes officer was in the building and were suddenly faced with an unknown person who jumped and turned toward them with a gun in his hand. Choice **b** was not a mistake for the same reasons. Choice **c** was not a mistake since all the bullets did not strike the trooper. Choice **a** was not a mistake; the troopers were assisting the first uniformed trooper.

84. a. This fact is specifically stated in the paragraph. The other choices are not mentioned.

85. d. The other three options are responsible for mistaken witness identification, not the majority of wrongful convictions.

86. d. Although Donovan could be sued civilly for ordinary negligence, his conduct was not criminally negligent. Choice **a** is incorrect since the child did not die. Choice **b** is incorrect; from Donovan's perspective, the failure to perceive the soccer field was not a gross deviation from the standard of care a reasonable person would observe in the situation. Choice **c** is incorrect for the same reason as choice **b**, and also because the child did not suffer a serious injury.

87. b. The failure to perceive the reasonable possibility that people were in the area where he was shooting the gun was the kind of gross deviation that amounts to criminally negligent conduct. Choice **a** is incorrect because the child did not die. Choice **c** is incorrect because the child did not suffer a serious injury.

88. c. His awareness and conscious disregard of the substantial and unjustifiable risk that people were nearby constitutes reckless conduct, and the child suffered a serious injury. Choice **a** is incorrect because the child did not die. Choice **b** is incorrect because the conduct was more serious and culpable than criminal negligence, and the child suffered a serious injury.

89. c. His awareness and conscious disregard of the substantial and unjustifiable risk that people were nearby constitutes reckless conduct, and the child died. Choice **a** is incorrect because the child died. Choice **b** is incorrect because the conduct was more serious and culpable than criminal negligence.

90. d. Donovan's reckless conduct created a grave risk of death, evinced a depraved indifference to human life, and caused serious physical injury. Choice **a** is incorrect because the child did not die. Choices **b** and **c** are incorrect because Donovan's conduct was more serious and culpable than criminal negligence or recklessness.

91. d. Donovan's reckless conduct created a grave risk of death, evinced a depraved indifference to human life, and caused death. Choice **a** is incorrect because the child's death is a more serious result than serious physical injury. Choices **b** and **c** are incorrect since Donovan's conduct was more serious and culpable than criminal negligence or recklessness.

92. a. Blue pants, gray sweatshirt, and a hood are the elements repeated most often by the eyewitnesses and are therefore most likely correct.

93. d. Hispanic and dark skinned are the elements repeated most often by the eyewitnesses and are therefore most likely correct. The ages given in choices **a**, **b**, and **c** are different from the other answers; therefore, choice **d** is the best answer regarding age.

94. c. Between 5'8" and 5'10" and 160 pounds are the elements repeated most often by the eyewitnesses and are therefore most likely correct.

95. d. The witnesses agree only that it was a handgun. No other elements are repeated often enough to merit reliance on their accuracy.

96. d. This matches the most likely descriptions obtained. Choices **a**, **b**, and **c** are incorrect because they include less likely descriptions obtained.

97. b. Descriptions #2 and #3 both match the suspect. Choice **a** is incorrect; although description #2 matches the suspect, #1 does not. Choice **c** is incorrect; although #3 matches the suspect, #4 does not. Choice **d** is incorrect; although #2 matches the suspect, it is not the only one that matches, because #3 also matches.

98. d. Choice **d** is correct; the language used in robbery #3 most closely matches the language in the convenience store robbery. Choice **a** is incorrect because the language does not match. Choice **b** is incorrect; although #3 matches, #2 does not. Choice **c** is incorrect; although #3 matches, #4 does not.

99. a. The only reasonable choice is to ask the resident to keep the noise down and leave. Even though the resident is drunk, he is of the legal drinking age and appears to be cooperative. Hence, no further action is necessary. The situation does not require backup and does justify the trooper pulling out his weapon. He does not have a warrant and absent exigent circumstances, he cannot enter the resident's home.

100.c. The officer should try to solve the problem by talking to the resident, but if the resident becomes increasingly aggressive, he should be arrested to avoid a possibly dangerous situation. The officer should not just walk away as the problem was not solved. He cannot barge into the resident's home without a warrant. Cursing and yelling at the suspect is unprofessional and serves no true purpose; it would most likely escalate the situation.

CHAPTER 18 ▶ THE ORAL APPRAISAL EXAM

CHAPTER SUMMARY

Not all state police agencies include an oral appraisal exam in their hiring procedures. The major reason for this is that it is a costly and time-consuming process to have each candidate questioned by an interview board at a centralized location. Agencies that do use an oral appraisal generally record the interview and retain the tape in the event a candidate lodges a challenge to this portion of the hiring process. One agency that includes an oral suitability interview in its hiring process is the ISP. The interview lasts an hour and applicants are ranked based on its results. The PSP also conducts an oral interview and provides detailed information about the process on its website.

Generally, even if there is not a formal board interview, candidates will have spoken to employees of the agency sometime during the hiring process. Although these conversations may seem informal, they are an opportunity for you to present yourself in the best possible way. Maybe you spoke with a human resources official when you sought information about the job; maybe you spoke with a trooper assigned to the recruitment unit at a job fair or received the application in person from the agency's headquarters. It may be true that these people make no employment decisions, but you have an opportunity to present yourself in a professional way and to get a sense of what behavior would be appropriate in the agency you hope to join. Look at how people are dressed; listen to how they speak to you. You have no way of knowing whether any of these initial contacts with the agency are people you will see again. Particularly in smaller departments, there is a good chance you will cross paths with these individuals again, and what is said about first impressions being lasting impressions is true.

Physical Appearance

While there is no need to dress formally to go to headquarters to pick up an application, you should look presentable. If you speak with a recruiter at a state fair, it is expected that you will dress differently than you would if the meeting were at a college job fair. Some colleges now require that students attend job fairs in business attire. Certainly if your selected agency conducts an oral appraisal exam, you should plan to dress in such attire. This may not mean a suit and tie everywhere in the United States, but it means at least a button-down dress shirt and slacks with a pressed crease for men. A man should not appear at his oral interview in sneakers, a polo or T-shirt, or jeans. Women applicants need not wear a dress, but should also wear a button-down blouse and a skirt or a suit. Just as for men, sneakers, any polo or T-shirts, or jeans are inappropriate. For both men and women, hair should be tidy, shoes should be shined, and jewelry should be kept to a minimum.

The PSP advises candidates that business attire is expected at the oral and polygraph exams and for the background investigation interview, noting that gym attire is appropriate only for the physical fitness tests and the medical and psychological evaluations. Do not assume that this is the same for all agencies; check before you show up at any stage of the hiring process in gym or casual clothing rather than in business attire.

Successful Interview Techniques

If your selected agency conducts an interview, you might consider practicing in front of a mirror or talking to adult businesspeople. You might even record yourself talking and try to eliminate from your speech habits known as *verbal tics*. Verbal tics include injecting into each sentence words such as *like*, *you know*, or *I mean*. Do not start sentences with the word *well*,

and do not use any curse words or racial, ethnic, or sexist slurs. Higher-pitched voices sometimes tend to sound more tentative than a voice in a lower timbre. Although you cannot totally change your speaking voice and style, you can minimize the tendency to sound unsure of yourself by not letting your voice go up at the end of each sentence to make it seem you are asking a question rather than answering one. You want to sound self-assured and confident without sounding like someone who knows it all.

Your posture is also important. Remember not to slouch or wiggle around in your seat. If you are more comfortable crossing your legs, do so at the ankle rather than swinging one leg across the knee of another.

Answering Questions

While you will be asked factual questions at the interview about yourself, such as what you majored in at school and why, or why you want to become a law enforcement officer, the primary purpose of the oral interview is not to learn the answers to these questions as much as for agency personnel to see how you perform under stress and to get a sense of your ability to analyze problems and converse with others. Some interviewers will ask probing questions that try to assess your character; some will ask you if you have any questions for them so that they can get a sense of your communications skills and of whether you have sincerely thought about what a career in law enforcement entails.

Listen carefully and learn the names of those on the appraisal board. When someone asks you a question, respond using the rank and last name of that person, and make eye contact with the questioner and with others on the panel. Do not look down at your shoes or at your fingers while you speak. Be sure also to get the name, its proper spelling, and the proper title of the person heading the interview panel, since you might want to follow up with a short note thanking the panel for the opportunity to meet with its members and reinforcing your interest in joining the agency.

Sample Interview Questions

Not all oral appraisals follow the same format, but some questions that you can be fairly sure you will be asked include:

- Why did you select this particular agency to apply to?
- What are your strengths?
- What are your weaknesses?
- What do you think you will be doing in this agency during your first year of service? Your fifth year of service?

Behavioral questions are becoming more commonplace during interviews for almost all law enforcement positions. Responses to such questions should be based on the STAR approach. This approach can be difficult because it requires you to pick events from your past, either professional or personal, that help illustrate your best character traits or work strengths.

- **Situation or Task:** Begin answering the question by explaining a past situation you were in or a past task that needed to be accomplished. Be specific about the example and do not speak in generalities.
- **Action you took:** Next, talk about the action that you took to try and resolve the situation or problem and/or accomplish the task you were given. Again, be very specific about what you did.
- **Results you achieved:** Last, what was the result of your action? Was it positive or negative? What did you learn?

Responses to interview questions using this format will be more successful than responses that do not utilize this format. Always keep the focus on yourself and highlight your achievements. If something did not work the way you planned, talk about the lesson you learned and how this lesson will help you improve

the way you handle similar situations in the future. Following is a list of possible questions that could be asked during an oral appraisal exam. Read them over and think about the answers you would give to each question based on the STAR method.

- Describe a situation in which you were able to use persuasion to successfully convince someone to see your side.
- Describe a time when you were faced with a stressful situation that demonstrated your coping skills.
- Give me an example of a time that you used good judgment in solving a difficult and complex problem.
- Give me an example of a time that you had to adhere to a policy that you did not agree with.
- Tell me about a time that you had to go over and beyond your job duties.
- Tell me about a time when you had to deal with conflict in the workplace.
- Tell me about the most difficult decision you ever had to make.
- Give me an example of a time where you tried really hard to accomplish a task but failed.
- Talk about a time where you had to show initiative and take the lead.
- Describe a situation where you were able to have a positive influence on others.
- Give me an example of a difficult goal you achieved and how you reached it.

Describing Yourself

You must be prepared for a general "tell us about yourself" question. Here, as in all the questions, you want to answer honestly and briefly. "Tell us about yourself" does not mean to replay every detail of your life up to this point. It is fine to talk briefly about your family, schooling or military experience, any jobs you've held, and why you want to be a state trooper. Similarly, when you discuss strengths and weaknesses, think about these in a professional sense. You might consider describing weaknesses that can be turned into strengths, because you want to illustrate that while you are not perfect, you also have the capacity to improve yourself.

Hypothetical Questions

Another line of questioning might be similar to the problem solving questions on the written exam. This means you might be asked a hypothetical question that gets to the point about how you would act at a crime scene or an assistance call.

You might be given a set of facts and asked what you would do first when you arrived at the scene. For instance:

- You are dispatched to a neighborhood park where young people are reported to have been noisy and possibly drinking alcohol and smoking marijuana. When they see you arriving, they disperse in a number of different directions. What would you do? How would you determine who to chase? Would you fire a warning shot into the air? Would you shoot at any of the fleeing youths? Would you take down the license number of a vehicle you see three of the youths get into and drive away?

Or you might be asked a question that delves into your personal ethics, such as:

- You overhear a colleague making racist or sexist remarks about a coworker; what would you do?
- You stop a motorist on a deserted stretch of the interstate, and he offers you $100 not to write a ticket; what would you do?

Although you may have thought about these or similar types of questions, the oral appraisal may raise some issues you had not given thought to before. Try to answer carefully but honestly because if you lie, a later question may bring you back to the same situation, and you will find yourself stumped if you do not recall what you said earlier, or if it becomes obvious that your answer sounded good but doesn't reflect your beliefs at all.

Asking Questions

Generally, the last phase of the appraisal gives you an opportunity to question the interviewers on the panel. Try to have at least one good question to ask, because asking no questions may be interpreted as a lack of real interest in the agency. If you have nothing specific to ask, ask about the future steps in the hiring process, which shows your interest in continuing as a candidate. You might also consider making a short closing statement that reinforces your interest in the position and your belief that you will be able to fulfill the responsibilities of the position. However, you do not want this to sound too rehearsed, as if you'd practiced it word-for-word for the last month.

THE PHYSICAL, MEDICAL, AND PSYCHOLOGICAL EXAMS

CHAPTER SUMMARY
Of these three exams, the physical is the only one that that a candidate can really "study" for. Since medical and psychological exams may differ, having a general knowledge of what these tests consist of will best prepare you for them.

Many agencies provide details about tests on their websites or in materials sent to candidates who have passed the earlier steps in the hiring process. However you obtain material from your agency of choice, read it carefully and follow the instructions provided. Many agencies place these steps late in the hiring process, so you will have already passed a number of hurdles on the way to employment. It would be unfortunate at this stage to be disqualified because you failed to follow instructions rather than because of any medical or psychological bar to employment.

Physical Exam

For many applicants, especially candidates who have been inactive for most of their lives, the physical exam may be as big—or even bigger—a hurdle than the written exam. Sometimes, even for those in good physical condition, the physical exam becomes a psychological barrier. But there is no reason for this; as with the written exam, you can study for the physical exam. In fact, some agencies post on their websites exactly what the physical exam will consist of, meaning that your studying for it can be even more directly targeted than your studying for the written exam.

Two agencies that tell candidates what will be expected of them at the physical are the NYSP and the PSP. Because these exams are fairly typical, and actually are on the more difficult end of the spectrum, their requirements will give you an excellent idea of what will be expected of you.

The NYSP calls its test physical ability testing, or PAT. The test is generally scheduled about six months prior to the start of an academy class. To do well, candidates need to start getting in shape about one year before they hope to enter an academy class. Candidates are invited to the PAT according to their rank order on the written exam, which means that you will be called sooner if you scored high on the written exam. The good part of this is that you have an early chance to move into an academy class. If you haven't been taking care of your physical conditioning, though, you will need to start a physical fitness program almost immediately upon receiving your score.

The NYSP assists candidates in passing the PAT by stressing training in three areas: flexibility, dynamic strength, and cardiovascular endurance. Generally, recruiting offices across New York state schedule seminars to help candidates prepare for the PAT and understand the techniques for performing the various physical tests.

The PSP provides one of the most detailed explanations of its physical testing requirements of any state police agency. It is also one of the most rigorous. Regardless of the agency you are interested in applying for, you should visit the PSP website (www.psp.state.pa.us) to gain an understanding of what your agency of choice may expect of you. The entry level physical standards for the PSP as of 2009 included completing a 300-meter run in 67 seconds, completing 30 sit-ups in one minute, completing 13 push-ups with no time limit, obtaining a vertical jump of 14 inches within three tries, and completing a 1.5-mile run in just under 17 minutes. These are the standards for entry; you will be expected to have improved your fitness by the time you graduate so that you are able to complete the 300-meter run in 56 seconds, complete 37 sit-ups in one minute, 30 push-ups with no time limit,

raise your vertical jump to 18 inches, and complete the 1.5-mile run in 14 minutes and five seconds.

Many state police agencies, unlike the vast majority of municipal police departments, expect you to maintain your physical ability throughout your career. Many troopers are tested annually for physical fitness. The NJSP, another agency with stringent physical standards, requires all troopers to take part in an annual fitness test, which includes a 1.5-mile run. This agency makes no adjustments for age or sex under the assumption that those running from the police do not stop to determine whether the trooper chasing them is young or old, or male or female.

To help those who are not fit and agile, many agencies provide fact sheets on how to study for the physical exam and on the best techniques for mastering the skills required to pass. Although many candidates do not realize it, there are better and worse ways of running, jumping, and particularly, making it over a five- or six-foot wall or dragging a 150-pound dummy. Knowing how to bend your body, when to rely on leg strength rather than upper body strength, and how to conserve energy for that last push of effort are things that can be learned. Healthy habits and diet to decrease your weight and increase your cardiovascular capacity can also be learned. A number of agencies also schedule pretraining sessions for candidates, and some conduct a pretest that is given under conditions similar to the actual test to give candidates an opportunity to learn what they do well in and what they might need to focus on before the actual test. This is an excellent reason to keep visiting the website of the agency you have applied to, because training sessions may be announced regularly.

Regardless of your physical condition, you must be prepared to undertake a fitness program to pass the majority of state police physical ability exams. Unlike applicants for local police departments, you may not be able to participate in pretraining that is conducted near your home. This means you will need to use the material provided by your agency to develop a program that you can work on alone. To maintain your motivation, you might consider joining a gym where you can obtain some assistance from professional trainers. If you are still in college, you might consider asking someone in the athletic department to guide you. You might also try to learn from your recruiter if there are other candidates in your immediate area so that you can form a workout group to help and to motivate one another.

Medical Exam

If you were not tested for drug use during the physical ability portion of the applicant process, it is likely that this will be done during the medical exam. Although at one time almost any drug use was an automatic disqualification for police employment, that is no longer the case. Different agencies have different policies regarding past experimentation with drugs, but you will not be hired by any agency if you test positive for drug use at the time of your medical exam. Find out the policy of the agency you are testing for so that you are prepared at the time of testing. If your agency accepts candidates who have experimented with drugs in the past, do not lie about the last time you used any of the permissible drugs, because the truth may be determined during your background investigation, and you will be automatically disqualified—not only for the drug experimentation, but also for having lied.

Many agencies once placed the medical exam early in the hiring process, but considerations based on the Americans with Disabilities Act (ADA) have moved it further along in the process. The ADA, which was signed into law in 1990, extended various protections to candidates who may have disabilities that do not preclude them from performing a full range of police tasks. To comply with this law, the PSP, for instance, in 2006 placed the medical exam as step six of seven steps prior to appointment. Prior to the medical exam, a candidate for the PSP will have completed an application, passed the qualifying written and oral exams, completed fitness tests (including drug screening), and passed a polygraph and a background investigation.

The PSP provides an applicant with detailed instructions for completing medical documentation by a physician of the applicant's choice and at the applicant's expense that includes a physical exam, a certificate of visual efficiency, and a dental exam. The material is reviewed by the State Police Medical Officer. Although there are no specific height and weight requirements, applicants must pass audiometer screening, must have healthy gums and a full set of teeth, and must meet very specific vision standards. The PSP is unusual because it directs the applicant to go to a private physician to meet the medical requirements; many agencies expect the applicant to appear for a medical exam conducted by doctors employed by the agencies specifically for this purpose.

There are many reasons why police agencies want to hire only candidates who are in good health. The most immediate reason is that the academy is very strenuous, and it would not be a good use of time or money to hire candidates who were not in sufficiently good health to complete the training and accept assignment as officers. The longer-range reasons are to ensure that candidates are not injury-prone, and do not suffer their own medical emergencies while responding to police emergencies, and to minimize the number of officers who retire early due to illness at considerable cost to the agency. Recently, a small number of law enforcement agencies have sought to keep their employees healthy by prohibiting officers from smoking in public or even from smoking at all. If such a prohibition applies in the agency you are applying for, you will be told that not smoking is a condition of employment, and that if you claim not to smoke and are found to do so, you will face disciplinary action up to and including termination. A number of state courts have upheld these policies despite challenges by applicants, so you should inquire what health-related requirements (smoking, drinking, or other prohibitions) the agency you are applying for may have in place.

Psychological Exam

The psychological assessment is another exam that it is almost impossible to study for. It is difficult to believe today that it has been only in the past 30 years that police agencies have relied heavily on psychological assessments of their candidates. Today it is common for applicants to be given a battery of paper-and-pencil tests and to undergo an interview with a licensed psychologist who is familiar with law enforcement officers' job responsibilities.

Although some agencies inform applicants of the tests that will be administered, the best advice is to answer questions honestly and not to try to be clever or cunning. Most of the tests ask the same questions more than once in slightly different formats, so it is virtually impossible to trick the test and lie consistently and successfully. Some of the more commonly used tests are the Minnesota Multiphasic Personality Inventory (MMPI), the California Personality Inventory (CPI), the Wechsler Adult Intelligence Scale—Revised (WISC-R), and the Inwald Personality Inventory (IPI). Questions are designed to ferret out those who have impulse control problems, lie or are evasive consistently, are substance abusers, have high levels of stress, or have difficulty managing anger. Many of the questions are also aimed at eliminating candidates who exhibit high levels of hypochondria; this is often a symptom of psychological problems and may also indicate that an applicant has a high possibility of being absent too often due to illness or injury, and then attempting to retire early.

Probably the best way to prepare for the psychological exam is to relax. Spending time at home or with loved ones, rather than socializing with those who may contribute to your uncertainty and concern, will reduce stress levels. Sleeping well and following a healthy diet and exercise regimen prior to the test may also aid you in being clear-minded and alert when filling out paper-and-pencil tests, and certainly when speaking with a trained psychologist or psychiatrist.

ADDITIONAL ONLINE PRACTICE

Whether you need help building basic skills or preparing for an exam, visit the LearningExpress Practice Center! On this site, you can access additional practice materials. Using the code below, you'll be able to log in and take two additional state trooper practice exams. These online practice exams will also provide you with:

- **Immediate scoring**
- **Detailed answer explanations**
- **Personalized recommendations for further practice and study**

Log in to the LearningExpress Practice Center by using this URL: **www.learnatest.com/practice**

This is your Access Code: **7359**

Follow the steps online to redeem your access code. After you've used your access code to register with the site, you will be prompted to create a username and password. For easy reference, record them here:

Username: _____   Password:_____

With your username and password, you can log in and access your additional materials. If you have any questions or problems, please contact LearningExpress customer service at 1-800-295-9556 ext. 2, or e-mail us at **customerservice@learningexpressllc.com**.